Raza Sí, Migra No

Justice, Power, and Politics

The Justice, Power, and Politics series publishes new works in history that explore the myriad struggles for justice, battles for power, and shifts in politics that have shaped the United States over time. Through the lenses of justice, power, and politics, the series seeks to broaden scholarly debates about America's past as well as to inform public discussions about its future.

More information on the series, including a complete list of books published, is available at http://justicepowerandpolitics.com/.

Raza Sí, Migra No

Chicano Movement Struggles for
Immigrant Rights in San Diego

· ·

JIMMY PATIÑO

The University of North Carolina Press Chapel Hill

The University of North Carolina Press has been a member
of the Green Press Initiative since 2003.

Library of Congress Cataloging-in-Publication Data
Names: Patiño, Jimmy, author.
Title: Raza sí, migra no : Chicano movement struggles for immigrant
   rights in San Diego / Jimmy Patiño.
Description: Chapel Hill : University of North Carolina Press, [2017] |
   Includes bibliographical references and index.
Identifiers: LCCN 2017020717 | ISBN 9781469635552 (cloth : alk. paper) |
   ISBN 9781469635569 (pbk : alk. paper) | ISBN 9781469635576 (ebook)
Subjects: LCSH: Chicano movement—California—San Diego—History—
   20th century. | Mexican Americans—California—San Diego—History—
   20th century. | Mexican Americans—Ethnic identity—History—20th
   century. | Illegal aliens—Mexico. | United States—Emigration and
   immigration—Government policy.
Classification: LCC E184.M5 P3727 2017 | DDC 305.8680794/985—dc23
   LC record available at https://lccn.loc.gov/2017020717

Cover illustration: Photographs from the National Protest March against
the Carter Curtain, February 11, 1979 (courtesy of the Herman Baca
Collection, Special Collections and Archives, University of California,
San Diego). "No! Vietnamization of San Diego" poster designed by Yolanda
López visible in lower photo.

Chapter 2 was previously published in a different form as " 'All I Want Is
That He Be Punished': Border Patrol Violence, Women's Voices, and Chicano
Activism in Early 1970s San Diego," in *The Chicano Movement: Perspectives
from the Twenty-First Century*, ed. Mario T. García (New York: Routledge
Press, 2014), 21–46. Reproduced by permission from Taylor and Francis
Group, LLC, a division of Informa PLC.

To Jimmy III and LunaBella.

Mom and Dad.

Mis abuelos/as y familia.

And mi gente.

Contents

Acknowledgments

Peace. Writing this book coincided with twists and turns, moves and migrations, crises and miracles . . . quite simply life, which is really the people and relations that are in it. This book was written with the support of a dynamic and awe-inspiring community.

Sociologist Jacqueline Hagan at the University of Houston in the early 2000s saw the potential of a *pocho* Chicano kid finding his voice. The UH Center for Mexican American Studies honed my scholarly explorations. My comrades in the Movimiento Estudiantil Xicana/o de Aztlán de UH (MEXA, aka, MEChA) struggled with me, rooted me on as an activist scholar, and created a dynamic space at the intersection of the intellectual and on-the-ground struggle. Scholars including Guadalupe San Miguel, Raul Ramos, Martin Melosi, John Mason Hart, and Gerald Horne were supportive and formative. The brilliance of Dr. Horne in particular has reverberated through the years—our conversations grounded me in a dialog about radicalism, the global struggle of the Left, and a history of black–brown solidarity. La Colectiva—our Chicano/a-Latin American Studies graduate student collective—introduced an intellectual political practice of solidarity and exchange that I bring with me everywhere. I send a shout-out to the *colectiva* diaspora and a special thank-you to my *compa* Felipe Hinojosa—thanks for being a trusted *hermano*, intellectual confidant, and source of support in and outside the academy, from back in the day to the time of writing this book.

Mil gracias to Luis Alvarez, who opened doors for me, supported me, and demonstrated what radical mentorship looked like. I also learned from him that no matter how repressive the circumstance, it is our responsibility as scholars to remind others that oppressed people lived, loved, practiced, resisted, and made decisions—and always held dignity and created the raw material for new horizons. Arriving in Luis's hometown of San Diego brought me to the borderlands where I gained insight from Chicano historian David G. Gutiérrez. San Diego and Dave G. taught me that immigration and migrants are not tangential to Chicano/a history, but central to the future of ethnic Mexicans in the US and society more broadly. Dave's support, challenges, and inspiration were crucial to the writing of this book. So many other mentors emerged at UCSD (University of California San Diego), primarily Daniel Widener, Nayan Shah, and Lisa Lowe. How privileged I was to develop seeds of thought in dialog with these preeminent scholars.

My move to Minnesota was also a significant part of creating the community that enabled me to write this book. Colleagues in the Ethnic Studies Department at St. Cloud State University were crucial in helping with the particular struggles of a new professor of color in an unfamiliar place. The University of Minnesota has a dynamic community of scholars and students centered on the study of race, indigeneity, gender, and sexuality. There are too many amazing colleagues to name, but specifically Catherine Squires, Lisa Sun-Hee Park, David Pellow, and Roderick Ferguson enthusiastically welcomed me. Yuichiro Onishi was also most welcoming, and has become a trusted mentor and compañero from whom I've learned much, while sharing plenty of laughs. Thanks to Yuich and Keith Mayes for inviting me to collaborate on creating Chicano/Latino, African American, and Asian American history curriculum in Minneapolis public schools. This opportunity was sustaining and generative work that provided me with reflection on the significance of this book.

In the Department of Chicano and Latino Studies, I became part of a dynamic community that spills into the streets of Minneapolis and St. Paul and provided the support to finish this book. Louis Mendoza was chair when I arrived and was a prolific mentor and leader. Edén Torres also served as chair during a tumultuous three years after Louis left for new horizons. We struggled with our community to replace him for the next two years—what an honor to struggle alongside Edén. While often frustrating, this struggle grounded me in the department, its community of students, alumni, and allies, and the Twin Cities Latino/a and activist community more broadly. Thank you all. My compañera and community lifeline in the department, Lisa Sass Zaragoza, taught me so much about solidarity and struggle. Rest in Power, Jesús Estrada-Pérez; it was an amazing experience to get to know you in struggle just before you moved on to the other side. As Freire reminds, students can teach teachers as much as the other way around, so thank you to the student activists of the Whose Diversity Movement. My colleague Zobeida Bonilla is a brilliant scholar to bounce ideas off of and a dear friend. Bianet Castellanos has been a staunch advocate for the department and a mentor who encouraged me during a crucial time. Erika Lee served as a trusted mentor who always gave me support, encouragement, and brilliant advice. David Chang always checked up on me and cheered me on. Thanks to David Karjanen for the support and bringing me into the Never Too Late Social Club. Juan Telles! Here's the book you always encouraged me to finish and asked me about *every time* I saw you! *Gracias, compa!* Thanks to Vichet Chuuon for the support and back porch reflections on the implications of being POC (people of color) professors. And to my colleague Clint Carroll—thanks for all those conversations about what would become this book and plenty of other topics that were so crucial—thank you, brother.

My support network within the cadres of brilliant scholars across North America in Chicano/a history, ethnic studies, Latino/a studies, and beyond truly formed the foundation to bring this book into fruition. My UCSD community—Cutler Edwards, Israel Pastrana, Alicia Ratterree, Gloria Kim, Jesús Pérez, Lorena Márquez, Myrna García, T. J. Tallie, Long Bui, Martha Escobar, José Fusté, James Schrader, Anita Casavantes Bradford, Miguel La Serna, Ricardo Fagoaga, Barbara Cortes Zepeda, James Gordon Williams, Harry Simon, Angelica Castillo, Zachary Britsan, Reese Hazen, Matthew Shindell, Stevie Ruiz, Mychal Odom, Iris Ruiz, Sara Sanders, Elizabeth Sine, Matt Johnson and many my memory fails to acknowledge—created, and continue to create, a dynamic intellectual community that ties scholarship to action. Rest in Power, Dryden Hull—our conversations about what the role of a scholar should be will always be a part of my walk forward. Also at UCSD, Lynda Claasen and her amazing crew at the Mandeville Special Collections Library enabled me to write a much better book.

Of course the San Diego community was the basis of this book, and I thank the veteran activists whose actions and reflections make up this narrative. Thank you for sharing your stories with me and welcoming me into your homes and communities. First and foremost, Herman Baca spent hours with me sharing his memories and insights. An organic intellectual, I learned so much from our conversations—both formal and informal. Thanks to Nadine Baca and the rest of the Baca family for treating me like family. Thanks to Roger and Norma Cazares for sharing your stories and welcoming me into your home. I also thank Augie Bareño, Gloria Jean Valderrama, Jerry Apodaca, Carlos "Charlie" Vásquez, Olivia Puentes Reynolds, and David Avalos for spending time with me and for the conversations and oral histories they shared with me.

Scholars emerged all over the country and gave me undying inspiration and support. Thanks to Patricia Nguyen for reminding to "do the work your soul must have." Yuridia Ramírez Rentería became a supportive friend, always down to listen to my concerns, struggles, and hopes. Thanks homie. Roberto D. Hernández was a trusted *hermano* in a trying moment that became an opportunity to grow and ground my ideals with my personal life. *Gracías, compa.* Abby Rosas, Ana Rosas, Max Krochmal, Gordon Mantler, Lauren Araiza, Milo Alvarez, Mireya Loza, Romeo Guzmán, Kency Cornejo, and many others shared key conversations, insights and/or inspiration for me and this book. Thank you all of my peers, especially within Chicano/a History and Ethnic Studies across the land—too many to name—for creating and holding space for our work. The prolific George Lipsitz gave indispensable feedback on this project that will serve me well beyond the book. Thanks as well to Kelly Lytle Hernandez and George J. Sanchez, who also gave me brilliant feedback. Ben Olguín played a crucial role in giving me feedback on the book project and contemplating how to present it to the world. Other scholars who gave me feedback on the book project through the years include Stephen Pitti, Matthew García, Gabriela Arredondo, Jose Alamillo, Josef Barton, Michael Ines-Jiménez, Ernesto Chávez, Mario García, Juan Mora Torres, Juan Gómez-Quiñones, Larena Oropeza and Lisa Ramos. Thank you all; this is a better book because of sharing community with you.

Chapter 2 of this book entailed an important rethinking of key premises of the manuscript and I wish to thank Ramón Gutiérrez, the Twin Cities Chican@ Studies Writing Group, especially Lorena Muñoz, Cindy García, and Yolanda Padilla, and Mario García and all the participants of the Conference on the Emerging Historiography of the Chicano Movement in February 2012 for solidarity and dialog regarding the writing of this chapter.

For the financial support crucial to the completion of this book, thanks especially to the Ford Foundation and community; and at the University of Minnesota, the Institute of Diversity Equity and Advocacy, the College of Liberal Arts Office of Faculty and Academic Affairs, and the Department of Chicano and Latino Studies.

I've grown to love the Minneapolis/St. Paul community because of its amazing, brilliant, and passionate people, who envision a better world and have loved me like their own family. I send a shout-out and much love to the Spokes Thugs and Harmony Crew—Chaun Webster, José Luis Villaseñor, Aaron Mallory, and Reverend Anthony Jermaine Ross. Talking so much of what Chaun calls "that good ish" grounded me here and always reenergized me, reminding me why my writing was important. Another bike ride and round! I extend a special thank-you as well to my compañera Jessica Lopez Lyman—my writing comrade and intellectual confidant; I appreciate your supportive energy, and persistent feedback. I can't wait to read your book! My brother Filiberto Nolasco Gómez was always down to share some Chicano time together—often needed in Minnesota—and urged me to consider ways to get my work to the masses, tied me to crucial activists and community members within the labor movement in Minnesota, and came real with emotional and moral support, too. Thanks, dawg! Michael Dueñes and his family gave me space to talk and rest in a crucial transitional moment. Darlene St. Clair gave me friendly support and feedback as well. Pratik and Gouri Jagtap also opened their home to me. Working with Hal Huggins was also so important. Thank you. To the rest of my Minneapolis peeps—too many to name—thanks for your time, energy, and support. Shout-out to the Left Wing/Futbolista crew all over the continent: 2-2! I'm so fortunate to have all these amazing people in my life that gave me grounding to write and reflect.

Thank you to the University of North Carolina Press for what was a wonderful experience. Thank you to Joseph Parsons for listening to my pitch and seeing the value of my study. Brandon Proia took the reins and was always transparent about the process, realistic about explaining the decisions that needed to be made, and supportive about the ideas and story I'm telling in this book.

I want to thank Nova Cortez for bringing our kids into the world and co-parenting with me. Thanks as well for the many opportunities to learn and grow as a human being. To Martha and Jim Sheldon, thank you for supporting the kids and me for all those years, and for your continued support—it still means so much to me. I thank the rest of the Hernández and Cortez family for the hospitality, love, support, and laughs you all shared with me—and continue to share with the kids—it was truly memorable.

Thank you to my strong and brilliant mother, Linda Patiño, for your constant support and for planting in my mind and soul long ago the seed to do what is right and to believe in myself. Thanks to my sister Linda for always having my back and being a phone call away, and to her family—my B-law Raul, and my sobrinos/as Julian and Mya for your love and support. Shout-out to my brother Charles and his wife Andrea—love y'all, especially my beautiful niece and nephew, Celine and Angelo. Thanks for the love and support from my aunt Toni and family, the Martínez family, and to my Papa—Charles Cordova Patiño—your stories called me to be a historian. Rest in Power, Dad, Nana and Granny; you inspire me still.

And to Jimmy III and LunaBella: thank you for your joy, your voice, your love, your honesty, and most of all, your patience with me. I hope you think Dad is kinda cool because I wrote a book. More important, I hope you see how you inspired the passion and calling to write and finish it—and the legacy of struggle you are a part of. Keep shining.

Raza Sí, Migra No

Introduction

We Gotta Get on This Immigration Issue

• •

Let us examine the character of the Mexicano family, of the family of *La Raza* [our people]. In every family, there are those who were born here, those from the other side [of the border] with documents, and those here without documents. . . . What are we going to do—deport all our grandparents and their friends who don't have documents? This was our territory!

—Bert Corona, *Bert Corona Speaks on La Raza Unida Party and the
"Illegal Alien" Scare*

All U.S. workers are suffering deeply from the persistent economic crisis that is shaking the U.S.A. But, as always, under the capitalist economic order those least able to exist and defend themselves are those that are the hardest hit. In this instance, it is the immigrant workers, with or without visas, nonwhite workers, workers that are not unionized, and of course women workers.

—Soledad "Chole" Alatorre, "Plight of Immigrant Workers in U.S."

The Chicano movement took it (immigration) up as a number-one type of priority. This was an issue affecting our people across the board whether we were citizens, whether we were documented or undocumented—this was something that was aimed at our efforts to enfranchise our community.

—Herman Baca, Interview with author

One evening in the early 1970s San Diego area, Chicano movement activist Herman Baca received an unannounced visit from his political mentors, veteran Mexican American labor activists Bert Corona and Soledad "Chole" Alatorre. While conversing with a group of friends for a few moments in Baca's print shop, which doubled as headquarters for the local chapter of the Mexican American Political Association (MAPA), Corona requested that Baca meet him in another room for a private conversation. "What's going on?" asked Baca in the next room. Corona urgently replied, "We gotta get on this immigration issue." Baca recalled thinking to himself, "You on peyote or something? What does that got to do with us?" Corona insisted, "We gotta get on this, this is an issue that is going to be with us probably until the year 2000."[1]

Conspiring with forces set into motion around 1968, this conversation initiated a process in which Baca and a contingent of Chicano movement activists in San Diego would bring the plight of undocumented Mexican immigrants into Chicano movement mobilizations. Building on the efforts of veteran activists such as Corona and Alatorre, who had battled border enforcement policies since the 1930s and 1950s, respectively, grassroots activists in San Diego—through organizations such as MAPA, the Center for Autonomous Social Action (Centro de Acción Social Autónomo; CASA), the local chapter of the La Raza Unida Party (LRUP), and the Committee on Chicano Rights (CCR)—adjusted Chicano movement activism to address the increasing violence emanating from militarized Border Patrol efforts to control the rising number of border crossers from the 1960s into the 1980s. Baca and Corona's backroom conversation represents the conferring of an immigrant rights, community-based, and transnational ethnic Mexican activism to a new generation. It marked the beginning of a conflictual yet significant process in which Baca and this group of San Diego activists contributed to a larger reorientation of the way the relationship between Mexican Americans and Mexican immigrants was conceptualized within the Chicano movement.[2]

This process is reflected in Baca's above quote, highlighting an ideological shift in Chicano movement mobilizations by conceptualizing immigration as a myriad of challenges and structural barriers among ethnic Mexicans "across the board . . . whether we were citizens . . . documented or undocumented."[3] Making it a "number one type of priority" widened the struggle onto transnational terrain and deepened activists' analysis of the ways global capitalist relations created systems of rightless people and workers. This book seeks to document the historical unfolding of this site of struggle and record these activists' ideological and identitarian shifts to demonstrate the potent critical analyses and sustained resistance that evolved to ultimately call for the abolishment of an exploitative regime of illegality—a deportation regime—projected through restrictionist immigration policies.[4]

From 1968 to 1986, San Diego Chicano/a activists linked with past and ongoing struggles against border enforcement policies and reconfigured their conceptualization of identity, strategy, and analysis of power and resistance in relationship with Mexican migrants. Veteran activists such as Corona urged Chicano/a activists to "redefine what is meant by unity" beyond the boundaries of U.S. citizenship and society. Corona sought to interconnect the mobilizing basis of the Chicano movement around ethno-racial unity (*la raza*) and indigeneity ("This was our territory!") with the longer struggle against the class antagonisms embedded in border enforcement policy by including undocumented workers (our grandparents and their friends) as important parts of the struggle of "our people."[5]

Using Baca's experience, this book documents how one localized expression of this sentiment unfolded in key activist organizations in San Diego that ultimately affected the larger state of California, the cross-border San Diego–Tijuana region, larger U.S. and Mexican society, and global debates on undocumented migration. In this regard, the book explores the rise and fall of a social movement that began by simply considering that immigration issues might "have something to do with us."[6] Yet the movement gradually and unevenly evolved to a conception of community that was inclusive of both Mexican Americans and Mexican immigrants (Raza Sí!/Our People Yes!) and identified the deportation regime as a systematic force that targeted ethnic Mexicans in its very functioning (Migra No!/The Border Patrol No!). This movement tied the exploitation of undocumented labor with other regimes within racial capitalism, including indigenous conquest and colonization, chattel slavery, Asian exclusion, past xenophobic movements, and racial segregation. These conceptual foundations interacted with on-the-ground events in the local border region, particularly in the form of legal violence, to contextualize an unfolding Chicano/Mexicano activism against the deportation regime. Through an ideological prism of Chicano self-determination, these Chicano/Mexicano activists reached an abolitionist political perspective on immigration by the late 1970s and the early years of the 1980s.[7]

This abolitionist perspective argued that the making of "illegal" immigrants, continually subject to expulsion from the country, was systematic and routinely used to create a cheap, subjugated workforce for particular business interests, in league with state powers in the United States and Mexico.[8] By 1981, San Diego Chicano/Mexicano activists convened hundreds of grassroots organizers from throughout the United States to demand an "abolishment of the INS [U.S. Immigration and Naturalization Service]/U.S. Border Patrol . . . and of the militarization policy between the U.S./Mexico as a solution to the immigration issue."[9] Up to the federal passage of the

Immigration Reform and Control Act (IRCA) in 1986, Chicano/a immigrant rights activists battled to put forth this grassroots, abolitionist perspective as part of the (inter)national dialog on immigration. This book is the story and critical narrative of this uneven, limited, yet powerful history of struggle.

Raza Sí, Migra No

Rather than a biography of Baca, therefore, the book explores the dynamic community activism that enabled his leadership—among students, migrants, women, workers, and other barrio residents and transients—mobilizing around a notion of "Chicano/Mexicano" identity, and the intertwined struggle for immigrant rights and self-determination. This Raza Sí, Migra No activism in part emerged from the late 1960s to the mid-1980s in the San Diego border region, and analysis of Baca's participation in a number of Chicano movement organizations there—MAPA, LRUP, CASA, and CCR—create the archival and oral history basis to analyze the evolution of Chicano/Mexicano sentiment between 1968 and 1986.

Chicano/a immigrant rights activism was conceptualized in the emergent protest slogan, "Raza Sí, Migra No/Our People Yes, The Border Patrol No!" Rather than engaging the immigration debate as advocates for "immigrants" who were a separate group from Mexican Americans, Chicano/a immigrant rights activism forged a transnational identity and politics that included migrants of all statuses as part of the same community, that is, part of *la raza*, which they articulated as "Chicano/Mexicano," and later, "Chicano/Mexicano/Latino."

Part and parcel to this identity and its politics was, as the slogan Raza Sí, Migra No reveals, recognition that the Border Patrol and deportation-oriented immigration policies were counter to the well-being of *la raza*, both Mexican Americans and Mexican immigrants. Indeed, the racial profiling and anti-Mexican sentiment embedded within the deportation regime and enacted at the border formulated the structural context in which a transnational Chicano/Mexicano identity was forged. The transnational social ecology of San Diego is therefore a significant site in which to document this sociopolitical phenomenon, a region where hundreds of people cross the border routinely each day in both directions to work, shop, spend time with loved ones, and reside.[10] This was a crucial space in which a Chicano/Mexicano transnational identity and politics emerged as activists and community members lived, learned, and developed political positions in a context where the *migra* (Border Patrol) subjugated, harassed, and brutalized Mexican Americans, Mexican immigrants, and other Latinos/as of all legal statuses.[11] In this local context, this book identifies the racial, ethnic, class, and gendered foundations on which activists reimagined the boundaries of the Chicano/a community beyond divisions of citizenship status and nation in a context of state-sanctioned violence.

Critically analyzing the archival and oral history data of the many organizations Baca led, however, entails paying close attention to how the construction of an immigrant rights politics among Chicano movement activists was also limited within the power dynamics of legal status, gender, and sexuality. In this regard, the book not only explores what the oral history and archival data reveals about the content evident in Baca and Corona's backroom conversation but also considers, investigates, and imagines what might have been said in the front room where Chole Alatorre was left with other activists. As Alatorre's above quote reminds, a difficult task within social movements in general, and the struggle for Chicano/a liberation and immigrant rights in particular, is the ability to tie together a number of struggles and different positionalities within capitalist state hegemony at the intersection of race, class, legal status, gender, and sexuality.[12] In the quote, Alatorre insists that the crises and repression unleashed by capitalism is experienced differently and to differing degrees among workers of color, immigrant workers, and/or women/feminized workers. Indeed, these particular groups of working-class people are often "the hardest hit," calling for an analysis and mobilization based on recognition of the divisive privileges extended to groups of workers that may be male, white, and/or citizens. In light of the intersecting regimes of capitalism, white supremacy, and heteropatriarchy highlighted by Alatorre, the book seeks to identify the particular experiences of repression that play out according to differing social identities and positionalities, and acts of solidarity that give priority to the voices of those who are "hardest hit"—"immigrant workers, with or without visas, non-white workers, workers that are not unionized and of course women workers."[13] The absence of Alatorre from Baca and Corona's backroom conversation therefore gives insight to this project, calling for an analysis of the degree to which Chicano/a immigrant rights activism was able to achieve this type of solidarity for "those hardest hit" in its ability to not only address the injustices of race, class, and repression of the undocumented but also gender, sexuality, and other categories that capitalist society utilizes in its day-to-day functioning.[14]

The Chicano movement was a series of mobilizations beginning in the late 1960s based on an ethnic nationalism that sought to unite Mexican

Americans as a people (Chicanos) through celebration of their racial and cultural difference from white Anglo society, recognition of a history of racial oppression, and a strategy of forging community self-determination as a way of organizing for basic civil and human rights.[15] While the Chicano movement put forth a vehement rejection of white supremacy and assimilation strategies and celebrated Mexican culture and identity, it was for the most part silent on the issue of Mexican immigration in its early years during the late 1960s. Therefore, transformation of Chicano movement activism toward a Raza Sí, Migra No perspective was important because Chicano activism was not initially concerned with Mexican immigrants, migration, and legal status issues. As the immigration issue emerged in the late 1960s and early 1970s, many movement activists responded with ambivalence, dismissiveness, and even hostility toward migrants. Indeed, Baca's initial thoughts about Corona's request ("You on peyote or something? What does that got to do with us?") revealed the struggle to address the implications of transnational migration. Chicano/Mexicano identity formations and Raza Sí, Migra No political perspectives were therefore monumental shifts away from nationally bound sentiment due in part to the ways quotidian migrant struggles and Chicano grassroots activism melded in the transnational San Diego border region. In this border context where the local met the global, grassroots activists could not ignore the presence of migrants in their communities, the ways in which undocumented Mexicans were increasingly scapegoated in the local and national media, and the accumulative instances of brutalities against both Mexican immigrants and Mexican Americans by law enforcement agents at the U.S.-Mexico border. Indeed, alongside Baca's initial bewilderment about Corona's request to take on the immigration question, Baca recalled, "I already knew there was something out there that wasn't right."[16]

Racial Capitalism and the Rise of the Deportation Regime

The mechanisms of deportation and immigration policies that Raza Sí, Migra No activists confronted in the San Diego Chicano movement from the late 1960s into the 1980s were part of a longer history of evolving racialized labor regimes that were central to the development and expansion of the United States and the interrelated colonial histories of the wider Americas. From formal systems that subjugated and accessed indigenous laborers to participating in the African slave trade, the very foundations of the U.S. nation-state and its role in the growth of capitalism lie in the seizure of land and labor as facilitated and justified through racial systems of knowledge, at the intersection of gendered notions of hierarchies and naturalization of class inequality. As theorist Cedric Robinson articulates in the notion of "racial capitalism," the development of this new economic regime as it began within Europe involved notions of difference to define which groups were deemed "racially inferior stock for domination and exploitation" and assigned certain types of labor. Racialist conceptions facilitated the construction of multilayered class hierarchies.[17]

These notions of difference were part of the colonial projects of differing European expansionists. These systems from the seventeenth to the nineteenth century created the resources and labor power to develop capitalist modes of production expanding from the U.S. Northeast and facilitating trade on the global market. Global markets emerged from European colonization in the Americas, Africa, and Asia, and established systems of racialized labor while redirecting resources from the colonized south to settler nations such as the United States and to Europe. Within Europe and settler nations, regional differences developed concerning the local resources and the particular character of labor exploitation regimes, such as the role of the plantation in the U.S. South, and its particular racial regime of chattel slavery, which provided cotton and other raw materials to the U.S. Northeast factories and the global market.[18]

Immigration was a key part of capitalist development in the recruitment of more laborers as industrial centers and factories were established alongside the forced migrations of the African slave trade. European migrants from Britain and Ireland, and later Eastern and Southern Europe, actors that often migrated in relation to displacement and capitalist development in their homelands, filled labor needs of the developing North and urban centers in the expanding nation throughout the nineteenth century. The differing national and ethnic backgrounds of these migrants doing unskilled labor also followed the logic of racial capitalism. Ethnic, religious, and national differences, alongside foreign status, hardened to race-like social categories that in many cases justified the low-wage work many of these migrants did to limit their participation in the citizenry of what Alexander Saxton calls the "White Republic."[19] Navigating the shifting boundaries of whiteness and U.S. citizenry, participation in the settler colonial projects of expansion and the development of the U.S. working class as "white" facilitated many of these migrants' and their descendants' uneven integration into U.S. society, a social formation particularly juxtaposed to black, Asian, Native, and Mexican communities.[20]

As the U.S. empire expanded, racial capitalism developed different matrixes of labor regimes, as indigenous land and practices were usurped and colonized, and the Mexican–American War completed the acquisition of northern Mexico, which by 1848 became the United States Southwest. The justifying racial logic used for the acquisition of indigenous and Mexican land marginalized and subjugated those populations now residing in the United States.[21] This was a complicated process as Mexican mestizos/as participated in or were descendants of accomplices to the settler projects of the Spanish empire and subsequent racial hierarchies in Mexico. U.S. dominance naturalized a white supremacist notion that indigenous peoples and mixed-race Mexicans were culturally inferior to Anglo-Americans, and these populations fulfilled initial labor needs as the infrastructure of the Southwest was developed further. Beginning in the second half of the nineteenth century, migrant workers, increasingly from Mexico and Asia, as well as the eastern United States and Europe, came to "the West."

The case of Chinese migrant workers in particular reveals the making of new racial regimes of labor that entangled within them government policy on immigration, accessing these populations for their labor, but then barring them from citizenship, as best exemplified by the Chinese Exclusion Act in 1868. This act, and later the Gentlemen's Agreement with Japan and a number of court cases, established that race could be formally used to determine which migrant populations were eligible and worthy of citizenship.[22] Of course, the determinant was whether these populations were "white" as had been established by the Naturalization Act of 1790, a notion that was a cornerstone of immigration law until the 1960s.[23] By 1924, all Asian groups were deemed ineligible. This racial logic was a structural component of creating a racialized labor hierarchy after the fall of plantation slavery. The category of "coolie" applied to Asian migrant workers signified the rise of a more flexible racialized labor regime following the demise of the slave system, referring to the "captive" nature of slavery simultaneously with the "free" nature of this type of foreign, immigrant laborer.[24] The use of race to determine eligibility for citizenship in the Asian Exclusion law—a population recruited for their labor contributions—worked as a prototype of the regime of illegality and deportation.

These racialized labor regimes developed in the U.S.-Mexico borderlands in relationship to the way capitalist development went hand in hand with the United States' imperialist ambitions westward. While ethnic Mexicans in the former territory of northern Mexico gained all the rights of other U.S. citizens under the Treaty of Guadalupe Hidalgo, the community was racialized in practice. An apartheid system—coupled with what historian Albert Camarillo calls the "proletarianization" of the majority of ethnic Mexicans as individual properties were systematically acquired by Anglo-American arrivals—developed in the Southwest through the rest of the nineteenth century.[25]

Of course, this situation was compounded at the turn of the twentieth century when economic restructuring on both sides of that political border set millions of people in motion. The infrastructural economic development of Mexico between 1870 and 1910—and especially the concentration and consolidation of land holdings by a tiny elite in that period—displaced millions of working people from their homes and livelihoods, driving them into a growing internal migration stream within Mexico. These capitalist developments in Mexico were facilitated by dictator Porfirio Diaz's policy of attracting foreign investors, particularly financial barons from the United States as well as Great Britain, France, and Germany. At almost the same time, the gradual extension of the rail network and expansion of massive irrigation systems in the U.S. Southwest opened up vast new territories to development and, in turn, increased the demand for labor. The convergence of these developments laid the foundation for a rapidly increasing circulation of laborers from Mexico into the United States (and often back again), increasing the ethnic Mexican population from approximately 100,000 in 1848 to 1.4 million by the end of the 1920s.

The rise of an immigration policy based on deportation—a deportation regime—facilitated the continued management of this transnational circulation of Mexican workers. The regime worked as a new racial system initiated in the Immigration Act of 1924 with the creation of the U.S. Border Patrol. The act appeased nativist concerns about a nonwhite influx of immigrants as well as capitalist desires to maintain a subordinated noncitizen workforce.[26] This regime centralized "illegal aliens" as the primary concern of immigration policy, unleashing a law enforcement system that came to target ethnic Mexicans in particular. As historian Mai Ngai asserts, "Illegal . . . became constitutive of 'Mexican,' referring, not to citizens of Mexico, but to a wholly negative racial category, which comprised both Mexicans and Mexican Americans in the United States."[27] The category of "illegal alien" would take the mantel of deeply rooted anti-Mexican sentiment and the long held (and counter factual) assumption that Mexicans, despite where they were born, were foreigners to the United States. Deportations, concerns with "illegal aliens," and the historical anti-Mexican sentiment accessed within these policies racialized ethnic Mexicans across nationality, as evidenced in the first mass deportation campaigns in the 1930s, in which up to 60 percent of the repatriates were U.S. citizens.[28] Just as ethnic Mexicans in the United States resisted the imposition of apartheid conditions and racialized labor regimes that were implemented following the Mexican–American War through forms of ethnic solidarity, demands for labor-racial-gender justice, and an array of barrio institutions, organizations and spaces in which to convene, organizations moved forward to battle the immigration regime as well. This book chronicles how the history of this resistance as interconnected with sustained struggle against the deportation regime.[29]

Narrative

In the context of an evolving racial capitalism in the history of the U.S.-Mexico borderlands, ethnic Mexicans struggled against state sanction and informal violence, land theft, subordination in housing segregation and employment, and an array of tactics to disenfranchise their citizenship granted by the 1848 Treaty of Guadalupe Hidalgo. By the 1920s and 1930s, these struggles encountered the ways emergent immigration policies implemented new forms of subordination. Many forms of convening emerged, such as *mutualistas*, or Mexican cultural practices of mutual aid. These working-class organizations that existed within ethnic Mexican communities addressed the survival needs of migrants beginning in the nineteenth century. The emergence of civil rights organizations and the incorporation of ethnic Mexican workers into labor unions were also critical organizational units that addressed the problems emanating from deportation-oriented immigration policies and mass migration.

This book sees the convening of ethnic Mexican community members in organizations, conventions, conferences, and gatherings as sites of encounter, or *encuentros*, that deliberated on the legal violence exerted on their communities by the deportation regime. These *encuentros* created processes of collective solution making that enabled the praxis of creating alternatives to the hegemony of the nation-state and capital intertwined in the immigration regime.[30] Chapter 1 reveals the history of Mexican American immigrant rights organizing in San Diego and greater Southern California at the intersection of ethnic and labor politics from 1924 to 1968. This chapter reveals that Chicano movement struggles against the deportation regime are part of a longer tradition of Mexican American social movements across generational divides. The chapter begins by exploring the creation of the

Border Patrol and the invention of the "illegal alien" category in 1924 to detail how it came to primarily target the ethnic Mexican population. The chapter then follows the immigrant rights activism of ethnic-based labor movement organizations, primarily the Congress of Spanish-Speaking People, which convened antiracist labor activists, many members of the Communist Party, and trade unionists from affiliates of the Congress of Industrial Organizations (CIO) in the 1930s and 1940s. These labor movement and community organizing spaces featured a transnational notion of peoplehood among ethnic Mexicans that included both immigrant and U.S.-born residents, and called for a radical reform of immigration policies as part of the struggle for workers' rights, antiracist activism, and a critique of U.S. imperialism in Mexico. I highlight the 1950s and 1960s activism of the immigrant worker advocacy group, La Hermandad Mexicana (the Mexican Brotherhood) in San Diego and some chapters of MAPA throughout Southern California that continued to voice community concern about deportations, labor exploitation, and an end to racial segregation.

Chapter 2 explores the process in which some Chicano movement activists in San Diego began to identify immigration as central to their struggles for self-determination and Mexican immigrants as part of their broadening notions of Chicano/a community. Furthermore, it highlights how beginning in the late 1960s and early 1970s this process was greatly influenced by different forms of violence emanating from the U.S. Border Patrol, customs agents, and local law enforcement in the San Diego border region. By focusing on the perspective of undocumented and Mexican American women who spoke out against Border Patrol and customs agents' perpetration of sexual violence, unauthorized strip searches, and other cases of harassment and brutality, the chapter outlines how race, legal status, and gender organized both border policing activities and Chicano movement activists' formulations of a transnational, Raza Sí, Migra No identity and politics. Furthermore, these women's voices, critiques, and complaints evoked a vision of holding customs and border agents accountable and the particular ways legal violence, in its racial, national, and gendered articulations, was embedded in the systematic and official practice of border patrolling.

Chapter 3 contributes to the larger scholarship on CASA (the Center for Autonomous Social Action), a national Chicano movement organization based in Los Angeles, by being the first analysis of its San Diego chapter, CASA Justicia. It reveals CASA Justicia as a significant political space that introduced younger Chicano movement activists to elder organizers who had struggled against the deportation regime in earlier decades. CASA's offering of legal and social services to immigrants suffering the perils of undocumented legal status unleashed a wave of migrant agency, which infused Chicano movement ideological narratives and influenced the mostly Mexican American administrators of CASA to a point where their own identities shifted. Migrants infused their narratives with accounts of the way border enforcement policies were an intensely repressive presence in their day-to-day lives, determining their ability to be present in their familial relationships, to provide sustenance and economic well-being, and to freely move about. U.S. Chicano/a activists in this context shifted their identities and political positions to more fully embrace the migrant struggle as part of the struggle for Chicano liberation. The chapter concludes by exploring the demise of this significant organization beginning in 1975 after a faction split from CASA Justicia due to intense ideological debate and different approaches to strategies about engagement with migrants and the larger ethnic Mexican community.

Chapter 4 continues the exploration of intense debate within Chicano movement circles over the immigration issue through analysis of differing positions among Raza Sí, Migra No activists and Chicano Democrats who were deeply influenced by the popular United Farm Workers (UFW).[31] Beginning with the story of an early 1970s meeting in which Herman Baca met UFW leader and emerging icon César Chávez, the chapter outlines how the first encounter led to "heated" disagreement between Baca, alongside his mentor Bert Corona, and Chávez over their relationship to undocumented workers. This divisive rift in the early 1970s indicated a larger context of political fragmentation within the Chicano movement, with Baca and Corona representing proponents of a transnational vision of Chicano community that included Mexican Americans and Mexican immigrants while emerging numbers of Chicano Democrats, recently elected to office through movement efforts, argued alongside Chávez, the UFW, the larger AFL-CIO (American Federation of Labor and Congress of Industrial Organizations), and other pertinent organizations that undocumented immigrants damaged the economic opportunities of Mexican American and other U.S.-born workers. The manner in which Chicano/a immigrant rights activists debated these Chicano Democrats is explored through Baca's debates with his former ally, San Diego assemblyman Peter Chacón, over California legislation that sought to address the problem of undocumented immigration. This legislation, the Dixon Arnett bill, was debated among Chicanos/as and others from 1970 to 1972, before, during, and following its passage in 1971. Analysis of these debates among Chicano/a activists with vastly differing positions on their relationship with Mexican immigrants and the immigration crisis helps assess the evolution of immigrant rights politics emerging from San Diego in MAPA, CASA Justicia, and the Ad Hoc Committee on Chicano Rights.

Chapter 5 continues the story begun in chapter 4, when a split between Chicano Democrats and Chicano/Mexicano immigrant rights activists led to the exodus of the latter from the statewide MAPA organization to the seemingly more radical politics of La Raza Unida Party, an ethnic third party effort. The chapter explores how this moment led to debates between various factions of the California La Raza Unida Party in which San Diego Chicano/Mexicano activists participated from roughly 1970 to 1975. Community activists in San Diego LRUP challenged a persistent narrow nationalism in the broader LRUP that, despite rhetoric otherwise, de-emphasized the noncitizen migrant experience and struggled to embrace the diverse political positions within the ethnic Mexican community. San Diego Chicano/Mexicano LRUP organizers maintained engagement with the diverse ethnic Mexican community in their registration efforts, as they continued to learn about the limits of voting strategies in their mixed legal status community. At the state level, the California LRUP, despite its progressive internationalist rhetoric, struggled to create a concerted solidification toward transnational unity across legal status due to prevalent suspicions of "outsiders" that threatened Chicano solidarity. Factions within the LRUP, basing their platform on an imagined "authentic" Chicano politics, successfully marginalized an emerging solidarity that would link movement politics to the goal of dismantling the immigration deportation system. This was tragically accomplished by policing the ethno-racial and political authenticity of participates in LRUP, thereby falling short of the radically democratic praxis encouraged and required in a struggle that advocated for undocumented migrants.

Chapter 6 explores how Baca and San Diego Chicano/Mexicano activists who had navigated MAPA, CASA, and the LRUP created the CCR in 1976. This group of course had struggled against local manifestations of the deportation regime, including racialized legal violence by local law enforcement and police entanglement with the Border Patrol. Undoubtedly a precursor to contemporary "show me your papers" laws and practices in contemporary Arizona and other states, these activists fought the San Diego Sherriff's Department's order in 1972 for taxi cab drivers, under penalty of citation and fines, to report to their offices for apprehension any of their clientele who they "felt" might be undocumented. The San Diego

Police Department, under the administration of San Diego mayor (and future California governor) Pete Wilson, followed suit in 1973 by assuming the responsibility of determining residents' legal status and apprehending the undocumented to assist the U.S. Border Patrol. The emergent CCR and their allies had challenged these racial profiling policies targeting ethnic Mexicans and other Latinos/as, revealing again how racializing policies and procedures practiced by tentacles of the law enforcement regime facilitated ideological and identitarian transformations among U.S. Chicanos/as. This racialized structural repression through law enforcement—from Border Patrol agents to local city police—enabled Chicanos/as to assert solidarity and communal ties with undocumented migrants, and, as will be further explored, other communities of color, particularly African Americans. Indeed, police repression revealed a shared experience of legal violence and racialization across differences in legal status, as black and brown people who were U.S. citizens were subjected to what activists perceived as the same regime of police violence. This culminated in the founding of the CCR through the struggle on behalf of the family of a Puerto Rican barrio youth, Luis "Tato" Rivera, killed by a National City police officer. The CCR asserted a politics of Chicano self-determination by engaging with localized community concerns, particularly police violence, as demonstrated in the tragic Rivera struggle. Through localized dialog and grassroots decision-making processes, a movement of Chicano/Mexicano organizers and a group of black activists sought justice for Tato, collectively engaging the local governing process and choosing to struggle for a recall of the entire National City Council. This mobilization provided a framework for holding accountable, and even attempting to abolish, governmental entities that unleashed violence on racialized communities. Such organizing worked as a template for further struggle against border policing as migrants and citizens of color would be subject to further legal violence by border policing agents, as explored in the final two chapters of the book.

Chapter 7 explores how the CCR rose to international prominence by criticizing President Jimmy Carter's 1977 proposal to further militarize the border (alongside a limited amnesty) while calling attention to an announcement by the infamous Ku Klux Klan (KKK), which planned on implementing a Border Watch Program to assist the Border Patrol in apprehending migrants. Focusing on the years 1977 to 1979, this struggle revealed that the nationalization of the immigration issue led to a widening notion of Chicano/Mexicano transnational community from beyond the borderlands in relation to other Latino/a communities throughout the country and beyond the context of the United States to further engagement with Mexico and Mexican civil society. From the purview of the CCR and other activists, over the past decade Border Patrol agents in conjunction with local police had invaded homes, churches, and schools; jailed, deported, and at times brutalized both Mexican immigrants and Mexican Americans; and daily searched, questioned, and detained border crossers, often under dubious circumstances. The CCR used the sensational event of KKK involvement at the border to argue that their overt racism was a manifestation of the implicit racism of border patrolling policies in general, particularly that proposed by President Carter. The 1977 March Against the Carter Curtain, which began a national dialog among grassroots Chicano/a and immigrant rights activists, set the tone for a sustained immigrant rights struggle calling for an elimination of border patrolling over the next several years.

Chapter 8 analyzes collective Chicano/Mexicano processes of asserting independent solutions to the immigration crisis by convening the space for grassroots organizers from throughout the United States to participate in a radically democratic practice of decision making. On April 11, 1981, the CCR reconvened a number of the one thousand grassroots activists who had participated in the National Chicano Immigration Conference the year before to hear the voices of several survivors of *migra* brutality and remember those who did not survive the abuse of militarized immigration policy. The chapter argues that through the tribunal, the CCR demonstrated an alternative practice of belonging, challenging the legitimacy of immigration policy and disrupting the related discourse of the nation-state by revealing its collusion with capital. Furthermore, the National Chicano Immigration Conference, held in 1980, was a process in which activists, community members, and advocates collectively constructed solutions to the immigration crisis from the perspective of the transnational "Chicano/Mexicano/Latino" community. These events intensified a dialog between the CCR as a significant part of the wider Chicano/Mexicano leadership and the U.S. state on abolishing the deportation mechanism of immigration policy. The CCR also facilitated an intensified dialog with the Mexican state and civil society. The tribunal demonstrated a practice of autonomy by Chicano/Mexicano/Latino communities as independent from, but in dialog with, both the Mexican and U.S. states, suggesting an enactment of a working-class transnational community formation—a critical mass articulating alternatives to not only the immigration regime but also global shifts toward neoliberalism.

The conclusion is a brief analysis of how the 1986 Immigrant Reform and Control Act (IRCA) both conceded to and fragmented the Chicano/

Mexicano immigrant rights mobilizations facilitated in part by the CCR. Signed by a Republican, President Ronald Reagan, it was the first mass amnesty act revealing the influence of the human rights components of Chicano/Mexicano organizing that activists in San Diego had taken part in formulating beginning in the late 1960s. Yet the act also marginalized the abolitionist position of the movement, giving concessions by providing amnesty to a subsection of undocumented migrants, while further militarizing the U.S.-Mexico border. The chapter concludes with an analysis of two divergent responses by Chicano/Mexicano activists to the new law: those who invested their energies in politicizing and assisting undocumented migrants who qualified for the amnesty provisions of IRCA by working with immigration state mechanisms and other activists who continued to criticize the "carrot and stick" immigration policies and maintain the call to abolish immigration state apparatuses. The latter group argued that the law ensured a reproduction of an exploitable undocumented population through the law's failure (or deliberate maneuver) to address the roots of illicit migration from the global south to the north that catered to the insatiable needs of an increasingly mobile capitalist class.

Taken together, the chapters trace the longer history of ethnic Mexican resistance to the immigration regime and reveal that these struggles required organizing across differences in nationality and legal status, among others. Forging a shared struggle among and solidarity between Mexican Americans and Mexicans immigrants was not a given, but much rather built on specific struggles against the state violence of border police and officials, an environment of xenophobia emerging from media sources and providing political capital for particular politicians, and the day-to-day needs of working people. Grounding these struggles in San Diego, the chapters piece together a story that reveals everyday people—undocumented women, migrant workers, families, Mexican American students, Chicana activists, and many others—rising up to do something about the injustices of their fellow community members in their own backyard. When an organic intellectual such as Herman Baca emerged ready to articulate these concerns, hundreds of Chicano/a and Mexicano/a community members and their allies heeded the call. Who was to speak, what was included in the analyses of why these injustices were happening, and what the solutions should be were always in tension and under debate, shifting and being contested. The chapters trace these contestations within and around the historic mobilizations of the Chicano movement struggle against the immigration regime to narrate how these hundreds, and even thousands, of people arrived in support for an abolishment of border policing and immigration policies rooted in the logic of deportation. This is their story—even if they did not always appear in the archive—their images in pictures and in reports reveal they were there, and without them, there is no story or leaders.[32] As one declaration reminds us, "Sometimes the people take up a name in order to say they are taking up a flag."[33]

Part I   **The Mexican American Left and Early Struggles against the Deportation Regime, 1924–1968**

1 Historical Rights in the Territory

Struggles for Mexican Immigrant Rights from El Congreso to La Hermandad

. . . .

In April 1939, San Diego delegates attended the first *Congreso del Pueblo que Habla Español* (Congress of Spanish-Speaking People) in Los Angeles. Luisa Moreno, a labor activist in Los Angeles and San Diego and a major Congreso organizer, brought forward a number of Mexican, Mexican American, and other workers to provide testimony of their suffering to the nationally convened group of activists. Humberto Lozano's face was burned by chemicals while working in a factory. Ambrosio Escudero had lost three of his fingers while working as a machinist. The Congreso's focus on labor inequity also brought forth ethnic Japanese and Filipino workers who shared their experiences of racial violence in rural areas where they farmed in California.[1]

Mexican and Mexican American labor organizers in San Diego had mobilized along with other workers to address these types of abuses in the midst of vigilante KKK harassment and "illegal alien" roundups by the newly created Border Patrol during the repatriations of the 1930s. Congreso chapters emerged in San Diego proper and in the San Diego County towns of Escondido, National City, and Oceanside to organize ethnic Mexican workers and face KKK and Border Patrol repression.[2] Congreso members in the San Diego borderlands forged solidarity among Mexican-origin workers across differences in legal status independently and through ongoing efforts of the CIO's movement to organize historically unrepresented workers—blacks, ethnic Mexicans, women, immigrants—across the United States during the Great Depression. The Congreso emerged to articulate what activist Bert Corona called "the Mexican American Left" as an innovative new voice that privileged the experiences of abused racialized laborers and noncitizens to develop a politics at the intersection of ethno-racial autonomy and labor rights.[3] Indeed, Tejana Communist Emma Tenayuca and other radicals in the Mexican American Left network asserted key concepts by articulating an analysis of deportation-oriented immigration restrictions that asserted that Mexican nationals held "historical rights in the territory . . . regardless of their citizenship . . ." and called for "the abolition of all restrictions—economic, political, and cultural—and for the due recognition of the historic rights of the Mexican people and territory."[4] Another leftist union organizer, Luisa Moreno, later tied these "historical rights" in regard to land with the human entitlements embedded within acts of labor. She asserted, "These people are not aliens—they have contributed their endurance, sacrifices, youth and labor to the Southwest."[5] Tenayuca's outlook, while unclear about the relationship between Spanish-speaking and indigenous peoples, asserted historic rights among ethnic Mexicans to critique the settler-colonialism of the United States takeover since the Mexican American War of 1848 and, alongside Moreno's critique of capitalist exploitation of migrant labor, countered the emergent logic of deportation.[6]

This chapter demonstrates that such positions emerged from the 1920s to the 1960s within important manifestations of Mexican American activism in Southern California. It emerged out of localized community struggles in conjunction with the burgeoning labor movements in the United States to articulate an intersecting ethno-racial and working-class identity that enabled advocacy for undocumented immigrants as fellow coethnics and workers. The rest of the chapter highlights the activism of ethnic-based labor movement organizations such as El Congreso, the Asociación Nacional Mexicana (ANMA), and La Hermandad Mexicana in their struggles to protect undocumented workers as part of the mixed-status ethnic Mexican community. These *encuentros* convened by these organizations nominally accomplished an understanding of power that centralized workers' oppression, and as evidenced in the leadership of many women organizers, accomplished a nuanced understanding that racism and sexism conditioned and intensified the oppression of workers. As the Great Depression, World War II, and the Cold War shaped and reshaped the material conditions and political possibilities that were imagined, these struggles laid the groundwork for a working class ethnic Mexican community critique of immigration policy and deportations, and their ties to racial, gender, and labor exploitation for future generations.

Cross-Citizenship and Transnational Resistance: El Congreso

As early as the 1910s and 1920s, a number of observers commented on the contradictions created when people with different nationalities but very similar class positions and linguistic, religious, and cultural traditions encountered each other as parts of a multinational labor force toiling within the territorial jurisdiction of the United States.[7] The development of temporary foreign labor programs during both world wars tended to exacerbate the complexities of Mexican/Mexican American interactions as both groups grappled with questions of their own senses of national and cultural affiliation; issues of cultural "authenticity"; and, of course, their attitudes toward one another.[8]

One of the perennial issues that ethnic Mexican activists in the United States faced after the emergence of a deportation-based immigration regime in the 1920s, therefore, was how best to struggle for full citizenship rights while a large proportion of their constituency were noncitizens. Throughout the twentieth century, ethnic Mexican politics in the United States was fragmented along the lines of nationality (American and Mexican) and citizenship status (U.S. citizen, documented migrant, and undocumented migrant).[9] For Mexicans in the United States, the pressures of being racially marked as perpetually "foreign" and inferior, a legacy of the Mexican–American War, were exacerbated further by the establishment of the Border Patrol in 1924 as an agency that more strictly enforced the divide between citizens and noncitizens, chiefly at the U.S–Mexico border.[10] Due to these pressures, on the one hand, many Mexican American activists, most prominently the League of United Latin American Citizens (LULAC) beginning in the 1920s emphasized their U.S. citizenship in juxtaposition to the noncitizens in their own communities. On the other hand, a number of ethnic Mexican activists, particularly those involved in the labor movements of the Depression era, enacted an ethno-racial solidarity among Mexican Americans and Mexican immigrants that was often grounded in an intersecting working-class identity.

Important to ethnic Mexican activists in the labor movement of the Depression era was how the CIO and radical activists, particularly the Communist Party of the United States of America (CPUSA) successfully ventured into communities of color, including a number of Latino/a workers, in their drive to address the dire economic circumstances of the era through organizing groups of workers historically marginalized by dominant labor unions.[11] It was in this context that a contingent of ethnic Mexican community members in San Diego and wider California formulated a concerted response to the mechanism of racialized noncitizen exploitation and the related system of deportation across the imposed differences of nationality and citizenship status. Many scholars have noted that *El Congreso del Pueblo de Habla Español*, a coalition of labor activists, liberal politicians, and leftist artists and organizers, was paramount to a working-class assertion of ethnic Mexican, and to a degree broader panethnic Latino, politics in the United States that crossed lines of citizen and noncitizen via cross-border ethnic ties, identity as workers, women's rights, and protection of immigrants as vulnerable members of the workforce. Congreso reoriented ethnic Mexican identity to battle the deportation regime and tie ethnic Mexican struggles to larger class concerns across borders.[12]

Mostly ethnic Mexican labor activists, alongside a small contingent of Puerto Rican, Cuban, and Spanish-origin participants, and their Anglo allies, convened a national meeting of grassroots organizers to determine action against, among other things, the repatriation drives from the perspective of the racialized communities under attack. Repatriation in the 1930s—what historians have called "A Decade of Betrayal"—put into practice the anti-Mexican mechanism of deportation and other coercive measures, resulting in at least half a million Mexican-origin people, about half or more of which were U.S. citizens, being returned to Mexico.[13] Within this hostile context, the Congreso held its first meeting in Los Angeles in 1939, where members identified border enforcement policies and deportations as a primary method of worker repression and exploitation, and called for the immediate end to deportations and adjustment of noncitizen workers' status.

The Congreso convened for "unity of the Spanish speaking people of the United States" to struggle for "the defense of Mexican homes in the United States, seeking to prevent their disorganization frequently caused by deportations."[14] Congreso identified deportations as a threat against "Mexican homes" across lines of official citizenship status. Indeed, the Congreso asserted that the repatriation effort more specifically had been "distorted by forces hostile to the Mexican and Spanish-American people in the United States" leading to "abuses upon our people." The Congreso opted to work independently toward informing noncitizens and other interested parties about the violation of rights and the antilabor effects of repatriation and deportation.[15] Furthermore, the Congreso sought to amend "the naturalization laws to permit all noncitizens, who wish to do so, to become American citizens."[16] Their primary reasoning was that fees for naturalization were too high for the working-class wages made by most of these noncitizens, that red tape and bureaucracy worked to bar access to citizenship, and most important, that "in every way except the possession of citizenship papers they (noncitizens) are as thoroughly a part of American society as the citizen population."[17] The Congreso's political and social platform made clear that such arguments for an easier path to U.S. citizenship did not require an assimilationist strategy that would de-emphasize the maintenance of transnational connections to Mexico and bicultural identities.

These postulations by the Congreso were part of a call for unity as an ethnic group that transcended the boundaries of the nation-state and crossed lines of nationality and citizenship status in a new era in which noncitizens, particularly those of Mexican-origin, were the targets of state repression. Parting ways with middle-class civil rights organizations by emphasizing shared cultural and working-class concerns among Mexican Americans and Mexicans immigrants, Congreso unleashed a critique of U.S. interests that exploited the labor of this community while creating barriers to fundamental life chances.[18] Utilizing ethnic identity as a basis for a structural critique of capitalism and larger solidarity with the international working class, Congreso carved out a space of struggle that utilized racial unity to contribute to class struggle on transnational terrain.

By organizing as an ethnic- and class-based entity, in the spirit of uniting with the wider working class, Congreso asserted an autonomous space from which to struggle, build coalition, and locally root radical activism while interconnecting it with transnational and global processes. The Congreso was part of a Communist popular front to address racial issues and incorporate workers of color into the ranks of the labor movement. Like other workers of color, ethnic Mexicans and other Latinos/as utilized the infrastructures of the Communist Party and CIO unions to assert a "politics of opposition" that enabled activists to enact their own, independent political perspective around the notion of ethno-racial identity as it intersected with class oppression as well as gender positionalities.[19]

Indeed, about 30 percent of Congreso's membership were women, many of whom held leadership positions, including cofounder Luisa Moreno as well as Josefina Fierro de Bright in the central Los Angeles chapter, and in San Diego women such as Cesaria Valdez, Celia L. de Rodríguez, Aurora Castillo, and Margarita Flores, who battled gender discrimination in the workplace, domestic abuse, and environmental ills.[20] Congreso's official stance on gender oppression, as designed at another 1939 conference, asserted that "The Mexican woman, who for centuries has suffered oppression (and) double discrimination, as a woman and a Mexican" and that in response chapters would create women's committees "so that she (the Mexican woman) may receive equal wages, enjoy the same rights as men in social, economic, and civic liberties, and use her vote for the defense of the Mexican and Spanish American people, and American democracy."[21]

Therefore, the Congreso acted as an autonomous voice for grassroots community and labor activists creating a program to address the intersection of race, class, and gender repression as a transnational entity rooted in the United States but situated in between the United States and Mexico, and even wider Latin America. Congreso worked as a transnational entity in its unequivocal stance that Mexican and wider Latino/a culture and community, built in reaction to a history of class racism for protection and perseverance, as well as the current structural position of both Mexican Americans and Mexican noncitizens as primarily exploited workers, sought to build on connections that transcended the U.S.-Mexico border. Indeed, Congreso put forth a transnational identity as both "American" and "Mexican" from the beginning of the 1939 conference when both the U.S. and Mexican national hymns were honored. The resolutions of the Congreso called for the preservation of Mexican heritage, the establishment of Spanish as another official language on par with English in areas of the country where there were large numbers of Spanish-speaking people, and even for a prototype of Chicano/a studies that would educate U.S. residents about the long history of Spanish-speaking peoples in what is now the United States.[22] This political stance on cultural identity perceived no contradiction between the transnational practice of Mexican ethnicity and ethnic Mexicans' place as part of U.S. society. The Congreso's expression of a Mexican identity within the United States facilitated its advocacy for and identification with undocumented migrants on the basis of both ethnic and class solidarity.

While historian George J. Sánchez notes that the Congreso signaled a shift from a Mexico-oriented to a "Mexican American" political posture rooted in the politics and context of the United States, the Congreso's embrace of Mexican and Latino/a heritage and communion with Mexican migrants as part of their community inextricably maintained ties to Mexican society.[23] One participant in the 1939 Congreso convention stated, "The basic objectives pursued by the Spanish-Speaking Congress involve the unification between American citizens of Mexican descent and Mexican nationals as well as the friendship between the peoples of the United States and Mexico."[24] The Congreso demonstrated that the structural reality of migration and the intertwined economies of the United States and Mexico created possibilities for a politics that transcended the nation-state. While it is apparent that a shift in consciousness among ethnic Mexican politics moved toward focusing on life in the United States as indicated in advocacy for union activity, naturalization, registration, and voting in a generation that was majority U.S.-born and generally supportive of the politics of the New Deal, the Congreso also maintained a space that nurtured cross-border notions of belonging in its engagement with the voices and experiences of noncitizens. For example, one of the Congreso's early public demonstrations involved support for Mexican president Lazaro Cardenas's effort to expropriate U.S. and foreign oil companies from Mexico. Former member of the Congreso Bert Corona remembered: "These companies for years had unfairly exploited Mexico's oil resources. El Congreso organized a march against possible U.S. military intervention to regain the oil concessions. Eight or nine thousand people marched up Broadway Street in downtown Los Angeles in a protest that concluded at the Mexican consulate. The march scared the hell out of the city establishment—Mexicans had never before marched in Los Angeles in such numbers."[25]

Indeed, Cardenas's appointee to the Los Angeles Mexican consulate and former interim president of Mexico Adolfo de la Huerta attended the 1939 convention and offered support and advice. Other transnational interactions included attendance of a representative from the Mexican labor union, the Confederación de Trabajadores Mexicanos (CTM). The Congreso had invited the CTM's leader, Lombardo Toledano, but due to his radicalism he was not allowed to enter the United States. Instead, Toledano sent a representative.[26] Explicit engagement with Mexican politics, expressions of Mexican identities in the United States, and embracement of noncitizens as fellow community members with shared cultural and class experiences defined belonging as a transnational rather than a nation-state–based reality.

Congreso Activism in San Diego

San Diego served as an important site in which members of the Congreso sought to protect and organize noncitizen workers in its pivotal position at the U.S.-Mexico border. As a site of border crossing, recruitment of migrant labor, and prevalent racial terrorism, San Diego and the Imperial Valley was a challenging and significant place for the Congreso's efforts—particularly in battling the terror of the KKK and exploitation of migrants by coyotes.[27] Thousands of Mexican immigrants had lived and worked in the fields throughout San Diego County and adjacent Imperial County, and as such were the target of KKK and other white supremacists organizations. Evidence suggests that the Klan would raid, lynch, and kill ethnic Mexicans along the U.S.-Mexico border, targeting the many migrants looking to work on the citrus, walnut, and other farms and factories from which owners hired them to work. Tying Klan terrorism with border control policies, Congreso member Bert Corona remembered recovered migrant victims of murderous KKK violence at the border. He stated: "These cadavers represented the forgotten, the abominated. In a way, U.S. border authorities saw the Klan's deeds as a form of Mexican repatriation in the 1930s."[28] Indeed, the racialization of ethnic Mexicans through official repatriation efforts fueled Klan activity. While capital depended on the exploitation of the ethnic Mexican workforce, when their numbers increased in the 1920s they became a threat to white capitalist accumulations. Like other situations, such as Chinese exclusion just a few decades before, the state invoked the whiteness of the citizenry to discipline ethnic Mexicans through affirming outcries for immigration restrictions.[29] In the U.S.-Mexico borderlands, the state granted the concessions to the "white" citizenry by exhibiting complacency toward Klan activity and encouraging white supremacist terrorism through the racialized practice of deportation regime immigration policies.

In the San Diego area, Congreso chapters were founded at National City, Oceanside, and Escondido, as well as the wider lettuce, cotton, citrus, and cannery industries in conjunction with trade unions.[30] Seeking to organize workers across ethnicities, Congreso members, including Philip and Julia Usquiano, Roberto Galvan, Cesaria Valdez, Carlos Montalvo, Aurora Castillo, and Margarita Flores, worked with wider Southern California Congreso leaders based mostly in Los Angeles, including Luisa Moreno, Josefina Fierro de Bright, Carey McWilliams, Bert Corona, and "Smiley" Rincon, to challenge a system of labor exploitation. Capitalists used the Border Patrol, local police, and the KKK to terrorize workers of color and break down unionizing efforts. Bill Karn, a grower in Fallbrook in northern San Diego County, exemplified this systemic practice in that he was both a San Diego County Supervisor and a KKK member. Furthermore, he reportedly used the Border Patrol to break up attempts to unionize by Mexican workers he employed.[31] The Klan and businesses that utilized noncitizen laborers and border enforcement policies formally and informally worked together in Southern California to disrupt the Congreso's organizing efforts.

The Congreso in San Diego sought to challenge this racism and labor exploitation through a strategy of organizing and uniting citizen and noncitizen workers within the trade union movement. In 1937, founding member of the Congreso Luisa Moreno arrived in San Diego to organize the fish and cannery workers throughout Southern California.[32] As chief organizer of the United Cannery, Agricultural, Packing, and Allied Workers of America (UCAPAWA) in Southern California, by the 1940s she successfully negotiated with a number of industry leaders to gain, among other things, a non-discrimination pledge from the Royal Packing Plant that packed Ortega chiles in San Diego.[33] During the spring of 1939, operatives at the Van Camp Seafood Company, a tuna cannery in San Diego, organized Local 61 of UCAPAWA. After a year of struggle, the firm signed a contract recognizing the union. According to historian Vicki Ruiz, "In 1942 local members and management hammered out a new agreement (providing) the predominately Mexican work force" with the highest wages in the tuna packing industry.[34] This accomplishment demonstrates how Congreso members applied their goals of including noncitizen workers and wider racial justice issues in the campaigns of unions within the CIO. UCAPAWA activism in the cannery industries was a prime focus for Congreso efforts, particularly because vulnerable noncitizens and workers of color were well represented in these workforces. In relation to these struggles, Moreno wrote "Caravans of Sorrow" in 1940 to argue that noncitizens were indeed a part of the American working class, and in the process, attempted to advance a bold new definition of belonging. She explained of noncitizens: "These people are not aliens—they have contributed their endurance, sacrifices, youth and labor to the Southwest. Indirectly, they have paid more taxes than all the stockholders of California's industrialized agriculture, the sugar beet companies and the largest cotton interests that operate or have operated with the labor of Mexican workers."[35]

In San Diego, this cross-citizenship organizing brought the wrath of the KKK, particularly as the activities of CIO organizers reached rural areas where farm workers toiled in the vast agricultural industries of the borderlands of San Diego and Imperial Counties. Like the organizing work in the canneries, the women's committee of the Congreso, the Comite de Damas del Congreso (Ladies of the Congress Committee), in San Diego worked to improve the lives of farm workers in borderland fields. One member, Margarita Flores, was brutally beaten by members of the KKK in Brawley, Imperial County. She lost her right eye and several teeth. The KKK in Orange County near Anaheim also beat Celia L. de Rodríguez.[36] A few *damas* disappeared and were never seen again in east San Diego and Imperial County. According to Larralde, Luisa Moreno thought they were left somewhere in the desert in rural Imperial County, victims of Klan violence.[37] San Diego Congreso members struggled to get the word out about the prevalence of KKK violence at the border since few mainstream newspapers reported on it.[38]

World War II and Congreso Organizing

The U.S. entrance into World War II shifted Congreso's efforts in the California borderlands in significant ways, namely, by moving forward with a popular front strategy, addressing the massive influx of immigrant workers in response to the wartime demand for labor, and confronting the domestic social environment that touted a patriotism that was often exclusive of people of color. Congreso members united with the U.S. effort against Hitler due in part to the American Communist Party's call to forge a popular front against fascism to maintain democratic principles in which change could be fought for, and in the interest of battling white supremacy.[39] Yet the popular front strategy also diminished the Congreso's civil rights work as members joined the war effort or diffused into other organizational fronts.[40] In San Diego, growth of the defense industry and the parallel growth of an exclusive promilitary ideological environment put Congreso members in a position in which they continued unionizing efforts across citizenship ranks while having to battle the increased maltreatment of communities of color who were too often perceived as not truly American and thus a threat to the war effort.

Moving to San Diego in 1940, Moreno continued organizing cannery workers in the context of a wartime economic boom. With Congreso member and secretary treasurer of the United Fish Cannery Workers Union Roberto Galvan, Moreno organized the UCAPAWA Local 64, enlisting hundreds of workers in San Diego's largest canneries, including California Packing Corporation, Marine Products Company, the Old Mission Packing Corporation, Van Camp Sea Food Company, and Westgate Sea Products.[41] This continued labor organizing was significant because World War II brought thousands more Mexican immigrant workers to the San Diego borderlands due to the industrial development that grew around the transformation of San Diego into a naval center.[42] Thousands of soldiers and sailors moved in and out of the region, while the wartime economic boom brought more Mexican migrants to fill important labor demands. By 1943, these informally recruited migrant workers were joined by bracero workers who arrived as part of an agreement between the United States and Mexico. Known as the Bracero Program, the two governments worked to bring Mexican laborers to temporarily fill labor needs left open as U.S. workers went to fight overseas. Just years after hauling Mexican workers away for "stealing jobs," they were now being officially recruited by the U.S. government.

The treatment of Japanese Americans as suspected enemies within the United States reflected the narrow nationalism exerted in an environment of wartime patriotism and reveals how race and ethnicity continued to be key factors in defining who was "American." Congreso members' responses to the internment of Japanese Americans beginning with Executive Order 9066 in 1942 provides evidence that its focus on worker's issues facilitated multiracial organizing and activism. For example, the San Diego Comite de Damas del Congreso consisted of members who were Anglo, Asian, and "Hispanic" according to one description of a meeting in the city's downtown.[43] Moreno and other Congreso members spoke out against the relocation of Japanese Americans to camps.[44] San Diego played a vital role in Congreso efforts to smuggle Japanese and Japanese Americans into Baja California to avoid detention. San Diego Congreso members Phil Usquiano and Carlos Montalvo assisted Los Angeles-based activists, especially Armando Davila and Alfredo Montoya, in these efforts. Addressing multiracial workforces in Southern California, Davila encouraged Japanese and Mexican Americans to take charge of their own lives in the face of brutal discrimination. Asserting a transnational political approach, Davila also pressured both the Roosevelt administration and the Mexican government to cease the mistreatment of the ethnic Japanese community while advocating for improved working conditions for ethnic Mexicans and other workers.[45] San Diego Congreso member Roberto Galvan reportedly assisted Japanese American internees at the Manzanar Camp northeast of Los Angeles by helping them sell their personal belongings and providing storage for many of the interned families' goods. He also reportedly assisted Japanese Americans into Mexico to escape internment. Many Congreso members, including Galvan, who was a close friend of the Okimoto family, had neighbors and compatriots who were Japanese Americans.[46] San Diego Congreso member Cesaria Valdez worked with her secretary, Junko, in her attempts to initiate government programs that addressed poverty in rural areas and farm worker communities. Junko was later interned.[47] This engagement with the Japanese American community and other communities of color was reflective of the grassroots attempts to organize the workers in the agribusiness and cannery industries, who tended to be Filipino, Japanese, and Mexican.[48]

The exclusive notion of wartime American identity also affected the Mexican American community and other communities of color. Indeed, ethnic Mexican, African American, and other youth who were participating in the jazz and zoot suit subculture of the era, were also targeted as a threat to the nation from within.[49] This wartime policing effort was best exemplified by events in Los Angeles, including the Sleepy Lagoon incident in 1942 and the Zoot Suit Riots in 1943. In clashes between these mostly Mexican American youth and military personnel the press depicted the youth as criminal gang members who held a disregard for authority and the war effort. These sentiments erupted in 1942 when a group of Mexican American youths was charged with the murder of Jose Díaz in Sleepy Lagoon in south-central Los Angeles and in June 1943 when sailors in Los Angeles attacked mostly Mexican American zoot-suiters.[50] The press and local leaders exerted anti-Mexican sentiment over concern for these "pachucos," or street youth, by using racializing language that defined Mexicans as primitive and barbaric. The wartime environment led many officials to conflate advocacy for these youth and against the racist sentiment being exerted on them with disloyalty and even Communist-inspired conspiracy to attack the United States from within.[51]

In San Diego, fear of the "pachuco menace" merged with ever-prevalent hysteria over "illegal aliens" to intensify the racialization of ethnic Mexicans in the border region. Moreno worked with Galvan to educate rank-and-file union members in San Diego about the issues involved in the Sleepy Lagoon Case in nearby Los Angeles. As a key member of the Sleepy Lagoon Defense Committee, Moreno argued, "The hysteria against the Sleepy Lagoon defendants and the Pachucos over all was the outward manifestation of a complex fear in Southern California that Mexicans were moving more into the essential industries like agriculture, the food-processing commerce, the garment commerce, construction and other businesses."[52] The riots of 1943 extended into San Diego, making visible ongoing conflicts between the military presence so prevalent in the emergent naval port and the area ethnic Mexican community. The San Diego City Council investigated a number of fights at local bars attended by both civilians and servicemen. On June 10, 1943, the *San Diego Union* reported that groups of servicemen took to the streets of downtown San Diego in response to a rumor that zoot-suiters had arrived in San Diego from Los Angeles. About one hundred sailors and marines chased zoot-suiters out of the area. San Diego police were told to search suspicious individuals that "appeared to be members of a Pachuco gang."[53] Seeking to disrupt the notion of wartime unity in San Diego, Luisa Moreno led a campaign in San Diego that attempted to force local officials to address the routine violence exerted by military personnel on ethnic Mexican communities. Allying for a time with San

Diego city councilman Charles C. Dail and Mexican consul Alfredo Elías Calles, Moreno sought to address the systematic conflict between the military and the ethnic Mexican community.[54]

Moreno argued that several cases of military personnel inflicting violence against the ethnic Mexican community were going unreported. Despite activist efforts to bring these incidents to the attention of both city and navy leadership, the problem was ignored because officials worried it would affect morale and the overall war effort. In other words, ethnic Mexican concerns were ignored due to the perception that their problems were at odds with national unity for the war. Moreno argued: "We will never know much about the San Diego civilian casualties. The Navy and the local newspaper ignored the violence since most of the victims were Mexicans."[55] Moreno alerted a number of *San Diego Union* reporters to several conflicts between minorities and the police and navy personnel.[56] She also expressed concern for Latino/a military personnel. Councilman Dail informed Rear Admiral David Bagley about the problem of civilian–military conflicts and their prevalence in San Diego. In the context of the San Diego borderlands where Mexican migrant laborers worked and passed through looking for work, Admiral Bagley had once reportedly joked, "Mexicans came cheap by the dozen and could be bought for ten cents each," and if "the Japs bombed Mexico City, it would cost fifty cents to replace it."[57] Moreno and Dail aimed to confront Admiral Bagley about the comments and invited him to meet. Bagley refused the offer.

In the new wartime context, elites threatened by the continued efforts of Congreso members and the wider labor movement to advocate for workers of color responded by using the old tactic of questioning the patriotism of unionists, deploying the strengthening vitality of red-baiting, and threatening to deport immigrant activists. In this emerging circumstance, the attempts to address the problems between military personnel and local ethnic Mexican residents in San Diego deteriorated when Admiral Bagley allied himself with state senator Jack B. Tenney, a master of red-baiting tactics. Moreno's sole ally on the San Diego City Council, Charles C. Dail, soon refrained from his earlier position for fear of Tenney's state-level Un-American Activities Committee. Congreso ally and attorney Carey McWilliams continued to assist Moreno, even while Tenney issued an indictment of Moreno publicly accusing her of participating in a Communist conspiracy. Tenney blamed the Zoot Suit Riots in Los Angeles on a Communist publication on the West Coast, the *People's Daily World*, and attacked the Sleepy Lagoon Defense Committee.[58] Moreno argued, "A desperate Tenney has used the

Sleepy Lagoon case and Red-baiting to support segregation, oppose miscegenation and to divide the Mexican community in Southern California." As Moreno later recalled, San Diego leaders, more interested in urban development and erasing the city's image of being a sailor's hangout, ignored harassment of the ethnic Mexican community by area military personnel and succumbed to the Tenney committee's bullying role. The racism against pachucos/zoot-suiters was extended to larger suspicions of disloyalty among all Mexican-origin people during World War II. This anti-Mexican sentiment was also tied to the deportation regime, as Moreno remembered that Mexican American veterans of World War II were denied service in most cafes and restaurants in the San Diego area and when they left the military, several were deported as aliens.[59]

In the San Diego borderlands, the racialized practice of border enforcement policy was conflated with the practice of policing Mexicans, whether citizens or not. In this environment, citizenship status did not spare Mexican Americans from harassment, suspicion, or even deportation among war veterans who had spilled their blood to prove their allegiance to the United States. Recalling the hysteria over "illegal aliens" during the Depression era, one historian refers to the "pachuco menace" as the World War II–era representation that continued the racialization of the broader ethnic Mexican community.[60] This shifted the priorities of the Congreso and the wider Mexican American Left to the domestic issue of public harassment and demonization of a Latino/a youth subculture, in addition to labor struggles, battles against segregation, and immigrant advocacy. In this way, former Congreso members continued the struggle to assert the rights of the ethnic Mexican community as a people within the United States by invoking President Roosevelt's commitment to assure the rights of minority groups globally regarding the world war, demanding that the same be done at home.[61] Although El Congreso declined during the war era and ceased by the end of the war, ideas of ethnic self-determination and autonomy as a convening mechanism through which to address class struggle in a transnational context would continue to be exerted as hysteria over migration would reach an unprecedented high mark in the next decade.

Rise of Cold War Repression

The momentum of the labor movement was countered in part by the rise of officially sanctioned hunts for "Communists," "Socialists," or others "deemed subversive" as enemies within the United States.[62] This second Red Scare was mobilized to disrupt the labor and civil rights organizing by CIO unions and organizations such as El Congreso as the United States rose to its super-power prominence in its standoff with the Soviet Union following World War II.[63] This was most visible with the passage of the Internal Security Act in 1950 followed by the McCarran–Walter Act of 1952. The former leg-islated the means to prosecute any person formally participating in Com-munist, Socialist, or other organizations deemed subversive. The latter declared that any noncitizen who had entered the country after 1924 would be subject to deportation regardless of his or her character, length of stay, employment record, or relationship to U.S. citizens.[64] Taken together, the Internal Security Act and the McCarran–Walter Act asserted that a natu-ralized immigrant could lose citizenship and be deported if deemed a subversive.

While the Congreso's demise was primarily due to a shift in priorities in support of World War II, the immigrant-inclusive Mexican American activism exerted by its members in other venues, that is, UCAPAWA, other CIO unions, and so forth were stamped out by a combination of Cold War repression of "subversives" and the deportation mechanisms against which the Congreso had struggled so vehemently. These Red Scare events began in the late 1940s and climaxed in the 1950s, displaying how immigration policing was deeply implicated in domestic wars against dissent expressed by working-class and racialized communities. The San Diego borderland region was a significant location in which these events played out due to its position at the border where the processes of expulsion took place. It served as a major site where militarization and intimidation became further embed-ded in the day-to-day existence of the ethnic Mexican community in par-ticular and the repression of radical politics throughout the nation.[65]

A number of Congreso members in San Diego and wider Southern Cali-fornia faced the State Senate Committee on Un-American Activities (hence-forth referred to as the state committee), part of a larger national entity of powerful state actors in charge of locating and interrogating so-called sub-versives. Congreso activists including Luisa Moreno, Josefina Fierro de Bright, Roberto Galvan, Phil Usquiano, and many of their allies in the CIO faced the state committee. Moreno's case in particular demonstrates that state-sanctioned witch-hunts for "subversives" were coupled with deporta-tion proceedings as a means through which powerful interests dismantled working-class social movements. Furthermore, Moreno's Red Scare harass-ment by state officials in San Diego located the city as a site of reactionary American nationalism that extended the practice of maintaining a physical border that divides "citizens" from "noncitizens" to police ideological borders as well.

In a hearing, Moreno revealed the contested notions of citizenship exerted by the Congreso on the one hand and red-baiting state actors on the other. Moreno exposed the hegemonic usage of official citizenship to divide workers with similar struggles and demonstrated that the practice of dividing citizens from noncitizens was at odds with democracy. The state committee, headed by Senator Tenney, subpoenaed Moreno in September 1948. Hearings were held at the San Diego Civic Center from September 8 to 10, 1948. Moreno remembered: "While the members were cautious and passive, Tenney was a bully with a scathing tongue. He reduced his victims to tears. By the time he finished with them, they felt depleted."[66] She evoked the Fifth Amendment when asked if she had ever been a member of the Communist Party. Richard E. Coombs, chief council for the delegation, asked her pointedly whether she might not be risking the right to become a fullfledged citizen by refusing to answer his question. "Citizenship," Moreno responded, "means a lot to me, but the Constitution of the United States means more." Listeners applauded in defiance of the customary Tenney edict that prohibited displays of audience sentiment. One youth was even removed from the room by officers. "I told Coombs," recalled Moreno, "that I had taken an oath to uphold the U.S. Constitution when applying for naturalization and that was what I intended to do in the hearing." In the hearing, Tenney and the committee threatened to send a transcript of the proceedings to the INS. They agreed that Moreno was an insubordinate, and did indeed forward the transcript to immigration authorities with intentions to discipline her.[67]

State officials' usage of the mechanisms of the deportation regime to disrupt working-class movements was further demonstrated as Moreno awaited the final determination of her naturalization application in her home in San Diego. Her application for citizenship was still open despite her being warranted under arrest as an alien who supported an organization that is subversive to the United States. She soon found that her immigrant gardener, Manuel, was collecting her memoirs and other documents for the FBI (Federal Bureau of Investigation) in exchange for being granted citizenship. Moreno soon after destroyed all the documents she had in fear of indicting other activists under the tyranny of the search for subversives.[68] She was soon after interviewed at the INS office in San Diego to determine her status. Her deportation was finalized. As a final attempt by state officials to indict more labor activists, she was offered citizenship if she would testify against Australian-born CIO activist leader Harry Bridges. Moreno declined the offer.[69]

Moreno's case reveals the wider success by proponents of Red Scare tactics in breaking up labor and civil rights activist networks. The Red Scare of the 1950s successfully used tactics of divide and conquer, utilizing not only citizenship and ideological differences but racial differences as well. One way of avoiding persecution by being labeled a subversive was to have character witnesses vouch for you. Unfortunately, few activists came to Moreno's aid for fear of being labeled a Communist. Bert Corona identified race as an important factor related to the failure to support Moreno and other Latino/a activists under attack. He recalled: "Luisa would have fought the effort to deport her if she had sensed that it would have been a collective struggle rather than just an individual one. Unfortunately, the efforts by the left—specifically, the Communist Party—to defend labor leaders in similar situations extended only to those of European descent and not to Latinos. That same lack of effort also characterized the reaction of the CIO."[70]

The combined struggles of the labor movement and activism for racial justice exerted by ethnic Mexican activists and other people of color was deeply wounded by the prerogatives of the Cold War battle against communism and its domestic purging. Internal fragmentation along lines of race and citizenship status aided the state-sponsored destruction of the labor movement. Despite attempts by labor activists of color to address the tendency to disconnect class identity from the experiences of racial oppression in the labor movement, these activists, as exemplified through organizations such as El Congreso, were exponentially disabled by the workings of racism both within and outside its ranks. Former Congreso members and other Latino/a community activists including Josefina Fierro, Refugio Martínez, Humberto Silex, Armando Dávila, Frank Martínez, Frank Corona, Tony Salgado, and Fred Chávez, among others, were also deported.[71] San Diego Congreso activist Phil Usquiano faced the Tenney committee, and another, Roberto Galvan, was deported. Galvan asserted that the vision exerted by Congreso and other racialized, working-class, and immigrant activists would continue to struggle when he noted: "We the ordinary people can shape history instead of suffering it and create a new world. Something has to be done since your committee [the Committee on Un-American Activities] has created untold upheaval and caused California much grief."[72] Like Moreno, Galvan was monitored for the FBI by people close to him, colleagues Roberto Reyes and Randy Resendez, in exchange for U.S. citizenship.[73] San

Diego area activist Phil Usquiano also exclaimed to the committee in his hearing: "I am a laborer and short on words . . . (but) investigating subversives and everything here in San Diego, I think it is up to you to report to Congress when you make your report that there is such a thing as something subversive over here. We have a little over 20,000 unemployed, and . . . I think that that is more of interest to people than this smear that you are trying to put on."[74] These Congreso activists critiqued the disciplining mechanisms at play under the guise of national security. Furthermore, they identified the ways in which state mechanisms of deportation and hunts for "un-American activities" were not in the interest of "the ordinary people" and "laborers," but revealed state mechanisms such as the deportation regime's tie with capitalist interests. Transnational cross-citizenship Mexican American politics, while severely damaged, survived in the continued activism of those who weathered this purge in the emergence of new organizations that sought to defend the ethnic Mexican community in the continued struggle against race, class, and deportation regime oppression.

Operation Wetback and the Bracero Program

A few organizations continued advocacy for noncitizen workers as intertwined with that of the Mexican American community as a whole, including ANMA, the Committee for the Protection of the Foreign-Born, some CIO unions, and in San Diego, La Hermandad Mexicana. Other organizations, including the Community Service Organization (CSO), and later, MAPA, put forth limited advocacy for noncitizen rights in contrast to and in debate with other political approaches within these organizations that were less decisive or were opposed to advocacy for noncitizens.[75] Many former Congreso members and ethnic Mexican CIO unionists participated in these and other political channels in the repressive Red Scare politics of the 1950s. This continued activism was significant in a moment of heavy repression of not only activists but the ethnic Mexican community at large.

Policies based on the conflation of a fear of underground subversives with "illegal aliens" in the 1950s also disrupted a disturbing number of ethnic Mexican communities throughout the country. "Operation Wetback" replicated the repatriation drives of the 1930s to an unprecedented level, as the Border Patrol unleashed sweeps to deport as many "aliens" as they could identify. Of course, race served as the primary criterion for who was identified as illegal, resulting in U.S. citizens of Mexican origin being deported.[76] More than half a million ethnic Mexicans of all citizenship statuses were removed in 1951 and 1952. More than eight hundred thousand were removed in 1953, and in 1954, the INS claimed to have removed more than one million.[77]

Operation Wetback was in part the result of the rise in undocumented migration that paralleled the Bracero Program, an official agreement between the United States and Mexican governments through which Mexico would provide U.S. agricultural businesses with temporary workers. This program began to address labor shortages in 1942 as many working men were sent to battle in the theatres of World War II. Demonstrating the contradictions within immigration policies that a few years before had repatriated thousands of Mexican and Mexican American workers, the Bracero Program sought to avoid the problem of recruiting undocumented migrant laborers by developing an official program. Ironically, the Bracero Program further exacerbated and encouraged the flow of undocumented migration. Provisions in the program required that "braceros"—literally, "arms" in Spanish—be provided adequate housing, wages, and other protections. Growers soon learned that to avoid paying higher costs as required in the program, they could simply hire undocumented workers or encourage braceros to overstay their contracts in exchange for more work, or both. Furthermore, the braceros themselves sought to gain leverage by ignoring the assignments of the official contracts, which often failed to pay sufficiently or offer the amenities promised, to find other work.[78]

Therefore, while it seemed contradictory for U.S. officials to deport more than one million noncitizen workers while importing thousands of others through the Bracero Program, Operation Wetback in fact sought to maintain the exploitation of foreign labor by harnessing those workers operating outside of the officially sanctioned agreement. Bert Corona argued:

> In fact there was no contradiction at all—Operation Wetback in reality was in support of the bracero program. What was concerning the INS, in league with the agricultural industry and other employers of braceros, was that braceros were protesting their poor working and living conditions and that numbers of them were skipping out on their contracts and moving into cities to find work without documents. Hence, Operation Wetback was really a response to the weakening of the contract-labor system that regularized the pool of cheap labor, especially for agribusiness. It was meant to scare the braceros into remaining in their camps and accepting their conditions and, in this way, to preserve the revolving door of reserve surplus labor from Mexico.[79]

Rather than stop the flow of migrant workers from Mexico, Corona's analysis reveals that the state much rather sought to maintain the subordinated status of these migrants. As sociologist Néstor Rodríguez has asserted in analysis of more contemporary migration, the state in collusion with capital sought to halt the autonomous migration and political activity of migrant workers through border enforcement policies.[80]

While LULAC and the Mexican American veteran's group the American G.I. Forum continued to support the deportation of "wetbacks" in their attempts to authenticate the citizenship status of U.S. citizens of Mexican origin, groups such as ANMA continued the practice of interlocking labor struggles, racial justice for ethnic Mexicans, and immigrant advocacy, as did the Congreso of the past.[81] ANMA struggled for the rights of braceros and against sweeps of the Border Patrol and Operation Wetback. Like the Congreso, ANMA intertwined women's rights within its activism, as evidenced by a resolution adopted at its founding convention that sought to place women in all levels of leadership in the organization while creating its own women's committees.[82] Composed of Mexican Americans and Mexicano immigrants with and without documents, the organization worked to continue labor struggles, battled discrimination, and continued to work in a transnational context. For example, Corona, a leading organizer in San Jose, recalled that many ANMA workers struck in solidarity with workers' strikes initiated against the same companies in Mexico and other parts of Latin America.[83] Corona also visited Mexico City as a representative of the Mill-Mine worker's union, from which ANMA emerged, to gain support for the union's famous Salt of the Earth strike in New Mexico. Here Corona gained support from a number of Mexican unionists and radicals. Artists Diego Rivera and Frida Kahlo showed much concern for Latino/a workers in the United States. This transnational solidarity honed by cross-citizenship ethnic Mexican groups in the United States is greatly demonstrated by a message displayed on a photo of Corona, Rivera, Kahlo, and José Gordillo. It read, in part, "Greetings to my Mexican brothers in the U.S. who are fighting for the preservation of our national consciousness, our rights to complete equality with Anglo workers, to equal pay for our work, and for the preservation of our pride in being Mexican and friends of peace."[84] ANMA chapters also participated in demonstrations in support of the Cuban revolution; against the overthrow of Guatemala president Jacobo Arbenz by the Central Intelligence Agency (CIA); and in support of labor struggles in Chile, Bolivia, and Peru.[85]

Indeed, in struggles to protect ethnic Mexican workers from the on-slaughts of Operation Wetback, ANMA worked with the followers of the progressive administrations of Lázaro Cárdenas of Mexico and Jacobo Árbenz of Guatemala through the consulates.[86] ANMA staged a number of protests and demonstrations in front of INS facilities and other parts of cities heavily affected by the Border Patrol raids. Furthermore, ANMA assisted undocumented and other migrants by informing them of their rights to withhold information about their status and giving legal assistance.[87] Operation Wetback was a storm that had to be weathered. A few migrants avoided deportation using the services provided by ANMA. ANMA also participated in a number of strikes initiated by braceros protesting their living conditions and the failures by the growers to abide by the contracts. Corona argued, "One result of the bracero strikes was that many of the growers found it more difficult to obtain and exploit such workers."[88]

La Hermandad Mexicana Nacional

Resistance to the increasing repression of the 1950s faced significant challenges in the context of the U.S.-Mexico border in San Diego County. In addition to Operation Wetback, San Diego activists had to contend with the consistent harshness experienced by migrants passing through the border-lands and the hysterical hunt for them not only by the Border Patrol and local police but vigilante and white supremacist groups as well. Mexican workers since the 1940s, lured by the growing wartime and postwar U.S. economy, passed through the San Diego borderlands risking their lives in a hostile and unforgiving environment to find work and livelihood. As continues to be the case, migrants hid in various compartments of vehicles, including side panels, under the metal bars of car seats, and even in the gas tank. Many drowned crossing rivers or succumbed to the desert heat. In the late 1940s, concern by the San Diego chapters of Congreso focused on the division of families by these migrations and by border enforcement policies that deported them.[89] And Congreso leaders in San Diego reportedly required that fellow union members practice shooting and carrying weapons in defense of themselves against the KKK.[90]

The particular context at the borderlands produced a transnational, cross-citizen ethnic Mexican organization called the Hermandad Mexicana Nacional. Founded by former Congreso member Phil Usquiano, the Hermandad emerged in 1951 in the midst of labor and immigrant repression. Throughout the 1950s, Hermandad chapters were founded throughout San Diego County, including the city of San Diego, National City, and Oceanside. Composed of mostly Spanish-speaking immigrants, the group was founded to protect the rights of a special class of workers found uniquely in the borderlands: those who resided in Tijuana but who worked in the San Diego metroplex in the United States. A number of workers had acquired temporary visas during the economic boom of the war era but were unable to find housing due to shortages in San Diego. For this reason, they and their families resided in their native Mexico just across the border in Tijuana. In the early 1950s era of immigrant repression, the INS threatened to cancel their visas and the Hermandad was formed to address these cross-border workers' unique circumstances. Most of the workers were members of the Carpenter's Union or Laborer's Union. The Hermandad succeeded in defending these workers' right to work and reside in the United States.[91]

The Hermandad, as one scholar suggests, "resurrected" the politics of El Congreso in the 1950s.[92] Like Congreso, it organized on the principles and protections of the U.S. Constitution and at the intersection of race and class. In its founding document, the Hermandad asserts that all men are created equal "without distinction of race, creed, or economic, social or political position."[93] While based on liberal democratic notions of the pursuit of happiness, the Hermandad also challenged the primacy of the nation-state in its attempt to "organize a united front of all Mexicans in defense of their union, material and legal interests."[94] Through the inclusion of noncitizens as key members in its ranks, the Hermandad challenged conceptions of citizenship that excluded immigrant workers. Indeed, the Hermandad noted that all Mexicanos have the right to participate in its democratic functioning "without distinction in origin, creed, or political economic positioning."[95] Organizing ethnic Mexican workers without distinction in origin signals the cross-citizenship, transnational basis from which it was based, crossing key differences in nationality within the mixed-status ethnic Mexican community.

Beginning in the late 1950s and into the 1960s, local chapters of MAPA continued the legacy of advocating for noncitizens as equal members of the U.S. Latino/a community. Phil Usquiano also began a MAPA chapter in the San Diego working-class suburb of National City. MAPA-National City was a political facet of the Hermandad, which was also led by Usquiano. Like the Congreso, which worked to bridge the ethnic Mexican community with other CIO union activism, MAPA in National City, alongside the Hermandad, worked to bridge grassroots ethnic Mexican community issues with labor activism. Usquiano was also a member of the Central Labor Council in San Diego in the 1960s.[96] MAPA was a vehicle through which labor and ethnic activism sought to assert itself in the electoral arena. For example, Usquiano, alongside his daughter Julia and son Albert, organized local campaigns in support of Robert Kennedy's run for the Democratic Party's presidential nomination in 1968. MAPA National City helped mobilize the Mexican American/Mexicano working-class community to contribute over a thousand volunteers to the campaign.[97]

MAPA represented a coalition of middle-class and professional individuals alongside working-class constituents and trade unionists. Therefore, only some of the chapters throughout California reflected the working-class–based, transnational politics exerted by past organizations such as Congreso, ANMA, and the Hermandad. Indeed, at the founding of the organization in Fresno in 1960, debates regarding ethnic identity, coalitional politics, and autonomy were put aside in the interest of consummating the group. Former Congreso member Bert Corona, alongside other trade unionists and working-class activists, sought to explicitly identify as people of color and seek out coalitions with African Americans, Asian Americans, and Native Americans. The debate was put aside because a number of participants were uncomfortable with claiming a nonwhite identity. Corona recalled, however, that two years later a coalitional stance was adopted, leading to a number of joint struggles with other people of color.[98] This was a legacy of practices established by the combined labor politics of the CIO and that of Congreso among ethnic Mexican and Latino/a activists. Tying the politics of the Congreso activist Luisa Moreno to that of African American activist Charlotta Bass and editor of the newspaper *The California Eagle* in Southern California, historian Gaye Theresa Johnson argues, "Both women kept a steady emphasis upon the common oppressions suffered by Mexican-American, Black, and Jewish communities in Los Angeles and later San Diego."[99] The worker-centered, transnational politics of former Congreso activists prioritized cross-ethnic affiliation in its centering of labor politics, clashing with Mexican American political orientations that were narrower in their advocacy for their particular community and assimilationist in their reluctance to critique capitalist class hierarchies and advocate for their *inmigrante* neighbors.

MAPA became the meeting place where the vision of grassroots organizing, explicit embrace of Mexican identity, at least rhetorical calls for gender equality, and working-class union struggles by Mexican American Leftists such as those in the Congreso encountered a new generation of activists calling themselves "Chicanos/as." Mexican American Left activists such as Corona and Usquiano passed down the idea that their communities were united across citizenship and struggled on transnational terrain.

· · · · · ·

More than a quarter century after the enactment of the Border Patrol, deportation mechanisms, and the legal category of "illegal alien" disrupted working-class transnational practices of Mexicano communities in the borderlands, the Hermandad and some MAPA chapters found ways to exist in the San Diego borderlands throughout the conservative 1950s and into the 1960s. Within the delicate alliances between liberal and radical community leaders, these organizations held the semblance of political practices enacted by the labor movement of the Depression era, when El Congreso emerged to put forth a transnational Mexican American politics that reimagined belonging in the United States as intricately connected to maintenance of Mexican cultural identity, community, and a mixed-status community. It would be former Congreso members who would tap into these continued practices within the Hermandad to reignite transnational, cross-citizenship ethnic Mexican politics in a moment of insurgent ethnoracial nationalism. The multiple manifestations of the Chicano movement mobilizations in the 1960s, after years in which explicit class struggle was heavily repressed, emphasized ethno-racial pride and identity as a basis for the emergence of new social movements. San Diego would play out as an important point of synergy in which old battles between proponents of border militarization and working-class transnational communities would be exacerbated by an unprecedented number of migrants passing through the volatile borderlands.

Part II   **The Chicano Movement Confronts the Immigration Question, 1968–1976**

. . . .

2 He Had a Uniform and Authority

Border Patrol Violence, Women's Agency,
and Chicano/Mexicano Resistance

· ·

In the midst of increasing brutality at the hands of immigration authorities, Martha Elena Parra López, a Tijuana resident, was raped by Border Patrol agent Kenneth Cocke on May 31, 1972.[1] A few days later, Martha Elena described the event to San Ysidro activist Alberto García, who, with area Chicano/a activists, created an uproar. San Diego Chicano/a activists, already incensed by a series of harassment and brutality incidents undertaken by U.S. Customs and Border Patrol officers against Mexicans and Mexican Americans, called for immediate action from authorities for this atrocious act against a woman they described as a "young attractive Mexican National" and "mother of two children."[2] For them, this brutality was part of a larger attack on *la raza*/"our people," as they called for a broader investigation of the local effects of deportation-oriented immigration policies. For Martha Elena, telling her story to Chicano/a activists and to the public was an act of defiance, as she later stated, "All I want is that he (Agent Cocke) be punished."[3]

The rape occurred after Martha Elena was apprehended with two companions, María Sandoval and Teresa Castellanos, while visiting their friend Vera León's Chula Vista residence in south San Diego County. Martha Elena was a resident of nearby Tijuana and married to a professional basketball player there. She was likely from "central Mexico," as one report noted that her eleven-year-old son was living with relatives there. She moved to Tijuana with her spouse six years preceding the incident.[4] Another report noted that she was a mother of two, suggesting that another child resided with her and her spouse.[5] She stated that while living in Tijuana she had only crossed the U.S.-Mexico border on two occasions, both times for brief visits. She had been in Chula Vista, only about fifteen miles from Tijuana and the border, for a week when she was apprehended.[6] Revealing the level of crisis growing among law enforcement agents concerning "illegal immigration," the Border Patrol was tipped off by Chula Vista police, who contacted INS officials after discovering Martha Elena, María, and Teresa were undocumented.[7] Agent Cocke apprehended the three women at about 6:30 in the evening and transported them to the San Ysidro Border Patrol Office.[8]

Demonstrating Cocke's emboldened attitude within his daily work at the Border Patrol, he began sexually harassing Martha Elena at the San Ysidro station, where she and her two companions were further interrogated and processed.[9] Affirming Agent Cocke's questioning about her marital status, Martha Elena reported that he then used obscenities as he remarked that she "must have many admirers" because she was "good looking."[10] Cocke then documented routine information, including Martha Elena's height and weight, and the number of children she had. He then checked her face and arms for any evidence of needle marks from drug use. Martha Elena was then "made to sign a paper" that she apparently did not understand; nor was she informed of what it was, although Cocke then gave her a copy of it.[11] The form most likely gave consent for a voluntary departure, an expulsion status wherein migrants admit to entering the country without documentation and are then immediately sent back to their home countries, particularly utilized to remove Mexican migrants.[12] Martha Elena was then detained in another room while each of her companions, María and Teresa, were also processed.[13]

Soon after, Cocke drove the three women to a major crossway, the San Ysidro border entrance, where the officer instructed only María and Teresa to follow the flow of pedestrians into Mexico. Revealing the women's insistence on staying together, María and Teresa reportedly responded to Cocke, "All three of us will leave or all three of us will stay."[14] The officer became visibly upset with the women's refusal to follow his orders and drove along the international border into an obscure area about fifteen to twenty minutes away from the San Ysidro border entrance. Martha Elena recalled, "I became very frightened when he insisted on dropping us off in the dark, out by the airport."[15] The airport under reference was Brown Field Municipal Airport, which is located about a mile north of the border, in the Otay Mesa community. A barbed wire fence, in bad repair and easily crossed, separated this part of the San Diego area from Mexico's La Libertad district of Tijuana at this time in the early 1970s.[16]

Once in this much darker, remote border site, Cocke again instructed María and Teresa to cross the border through the meager border fence. They again refused. Martha Elena recounted, "I wanted to also go with them but he grabbed me by the arm and threw me in the front seat."[17] Cocke then threatened the women, asserting that María and Teresa "better get going" or he would "do something" to them or to Martha Elena. As Martha Elena stated, "In other words he threatened us."[18] Given that María and Teresa had consistently refused Cocke's instructions to separate them, they made what must have been a painful decision to leave the scene (and Martha Elena) rather than test an armed law enforcement agent's threat of violence. Indeed, Martha Elena recalled the intimidating character of the officer: "He was a large, blond man. I was afraid of him from the start. He had a uniform and authority."[19]

Martha Elena defied Cocke's violating instructions. Interlacing official inspection procedures with sexual harassment, Cocke took out a flashlight and instructed her to take off her clothing "to see if they are real" and "so that I can see if you have concealed money or documents."[20] Martha Elena then claimed, "After a long struggle with this officer until my strength was out" he sexually assaulted her and said, "I hope you do not have any disease." Martha Elena completed her testimony of the event when she said, "he then told me to get dressed and to get out of the patrol car and go to my country."[21]

The next day, she contacted Vera León, whose home she was visiting in Chula Vista when she was apprehended, to inform her about what had happened. Vera contacted San Ysidro activist and notary Alberto García, who, a few days later on June 7, listened to Martha Elena's report of the incident and notarized an affidavit.[22] She also visited a San Diego area hospital where she was treated for bleeding due to the sexual assault, an injury she also reported in the affidavit.[23]

While Martha Elena Parra López was not a frequent border crosser and the actions of Agent Cocke were seemingly isolated and extreme, her voice is instructive in revealing how the increasing number of Mexican migrants entering the United States in the early 1970s were subject to arbitrary acts of harassment and violence through the official questioning and search procedures mandated by U.S. immigration policy after the end of the Bracero Program in 1964 and the contradictory results of the Immigration Act of 1965.[24] U.S. border agents consistently subjected migrants and other border crossers to procedural inspections that aimed to identify drug users, drug smugglers, people deemed to be "economic burdens," illegal aliens, and others who were perceived as potential hazards to the well-being of U.S. society. In 1966, Border Patrol apprehensions peaked back over one hundred thousand—a level they had not reached since Operation Wetback in 1954. By 1970, the rate reached half a million, on its way to reaching just under one million by 1977.[25] Through official Border Patrol procedures emerged cases of abuse, including physical assault, unwarranted strip searches, and, as in the case of Martha Elena Parra López, sexual harassment and rape.

Like Martha Elena, dozens of Mexican migrants and Mexican Americans refused to be silent about harassment and brutality in the early years of the 1970s. Their testimonies initiated new movements to battle the deportation regime. In particular, along with the dozens of complaints that came forth from Mexican immigrants, Mexican Americans, and other border-crossing women from 1970 to 1972 concerning the humiliating experiences of being strip-searched, Martha Elena's voice contributed to unmasking to a new set of activists in the burgeoning Chicano movement systematic acts of racial and class subjugation unfolding through immigration policies.[26] In particular, women's voices revealed that invasive and humiliating violations of one's self-possession were occurring within the everyday procedures of border patrolling, alongside physical beatings, verbal intimidation, and racial profiling, and while ethnic Mexicans of many backgrounds were subject to this legal violence, gender and legal status often shaped the severity of the experience.

Demographic Shifts and the (Re)Emerging Immigration Debate

The string of brutalities against ethnic Mexicans, including Martha Elena's survival of sexual assault, occurred amidst an unprecedented movement of people from Mexico to the United States. The total Mexican immigrant population in the United States was 454,000 in 1950, hit 760,000 in 1970, and by 1980 would reach about 2.2 million.[27] Mexican-origin people in the United States more broadly grew almost tenfold between 1960 and 1980, from 1.7 million to 8.7 million, in large part due to this migration.[28]

This rise followed a brief hiatus of migration from Mexico in the mid-1960s after the Bracero Program, a binational guest worker agreement, was ended in 1964.[29] The mid-1960s also witnessed an improving economy in Mexico called the "Mexican Miracle," which was credited in large part to U.S. investment. By 1967, this rapid development in Mexico created a widening gap between rich and poor as job creation failed to keep up with the needs of an increasing population.[30] As wealthy nations invested in global south countries to create export-oriented growth, commercial agriculture uprooted rural farmers in Mexico, who then crowded the industrial bases in urban centers. The Border Industrialization Program initiated by Mexico in cooperation with U.S. corporations in 1965 directed this migration northward. Many migrants eventually crossed the border for low-wage work in the United States.[31]

Mexican American activists successfully criticized the exploitative nature of the guest worker Bracero Program and pressured federal officials to terminate it in 1964. Yet the systematic dependence on foreign laborers, particularly in the Southwest, still needed to be met and exceeded due to the way global economic shifts that sent manufacturing jobs to developing nations led to the expansion of a service economy.[32] In addition to the nearly century-old practice of recruiting migrant laborers to work for agribusiness in the United States, expansion of the service economy in the 1970s, alongside other industries such as construction and domestic work, continued and increased their reliance on migrant labor, which, whether a guest worker program was in effect or not, was often undocumented.[33]

With guest workers now out of the equation but the need for migrant labor still fully intact and increasingly relied upon, the Immigration Act of 1965 created an administrative situation in which undocumented immigration dramatically increased, leading to intensifying contact and conflict with the Border Patrol. While important for its elimination of racial quotas, the 1965 act also placed annual quotas on immigration from the Western Hemisphere for the first time, with a 40,000 person quota on any one nation. With about 200,000 migrant laborers from Mexico projected to be needed in the U.S. labor market, alongside another 35,000 Mexicans with applications for regular permanent residency, the number of "illegals" would inevitably exceed the scant new quota.[34] Employers in industries reliant on migrant labor would continue to recruit migrants regardless of their legal status.[35] While the end of the Bracero Program was in large part due to the work of Mexican American activists battling against the exploitative nature of the program's inability to abide by its human rights components, its end marked the emergence of a dramatic increase of undocumented migration as employers continued and expanded informal decades-old processes of migrant labor recruitment.[36]

The increase in migration from Mexico in the 1960s and 1970s was also characterized by intensifying participation of women. The Bracero Program actively recruited Mexican men, and following its termination, Mexican migrant women's participation and network creation ensued and expanded.[37] With the rise of the maquiladora industry at this time, scholars have noted that employers of these assembly plants in the border region targeted Mexican women as a cheap, exploitable labor force both in Mexico and the

United States.[38] In Mexico, this shifted gender relations and migration patterns as industrial work was not provided at the same levels for under- and unemployed men.[39] This process, thought to develop Mexico, socialized many Mexican women to rely on industrial work while maquiladora jobs failed to provide needed stability, inducing migration to other industrial jobs, often along the border and the United States in industries such as microelectronics and apparel manufacturing.[40] U.S. industries intensified the recruitment of jobs historically circumscribed for Mexican migrant women in the United States, including domestic work as maids, elderly care, house and office cleaning, childcare, and health care. Employer preference for female migrants in these industries, particularly Latina and Asian workers, combined patriarchal and racist assumptions that women should receive lower wages and are more suited physically to certain kinds of meticulous and repetitive work.[41]

The rising number of Mexican immigrants was met in the United States with the discourse of the "illegal alien." While based in a history of anti-Mexican sentiment rooted in the Mexican–American War of 1848 and the racial nativism of the repatriation/deportation drives of the 1930s and 1950s, the new anti-immigrant discourse of the early 1970s again depicted migrants as a drain on U.S. society in a moment of recession. Indeed, a series of hearings led by Representative Peter Rodino (D-New Jersey) in 1971 produced a five-volume congressional document on the dangers and negative effects of undocumented migration on U.S. citizens, particularly regarding employment and wages. Concerns were also mounting regarding the suggested migrant tendency toward crime and association between Mexico and illicit drugs.[42]

With this discourse proliferating within public debate, Mexican immigrants, usually imagined as male unskilled workers, were characterized as occupying jobs in place of U.S. citizens, bringing their families to consume public services, and engaging in criminal activities. Mexican women were characterized as not only invaders but reproducers of the invading population. Analyzing national magazines since 1965, anthropologist Leo Chávez identifies three themes relating to fears of Mexican women's reproduction: (1) high fertility and population growth, (2) reconquest, and (3) overuse of medical and other social services.[43] Local and national elites depicted the entrance of "illegals" as a crisis, reinforcing the logic of militarized law enforcement efforts.[44] Indeed, concern about immigration among politicians and the media was increasingly articulated in military language depicting the need to stop an invading force. As a 1972 *Los Angeles Times* article exclaimed, "Holding the line against the tide of illegal entrants are 350 U.S. Customs, Immigration and Border Patrol officers."[45] While at times considering the immigrant side of the issue, the media often depicted federal border officials as weary combatants protecting the country against "illegal entrants."

Border Patrol Violence and the Chicano Movement in San Diego

The Chicano movement emerged in the late 1960s across the country in a variety of settings—calls for farmworker rights in California, historical land claims in New Mexico, a La Raza Unida Party in South Texas, and a Chicano Youth and Liberation Conference in Denver, Colorado, among other manifestations. In San Diego, these calls of Chicano Power flowered within local support for the farmworkers movement, campus struggles for Chicano studies at San Diego State University, a Lumumba-Zapata third world college at University of California, San Diego, the rise of local chapters of the Brown Berets, and the community struggle in the historic barrio of Logan Heights for the founding of Chicano Park in 1970.[46] In particular, a group of mostly young men who grew up together in the barrios of National City led by the charismatic printshop owner, Herman Baca, founded local chapters of state- and nationwide Chicano organizations, including MAPA, LRUP, and later, CASA, right at the moment when Martha Elena let her experience be known. The voices of Chicanos/as and Mexicanos/as calling for accountability for the brutalities they endured from the deportation regime were a crucial spark that, along with other influences, conspired together to initiate a series of struggles asserting that the collective abuses experienced by Mexican immigrants and Mexican Americans at the hands of border agents were systematic attacks against "our people." Martha Elena's act of holding Agent Cocke accountable, alongside the many border women who came forward with complaints that border officials had unduly strip-searched them, influenced, contested, and informed Chicano movement calls for social justice.

The increased concern about "illegal entrants" alongside increasing numbers of border crossings from Mexico in the early 1970s made San Diego a primary site where routine acts of violence, harassment, and brutality against Mexican immigrants and Mexican Americans occurred through official border enforcement efforts of U.S. Customs and the Border Patrol.[47] In this context, Baca and other Chicano movement activists in the San

Diego borderlands were among the first to engage the immigration crisis in a new era. This was significant because while the Chicano movement rejected white supremacy and Mexican American assimilation strategies through an assertion of pride in Mexican heritage, it was largely silent on the issue of Mexican immigration in its early years.[48]

The exception was the 1968 founding of CASA, el Centro de Acción Social Autónoma, in Los Angeles by veteran trade unionists Soledad "Chole" Alatorre and Bert Corona. CASA sought to provide services to undocumented immigrants and worked to politicize them into Chicano movement activism. Indeed, Corona and Alatorre were key influences on the San Diego activists' thinking on the immigration issue in their interactions in MAPA. According to Baca, a rift developed within the Chicano movement in the early 1970s along the lines of those who advocated for undocumented migrants versus those who wanted to concentrate on Mexican American (U.S. citizen) issues separate from immigration issues. Baca, the head organizer of a MAPA chapter in National City and the San Diego County La Raza Unida Party, would help organize a CASA in San Diego later in 1971, in part influenced by migrants such as Martha Elena, who spoke out against Border Patrol brutality. Baca recalled, "There was a lot of misunderstanding, really a sense of irrelevancy that the issue (immigration) didn't have nothing to do with us."[49]

The Parra López incident and other testimony by ethnic Mexican survivors of border officials' abuse deeply influenced this contingent of local Chicano movement organizations who were already contemplating the ways immigration policing was affecting their communities and their struggle for Chicano liberation. MAPA and La Raza Unida encountered the issue in their door-to-door engagement with the community, where households often had undocumented members present. Furthermore, they were part of struggles against state legislation passed in 1971 that sought to fine employers who hired undocumented workers. In addition to these San Diego area chapters of MAPA and La Raza Unida, as early as 1970 the newly created Office of Mexican American Affairs in San Diego County, directed by former Urban League organizer Victor Villalpando, and Alberto García's United California Mexican American Association came to address immigration issues in response to numerous complaints from ethnic Mexicans of all citizenship statuses who were discriminated against by employers, detained, deported, racially profiled, and made the victims of Border Patrol and law enforcement violence.[50]

Ethnic Mexican Testimonials of Brutality

In 1970, noting how many of his friends had recounted Border Patrol harassment, local newspaper columnist Joe Viesca recounted this July 24, 1970, encounter:

> The official asked what I had done in Tijuana. Since I believe this was an insulting question, I merely told him it was a personal matter. This was sufficient for him to send me to the second inspection point . . . (where) an official took me by the arm and twisted it toward the spine, and if I would have resisted in the least he would have broken my arm. When I commenced to tell him that as an American citizen I was fully aware of my rights he said: "No B___ [*sic*], S.O.B. Mexican has any rights here." He took me, making a showing of unnecessary violence, to the office, where he ordered me to put all my personal belongings on the counter. He began to check all my personal documents and looked for "contraband" in the cards and papers that were in my wallet. When I tried to smoke, he slapped my face.[51]

Viesca's account reveals that Mexican Americans, despite a claim to official U.S. citizenship, could be subject to harassment and violence by border agents. Indeed, as a generic "Mexican," Viesca was informed he had no rights and, like Parra López, was subject to violence within the official procedures of the Border Patrol, being slapped and strong-armed as they searched through his belongings.

Also in 1970, a young Anglo-American woman and African American woman underwent an invasive strip search when crossing the border together with two Mexican American men who were pat searched. The Anglo woman's mother reported that a matron inspector checked her daughter's vagina and rectum with a flashlight. They were never put under arrest or told why they were being searched. Her mother explained: "My daughter told me it was a very humiliating experience. I asked her why she thought she had been searched, and she told me she had long hair, was wearing blue jeans and was with a black girl and two Mexican-American men and she thought she represented the counter culture to the customs officials."[52] Another woman who was a retail worker from National City and described her ethnicity as French and American Indian recalled how she was stopped twice in one week and strip-searched one time. For both stops she was accompanied by two African American and one Anglo-American acquaintance.[53] A registered nurse from Chula Vista, whose ethnicity was not revealed, recalled a similar experience when she was strip-searched on May 28, 1971, when crossing the border. As a nurse, she testified that the search, in addition to humiliating, was unsanitary. Revealing again the blurred line between harassment and official border authority procedures, another young woman reported that a male customs officer had twisted her arm and put his hand in her brassiere in a supposed search for narcotics.[54] In some cases, male crossers were also strip-searched, as well as beaten and abused. For example, a San Diego shipyard welder told of being strip-searched, internally examined, and slapped.[55] These cases reveal that the customs agents' and Border Patrol's concerns about concealing contraband often took the form of strip-searching women in suspicion that their bodies might harbor contraband. These cases seemed to reveal that race was a primary factor in deciding which female border crossers might be harboring such contraband. This practice seems to have extended to white women in a situation where they were accompanied by people of color.

These reports of harassment at the border came to the fore after Joe Viesca published his account in 1970, and especially when the account of Antonio Cuevas was reported in February of 1972. Cuevas was a Mexican American who claimed he was beaten twice attempting to cross back into the United States after visiting friends in Tijuana in December of 1971. He was beaten while in the presence of an Immigration Department supervisor, and beaten again when he remarked that he would report the Border Patrol agent, Agent Ecerkt, who beat him.[56] According to a letter from Vic Villalpando to Baca and other Chicano/a activists, the documentation of the Cuevas case represented an opportunity to record and publicize the wider harassment of Mexican immigrants and Mexican Americans by the Border Patrol. Villalpando asserted, "Heretofore, I have been appraised [sic] (verbally) of mal-treatment [sic] cases against Chicanos crossing the Border by Immigration and Customs officials, but I was never able to attain written statements that could be used in a court of law."[57] Villalpando's concern for "Chicanos" crossing the border undoubtedly included Mexican Americans and Mexican immigrants, as he referenced cases of brutality experienced by both groups. For Villalpando, the Cuevas case was also important because unlike the numerous other cases of Border Patrol brutality, it was recorded and covered by the media, and its exposure could work to reveal numerous other incidents embedded within ethnic Mexican life in the borderlands.

San Ysidro activist Albert García, leader of the United California Mexican American Association, asserted that after the *National City Star-News* ran a story on Cuevas's beating, he received more than sixty additional complaints charging U.S. customs and immigration officers with brutality.[58] Villalpando asserted, "We know, either personally or vicariously, that incidents of brutality by Border officials against our people are frequent and almost common-place."[59]

Indeed, activists began referring to Chicanos and Mexican Nationals as "our people" and members of *la raza*, even including undocumented migrants in their reference to the "Chicano community." In February 1972, Villalpando called for a "Border Project" that would document the harassment and brutalities that border communities often experienced in their everyday lives. With the notary Albert García of the United California Mexican American Association, he requested that Herman Baca's MAPA chapter and other Chicano movement organizations assist in this project. Here Villalpando publicized a kind of border sentiment held by both Mexican migrants and Mexican Americans ("our people"): a shared experience of racialization at the hands of border officials.

Many of the individuals who came forward to record what they perceived as harassment and abuse by border officials were women complaining about strip searches. As Chicano/a activists sought to document mounting cases of border violence against Mexicans and Mexican Americans, one source reported that by 1972 several hundred women came forth to complain about being strip-searched by customs agents.[60] These women, many if not most of whom were of Mexican origin, used the Chicano/a activist call to record the legal violence of border policing to reclaim their bodies and refuse the normalized practice of strip searches carried out by border agents. Indeed, their stories challenged the racial and gendered assumptions that underpinned the perception that the bodies of Mexican-origin women were probable harboring places of contraband. For instance, Roberta Baca (no relation to Herman Baca) filed suit against the San Diego INS District Supervisor Vernon Han after being strip-searched without explanation in January of 1972.[61] Roberta Baca's complaint was exemplary of a series of other complaints when she asserted that inspectors unjustifiably strip-searched and interrogated her upon her return to the United States from Mexico. She stated that for no apparent reason, she, her children, and a friend, Isabel Loranzana, were asked to go into INS offices at the San Ysidro border crossing on January 15, 1972. After being asked to empty their purses, inspectors confiscated Baca's identification card as well as that of Loranzana's boyfriend, which she happened to be carrying. Roberta and Isabel were denied explanation of why they were being detained as they were made to wait in the office. They were told that they could not make any phone calls because they were not under arrest. Furthermore, because they were not under arrest, they were told they had "no rights." A female inspector then took Roberta into a separate room where she was told to be quiet and stand in the corner. The officer asked Roberta if she had anything concealed on her body to which she replied that she did not. Roberta then testified that the inspector "had me bend over and through all this she kept asking me repeatedly if I had anything concealed on my body. . . . She then had me bend way over and place my hands on my buttocks and spread my buttocks apart. She proceeded to check the inside of my vagina with a flashlight, to see if I had anything concealed."[62]

After being instructed to put her clothes back on, the inspector asked if Roberta was on welfare, if her husband was the father of her children, and if she had ever been arrested. Isabel was then taken to the room where she was pat-searched and asked the same questions.[63] Revealing no probable cause other than the women's ethnicity and gender, the inspector's interrogation following the strip search reveals the perspective held by the INS that Mexican women in particular were threats to the well-being of the nation. Deemed to be potential welfare recipients, concealers of illegal substances, and reproducers of an unwanted population, these women, who appeared to have legal status in the United States, were assumed to be a threat. This account further revealed the role that gender and race played in the interface between the practice of immigration policy and popular stereotypes of Mexican immigrants. As anthropologist Leo Chávez observes in his analysis of post-1965 media coverage:

> Rather than an invading army, or even the stereotypical male migrant worker, the images (of Mexican immigrant women) suggested a more insidious invasion, one that included the capacity of the invaders to reproduce themselves. The women being carried into U.S. territory carry with them the seeds of future generations. The images signaled not simply a concern over undocumented workers, but a concern with immigrants who stay and reproduce families and, by extension, communities in the United States. These images, and their accompanying articles, alluded to issues of population growth, use of prenatal care, children's health services, education, and other social services.[64]

Furthermore, the accounts of Roberta Baca and other border-crossing women reveal Mexican-origin women as perceived threats to the idealized nuclear family, as they were suspected of having children out of wedlock or from a number of different fathers, or both. As Chávez notes, popular discourse post-1965 has dichotomized between Mexican-origin women's fertility as "irrational, illogical, chaotic and therefore threatening" in contrast to Anglo women's fertility as "autonomous, responsible . . . of sound mind, as in a legal subject."[65]

Based on these complaints of border official harassment, particularly by Mexican and Mexican American women, Villalpando and Albert García demanded a congressional hearing on the prevalence of strip searching and abuse at the border. Chicano/a activists perceived the proposed hearing as an opportunity for the "Chicano/a" community, including Mexican immigrants, to testify against the systematic practices of customs and the Border Patrol. Herman Baca and the MAPA-National City chapter urged state officials to investigate "a problem that has been prevalent in this area for too long . . . the continual violation of Chicano's and Mexican Nationals civil and God-given rights by the U.S. Immigration Department and the U.S. Customs Bureau." Baca accused the two departments of being "more representative of the KGB and the Gestapo than organizations that are supposedly representative of a constitutional government . . . we are tired of this type of attitude and treatment and whole heartedly support the investigation being called for by Mr. Albert García and Mr. Vic Villalpando."[66]

Responding to Chicano/a activist appeals was Mexican American congressman Edward Roybal, who, as chair of the Congressional Treasury Committee, which held U.S. Customs within its jurisdiction, agreed to hold a hearing on border issues in San Diego on April 28, 1972. Countering the INS's depiction of Mexican women as welfare-hungry, decadent child bearers, activists argued that Border Patrol, customs, and local law enforcement agents physically brutalized Mexican men and violated women's bodies, attacking what might be perceived as *la familia de la Raza*, a popular Chicano movement conception of a united ethno-racial community organized as a family.[67] Indeed, the gendered dimensions of Chicano movement activism were evident in the preparation for the hearings, where García categorized border brutalities in two areas, "women being searched illegally" and "men beaten or abused."[68] In García's testimony, he demonstrated the anti-family policies of the Border Patrol, for example, by recalling how a busload of Mexican children, ages eight to ten, returning from a visit to the San Diego Zoo were stopped and apparently "strip-" searched at the border crossing.

Chicano/a activists and border community members sought to counter the depiction of Mexican men and women as threats to the notion of the U.S. family by revealing the antifamily practices of the Border Patrol who strip-searched and harassed women and children, and physically abused men.

Ethnic Mexican victims of border brutality displayed their grievances to members of the House Appropriations Committee investigating the Treasury Department. Noting the role of women in the hearing, Roybal would report that out of the 1,800 women stripped and searched at the border in 1971, only 285 were found to be carrying any contraband. Of those carrying contraband, very few actually concealed it in their body cavities.[69] Like Parra López, these women struggled for the possession of their own bodies by protesting and making public the ways in which searches at the border subjugated them to humiliation and loss of dignity.

The accomplishment of the April 1972 hearing marked an important development within Chicano movement politics. The systematic Border Patrol violence on ethnic Mexicans across citizenship statuses and the testimonials the survivors shared led many San Diego Chicano/a activists to develop a cross-border notion of "Chicano" identity, inclusive of undocumented migrants, as a basis for struggle. Grappling with legal violence at the border, activists began constructing the parameters of a transnational Chicano community by speaking of a shared experience of brutality by both Mexican Americans and Mexican immigrants at the hands of border agents. A coalition of Chicano/a activists was part of the one hundred or so participants in a demonstration outside the federal courthouse in downtown San Diego against the variegated brutalities experienced at the border. The *El Mexicano* newspaper observed, "To the shout of 'Chicano Power', and 'Raza sí, Migra no' (Our people, yes, the Border Patrol, no!), a group of Americans of Mexican ancestry, walked in a great oval outside of the Federal Court, with placards and slogans that repudiated the attitude of customs and immigration agents."[70] According to *El Mexicano*, more than one hundred Chicano/a activists led by Herman Baca sought to call attention to the federal hearing inside the courthouse and the repeated brutalities of the Border Patrol and customs agents.[71] As these Raza Sí, Migra No activists asserted, "The issue of immigration brutality, both psychological and physical, is one that affects all Chicanos and Mexicanos throughout the *frontera* of the Southwest."[72] Through Chicano movement mobilization as a united *Raza*, activists created space through which abused ethnic Mexicans of all citizenship statuses could voice their resistance. Yet mobilization as a united community was limited in its ability to articulate the complex ways that legal status and gender differences within the Mexican-origin community shaped social relations at the border in the early 1970s. As the mostly male, U.S.-born Chicano response to the Parra López case reveals, there were also significant limits to the gendered construction of *Raza*. Furthermore, most of the women and men who spoke out in the hearings were U.S. citizens—mostly Mexican American—suggesting challenges to grappling with the unique and subjugated experiences of the undocumented.

Chicano Movement Activists Respond to Rape

The rape of Martha Elena Parra López further reveals that the particular violations of women's bodily possession was a key experience of subjugation for Mexican and Mexican American female border crossers in the early 1970s. Scholarship on more recent periods in the 1980s and 1990s suggests that rape is a prevailing experience among undocumented women, revealing how gender and legal status make some ethnic Mexicans more vulnerable to border official violence than others. Indeed, it reveals that the hierarchy between the protections offered by documented and undocumented status is normalized by border officials' rape of undocumented women. With the "low-intensity warfare" bases of border militarization, sexual violence by officers and others is deemed an "inevitable consequence," unmasking its systematic and routine nature.[73]

Like the other forms of legal violence reported by border crossers and Chicano/a activists, Agent Kenneth Cocke's rape of Martha Elena occurred within the militarized procedures of border policing. Agent Cocke's remark following the rape, "Now go back to your country," reveals the act as part and parcel of the deportation process, as Martha Elena was literally expelled into Mexico following the assault. Cocke's comment that "I hope you do not have any disease" reflects the larger anti-immigrant narrative foundational to the deportation regime in that it characterizes unauthorized Mexican immigration, particularly female migration, as a threat to the cultural and racial "health" of U.S. society. These hierarchical discourses on race and nation further legitimized a labor system of superexploitation as "illegal" status maintained and reinforced the subjugation of a racialized labor force that was, and continues to be, a permanent feature of the U.S. economy.

Furthermore, the redeployment of violence targeting women of color indicated the ways authorities responded to the increasing incidents of female border crossing within the economic shifts that deliberately recruited migrant women labor beginning in the late 1960s.

The intersections of nation, race, gender, and sex within border policing are important in relation to how research has explored these intersections within Chicano movement activism. Chicano movement research has revealed that while activism asserted counterhegemonic politics that challenged racism and discrimination, many organizations tended to reproduce structures of patriarchy practiced within and outside of the ethnic Mexican community. Historians note that the assertion of Chicano masculinity was central to movement rhetoric, within concepts such as *la familia de la Raza* (collective practices of community extended from the notion of family) and strong male symbolism depicted from Aztec and Mexican history.[74] This counterassertion of masculinity responded to a history of social emasculation and cultural negation implemented by the imposition of a white supremacist U.S. society onto Mexican and Mexican American communities. These precedents often normalized almost exclusive male leadership in many cases, centralized male subjectivity within dominant articulations of "Chicano" identity, and reproduced notions of Chicano men as the rightful protectors and proprietors of the Chicana body.

The archives reveal that these patriarchal assumptions were a key part of how Chicano movement activists struggled for justice on behalf of Martha Elena Parra López. Coverage of the rape in the San Diego County *La Raza Unida Newsletter* describes her on two separate occasions as "attractive" and a "mother." By highlighting Martha Elena's sexual appeal, the description "attractive" implies that her sexuality was taken by the Border Patrol agent from its proper place under the protection of Mexican men. Indeed, in reporting on Martha Elena's affidavit, the article reiterates her affirmative answer to Cocke that revealed her marital status. While this is seemingly objective in its reporting of what Martha Elena stated in the affidavit, matched with the article's description of her as "attractive" and a "mother of two," the event is framed within the confines of the domestic sphere. The article suggests that Martha Elena's "attractive" sexuality was displaced from the appropriate domain of her (Mexican) husband and her duties as nurturer to her children.[75]

Placing Martha Elena's sexuality and role as "mother" within *la familia de la Raza* was a key way Mexican immigrants were imagined as "Chicanos" and part of the same *Raza* as Mexican Americans. Furthermore, it reveals how developing notions of transnational community were articulated through the patriarchal notion of the nuclear family, mobilizing to assert a Chicano/Mexicano masculinity in competition with hypermasculine state violence. Activists advocated for Parra López and other victims of *migra* repression in part by acting as defenders against the disruption of ethnic Mexican families who protected Mexican women from being taken away from their roles as wives and mothers by the invading Border Patrol. This type of description worked as a strategy in bolstering Chicano movement activists' claims against the brutality of border enforcement policy on their community by highlighting the Border Patrol's role in disrupting family life, in this case violating women's roles as wives and mothers.[76] At the same time, while these transnational Chicano movement proponents criticized the hegemonic practice of immigration policy and border enforcement, they did not consider how the notion of the nuclear family itself upheld hierarchies within and outside of their community.[77]

In addition, by ignoring the patriarchal dimensions of the rape and publicizing it as only another attack on *la raza*, Chicano/a activists failed to conceive of the ways in which the Chicana/Mexicana experience at the border could not be deduced to racial oppression without considering its intersection with sexist practices both within and outside of the Mexican and Mexican American community. Instead, Chicano movement activists painted the event as another case of the Border Patrol embodying the white political structure's attack on their transnational ethno-racial community. After San Diego County district attorney Edwin Miller failed to bring Cocke up on charges, arrest him, or even question him, Herman Baca criticized him for dragging his feet, arguing, "If the suspect would have been a Chicano, he would have been in jail long ago."[78] Baca also exclaimed, "This travesty of justice only serves to symbolize the immorality, brutality, and all the injustices that are committed against *Mexicans* and *Chicanos* [my emphasis] daily along the international border by the racist Immigration Department."[79] In a later critique of officials in handling the case, other Chicano/a activists in MAPA, commenting in the *La Raza Unida San Diego County Newsletter*, used it as evidence of a systemic "double standard . . . one for whites and the other for non-whites."[80] By modifying the rape into the domestic sphere via race as family and then eliding the gender and sexual categories of power at play within this act by defining it as solely an attack on their ethno-racial community, Chicano/a activists deployed traditional gender roles of male breadwinner/protector and female domestic caretaker to forge Chicano/Mexicano notions of transnational community.[81]

Nevertheless, Chicano/a activists never wavered on Martha Elena's assertion that she was raped by Agent Cocke, even as other advocates and officials suggested that the sex was consensual. Indeed, officials whom activists demanded actions from on the incident seemed reluctant to even handle the case. San Diego County district attorney Ed Miller refused to file charges in the local jurisdiction, calling it a federal matter and citing a lack of evidence to convict the accused of rape.[82] Appealing then to the district attorney of the state of California, Evelle J. Younger, Chicano/a activists were disgusted to hear him defend Miller's decision and argue that a rape did not occur. Younger explained, "While the evidence does reveal that an act of sexual intercourse did occur . . . the evidence also reveals that the Border Patrol officer did not use such threats of force" that would fall within the description of rape under the California Penal Code.[83] In other words, the San Diego County and California State district attorneys agreed with the alleged perpetrator Kenneth Cocke's assessment that the sex was consensual. Later, in 1974, the newly appointed INS commissioner General Leonard Chapmen responded to continued pressure from Chicano/a activists to address the rape case by reasserting Cocke's contention that he gained consent from Parra López. The INS did proceed with misconduct and removal action against Cocke, under which he resigned in October 1972. No criminal charges were pursued. Congressman Roybal criticized officials for failing to act, but also considered Cocke's assertion that he gained consent from Martha Elena. Roybal asserted, "He (Cocke) must be guilty of something, even if the girl consented."[84]

Chicano/a activists were appalled because there seemed to be ample evidence that could bring the Cocke case to a grand jury. Aside from Martha Elena's statement that she was indeed abducted and raped, her companions whom Cocke forced to leave the situation, María Sandoval and Teresa Castellanos, were witnesses to the events. Furthermore, a medical examiner at University Hospital in San Diego verified that there were physical indications of bruising, vaginal bleeding, and use of force.[85] The San Diego district attorney, California attorney general, and INS's failure to proceed with criminal prosecution led Chicano/a activists to draw conclusions on and dramatize the role that race might have played. García revealed the frustration experienced by activists in this case when he deduced, "I understand this rape case was stopped in Washington so that no further publicity would be issued."[86] Indeed, with the failure to even put forth a trial on these offensive allegations, Chicano/a activists learned that state actors were not to be relied upon.

· · · · · ·

Martha Elena and other border women entered the realm of Chicano politics to contest its limited framework that tended to value women only in the domestic realm. Chicanas and Mexicanas at times used domestic identities such as "mother" or "wife" as a way of asserting their rights while simultaneously rejecting these roles as limits to other identities and participation in community. Indeed, Martha Elena's insistence on sharing her terrifying experience with the public reveals the agency, although fragmented within the archival sources, of an undocumented migrant woman that suggests an alternative political subjectivity beyond the domestic realm. Her friends' refusal to leave her side demonstrated an oppositional solidarity among Mexicanas who were all too aware of the consequences of being left alone with a *migra* officer.[87] This Mexicana oppositional sentiment revealed a consciousness of and resistance to not only systematized national/racial exclusion and exploitation of physical labor but also routine exploitation of their bodies as sexually objectified and violated in a way that subjugated Mexican immigrant women in particular. Martha Elena also worked with her friend Vera León to document her story with activist Alberto García, revealing cross-border Chicana/Mexicana networks of support and solidarity across differences in legal status. Furthermore, that Martha Elena shared her story with León reveals her refusal to accept sexual violence at the hands of a U.S. state official as routine, and a struggle for the possession of her own body and dignity despite her undocumented status.

This Chicana/Mexicana solidarity shows an awareness of and resistance to forms of sexual exploitation not only at the border but within work sites, community life, and relationships. Indeed, the experiences that Martha Elena and her compañeras struggled through reveal a class experience shaped by legal status, gender, race, and national affiliation.[88] Therefore, Parra López's refusal to remain silent might reveal a nuanced transnational Mexicana politics beyond the domestic realm of wife and mother, and the limited rhetoric articulated by Chicano movement activists. Martha Elena and other survivors revealed migrants' agency and its influence on developing Raza Sí, Migra No activism within the Chicano movement, while the voices of undocumented women in particular also reveal its intersectional possibilities and heteropatriarchal limitations.[89]

The voices of these ethnic Mexican borderlands residents who refused the routine violence of border officials in the early years of the 1970s were central to mobilizing San Diego Chicano movement activism that perceived the deportation regime as an attack on all of *la raza*. The activists, particularly those community mobilizations under the leadership of the vocal Herman Baca, had not yet asserted specific strategies or analysis of the deportation regime. While a liberal/moderate strategy sought traditional mechanisms of redress to serve as a corrective to glitches in the otherwise democratic practices of U.S. society, a transnational Chicano/Mexicano politics was also emerging to criticize immigration policy as a systematic practice that served the globalizing interests of capital. To parse this process out, the remaining chapters will explore the debates, tensions, and visions that evolved within each of the organizations Baca led, including CASA, MAPA, La Raza Unida Party, and later the CCR. Indeed, the Raza Sí, Migra No activism initiated at this moment, the book argues, fundamentally shifted the priorities and scope of these state and national organizations—and the Chicano movement itself. Unfortunately, the crisis of immigration would lead to further harassment, brutality, and scapegoating of so-called illegal aliens—which as the above testimonials reveal, deeply affected Mexican Americans as well and ensured a longer struggle. With intersectional struggles of race, class, gender, and legal status especially revealed by Chicana/Mexicana testimonials, subsequent chapters explore how the set of debates and positions that emerged within the Chicano movement and broader ethnic Mexican community in San Diego would unfold in broader California, the United States, and Mexico for the next decade and a half.

3 For Those Families Who Are Deported and Have No Place to Land

Building CASA Justicia

• •

CASA, the Center for Autonomous Social Action, has been the major organization through which Chicano/a historians have researched immigrant rights activism within the Chicano movement. Founded in 1968 by the unionist activists Chole Alatorre and Bert Corona, it emerged out of the *mutualista* tradition, a historic organizing practice among the Mexican working class. This included working as a dues-paying organization and providing legal and social aid to community members, with CASA focusing particular attention on undocumented migrants. CASA served an important function as an *encuentro* between Mexican Americans and Mexican immigrants, facilitating solidarity in a context where, of course, these groups often conflicted.[1] As CASA member Augie Bareño remembers, a common sentiment growing up Mexican American in San Diego barrios was that anything remotely Mexican was derogatorily labeled *tijuanero*, meaning from Tijuana. According to Bareño, the Chicano movement's celebration of Mexican culture was often a huge barrier to recruiting youth and students into the movement due to the negative sentiments among Mexican Americans toward Mexican culture. He remembers that many youth, including him, would reply to invitations to Chicano movement events by exclaiming, "I ain't tryin' that fucking *Tijuanero* thing!" Bareño explains further:

> cause we were of that generation where my father played Pedro
> Infante and . . . I didn't want to hear that shit. . . . we used to fight
> the guys from Tijuana. At the dances and stuff. . . . Some of the best
> fights we ever had, we'd go to Tijuana . . . the bars. . . . You fight as
> a community, so we were fighting Tijuaneros. We were fighting
> alongside white guys against Tijuaneros. We were fucking them up.
> They'd fuck us up. That's how it was. Cause we grew up with white
> kids. And I had cousins and shit (from Tijuana) and I didn't even
> want to be associated with 'em. They'd come over our house and
> (I'd say) "damn!" So that's the honest truth.[2]

Bareño's frank memories of his relationship as a Mexican American youth in San Diego to Mexicans and Mexican immigrants reveal the crucial ideological work that the Chicano movement and the CASA contingent in particular, accomplished. While many Mexican Americans had familial histories that deeply connected them to Mexico and immigration, this did not necessarily lead to feelings of solidarity, as Bareño's thoughts about being ashamed of his Tijuana cousins discloses. To get Mexican American youth to join an organization such as CASA, as Bareño eventually did, required a cultivation of interest in forging ties and emphasizing shared histories, families, communities, and cultural practices with Mexican migrants. Once in a critical activist space such as CASA, migrant agency and dialog with U.S. Chicanos/as inextricably revealed their interconnectedness while identifying the severe repression experienced by the undocumented.

Scholarship on CASA has largely concentrated on its 1974 leadership shift to younger activists, many of whom were students, who sought to deemphasize the organization's social service component and move toward a commitment to an explicitly Marxist-Leninist theoretical education and political program. The shift in leadership sought to implement a "commitment to the development of an active political base as opposed to a social service organization."[3] Scholars such as David G. Gutiérrez, Ernesto Chávez, and Laura Pulido have analyzed CASA's explicitly Marxist turn as a powerful attempt at reorienting Chicano movement mobilizations toward an ideologically potent, yet internally fractured, emphasis on class struggle, cross-border identity, and the radicalized notion of the U.S. Third World Left.[4]

While the explicitly Marxist-Leninist politics of the second round of CASA leadership is important in the intellectual and ideological debates among Chicano/a activists in 1970s, CASA's activism as initiated in its earlier service form of mobilization marks a largely unexplored matrix of immigrant rights activism. CASA Justicia, as the San Diego area chapter was named, was formulated in a context of ongoing struggle in Chicano movement organizations, including MAPA, LRUP, and the emerging CCR. CASA Justicia was supplemental to these efforts to enfranchise the Chicano/a community through electoral means, consciousness raising, and representation of working-class ethnic Mexican concerns to mobilize against the social problems that plagued the barrio, including police brutality, inadequate schooling resources, and poverty. Therefore, analysis of CASA Justicia initiates an exploration of the ways organizing undocumented immigrants facilitated localized struggles within the Chicano movement and the earlier form of activism within CASA that emphasized providing legal and social services from 1971 through the Marxist-Leninist shift in 1974–75. CASA Justicia in San Diego County viewed the shift to the new ideologically charged student leadership negatively; these activists maintained the practice of providing social and legal services to the undocumented as a primary means of politicizing migrants. Furthermore, CASA Justicia demonstrated a continued practice of implementing a class analysis of immigrant rights and Chicano politics without explicitly calling for a stringent system that policed its members to gauge differing levels of understanding Marxist thought. Finally, the San Diego chapter revealed the significant importance of maintaining focus on assisting migrants in their unique context at the site of border crossing. As Alatorre noted, the San Diego chapter was of particular significance because of its location at the U.S.-Mexico border "for those families that are deported and have no place to land."[5]

CASA Justicia was an activist site in San Diego that developed alongside the efforts documented in chapter 2, as Herman Baca led MAPA and the local LRUP, in a context of increasing legal violence against migrants and Mexican Americans in this volatile border region. Analysis of CASA Justicia therefore reveals how the social service component of CASA was central to the development of a Raza Sí, Migra, No! identity and political reorientation that emphasized solidarity and a shared community between Mexican Americans and Mexican immigrants, as fellow workers and members of *la raza*. Engagement with Mexican immigrants, undocumented community members, and the myriad of cross-border identities that existed in the border region influenced and deepened U.S. Chicano/a activists' consideration of immigration through the interchange within its service-oriented activism. CASA's offering of services to immigrants suffering the perils of undocumented legal status unleashed a wave of migrant agency— which infused and shifted Chicano movement ideological narratives—and educated the mostly Mexican American administrators of CASA. This migrant agency shaped the trajectory of emergent immigrant rights politics practiced by some contingents within the Chicano movement in the early 1970s. Migrants shared their stories and asked for assistance with the ways in which the immigration regime worked as an intensely repressive force in their day-to-day lives, from impeding their health needs to the quality of their familial relationships, and their ability to provide sustenance and economic well-being, to the right to freely move about. Out of survivalist necessity, Mexican migrants, particularly the undocumented, pushed Chicano/a activists toward forging a critical, grassroots political perspective on the immigration regime and instructed a more apt analysis of the working-class context and prescriptions for struggle within intensifying global capitalist arrangements at the end of the twentieth century.

Establishment of CASA Justicia in San Diego

It is important to note that migrants, particularly without papers, have extensive networks and community bases that sustained their movement and day-to-day lives informally. Bareño recalls, for example, a group of "Señoras" in the San Diego border area who "single-handedly operated an underground railroad" for undocumented migrants. These "Señoras," Bareño remembers women named Carolina Valverde, Virginia Martínez, and Lilia López, provided needed resources to the undocumented community settling or moving through the border region. Bareño argues that these women did "more informally" than many formal Chicano movement organizations did combined.[6] This reminds that these kinds of supportive networks of subaltern self-activity exist on a day-to-day level, often operated by women in the community. In many ways, CASA attempted to tap into and formalize these informal communal practices.

Cofounder Chole Alatorre described CASA's purpose and functioning as one that provided aid to poor families—employment, housing, food, clothing, and legal aid, especially with regard to immigration status.[7] Alatorre reported that CASA assisted over thirteen thousand families in the past year. There were CASA chapters in Los Angeles, the San Fernando Valley, Santa Ana, San Diego, Oakland, San Antonio, Chicago, and Greeley, Colorado. CASA was founded in 1968 by Alatorre and Corona in Los Angeles, an extension of the work for immigrant workers done by La Hermandad Mexicana Nacional (see chapter 1) in the 1950s. Alatorre was an immigrant herself from San Luis Potosí, Mexico, whose father was a railroad unionist. As a swimsuit model, she organized garment workers in Los Angeles and later struggled with the teamsters, Maritime, auto, and farmworker unions. Bringing the strong tradition of ethnic Mexican organizing at the intersection of labor, immigrant rights, and antiracist struggles to the Chicano movement, CASAs were formulated to more fully concentrate on administering the legal and social services offered to immigrants and build a large staff of mostly U.S. Chicanos/as who were professionals or students to assist in this.[8]

At Corona and Alatorre's encouragement, CASA Justicia was founded out of the grassroots political activism emanating from the National City (a San Diego suburb) chapter of MAPA. In many ways, the founding of CASA was a move away from MAPA and toward a concentration on the struggles of immigrants and workers. Indeed, Corona remembered resigning from MAPA at this time due its elitist politics led by lawyers and Democratic Party leaders to the exclusion of workers, and a disagreement with the United Farm Workers' leaders Dolores Huerta and César Chávez, who "developed a harsh attitude toward undocumented workers."[9] In this context, Charlie Vásquez remembers, "Bert said, 'You guys are closer to the border—you have to do something. You guys are more important because we can't do it in LA,' so that was what sparked our interest."[10] These San Diego area activists were engaged in a number of struggles through their local MAPA and LRUP chapters, which initially sought to create a Mexican American voting bloc, but soon became consumed with seeking retribution for violence and harassment at the hands of the Border Patrol and local police against both Mexican immigrants and Mexican Americans (see chapter 2). Furthermore, as San Diego-area MAPA organizers attempting to register the ethnic Mexican community to vote, these activists had already encountered the ways that immigration and legal status worked as a key barrier to their electoral goals. Attempting to register voters, knocking door-to-door, and engaging community members, MAPA organizers were told time after time by families that they could not register because of their legal status. They often found that some members were undocumented, some were legal residents, and some were citizens. Often even Mexican American U.S. citizens opted not to register to avoid unwanted attention to their undocumented relatives.[11]

Five members from MAPA National City volunteered to work for CASA Justicia and to be trained to provide legal and social services to undocumented community members and migrants in 1970—Carlos "Charlie" Vásquez, Norma Mena, Augie Bareño, Gloria Jean Valderrama, and Nick Inzunza. CASA Justicia used the resources of the Volunteers in Service to America, or VISTA, program, offered as part of the federal government's War on Poverty programs and as a domestic component of the Peace Corps. These members were certified as VISTA community organizers, and wrote up the bylaws and goals of CASA Justicia to assist and counsel the undocumented population. They brought in immigration and human rights attorney Peter Schey to train them further on how to navigate immigration law to provide legal assistance to their members. CASA Justicia workers learned to put an immigration file together, petition for legal standing or citizenship, or both, and to call and facilitate court hearings. Like CASA in Los Angeles and elsewhere, CASA Justicia recruited undocumented community members by offering them services in exchange for becoming members, paying dues, and attending fund-raising and political events.[12]

As Herman Baca remembers, CASA Justicia became a resource to migrants, but also an important way that the organizers learned about the multifaceted problems, concerns, and needs of their communities, and contemplated ways to struggle against the particular injustices facing Mexican Americans and Mexican immigrants. He explains: "CASA Justicia started out as (addressing) immigration . . . but then welfare, and then schools, and then police brutality. . . . We used to charge fifteen dollars for a year membership, and like I said, bring in every imaginable problem you can think of, from wife beating to kids getting kicked out of school, how do we get food stamps, how do we get welfare."[13] CASA Justicia worked with the Mexican American Advisory Council (MAAC), another organization that used VISTA workers to provide services. MAAC was an organization formed by a number of Mexican American associations that addressed social service and poverty issues, founded by the aforementioned Laborers Union Local 89 and the Hermandad Mexicana, headed by Phil Usquiano, among others.[14] When CASA Justicia was unable to address the many social problems their clients brought in, they would often send them to MAAC to further assist them with immediate and long-term needs in housing, jobs, health, and other issues.[15]

Baca's quote reveals a key lesson that Chicano/a organizers learned: addressing immigration problems was entangled with the day-to-day problems the ethnic Mexican community experienced as an oppressed people. This is central to understanding the framework through which CASA Justicia and this contingent of activists in South San Diego incorporated immigration issues as part of the Chicano liberation struggle—that it was a set of policies through which structural racism affected the entire community across differences of legal status.

Undocumented members who joined CASA Justicia would get a "green card"—one issued by CASA Justicia themselves—that identified them as members, so that if they became entangled with immigration officers, CASA leaders could assist them. In this way, Chicanos/as used their legal status as U.S. citizens—even emulating the state by issuing "green cards"—to assist their undocumented neighbors. Furthermore, this performance of legitimacy and offering services significant to the day-to-day struggles of undocumented migrants facilitated CASA's goal of attracting and then politicizing migrants. Vásquez recalls what they would tell potential undocumented members, explaining to them, "We are going to save you a lot of money [in getting their legal documents]. But you need to be part of the community. . . . We would call for meetings with members [where] we'd explain the situation [of Chicano politics in the United States]. They [the immigrants] were very vocal on what problems they were having—work, their kids at school, small claims, house loans, driver's licenses, cops harassing, DWI's—and we'd politicize them on Chicano history. Some did become U.S. citizens and voted."[16] While Vásquez's emphasis on becoming citizens and voting as an indication of politicization reproduces the regime of citizenship and the logic of the nation-state, creating a space in which undocumented migrants asserted their material experience and injustice in capitalist society—calling for rectification of ongoing injustice and building collective identities as a racialized community—facilitated a critical contingent that was potentially subversive to the hegemonic context.[17]

In the Trenches

CASA Justicia became popular enough within the South San Diego community networks of Mexican migrants that a steady traffic of clients and membership for the organization was soon present. Migrants and community members would fully take advantage of services available and deeply influence U.S. Chicano/a activist workers within CASA Justicia. There was, for example, a memorable story about the Zarate family, who approached CASA Justicia for assistance with a decision by the American consulate that argued that their son, who had an intellectual disability, was inadmissible for entrance into the United States. The consulate ruled that immigration laws sought to limit the migration of individuals with medical issues who were not able to financially support themselves. The Zarate family had established a home in South San Diego County, where the mother, father, sister, and brother of the disabled son worked and pulled resources together to care for him. Charlie Vásquez, being certified to conduct negotiations in administrative law, led an action to argue to the U.S. consulate that the family's collective resources would not make the disabled sibling a burden to the state. They won the case, to the jubilation of the family. The family remained members of CASA Justicia, and the daughter, Rosalie Zarate, became a staff member. Vásquez remembers that after the case was won, one of the Zarate brothers, who managed a local Mexican restaurant, would insist that Vásquez, and any guests he had, enjoy a free meal. "To this day," Vásquez reflects, "the family thanks us."[18]

The community atmosphere of the CASA Justicia office, which was in the main business district of National City, next to Baca's own business, Aztec Printing, was an important part of the functioning of the organization. Previous and ongoing activism with MAPA, where Baca's print shop served as a headquarters, had already made this space known as the place to come for community concerns and problems. With the services offered to the undocumented through CASA Justicia, the space became more open and dynamic. Appointments for assistance were made by walking up to the offices, hanging out a bit, and catching up with open conversations. The administrators remember Enrique Ramos, better known as Señor Ramos, an elderly migrant, who would come by once a month or so to cook the staff carnitas. Fund-raisers for the organization, mostly achieved by throwing *tardeadas* and community get-togethers, received contributions from immigrant members who would mobilize their resources to cook and sell food at these events, and invite friends and other family.[19]

CASA Justicia became such a place for safety among undocumented community members that one member would use the "green card" issued to members of CASA as what he thought was legitimate documentation to cross the border back and forth. One day, a Border Patrol vehicle pulled up in front of CASA Justicia offices with this man in the backseat. The agents approached Vásquez and the CASA staff, asking them to explain to their member that the "green card" was not a legitimate way to pass through the border, and that he had been apprehended several times because of this. They left the man at the CASA Justicia offices, where staff members explained to him that his legal application for a legitimate green card was being processed and that he would need to stay in the United States to not jeopardize this. CASA Justicia leaders remember this story fondly and humorously, but it also reveals the level of legitimacy, trust, and safety that undocumented community members invested in this organization.[20]

CASA worked to communicate with and represent people both in Mexico and the United States who wished to immigrate to the United States, adjust their status, or do the same for family members. This was particularly true in the San Diego border region. Roger Cazares, a CASA Justicia administrator, remembers several examples of split-up families who lived in both San Diego and Tijuana. He explained that immigration policies in the United States required that adult members make enough income to cover each dependent. Often, primary bread winners only made enough to immigrate one or two family members in a larger household. Cazares gives the example of a couple he remembers that had three children. The father only made enough to bring one of the children to live in San Diego, where he worked. The mother and two other children stayed in Tijuana, and waited for the father to earn enough income to a point that he could satisfy the immigration official's requirement for financial support of all dependents. In many cases, family members without documentation would stay with family members with documentation in the United States as a means of keeping the family together. This was a common circumstance, Cazares explains, in San Diego–Tijuana.[21]

Letters from migrants to the Los Angeles chapter reveal the important role that CASA played in its social service roles as a method of engaging the transnational realities of the ethnic Mexican community that exemplify issues that also reached San Diego. One letter from Alvaro Camargo of Mexico City written in June 1973 refers to CASA as "the organization that helps Mexicans."[22] Unable to gain sufficient wages in Mexico to feed his wife and five daughters, and having the experience of working in the gardening, mining, and railroad industries in the United States before, Camargo requested CASA's assistance in migrating to the United States. Having all their legal documentation in hand, Camargo cordially asked for assistance assuring that he was able-bodied and prepared to work.[23] Similarly, Mercedes Alba thanked CASA in 1972 for sending her the forms she needed to gain documentation to immigrate, and asked for assistance so that her daughter could join her in the United States.[24] In all likelihood Alba became a CASA member as an undocumented worker and was able to use CASA's services to gain legal status in the United States. Responding to a member residing in Tijuana, a CASA representative informed Asunción Esparza Vera that they would need her union number to pursue the collection of a paycheck she was awaiting.[25] That CASA members were both in the United States and Mexico and were dealing with work-related, immigration, and other day-to-day occurrences reveals how CASA services functioned as an important way to tap into the on-the-ground transnational lives of the ethnic Mexican community in Southern California.

Several incoming and outgoing letters to and from the Los Angeles office also reveal the central role that family played in motivations to migrate and adjust legal status. For example, CASA administrators in several of these letters represented their members by informing immigration authorities that they were presently married to or had recently married an American citizen and urged action toward adjusting their legal status accordingly.[26] Many letters also requested assistance in reuniting a spouse (usually a wife), son, or daughter with a loved one in the United States. Others petitioned to stay in the United States to avoid being deported and separated from family members. One example was a couple living in Los Angeles who had a child born in the United States, who was therefore an American citizen. The couple, Lazara Emilia de los Rios Carrasco de Guerrero and Ignacio Eduardo Guerrero, petitioned as members of CASA to gain legal status so they could stay together in their daughter's country of birth.[27] This reveals the transnational and fragmented reality that many families existed under, or were under constant risk of, in the U.S.-Mexico border region. They were often split up and restricted from reuniting for different reasons. Whether possibly being deported, returning to Mexico voluntarily to avoid deportation, or possibly for attending to business back in Mexico, these families often existed across border lines. This practice was expanding in California as well, as letters from Salvadoran, Nicaraguan, and Guatemalan migrants reveal.[28] Deportation-oriented immigration policies greatly complicated this existence, slowed it down, restricted free movement, and kept families apart. These circumstances shaped the counterdiscourse that Chicano/a and immigrant rights activists' developed by centralizing the separation of families, much of which was developed by organizations such as CASA that dealt with these struggles and observed the intimate ways it affected households. At a fundamental level, the division of parents from children and of spouses from one another was a lived reality that greatly stressed and concerned migrants, as articulated in letters and the social service work of CASA.[29]

Most of the letters and oral histories collected identify notions of "family" in heteronormative terms. This may reflect dominant heteronormative practices within Mexican culture, but it is also prevalent in U.S. immigration law. Indeed, homosexuality was a health-based reason for exclusion from migrating, and this aspect of the law reached at least one case at CASA Justicia. A Tijuana resident was stripped of his green card when an immigration agent identified him as homosexual due to the way he walked. The man, described by CASA Justicia director Charlie Vásquez as "gay," came for assistance in getting his green card back. Vásquez and attorney Peter Schey worked together on the case and got a hearing called for their client to be medically examined and argued that he should be given back his green card. They prepared their client by asking him to "tone down" the feminized way he dressed and to prepare for an examination of his hands and feet by insisting that he not giggle. They also asked that he bring a witness to testify on his moral character.[30]

On the day of the hearing, Schey and Vásquez found that their client had defiantly dressed in a manner that Vásquez describes as "flamboyant," including what was described as a feathered shawl as part of his outfit. Furthermore, the witness, whom Vásquez identified as the client's boyfriend, was dressed similarly. Schey and Vásquez politely informed their client that his witness would no longer be needed, and became concerned that because of the client's dress, they would likely lose the case. During the physical examination at the hearing, their client did in fact giggle "like a girl," as Vásquez described it, against their suggestions. To Vásquez and Schey's pleasant surprise, however, their client was awarded his green card back. The defiant expression of this migrant's identity despite the risk of losing his legal status reveals the nature of the heteronormative leanings of U.S. immigration law as well as a small act of resistance to it.[31]

Dozens of letters to the CASA Los Angeles office also reveal that immigration bureaucratic agencies were antagonistic, or at least uncooperative, to applicants; the process of gaining legitimized documents to immigrate was a long one and required constantly urging immigration officials to take the next steps in moving a case forward. For example, Luis A. Aguilar was undocumented, having received a working permit in 1968, which had expired.[32] By 1973 when he wrote Bert Corona, his permit had run out and he ran into multiple obstacles in obtaining legal status and bringing his mother to be with him and his family. He married a woman who was born and raised in Douglas, Arizona, who had a child from a previous relationship they now took care of together. In addition, Luis and his spouse had had two additional children together. When attempting to gain legal status, he was denied because his spouse had previously used welfare benefits. Furthermore, Luis's mother, who was in Mexico, was actually a U.S. citizen. Born in Cleveland, Ohio, while her parents were most likely working there, after four years she moved back to Mexico as a child, and lived there into adulthood. For this reason, Luis was born in Mexico but was actually the son of a U.S. citizen. Yet immigration services denied Luis's mother entrance into the United States because the citizenship application form was not applicable to U.S. citizens, indicating that Luis and his mother may not have possessed a birth certificate or documentation of his mother's birthplace. This circumstance, seemingly simplified by the legitimate birth of Luis's mother and spouse in the United States, revealed the adverse behavior immigration officials often displayed toward migrant workers from Latin America.

The struggles of the undocumented were not only articulated through CASA Justicia's work on particular legal status cases but also through dialog with the organization's board of directors, which was made up of undocumented community members. Carlos Vásquez remembers: "[the board] would actually voice what they felt, which was good because they participated. And that's what we needed in the 70s: people [who were] really affected [by immigration] would be part of what we were doing. And for us to show them the leadership . . . and why they had to be immersed in what we were doing. It was a good combination and we really found some real good people. . . . if you've ever been to a meeting with Mexicanos and the politics from over there, it's a sight to see, they get very boisterous."[33]

The board, consisting of seven members according to one report, would encourage Vásquez and Baca to get the word out regarding the plight of undocumented people, to continue to advocate for and recruit more people to the cause of immigrant rights.[34] Board members were among the most dedicated to the functioning of CASA Justicia, and to the political protests, demonstrations, and community fund-raisers put on by MAPA and La Raza Unida Party.[35] As chairman of the board, Baca would attempt to articulate at press conferences, in newspaper interviews, and at demonstrations the sentiment of the undocumented, giving him and the organizations he led a community basis to speak on such issues.[36] Migrants took advantage of the offer of assistance within CASA Justicia, voicing their emotional, political, and material concerns, thus shifting the political struggles within the Chicano movement onto the transnational terrain on which immigration politics were taking shape.

Chicano/Mexicano

In addition to the hundreds of cases CASA Justicia took on, and the many that successfully assisted migrants and undocumented community members, another gauge that might measure the significance of the collective's social service–oriented approach might be the ways it was transformative to the mostly U.S. citizen Chicano/a activists who administered it. In a context in the early 1970s in which many Chicano movement groups, labor unions, civil rights activists, and liberal politicians were adverse to undocumented migrants, CASA was a crucial challenge to ethnic and working-class activism of that time that was exclusive of noncitizens. For this reason, by 1974 when the Marxist-Leninist younger leadership emerged in the Los Angeles CASA, San Diego CASA Justicia, among other chapters, sought to uphold this older way of doing things to maintain a presence in transnational ethnic Mexican communities.

CASA Justicia influenced a generation of Chicano movement activists, revealing how engagement with the immigration issue, and interface between Mexican immigrants and Mexican Americans, forged new notions of identity and politics. While many CASA Justicia activists were Mexican American, they were often also the children of immigrants. Interaction with current migrants conjured experiences with migration and immigration laws, and revealed the longer history of struggle with deportation-oriented immigration policies among ethnic Mexicans. For example, Charlie Vásquez was the child of immigrants from Veracruz and Mexicali in Mexico. Both of his parents migrated to settle in National City, the working-class suburb of San Diego where Charlie was born and grew up. Vásquez recalled his parents' struggles with immigration policies in the first mass raids of the 1930s. He reflected, "My dad was already immigrated [after they got married] and he found out that she had gotten deported, so in the process she had to ask to be immigrated after being deported."[37] His father would have to travel to Ensenada, Baja California in Mexico, sometimes several times a day, in the process of providing the appropriate documents. His mother lived in National City, working with his father in the tuna canneries and harvest-packing factories while undocumented.[38] The challenges of legal status and immigration policy as well as the ease with which Vásquez's father traveled back and forth while his mother lived without documentation reveal the increased militarization that had since taken place at the border and its persistence and intensification in the lives of ethnic Mexican border residents since the 1930s. Histories their families had experienced with the immigration system reminded Chicanos/as such as Vásquez about their connections to these issues. These memories were conjured up when they engaged the contemporary struggles immigrants were experiencing, giving U.S. Chicanos/as a frame of reference with which to identify with the Mexican migrant experience in the early 1970s. It is important to note that Vásquez's mother contributed to Chicano movement activities, supporting the MEChA (Movimiento Estudiantil Chicano de Aztlán) that Charlie led as a student at Southwestern College where she managed the cafeteria. She made burritos for fund-raisers, and later supported the Committee on Chicano Rights, providing food for protestors and fund-raisers.[39]

Chicanos/as who joined CASA, like the Mexican American population more broadly, did not automatically identify with Mexican immigrants, even though many of them were the children or grandchildren of Mexican immigrants. In many ways, immigrant rights activism within the San Diego Chicano movement activism of CASA Justicia activated a historical memory of family ties to Mexico and struggles with the immigration regime. CASA Justicia member Norma Mena Cazares, for example, recalled that her mother, who was born in Miami, Arizona, was deported at eleven years old, along with her five siblings and parents. Norma's grandfather was targeted for his labor organizing work in the copper mines, and a local sheriff—in the pockets of the mine owners—used the 1930s anti-Mexican repatriation policies to deport him and his family. They landed in Juárez, Chihuahua, where Norma's mother grew up. In fact, this is where Norma's mother would meet her father, a Juarez native. As a U.S. citizen, Norma's mother got documentation for her father and they moved to San Diego, where Norma and her six brothers and sisters were born. Norma tied her political activism within the Chicano movement with the activism of her grandfather. As she explained: "The Sheriff told my grandfather that you either leave voluntarily tonight or you will be forced tomorrow. . . . I got a little bit of my grandfather in me as well."[40] Rekindling the ties to these family memories not only conjured feelings of identification with Mexican immigrants but revealed deportation as a method of political repression, labor control, and subordination of an entire community.

Norma's experience as one of the few women in a leadership position in CASA Justicia as well as MAPA and La Raza Unida Party is important to note, as it reveals the limitations of the Chicano/Mexicano community regarding gender hierarchies. Norma recalled, "Some of the guys were pretty domineering, Herman (Baca) certainly was." She worked closely with the charismatic Baca, however, and could "tell him he's full of it" when there came a need to challenge him and some of the other male leaders. Norma describes a core group of men surrounding Baca's leadership who were agreeable to him, which was at times challenging for her. Historian Marisela R. Chávez notes in her study of the CASA chapter in Los Angeles how Chicanas often experienced marginalization from the decision-making process and faced expectations to do secretarial sorts of tasks without a lot of acknowledgment.[41] Norma recalls that she and another important VISTA worker in CASA Justicia, Gloria Jean Valderrama, did most of the administrative work. Valderrama recalls, "We did all the paper work and the (typesetting) for the newsletter."[42] While this was certainly important work to these women, which they fondly remember as providing "support to *la gente* [the people]," the challenges of male chauvinism were apparent. "We spoke up," insisted Norma, when the chauvinism became intolerable, and when doing so, she asserts, "I think they did respect our opinions."[43] These experiences complicate the development of Chicano/Mexicano identities and community, as patriarchy and other forms of power operated within the Raza Sí, Migra No movement.

Roger Cazares, a member of CASA Justicia, recalled a family story that told of how his great-great-grandparents were born in what is present-day Arizona when it was still a part of Mexico. Roger himself was born just across the present-day borderline in the state of Chihuahua. It is interesting to note that Roger's family had to flee their town in Chihuahua because of pressure from the Mexican government for labor organizing. They migrated to Tijuana and eventually settled across the border in San Diego when Roger was about three or four years old. These family histories were made viable through Chicano movement celebration of Mexican history and culture, CASA's politics of immigrant rights, and solidarity work between Chicanos/as and Mexicanos/as.[44]

Even Chicano/a activists that did not have direct family connections to Mexico came to struggle for immigrant rights through CASA. Activist Herman Baca traced his family history to the original Spanish settlements of New Mexico in the 1500s. Many *manitos*, as Nuevomexicanos are called, emphasize their disconnect from Mexico due to their long genealogical histories in what today is the U.S. state of New Mexico. Also calling themselves *hispanos*, Baca asks of this disconnection with Mexican heritage, "but do they eat beans and chile?" Baca refers to a shared Mexican cuisine and culture among ethnic Mexicans in Mexico and those with historical roots in the present-day United States. Baca attributes his outlook on undocumented migrants as part of a shared "Chicano/Mexicano" community to the mentorship of Bert Corona and the political struggles in San Diego with policies that targeted "illegal aliens" but affected ethnic Mexicans of all statuses. In fact, all the CASA Justicia activists identified much of that ideological work of tying the identities and political trajectory between Mexican Americans and Mexican immigrants together to the labor organizing and influence of Bert Corona, whose activism spanned from the 1930s through the Chicano movement era. In addition to his role as an organizer, Corona was also present as an instructor in emergent programs in Chicano studies, including several classes at San Diego State University, where Norma Mena Cazares and other student activists first met him. Corona's analysis is encapsulated well in one of his many documented speeches where he "re-define(s) unity" by characterizing the "mexicano family" as "those who were born here, those from the other side (of the border) with documents, and those here without documents."[45]

Augie Bareño remembered Corona's approach and how he taught the younger activists through his own experiences of struggle since the 1930s. Bareño says, "Bert's approach to the undocumented back then was a sense of the 1930s idea that we're workers of the world, that we have something in common . . . and he knew enough about that workers-of-the world approach in his history to infuse it with what Chicanos need to be about."[46] What "Chicanos need to be about" in this "workers-of-the world" approach to transnational Chicano/Mexicano identities in CASA became deeply contested as CASA in San Diego, Los Angeles, and elsewhere fractured during the mid-1970s.

"A Major Break"

In 1973, the younger, mostly student members of CASA in Los Angeles gained control of the leadership from veteran activists Alatorre and Corona, putting the national organization on a new path. Instead of continuing to concentrate on service to undocumented workers and families, the students began to emphasize ideological rigor as they embraced Marxist-Leninism to facilitate their perceived role as the vanguard of a transnational ethnic Mexican worker's movement.[47] The new faction hoped "to transform CASA into a 'revolutionary vanguard' dedicated to the 'liberation of the Mexican people.' "[48]

These young people were members of other Chicano movement organizations in the East Los Angeles barrios, and important among them were Antonio and Jacobo Rodríguez; the former had ties with the student movement in Mexico and also lead Casa Carnalismo, a legal service organization.[49] Corona welcomed the politically experienced Rodríguez brothers into CASA. This emergent leadership widened the Chicano/Mexicano solidarity efforts to insist that there were no distinctions between Mexican-origin peoples in the United States and Mexico, to drop the term "Chicano" in favor of "Mexicano," to seek a reunification with Mexico, and to commit to struggling toward a socialist revolution. The emphasis on these ideals, however, led to a dramatic recomposition of the membership and strategy of CASA. Corona later commented that the young leadership wanted to focus on a group "composed primarily of young Chicano professionals and students—people like themselves."[50]

Corona remembered cordially turning over CASA in the Los Angeles area to these student activists, even though he disagreed with much of their strategy. Upon their exit from CASA leadership, Corona and Alatorre chose to concentrate more on organizing the immigrant-led units of the Hermandad Mexicana Nacional. Corona and Alatorre did insist that the new CASA leadership continue to provide services to undocumented migrants and maintain their files. As Corona puts it, the "Young Turks" then turned the CASA network into one in which they "decided they were to become almost a political party. It was to be a vanguard party, a Marxist-Leninist party."[51] He assessed: "The problem was that they could never pull it off. It was unnatural for such a party to be formed out of a social service organization. . . . What was wrong was that they were trying to substitute the vanguard for the working-class base. . . . It was putting the cart before the horse. . . . I warned them that this formula wouldn't work, but they insisted on taking a chance. They saw themselves as a vanguard, but it was a vanguard without a 'guard'—without a base!"[52]

Leaders in CASA Justicia in San Diego County disapproved of the new student leadership in part because it led to the resignation of CASA's founders Bert Corona and Chole Alatorre from their executive positions. Although Corona and Alatorre willingly left their leadership roles within CASA and maintained political relationships with the new leaders, their San Diego mentees later summarized the change of guard as when "the Rodríguez brothers (LA) dominate(d) a major break."[53] This statement may reveal how the leaders of CASA Justicia in San Diego remembered the emergence of the new leadership as a "major break," brought about in a manner in which one clique asserted its domination over the other.[54] This became apparent when CASA Justicia split in 1975 between those wanting to maintain the service-providing agenda they had been fulfilling for migrants and a group of students who opted to side with the Young Turk faction in Los Angeles. This faction in San Diego seemed to be demographically similar to the Young Turk group in Los Angeles; they were younger students from San Diego State University and the University of California, San Diego, who had begun joining the efforts of CASA Justicia in the early 1970s.[55] Similar to what Corona suggests about the CASA in Los Angeles, the break within the San Diego chapter and the conflicts that developed around it were primarily about organizing strategy. At stake were the ways in which Chicano/a immigrant rights activism would engage working-class ethnic Mexican communities and the growing number of immigrants. In the case of CASA in Los Angeles, San Diego, and other CASAs, these conflicts centered in part on the differently valued practice of providing legal and social services.[56]

In February of 1975, student members of CASA in San Diego announced to the new Young Turk leadership in Los Angeles and the wider national network that they had "severed" their relationship with Baca, Vásquez, and CASA Justicia in National City. Calling themselves "CASA San Diego," these volunteers wrote: "The rationale for this decision is based principally upon two essential considerations: One, that the concept and practice of the Hermandad General de Trabajadores (-CASA) and the struggle to organize undocumented workers is being ignored for the sake of providing social services. Two, that the politics and practices of the self-appointed 'Chairman' and 'Director' are undemocratic, arbitrary and essentially manipulative; for us to remain would serve only to validate and reinforce these reactionary tendencies."[57]

The first rationale reflects the desire to radicalize the organization from what CASA San Diego perceived as a mere "social service organization" to "an active political base." Focus on an "active political base" emerged from a new emphasis on applying interpretations of Marxist-Leninist writings and study. Like their Los Angeles allies, the San Diego Young Turks emphasized their vanguard role in what they perceived as an ideological evolution within the Chicano movement from cultural nationalism to class struggle.[58] As Young Turk supporters in San Diego asserted: "The concrete research and investigation necessary to combat the repressive forces was responsible for propelling elements with the organization theoretically beyond the stage of 'cultural nationalism' to the concept of *class struggle*. The notion of racism as the primary contradiction facing Latinos was replaced by the growing awareness that Capitalists *versus* workers, Exploiters versus Exploited, was the fundamental contradiction in society."[59] It is worth noting the use of "Latino" in this statement, as it may reveal how "Third World Left" organizations—radical activists of color in the United States that identified as explicitly Marxist and internationalist—successfully widened their identification with struggles in Latin America and the global south.[60] Class struggle, the Young Turks argued, must be "clear and directed to combat for workers"; providing social services did not fulfill this goal.[61]

The second rationale refers to claims that Baca and Vásquez acted undemocratically. The break came about after the contested process that organized the first general membership meeting for CASA Justicia in 1974. According to the San Diego Young Turks, Baca and Vásquez terminated three organizers within CASA Justicia just prior to the general meeting. Baca and Vásquez apparently reasoned that the termination of these organizers was because they had not put sufficient time and effort into the organization. The Young Turks charged that "the actual reason these volunteers were terminated was because their political work with the members and specifically workers, posed a threat to their continued dominating and manipulation of the centro." Afterward, the Young Turks claimed that "A 'Board of Directors' was arbitrarily selected by the 'Chairman' and 'Director' to legitimize this decision." They claimed further that one of the board members admitted to being "coerced" into signing the termination letters for the three dismissed volunteers without fully comprehending what they were signing. These charades, claimed the Young Turks in a February 1975 memo, were to "develop a staff of paid volunteers responsible only to the Board of Directors, thus eliminating the threat of 'outsiders', consolidating their (Baca's and Vásquez's) domination."[62] It is interesting to note that according to Norma Mena Cazares, VISTA funds had run out by 1972, leaving no other paid positions.[63] Relatedly, VISTA stipends were meager, at $200 a month. Vásquez and Baca recall that by 1974, CASA Justicia was in decline as VISTA ran out, and former organizers had moved on to other things.[64] Therefore, it appears that these San Diego Young Turks were referring to arrangements that had begun to decline and change years before.

As Baca, Vásquez, and other CASA Justicia administrators attested, there was a board of directors that was composed mostly of undocumented members. As discussed, Baca and Vásquez portray an amicable relationship with the board and the many migrant members of CASA Justicia. This aligns with the Young Turks' idea that the board of directors sided with Baca and Vásquez. It is unlikely that the board was created to legitimize firing these three individuals given that CASA Justicia's main activity occurred from 1970 to 1973. Nonetheless, it is clear that the Young Turks perceived this board as being loyal to Baca, Vásquez, and other CASA Justicia leaders.

About a month after CASA San Diego's break, the new CASA leadership in Los Angeles informed Baca, Vásquez, and CASA Justicia that they were no longer affiliated with CASA because of "anti-democratic" decision making and a failure to "participate in the political and organizational development" that was ongoing with other CASA chapters. In addition, the letter from the general secretary (*secretaria general*), Jacobo Rodríguez, informed Baca that all ties to Bert Corona and "all political contact, communication and work" with him were to cease.[65] Rodríguez sought to legitimate the new leadership of CASA by demonstrating that they had Corona's support. As has been established, however, CASA Justicia leadership saw themselves as aligning with Corona in maintaining social services to migrants as the primary manner of assessing the everyday needs of working-class ethnic Mexican community members. As Corona's aforementioned reflections on the Young Turks' actions make clear, he held significant critiques of their self-designation as a vanguard and their move away from engaging working-class migrants through social services and organizing migrants to speak for themselves.

Indeed, the move away from providing services by the new CASA San Diego chapter made it very difficult to create, much less maintain, a significant organizational base. The new leadership of CASA San Diego sought to engage community members by bringing them into its study circles. This goal was reflective of CASA's new national organization goal to develop a "disciplined National organization" committed to the "theoretical and political education of its members, as well as their integration into the political process." By early 1976, CASA San Diego established at least two study groups, one based in Chula Vista in southeast San Diego County, and the other at the University of California, San Diego. Furthermore, they happily reported to the CASA Los Angeles leadership that in an attempt to act on their study of class struggle, they had made contact with a local construction worker.[66] These study groups and work with the Eastwood Carpenters Local 2020, an AFL-CIO union in south San Diego, became the group's key projects as the latter prepared for a possible strike.[67] In July of 1976, CASA San Diego also began work with an organization of tenants at the Del Sol housing project. CASA San Diego gave Del Sol tenets organizational advice, disseminated information on forming a tenant organization via leaflets, and mobilized them as issues arose.[68] Yet over the long run, an emphasis on ideological rigor and discipline rather than the needs of workers, tenants, and other community members prevented successful partnerships between the community and the ambitious student leaders of the new CASA San Diego.

In working with the construction workers union and the housing project tenants, CASA San Diego placed emphasis on identifying the "most militant" individuals to participate in the study groups, placing stringent limits on the possibility of dialog and exchange. Indeed, CASA San Diego limited the number of workers who could participate in the study groups to six because it sought to invite only the "most militant."[69] The relationship with the Del Sol Action Council also seemed to sour because its members were not attending the study meeting to which CASA San Diego had invited some of its members. According to CASA San Diego's correspondence with the CASA Los Angeles chapter, Del Sol Action Council representatives explained that the tenants elected to forego the study group because "too much work was needed at the apartments."[70] CASA San Diego leader Juan Gutiérrez lamented, "The Del Sol Action Council is still meeting regularly but in essence I don't think they are doing the work properly."[71] Furthermore, he was particularly aggravated that the leader of the tenant's council missed a meeting with him. In essence, CASA San Diego's now top-down engagement with community groups and potential members was conditional on an expectation of ideological conformity and measures of "militancy" and "discipline."

This was seen clearly in another episode during this period. Describing the potential recruitment of a garment workers' union leader, Gutiérrez praised the unionist's critical assessment of the Mexican government, in line with CASA ideology, while criticizing the fact that he "still believes in U.S. democracy."[72] While he still requested permission from CASA Los Angeles to recruit him, these comments revealed the policing efforts at play that conditioned working with the group. The ideological narrowness of the student group made it difficult to organize the working-class constituency it claimed to represent.

In the end, CASA San Diego's failure to establish key spaces of community engagement in conjunction with intense theoretical study would lead them to place the blame for the organization's shortcomings on the community rather than their own mobilizing strategies. Gutiérrez argued that there "doesn't exist the clarity of who we are" in San Diego.[73] Furthermore, he explained that mobilization was difficult because "repression at this point is at a highest stage [sic], Migra raids, police brutality, drugs, and lumpenism among others set the objective field for someone to come and organize." "I'm doing what I can,"[74] he lamented.

However, Gutiérrez's assessment of the dire condition of the local organization served as a harbinger of CASA's fate at the national level. CASA San Diego, and wider CASA at the national level, would dissolve in 1978, but the symptoms of organizational decay were already well apparent in San Diego at least by 1976. Disconnecting from its older leadership, failing to consider the needs of community members to create a base, and concentrating on forging ideological conformity rather than engaging in active coalition building inevitably undermined any working relationship with community members and activists—and thus also undermined the lofty revolutionary goals the young activists had set for themselves. These practices greatly limited CASA San Diego's success in what was already an ambitious set of goals.

· · · · · ·

The Young Turks in San Diego sought to radicalize CASA Justicia by emphasizing class struggle explicitly as the goal of the Chicano movement, teaching Marxism to Mexicans *sin fronteras*, (without borders) and funneling their community into trade unions rather than into electoral politics and community services. They also sought to democratize CASA Justicia by reducing the roles of existing leadership. In all actuality, the Young Turks identified some limits to the decision-making processes that centered on Baca and Vásquez as leaders. Furthermore, the Young Turks began reflection and conversation that pushed Chicano radicalism toward struggle explicitly with capitalism and beyond liberalism. Yet, while their critiques and aspirations may have held some weight, they did not provide substantive alternatives.

CASA Justicia, as opposed to CASA San Diego, chose to continue an emphasis on providing social and legal services to undocumented migrants. They also chose to de-emphasize stringent acceptance of the ideological posturing that the new CASA leadership in Los Angeles and elsewhere were moving toward, instead opting to use CASA Justicia as a space in which to politicize migrants, with the goal of Chicano self-determination. As activists debated where they thought migrants should journey to, ideologically and politically, it is important to consider how migrants actually engaged these ideas and expressed their own agency. As indicated, many migrants journeyed to CASA Justicia organizers because they found solidarity with their day-to-day struggles and the material consequences of legal status, racism, and family separation within the deportation regime. These interactions reveal how social services were central to CASA not as an end in itself, but as a method of mobilizing defense of these migrants and the community at large. The emergent CASA San Diego appeared to be less successful at recruiting migrants to their version of mobilization due, ironically, to its rigid top-down decision-making practices, its insistence on hierarchical notions of "the most militant" members, and crucially, its de-emphasis on providing the social and legal services migrants found so useful. While CASA San Diego was radical in its rhetoric, CASA Justicia offered a practice of radicalism by assembling a space that migrants found useful for asserting their agency, calling forth new notions of belonging.

As CASA Justicia phased out due primarily to the end of the VISTA program, services to migrants were passed on to organizations such as MAAC and Barrio Station, which are social service–based groups that continue to exist. Yet Raza Sí, Migra No politics continued in direct actions meant to challenge the legal violence that continued against ethnic Mexicans in the borderlands. This politics was cultivated through deep engagement between U.S. Chicanos/as and Mexican migrants who insisted on telling their stories, voicing their concerns, and utilizing the day-to-day service work of CASA. As Charlie Vásquez asserted: "We saw it working through CASA. . . . there was no real division [between Mexican immigrants and Mexican Americans] because it affected everybody. An undocumented immigrant was married to a U.S. citizen and was afraid of being deported, or maybe the father and the mother were undocumented and the kids were born here . . . so there was all these crossings of problems . . . a lot of people had a different opinion, but we saw it different because we seen it. We were in the trenches with them."[75]

4 The First Time I Met César Chávez, I Got into an Argument with Him

California Employer Sanctions and Chicano Debates on Undocumented Workers

The first time Herman Baca met César Chávez, he observed a divisive rift with the UFW leader on one side, and veteran labor activist Bert Corona on the other. In Baca's recollection, he made clear which side he was on. He recalled:

> César and myself met at the Christ the King Church in Imperial (Imperial Beach in San Diego County). To be honest, it was hot and frank, the discussion. César's position was that they (undocumented workers) were breaking our strikes, that he didn't care who they were—that anyone who broke their strikes was the enemy and blah, blah, blah. So, I remember telling him . . . "Aren't these people (undocumented workers) also poor people? Aren't they trying to feed their families just like your people are? Aren't they also being exploited?" But we went around and 'round . . . that was the context of the time.[1]

It is in this heated context that Baca would confront other Chicano/a activists and a growing number of Mexican American elected officials who followed Chávez's position on immigration. This chapter will explore the contours of this debate within Chicano and Mexican American politics in California as it unfolded over Assembly Bill 528 (AB 528), a 1971 California State Assembly law that sought to sanction employers who hired undocumented immigrants.

In this context, Baca and Corona represented proponents of a (re)emerging transnational vision of Chicano/a community that included both Mexican Americans and Mexican immigrants, whereas Chávez and his United Farm Workers, the broader AFL-CIO, and emerging numbers of Chicano/a activists and elected officials tied to the Democratic Party argued that undocumented immigrants damaged the economic opportunities of Mexican American and other U.S.-born workers. The delineation of this debate between Chicano/a immigrant rights activists and Chicano Democrats is represented well by an impassioned exchange between Herman Baca and newly elected San Diego–area California State Assembly representative, Peter Chacón, over AB 528 and the broader struggle to address undocumented immigration.[2]

Raza Sí, Migra No activists such as Baca and Corona argued that employer sanctions in practice targeted undocumented workers as the problem rather than employers. They asserted that the growing hysteria over undocumented workers as job stealers and strikebreakers was part of a racialized discourse that was anti-Mexican. Indeed, they pointed out how Mexican Americans would also be affected by the stigma behind the scapegoating of undocumented immigrants during recession, because the pressure to prove one's citizenship would lead to interrogations against anyone who looked Mexican. Not only were these Chicano/a immigrant rights activists defensive in their posturing of the blame put on immigrants for high unemployment rates and adverse economic conditions, but they began to put forth nuanced analyses and solutions for the immigration crisis as it related to major economic and political shifts in global capitalism.

Chicano/a activists critiqued incoming neoliberal policies that made it easier for multinational companies to cross borders into places such as Mexico, disrupting the national economies there and encouraging workers to move toward the wealthier northern border looking for work. While these migrant workers were welcomed, and even recruited, by certain economic sectors, including agribusiness, construction, garment factory work, and domestic services, during times of economic recession, as witnessed during the 1970s and 1980s, the fear-based depiction of immigrants as invaders and job thieves heightened the urgency with which to address the problem of "illegal immigration." Raza Sí, Migra No activists argued that the focus on undocumented immigration as a primary cause of economic decline hid the underlying political-economic shifts indicated by the sending of U.S. manufacturing jobs overseas; growing dependency on immigrant and non-union laborers in several industries through long-established practices of subordinating particular laborers through race, legal status, and other social categories; and continued investment in wars such as that in Vietnam.

During these years of national recession from 1970 to 1972, and an unemployment rate in California that surpassed the national rate, the anti-immigrant politics of recession created a crisis among liberal and Left politicians, unionists, and activists, and fragmentation within the Mexican American community in the midst of the Chicano movement.[3] At stake in these debates between Chicano Democrats and Chicano/a immigrant rights activists was whether the very definition of "Chicano" could transcend the lines of U.S. citizenship. Further at stake was whether worker solidarities and the political struggles of the U.S. Left ended at the border or crossed it. The chapter will explore this through analysis of the Mexican American Political Association (MAPA), which had chapters throughout California, including San Diego, and was a primary site in which clashes between divergent positions emerged among Chicano/a activists and Mexican American politicos. These political clashes are further analyzed in the campaign to elect the first Mexican American member of the California State Assembly from San Diego County, Peter Chacón. Chacón requested the assistance of MAPA, National City, headed by Herman Baca, and emergent organizers and students galvanized by the Chicano movement to launch his campaign. The chapter ends after Chacón is in office and Baca, having earlier resigned from his campaign, is organizing for alternatives to the Democratic Party through La Raza Unida Party and against emerging anti-immigrant sentiment as expressed through AB 528, about which he and Chacón debated. The contingency exemplified by Baca and Chacón of course reflected the larger political fragmentation within the Chicano movement in the early 1970s, as the opening vignette reveals concerning arguments among César Chávez, Bert Corona, and Baca.

MAPA and Mexican American Politics in 1960s California

The Mexican American Political Association (MAPA) was an organization that emerged in 1960 with a goal to increase the number of Mexican American political officials and elected representatives. Part of this emerged through frustration with the Democratic Party in California, which many Mexican American activists felt had failed to support the election campaigns of candidates such as Edward Roybal, who ran for lieutenant governor in 1954, and Henry "Hank" López, who ran for state treasurer in 1955. Born out of frustration with Democratic governor Pat Brown's unwillingness to adequately address the issues of farmworker rights, the Bracero guest worker program, the lack of Mexican Americans attaining governmental jobs, and their underrepresentation in elected and appointed official positions, "MAPA declared independence from both major parties."[4] As former MAPA president Bert Corona puts it, "The party war-horses such as Pat Brown and Jess Unruh . . . felt a Mexican was not electable statewide."[5]

According to Corona, MAPA was a coalition of advocates that fractured along the lines of middle-class reformers tied to the Democratic Party who sought leverage that would enable them to move up the latter within the party system and community/trade union activists with roots in an ethno-racial organizing approach concerned with class conflict, immigrant rights, and at times, issues with sexism and patriarchy. Therefore, while MAPA emerged out of frustration with and a critique of the Democratic Party, there were fragments within the organization that had very different ideas and political practices. Corona explains that these factions chose to compromise with one another to come out of their initial 1959 convention with an organization, but the fractures are significant to note, particularly with regard to immigrant rights, political practice outside of the electoral context, and loyalty to the Democratic Party.[6] As will be noted later in the chapter, some of these fractures were revealed when issues of immigration emerged and Chicano movement notions of ethnic militancy sought to establish independence and self-determination from institutions such as the Democratic Party as well as a larger social system that activists began to understand as inherently white supremacist.

Many historians argue that the move toward more explicit ethnic militancy among Mexican Americans and other communities of color reflected the Cold War context in which it emerged. Historians note how the shift in political atmosphere by the 1950s toward anticommunism and purges of "subversives" enforced by various levels of the U.S. state led to the demise of important political practices among working-class communities of color within trade union activism and class-oriented ethno-racial organizations.[7] MAPA and other organizations such as the Community Service Organization (CSO) in California therefore emerged out of this tense context of anticommunism and purge of class-based struggles so important to many ethnic Mexican workers and immigrants, filling what historian Stephen Pitti calls a "vacuum" that was formerly held by labor-oriented organizations battered in the Cold War atmosphere.[8] Furthermore, immigration policy and deportation worked as a key mechanism through which ethnic Mexican activists were targeted, attacked, and demobilized in the 1950s.[9] According to Zaragosa Vargas, one observer argued that the threat of deportation "served as a very effective weapon to keep the Mexican people as a whole in bondage."[10] Therefore, coalitions within less overtly class-oriented ethnic organizations such as MAPA, with middle-class reformers and a focus on electoral politics, became a method through which grassroots organizers dedicated to critical class struggle within communities of color could regroup and continue a relatively safer mode of political engagement.

The repression of the U.S. Left in trade unions, the CIO, and the Communist Party during the Red Scare contributed to the rise of more ethnic and racial political organizing. The fertile historical environment toward ethnic unity and Chicano nationalism was also attributable to the emerging postwar struggles of the Black Freedom movement in the U.S. South and shifts among groups such as the Student Nonviolent Coordinating Committee (SNCC); proponents of black self-determination such as Malcolm X; the historical evolution of and frustration among Mexican American struggles for political empowerment in the electoral realm; and the influence of the nationalist movements toward decolonization in Asia, Africa, and Latin American, particularly the Cuban Revolution of 1959.[11] These developments at the local, national, and global level would provide substance for ethnic Mexicans and other communities of color in the United States to reorient powerful structural critiques and political efforts in the language of ethno-racial solidarity and activism. Furthermore, the continued racialized social structures of residential segregation, police brutality, housing discrimination, deportation repression, and exclusion from political and social institutions ensured that ethno-racial identities would be a central organizing focus through which intersectional struggles would be articulated by ethnic Mexicans and other communities of color in the postwar era.

MAPA's emergence in California indicated this continued momentum toward organizing based on a shared ethno-racial identity. MAPA also housed many veterans of the Mexican American Left of the 1930s–1950s who played key roles in orienting some MAPA chapters toward a grassroots base and mentoring new activists. Bert Corona remembered: "Some of us had been in the labor movement, where we had picked up lifelong organizing tactics. We'd gone out and organized workers. I and others had further experience in the National Congress of Spanish-Speaking Peoples and in ANMA. . . . People like this, who were the progressives in MAPA, could go out and call a meeting in a church, raise the issues that were hot at the time and come out with an organization."[12] The labor movement and community-organizing left wing of MAPA used the organization to provide the space through which new activists would cut their teeth in the fervent decade of the 1960s via grassroots organizing in dialog with the struggles of barrio residents throughout the state. Indeed, Chicano/a scholars have noted MAPA's emergence as part of what David Gutiérrez phrases as "the first phase" of the emergent Chicano movement, revealing that Mexican

American organizations had "significantly changed their political tactics" and indicating "new" and "more aggressive tactics."[13] George Mariscal adds that the emergence of MAPA and many other organizations in the early 1960s marked the beginning of an "era of elevated political praxis among Mexican Americans," indicating a moment when "a more militant ethnicity-based politics emerged throughout the Southwest."[14]

This may be indicated by the left wing of MAPA insisting on using the term "Mexican," and eventually winning the fight against more conservative forces within the organization in asserting a nonwhite identity and emphasizing forming coalitions with other communities of color. Mexican Americans had long debated their relationship to whiteness, as groups such as the League of United Latin American Citizens (LULAC) and others had found success in the courts by noting the legal white identity to which Mexican Americans had access to due to the historical particularities of the initial incorporation of Mexicans into the United States in 1848. Furthermore, there had long been anti-black and anti-indigenous sentiment in Mexican mestizo society, and Mexican Americans' "faustian pact with whiteness," as historian Neil Foley puts it, did not help change these hierarchical sentiments.[15] But the left wing within MAPA was insistent on using, unapologetically, "Mexican" in the organization's name and also insisted on a coalitional position, particularly in solidarity efforts with African Americans. Corona remembered:

> The name "Mexican" *had* [Corona's emphasis] to be included. It was important for the Mexican community to recognize itself. If we didn't recognize ourselves and instead shied away from using our name in order to be more acceptable to Anglos, we would be giving in to all of the discrimination and belittling that had characterized our political experience. Consequently, I was very strong for using the term "Mexican American"—with an emphasis on *Mexican* [also Corona's emphasis]—because I really felt that we needed to identify ourselves very clearly and not make any bones about it. Moreover, those of us who had had previous political experience in organizing Mexicans understood that Mexicans would in fact participate politically if they identified with our name.[16]

By the early 1960s, MAPA leaders continued to be frustrated by the failure of the Kennedy administration at the national level and Governor Pat Brown's administration at the state level to place Mexican Americans in important posts and attend to their concerns. This frustration was often interpreted by ethnic Mexican critics as subordination by Democratic policymakers of their particular issues—language and cultural rights, immigration and citizenship issues, and the struggle of farmworkers—to African American issues, especially in California.

By the mid-1960s, the United Farm Worker Organizing Committee, later to be named the United Farm Worker (UFW) union, had come to international acclaim as Dolores Huerta, César Chávez, and others led farmworkers to win contracts in its historic grape boycotts from 1965 to 1970.[17] The UFW struggles became synonymous with Mexican American civil rights struggles—and for good reason, as the majority of its members and farmworkers more broadly were of Mexican origin (among other groups, such as Filipinos) and were among the most exploited laborers in the country. Chávez pushed this notion when he lobbied Governor Pat Brown in 1963, stating, "The farm worker is synonymous with the Mexican-American in California, and the Mexican-American voter is synonymous with the Democratic Party in California."[18] Indeed, the UFW's struggles inspired and influenced ethnic Mexican youth, and stirred the emergence of the Chicano movement as these youth, students, and community activists supported the international consumer boycott of nonunion California grapes in supermarkets in their local, often urban environment. MAPA, like virtually all Mexican American organizations in the 1960s, fostered this support for the UFW and farmworker struggles as central to Mexican American issues, experiencing the frustration with the Democratic Party that brought MAPA into being in the first place. As historian Mark Brilliant describes, in addition to Governor Brown's failure to appoint more Mexican American representatives to important governmental positions, he also refused to assist Chávez and the UFW on a number of campaigns. In particular, Brown did not address a demand from the Agricultural Worker Organizing Committee (AWOC)—the Filipino-led precursor to the UFW—to raise the minimum wage and failed to call for a special legislative session to enact a collective bargaining law during the acclaimed UFW grape boycott in the gubernatorial election year of 1966. Brilliant attributes this tense relationship between Brown and Mexican Americans to Brown's loss to Ronald Reagan for the governorship in 1966. The inability to address Mexican American issues led to Reagan performing "more strongly in this community (38 to 40 percent) than any Republican had ever done."[19] With tensions between the Democratic Party and Mexican Americans, different political practices within organizations such as MAPA and the emerging Chicano movement, and, by the late 1960s, the rise of immigration as a significant issue, internal conflict among ethnic Mexican activists was set to boil over, not only with a movement away from the Democratic Party and toward the Republicans but much rather with a shift among community organizers that saw MAPA as a mechanism to achieve what they called "Chicano self-determination."

MAPA and the Chicano Movement

The emergence of the National City chapter of MAPA in 1968, with the dynamic, small print business owner Herman Baca as its leader, demonstrates how the organization worked across the state as a site off of college campuses where new Chicano movement activists engaged in applying the notions of Chicano self-determination within movement documents such as *El Plan Espiritual de Aztlán* (Spiritual Plan of Aztlán).[20] A working-class suburb of San Diego that was 40 percent ethnic Mexican, Baca founded the National City chapter to battle the issues he had grown up with as a barrio youth, including police brutality, poverty, employment issues, crime, and lack of access for ethnic Mexicans to positions of leadership and power.[21] Baca's political experience grew into the Chicano movement struggle for self-determination based in part on his experience growing up in the small town of Los Lentes, New Mexico, and the barrios of National City. The shift from the communal pueblos of New Mexico, where ethnic Mexicans predominated the cultural atmosphere, to the segregated barrios of the San Diego area, where authority figures were overwhelmingly white and often antagonistic, proved to be a striking experience for Baca. Indeed, his experiences in the San Diego area soon taught him painful lessons about how racism worked as an oppressive system continually present in urban working-class ethnic Mexican communities. Contrasting the racially exclusive circumstances of Southern California with an environment in which ethnic Mexicans occupied significant positions of stature in New Mexico supplied an intellectual basis for future analysis of Chicano oppression and the possibility for alternative political practices. Indeed, Baca's father, Nicholas Baca, served as a justice of the peace in Los Lentes when Baca was a child. While serving in an official position in a small-town environment required minimal responsibilities (Baca recalled his father ruling a reward of two chickens to the victim of a scuffle), that a Mexican American could occupy a position of relative power was an important contrast to the systematic exclusion of ethnic Mexicans from significant community positions in San Diego County.[22] Baca remembered: "When I look back, I remember the sheriff (of his home town) was a Mexicano. The mayor was a Mexicano. You know, the senator, the U.S. senator . . . (was) Dennis Chávez."[23] The unique history of New Mexico, an area with the highest concentration of Mexican-origin inhabitants among lands ceded by the United States after its war on Mexico, led a number of Hispano elites to maintain some of their prestige and access to positions of power, even as most of the population became subjected to various forms of exclusion and oppression.[24] This circumstance influenced the political trajectory of Baca. Baca also claimed that many of the leaders in MAPA were *Manitos* (Mexican-origin people from New Mexico), implying that their insistence on participation in politics was in part honed by an upbringing where Mexican Americans held positions of power and demographic majorities.

Yet Baca's move to the San Diego area at the age of seven was a dramatic shift in his life and in the broader social context where whites were in positions of power and Mexican Americans were consistently ridiculed and institutionally excluded. Baca recalled the ways this was experienced in everyday life, such as a gym coach in high school ordering "all you tacos" to get in a line. Ethnic Mexicans were pushed into shop classes. Baca got into many fights, and went to juvenile hall several times. As a teenager, the National City Police would consistently pull Baca and his friends over every time they crossed out of their neighborhood. He recalled: "I remember telling this reporter one time, 'The cops used to stop us so much that when they didn't stop us we felt like, "Hey, don't they like us anymore?"' Yeah. I mean, we'd cross National Avenue, National City Boulevard, and they would stop us. I mean, that was routine." Baca recalled further, "I had come out of a barrio-type environment, and out of all the friends I grew up with a couple were already dead, a couple were in jail, and some had gone over to Vietnam."[25] After graduating from Sweetwater High School and spending a few days in jail for being with a group of friends who broke into a store, Baca decided to fly straight and entered the printing industry, slowly moving his way up.[26]

Baca created MAPA National City with another close friend he grew up with, Carlos "Charlie" Vásquez. Vásquez founded a chapter of the Movimiento Estudiantil Chicano de Aztlán (MEChA) at Southwestern Junior College in nearby Chula Vista. Other neighborhood friends from the National City barrios would be among the first recruits, many of them veterans after being drafted to the Vietnam War. One of these neighborhood acquaintances, Augie Bareño, remembers:

I got drafted . . . (and) got out of the army in '69. Everyone from National City was going to Southwestern and we would all carpool with Charlie (Vásquez) . . . Charlie and Roger's (neighborhood friend and future activist Roger Cazares') brother, Hector, and Herman's brother, George. And Hector and George were veterans. . . . Charlie and Herman's brother, George, and some other guys started MEChA. . . . So Charlie started inviting people to go to MEChA and we were like, "I ain't trying that fucking *Tijuanero* thing, man." [Charlie would say] "No, no, no, no, there's broads there." And shit. Haha . . . that's basically how he got most of us to go. And then it was, like, MAPA, which is Herman. Early MAPA they would put on events and stuff. Back then the teachers would give you credit and extra points if you did community work and you attended an event. So when MAPA was doing something, Charlie was like y'all gotta go down there—they are doing something—you gotta get extra credit. It was bullshit like that (that led to Chicano activism). It just grew.[27]

Bareño's reflection reveals how early organizing in National City came from a tight-knit group of Chicano men who grew up together there. The community atmosphere of Southwestern College (even Charlie Vásquez's mother worked there in the cafeteria, where Bareño remembered her slipping them free food when they did not have any money) culminated in engagement with the emerging Chicano, Black Power, and antiwar politics of the times. Bareño's comments also reveal the homosocial and heteronormative social networks that were transferred from neighborhood life into campus and community political organizing, as assuring young Chicano men that "there's broads there" was apparently a central means by which to get them to attend meetings and get involved. These gender norms reinforced male dominance and reflected the larger context in which scholars have documented the struggles that cisgender Chicanas and Queer Chicanos/as confronted with regard to sexism and homophobia in Chicano movement political spaces.[28]

Indeed, scholars have argued that Chicano movement discourse and practice, particularly on campus, was often encouraged by Chicano nationalist insistences on unity. Women often experienced this as a control mechanism that prevented them from highlighting patriarchy and sexism, for which they would be charged with selling out and disuniting the movement. For example, Chicana student activist at California State University in Long

Beach and scholar Anna Nieto Gomez argues, "Back on campus it seemed the guys were role-playing the exaggerated stereotypical macho and forced women to play out their passive role." Nieto Gomez recalled that at least on one occasion her encounter working with Chicano men off campus was less exaggerated. She remembered, "I saw their male identity as being comfortable and part of who they were."[29] Bareño's comments reveal objectifying tendencies among Chicano men coming from the community (as well as the masculinist culture of the armed forces) to campus, and possibly points to how these tendencies might have been intensified within movement politics as students encountered Chicano nationalist discourse in the hostile institutional setting of the university. Indeed, many former Chicana students recall how sexual advances from their Chicano male peers in movement spaces were common and spilled over into political decision making. Chicano/a historians have documented this tendency, as exemplified by Leticia Hernández's reflection of her experience in the MEChA at California State University, Long Beach. Hernández remembered:

> The women felt that they were being used as far as sexuality within the movement. A lot of sexual double standards. It's a whole difference between men and women, too, you know. Girls go to college young, naïve, maybe they fall in love with someone, and so they go to bed with somebody and think that this guy is going to marry them. He's going to do her for a couple of weeks or maybe a couple of months and then drop her, you know. He has no intention of marrying her or anybody else. This would happen to women; they would pick up the pieces, and it would happen again they'd get a reputation, or else if they didn't go to bed with the guys the men thought the women who don't are lesbians, or that women are holding out for some reason, that they want to be men. This was a difficult position for women to be in within this kind of organizing.[30]

These contradictions were confronted by Chicana activists in the movement, leading to new analyses, critiques, and praxis of Chicana feminism that sought to reconfigure notions of solidarity and unity through consideration of the marginalizing experiences of women and other aggrieved identities within the ethnic Mexican community. Bareño's reflections also reveal that Mexican American women were, indeed, present in the MEChA at Southwestern, and later at San Diego State University (SDSU), where many of them transferred. As Chicana activist, former MEChA member and student at San Diego State University State, Olivia Puentes Reynolds described, it was a wider practice among many Chicano movement organizations at the time that men would make the decisions. Chicanas, among the broader activist community, would heed the calls through their networks to mobilize for a march or rally announced by the organizers, but to get into the decision making room, as Puentes Reynolds put it, you had to be attached to a man. Like the historiography reveals about other sites of Chicano movement activism, the issues of sexism and gender difference was navigated and challenged by Chicanas in the San Diego movement as well.[31] Similarly, movement activism also led to confrontation with other intracommunity differences and tensions, as Bareño remembers the divide between Mexican Americans and Mexicans across the border (*Tijuaneros*), and overcoming reluctance among the former to explore their connections to the renaissance and celebration of Mexican culture and identity that was ongoing within Chicano movement activities.[32]

Yet the politicized fervor of the movement in the 1960s attracted these young activists, as struggles against the racism they experienced growing up gave resonance and language to describing and challenging oppression. Indeed, Charlie Vásquez remembered going to the established MEChA chapter at nearby SDSU, where he later transferred, and being impressed by the likes of Black Power activists speaking there, including H. Rap Brown and Stokely Carmichael. Baca recalled visiting one of his first Chicano movement events held at SDSU in 1968: "That was the first time I'd ever seen that many Mexicans gathered in one place other than the church. . . . there was Gracia Molina de Pick . . . there was Alurista, there was Rene Nuñez. . . . and I remember thinking, 'this is the first Mexicans I've ever heard talk about something other than *brindis* [a toast] . . . here they're talking about politics.'"[33] Alurista, Molina de Pick, and Nuñez were faculty members of the newly established Mexican American Studies Department at SDSU. At SDSU, students formed the Mexican American Youth Association (MAYA), which later became MEChA, successfully pressing to found one of the earliest Chicano studies departments in the country in 1968.[34] Also in 1968, a MAYA chapter at the University of California, San Diego, in alliance with Black student activists, struggled to create a college for third world students, called the Lumumba-Zapata College.[35] Members of the National City group, many of whom would attend San Diego State University, including Charlie Vásquez, Augie Bareño, and Roger Cazares, engaged local manifestations of Chicano movement activism and the student militancy of the late 1960s there. Roger Cazares remembered being involved with an organization called BOMB (Black, Oriental, and Mexican Brothers) at SDSU, and meeting with the likes of Eldrige Cleaver of the Black Panthers, Stokely Carmichael of SNCC, Students for a Democratic Society (SDS), the Brown Berets, and the Young Lords. He was greatly influenced by Malcolm X's ideas in particular. Norma Mena Cazares recalled that as a student activist, "I think we [Chicano/a student activists] identified more with Malcolm X . . . a lot of it based on anger and seeing the injustices."[36]

Baca was not a student, but through his friendships with many people who were, such as Cazares, Vásquez, Bareño, and later, Mena Cazares, his political development shifted radically. As a printer, Baca was asked to print flyers and pamphlets for the numerous activities and speaking engagements his friends and other activists were engaged in. Establishing his own print shop in the barrios of National City, it served as a space in which political ideas of the day were discussed, piquing Baca's interest in the burgeoning era of protest. He remembered making the dramatic ideological shift from canvassing for the Richard Nixon presidential campaign to seeking Chicano self-determination in National City by founding a MAPA chapter there.

A number of other influences reached the San Diego Chicano movement, including César Chávez and the UFW's mobilization of mostly Mexican American farmworkers. The UFW reached international attention at the end of the 1960s and featured symbols that evoked the ethno-racial pride that resonated the militancy that attracted Mexican American youth, including a flag with an eagle at the center like the Mexican flag, banners that revered the brown Virgin de Guadalupe as the movement's and Mexican people's patron saint, and expression of Chicano/Mexicano art, identity, and politics in the Teatro Campesino (Farmworkers' Theatre) that emerged from the UFW struggles.[37] Other influences combined, as Cazares and Mena Cazares mentioned, including, antiwar student movements, the Black Power movement, and nationalist decolonization movements in the global south, which also persuaded students to formulate a radicalized political identity based on ethno-racial unity. Baca also remembered particularly the influence of Malcolm X. He recalled: "I was highly influenced . . . more by Malcolm X than Martin Luther King. What I dug about Malcolm X was his personal courage, you know, and his confronting the system, the white supremacist system, you know, which wasn't easy."[38] Chicano movement discourse fit with what Baca recognized as a courageous confrontation with the white supremacist system from the historical perspective of Mexicans in the United States. In this context of the 1960s, the Chicano student movement took an unrelenting stance against identifying with American culture and society through claims to an indigenous "Chicano" cultural identity based in the former Mexican territories of the Southwest United States. This stance was articulated best through the embracement of a "Chicano" identity, juxtaposed with the assimilationist "Mexican American" label, and an embrace of the conception of Aztlán as the territorial homeland of Chicanos located in the U.S. Southwest. As two generation of scholars have now documented, Chicanos took on a "brown" nonwhite racial identity that used depictions of indigenous Mesoamerican ancestors, farmworkers' connections with the land, and the impassioned recognition that the conquest of Northern Mexico by the United States in the war of 1848 created the oppressive circumstances of their community to imagine an alternative to the racism embedded in capitalist U.S. society.[39] Chicanismo focused on the conception of a racialized community (*la raza*/"the people") that would serve as a strategic rallying point (*carnalismo*, or brotherhood) for a unified antiracist movement.[40] Conceiving of themselves as a part of a "mestizo nation" within the United States, Chicano/a students and activists emphasized a right to self-determination. The *Plan de Aztlán*, in part authored by San Diego poet Alurista, asserted, "A nation autonomous and free—culturally, socially, economically, and politically—will make its own decisions on the usage of our lands, the taxation of our goods, the utilization of our bodies for war, the determination of justice (reward and punishment), and the profit of our sweat."[41] For the most part, Chicano/a students used this revolutionary and neoseparatist rhetoric to establish their own spaces on campus in which to learn about their cultural heritage, initiating Chicano studies programs and establishing Chicano movement student organizations, culminating in the establishment of the MEChA as a national student activist group in 1968.[42]

Baca was deeply influenced by Chicano movement calls for self-determination, but as a community member (rather than a student) he sought to apply chicanismo (the politics of being Chicano) in the working-class barrio in which he lived. This led to his engagement with MAPA and the creation of the National City chapter. Baca's experience with MAPA marked a key difference with the trajectory of Chicano movement activism among students, because present within MAPA were veteran labor activists such as Bert Corona, who since the 1930s had insisted on an embracement of Mexican heritage, community self-determination, and protest as central to bridging ethnic Mexican community politics to cross-ethnic class struggles. Therefore, Baca's experience with MAPA put him in contact with older Mexican American labor activists. Baca's experience paralleled that of other Chicano movement activists who got their political start among the dozens of other MAPA chapters that operated throughout California.[43]

These experiences go against the grain of many scholars who insist that the Chicano movement was fundamentally distinct from the so-called assimilationist politics of the Mexican American generation. Some MAPA chapters organized communities at the grassroots level, as practiced by the Mexican American Left of the previous generation, evolving into a new cohort of Chicano/a activists who gained access to ideological tools that combined class identities as workers and poor people with the cultural pride emphasized within the Chicano movement. Movement activists such as Baca, in many ways different from student activists in their presence in ethnic Mexican barrios, would apply notions of self-determination in relationship to the demographic shifts and structural realities within working-class ethnic Mexican communities.

In establishing the National City chapter of MAPA, Baca and his allies began dialogs with the statewide leadership, and met with the preexisting MAPA San Diego chapter, headed by veteran activist Phil Usquiano. Like Bert Corona and other MAPA leaders, including Herman Gallegos, Ed Quevedo, and others, Usquiano was a former member of the Congreso del Pueblo Que Habla Español and a labor leader in San Diego who utilized MAPA as a political facet of the ethnic-labor organization the Hermandad Mexicana Nacional. As discussed in chapter 1, the Hermandad Mexicana was a San Diego-area organization created in 1951 that mobilized mostly Mexican immigrant workers and controlled the Laborers Union Local 89.[44] Therefore, Baca's search for a community-level organization through which to address Chicano oppression brought him into contact with veteran activists such as Corona and Usquiano, and a history of immigrant rights activism interrelated to worker and antiracist struggles. Indeed, Corona also worked with Usquiano in 1968 to extend the Hermandad to the Los Angeles area, establishing the Centro de Acción Social Autónomo (CASA).[45] These ties to leaders such as Corona and Usquiano would have great influence on the younger Chicano movement activists emerging out of National City. This began when Usquiano worked with Baca and established the new MAPA National City chapter in 1968.

MAPA National City and the Peter Chacón Campaign, 1969–1970

Like many Chicano movement organizations, some of MAPA National City's first actions centered around supporting the United Farm Workers Grape Boycott struggle in 1968, holding strikes and protests in front of grocery stores and markets to influence consumers not to buy grapes from the UFW's enemies. MAPA National City's main focus, however, soon became electing more Chicano/a candidates to office, applying the notion of Chicano self-determination by simply attempting to create a united ethnic voting bloc. This entailed canvassing ethnic Mexican neighborhoods and holding drives to register community members to be eligible to vote. This also involved endorsing candidates, as statewide MAPA chapters had practiced for years, and campaigning for particular Mexican American candidates to achieve the goal of getting more of their people into office. Baca remembered the lack of Mexican American elected officials at the time, and MAPA activists' naïve assumption that "all we had to do was register people and get them out to vote and elect some Chicano candidates and, 'Hey, our problems are going to be over.'" Alex García from the Los Angeles area was the only Mexican American member of the California State Assembly. The only individual in the San Diego area of Mexican descent who was an elected official was Louis Camacho, council member of National City. But in 1968, Baca and the MAPA National City chapter assisted Ernie Azhocar, a former Mexican American liaison for a local assemblymember, in getting elected to the Sweetwater School District Board of Trustees. This success, coupled with Baca's outspoken manner of identifying racism as being at the root of Mexican American community problems and exclusion from mainstream institutions, began to gain attention. Baca became the campaign manager for Ben Moreno in his run for Board of Trustees at Southwestern Junior College. Baca remembered the criticism he and his MAPA chapter were gaining as "militants," "subversives," and "communists," and informed Moreno that if that emerging reputation was a problem, he would understand if Moreno did not want him as campaign manager. "To his [Moreno's] credit," Baca recalled, he said, "'Hey, that's the way I want it and the hell with them if they don't, if they want to see it in a negative light, you know, if they don't want to see it as something that, you know, coming out of our community.'"[46] Moreno won the race, becoming the first Mexican American Board member in an emerging junior college district serving Mexican Americans.

This success and ties to the ethnic Mexican community led to MAPA National City's involvement in Peter Chacón's campaign to become the first Mexican American assemblymember from San Diego county. Chacón was born in Tucson, Arizona, and moved with his family to the San Diego area in 1946 after a tour in the U.S. Air Force during World War II. A decorated war veteran, Chacón grew up working in the farm fields picking beets. Chacón attended college on the G.I. Bill and became a schoolteacher, and eventually a principal, at Sherman Elementary School in San Diego.[47]

As an educator, he observed how Spanish-speaking children were often sent to classrooms for students with severe learning disabilities.[48] He cofounded the Chicano Federation, a coalition of Chicano movement–era organizations in San Diego, serving as the first president in 1969.[49]

Baca was involved, of course, with the Chicano Federation and knew Chacón as the chairperson of that important community group. In late 1969, Chacón came to Baca's print shop, Aztec Printing, which had become an important community and activist meeting spot in National City for MAPA and other movement activity. There Chacón asked Baca to have MAPA National City involved with his campaign. Baca recalled his response, "And, I said—and this is one of the things that I've always tried to follow, you know. In politics, you need a consensus or a mandate from those that you're trying to affect. So . . . I said, 'You know what Pete,' I says, 'let me get a group of people from the community and let's sit down and talk about it.'"[50] So in the final weeks of December 1969, Baca called forth members of the Chicano/a activist community together for a meeting at the headquarters of the Mexican American Advisory Council (MAAC), an organization formed by a number of Mexican American associations that addressed social service and poverty issues, also founded by the aforementioned Laborers Union Local 89 and the Hermandad Mexicana headed by Phil Usquiano, among others.[51]

Chacón's initial idea was to run for San Diego County supervisor. Baca recalled how most of the activists in the room were under thirty and had little political experience. However, Usquiano, as a longtime veteran activist and labor organizer, suggested Chacón run for assemblymember of the 79th District. After revealing that Chacón was a grassroots candidate with little money, Usquiano made the case that the supervisor campaign would be much more expensive to run than one for the Assembly. Usquiano also reasoned that the 79th district was a traditionally blue-collar, Democratic district, with a large minority population, but at the time it was held by a Republican, Tom Hom.[52] The suggestion was that it would be less expensive and more feasible to win the race for Assembly. Chacón and the group agreed to run for the 79th district. Chacón also asked Baca to be the head manager and chair of the campaign at the meeting. Baca responded that he had to present it to his organization, MAPA, for approval. Soon after, MAPA National City approved it, and the group became involved with the Chacón campaign, with Baca as the campaign manager.[53]

Baca remembered giving a few conditions for serving as campaign manager, including running the campaign to win it, using the campaign to educate young Chicano/a activists on the game of politics, and to run all decision making through the group of organizers that would be doing the ground-work, knocking on doors, and telephone campaigning. Baca recalled meeting at Chacón's home every Monday for decision-making meetings, beginning in early January 1970, focusing on the primary election in June of the same year. Fund-raising was a problem, but it was in this context that MAPA state leaders and veteran activists, including Bert Corona and Abe Tapia, came in to assist in raising funds alongside Usquiano. Baca explained: "We brought in those people and then we, you know, so we made like around $6,000 to $7,000, which was a lot of money in those days. And so, it was a successful fund-raiser."[54] Reports revealed that Chacón would spend $7,621 on his campaign, of which $1,693 was his own contribution. This was compared to the $11,497 that incumbent Tom Hom spent in an attempt to win the Democratic Party nomination (as previously mentioned, Hom was a Republican) with a write-in campaign, and $15,531 spent by another candidate, George Koulaxes.[55] Chacón's campaign was truly a grassroots one, and he was an underdog in terms of spending. As Baca remembered, after gaining their first significant campaign contribution, the campaign team invested much of their own money: "So, I remember after leaving there . . . we (the MAPA campaign volunteers) each put [in] $100 and one of the persons there put in $100 worth of stamps. Where she got them, I don't know. But she put [in] $100 worth of stamps."[56] The central strategy was to focus on Mexican American voters in the district, reflected in centering the campaign headquarters in Logan Heights, or Barrio Logan, as many Chicanos/as referred to it, the oldest barrio and center of the ethnic Mexican community in the San Diego area. This strategy emerged through the ethnic-centered organizing of MAPA and the Chicano movement, as well as the awareness that white voters would most likely be less than sympathetic to the campaign, given the racism of the time. Baca explained: "There was a calculated effort to say, 'Look, we got to zero in on our community. We've got to register our community. We've got to politicize and we've got to get the word out to our community.' . . . So we mainly zeroed in on . . . the Chicano community, and that's where we did most of our walking. That's where we were headquartered at in Logan Heights."[57]

A core group of organizers formed a committee to elect Chacón, and they quickly learned that the Democratic Party was not very supportive of their efforts. Baca reflected on the outright resistance from party leaders: "The thinking, even of the 'liberal' Democrats was that civil rights was meant, or political involvement meant, the Black community, you know, because of their presence and their high visibility and activism. And, it was like, 'What are you guys (the Chacón campaign organizers) doing here?' you know. To outright being told, 'Hey, you guys ain't going to win. You guys (Mexican Americans) don't vote. You guys are not registered . . . you guys are . . . apolitical, your community.' "[58] This attitude that Mexican American candidates were not electable reflected the frustration of statewide MAPA organizers and broader Mexican American activists with the Democratic Party in the state since the early 1960s. In the Democratic Party primary, Chacón would compete with Marie C. Widman, an African American woman serving as interim chair of the San Diego County Democratic Central Committee, whom Baca identified as the "party favorite," and George Koulaxes, an engineer for defense industry giant General Dynamics and a Greek American war veteran.[59] As the Chacón organizing committee walked door-to-door in the community for the campaign, the June 2, 1970, primary election approached, and the Democratic Party leadership moved in to take charge.

The Democratic Party in California in 1970 was attempting to retake the governorship after Ronald Reagan defeated incumbent Pat Brown in 1966. Longtime Democratic Party chair in California, Jesse Unruh, would win the nomination over Los Angeles mayor Sam Yorty to face Reagan in November 1970. The California Assembly was split evenly, 40-40, so the opportunity for a Democrat to win the 79th District was of utmost importance. When Chacón's campaign began to demonstrate that it would seriously compete for the seat, it appears that party leaders shifted their concerns about his electability (and by extension, Mexican American candidates in general), and sought to control and manage the trajectory of the now viable candidate. Baca remembered waking up the morning of June 1, the day before the primary elections, and seeing an ad exclaiming "PETER CHACON is *that man*."[60] Baca explained:

> So we started to get outside contacts from some of the power structure individuals, you know, some of the power brokers (from the Democratic Central Committee). And, you know, "Okay, fine," you know, "we're trying to win," you know, "Hey, if that helps, then fine." But we [the MAPA organizers] would still make the decisions, you know, what was going to be done. . . . I get up in the morning and I'm reading the newspaper and there's an ad in the newspaper, you know. . . . So, I'm looking at this and I said, "Where does that come from?" A complete surprise to me, because it hadn't been discussed, and, "Where'd we get

this kind of money for the *San Diego Union*, you know? This thing's not cheap." It wasn't a full-page ad, but it was a good-sized ad.[61]

At the bottom of the ad, Baca noticed a caption that read,

PAID BY CITIZENS
TO ELECT PETER CHACON
DR. G. L. ODDO, CHAIRMAN[62]

With it being the last moments before the primary, Baca and Chacón were scheduled to perform last-minute duties checking in with the ballot officials, the organizers working to get people to the polls, and telephone bank volunteers. At the beginning of primary day, Baca showed Chacón the ad and asked, "Pete, what's going on man?" According to Baca, Chacón said, "Oh, that's just some people that wanted to help me out." To which Baca says he responded: "No. No. No. No. No. . . . That ain't what we had agreed on and that ain't what we have been working under. . . . I thought we had agreed that all of the decisions would be coming out of the committee of the people that were working every day?" When asked about the chairman label given to Dr. G. L. Oddo, Baca recalls that Chacón claimed it was a "tactical move." Baca remembered responding:

> You know what Pete? I'm out of here. . . . I'm going to see this thing
> through today . . . but next meeting we have . . . I'm resigning. And
> I want to tell you right now before one vote has been taken. . . . You
> know, this was not the agreement. If you're doing this and you're
> not even in office . . . what are you going to do once you get in there?
> And I'm going to tell you something before the votes come in tonight,
> so you don't say it's sour grapes . . . you're going to win. And the
> reason you're going to win is because you walked. They didn't.[63]

After a few days, the votes were finally tallied announcing Chacón the winner of the primary, thus set to take on Assemblymember Tom Hom for the seat in November.[64] Baca remembers attending the campaign meeting the next week at Chacón's home. Ready to announce his resignation, Baca recalled two unknown white men briefing Chacón on next steps and that they were dismissive of Baca's presence, which seemed symbolic of the takeover by Democratic Party insiders. Baca announced the resignation, to the surprise of many of the organizers, most of whom he recruited, according to Baca.[65] Carlos Vásquez also decided to resign when Baca informed him earlier about the ad incident. Vásquez described their decision to resign as the result of being forced out by party leaders. "After we won, the party came in and said, 'Get rid of the radicals,' meaning us," said Vásquez. "For us [Baca and Vásquez], it was the turning point away from traditional party politics."[66] While Baca does not describe his exit as one of being forced out, he did believe it was the goal of the party to wrestle control away from Chicano movement organizers using a grassroots strategy that focused on ethno-racial solidarity, based in Mexican American neighborhoods. Baca observes: "I'm sure after, after he (Chacón) won, that he probably thought that he got rid of a liability, you know. Because I, like I said, during all this period, I was still active . . . on the unpopular activist issues, you know, and some people probably decided it was a hindrance or, you know, it was a liability, or what have you."[67]

Chacón would go on to unseat the Republican incumbent, Tom Hom. Chacón and established local, state, and even national, Democrats attacked Hom's record, particularly on failing to support "minority issues," education, and the concerns of working people.[68] Hom's indictment on taking bribes from the Yellow Cab Company also assisted Chacón's victory.[69] The victory was part of a larger retaking of the California Legislature as Democrats gained majorities in both the Assembly and the Senate, but lost the governorship to Ronald Reagan again.[70] Upon entering office in 1971, Chacón authored a bill in bilingual education that was eventually passed and implemented through public schools in California. This earned Chacón the title "the father of bilingual education."[71] He was also one of the founding members of the Chicano Legislative Caucus in the California Assembly in 1973, a group he would chair for the next fourteen years. He was reelected as assemblyman of the 79th District a number of times and served twenty-one years, retiring in 1992.[72]

Despite the differences that led to the end of Baca and Chacón's working relationship, Chacón identified with the Chicano movement, and sought to address problems of discrimination, language, and cultural rights, labor, and systematic neglect to gain the Mexican American vote. Indeed, the Teamsters Union made contributions to Chacón's opponent Tom Hom, due to Chacón's support for the United Farm Workers grape and lettuce strike, to which the Teamsters were opposed. This support for Chávez and the UFW would play out when Baca and Chacón would come together again later in 1971, this time as adversaries debating the passing of AB 528 in the California legislature, a law that fined employers who hired undocumented workers. As Baca remembered from his experience as Chacón's campaign manager leading up to the primary and his resignation: "I got a political education. I said [to myself],

'You know what? This isn't just about registering people or electing candidates. It's a little bit more complex than that.' There's some structural things here that aren't just going to be done away with, you know, just like that."[73] Immigration and the undocumented population proved to be one of the central indications of "some structural things" that Chicano Democrats and Chicano/Mexicano activists clashed over later in 1971, revealing contested notions of the political trajectory of the Chicano movement.

Assembly Bill 528: The Dixon Arnett Employer Sanctions Law

For years, organized labor and Mexican American civil rights activists struggled against the exploitative Bracero Program, which initiated a guest worker agreement between the United States and Mexico during World War II, but lingered on into the 1960s. Activists and their allies were finally successful in their attempts to end it, as unionist such as César Chávez and Dolores Huerta perceived the exploitation of braceros as a major barrier to gaining farmworkers' rights in the early 1960s.[74] Their position was that growers were being allowed to bring in braceros when there were local workers already available. This drove down wages, they argued, and gave the upper hand to growers to exploit both braceros and local workers. Chávez and Huerta therefore put particular emphasis on ending the Bracero Program. But there's evidence that the targeting of the Bracero Program led to conflictual interactions with and a somewhat vehement depiction of the braceros by these unionists. After the end of the program in 1964, growers simply continued to recruit undocumented migrants to maintain the wage controls and disciplinary measures over the workforce. Border Patrol apprehensions of undocumented migrants in the Southwestern sector shot up from 32,519 in 1964 to 73,973 by 1967. By 1970, it reached 201,780, and increased almost every year until extending to a peak of more than 1.6 million apprehensions in 1986. The San Diego sector reflected this trend in its local context, growing from 4,521 apprehensions in 1964 to 196,981 by 1970, and 629,656 in 1986, by far the most in any crossing area (the next highest was El Paso at 312,892 in 1986).[75] This increase in the undocumented population was also brought on by first-time quotas placed on immigration from Mexico with the Immigration Act of 1965. An economic system dependent on Mexican labor dated to the late nineteenth century, and new quotas of 20,000—the same for all countries—failed to consider (or deliberately ignored) the unique relationship between Mexico and the

United States, and the reality that an average of 200,000 migrants were recruited by agribusiness and other industries in the United States yearly in the first half of the 1960s. For union organizers, undocumented workers replaced the problem of the bracero, particularly as they were recruited as strikebreakers during the days of the UFW struggles. In this context, the UFW held a position that sought the enforcement of deportation immigration policies, going so far as to call the Border Patrol when migrant strikebreakers would arrive, and by the early 1970s, patrolling the U.S.-Mexico border themselves to stop the migrants from entering California.[76] As highlighted, the UFW deeply influenced the Chicano movement, and this position on immigration was adopted by activists throughout the movement, including MAPA and emergent Chicano Democrats such as Peter Chacón.

As the opening vignette suggests, however, there were differing positions in Chicano politics concerning immigrants. Former MAPA president and founder of CASA, Bert Corona, recognized the need to organize undocumented workers and families after working with the campaigns of the UFW in central and northern California in the mid- to late 1960s. Corona interpreted the problem of the growers' ability to bring in undocumented as strikebreakers differently than Chávez. Corona explained: "We understood César's dilemma but rejected his strategy. We believed that these undocumented farmworkers who were being used to break strikes also had to be organized. Unless we directed ourselves to educate them politically and to organize them, they would always be at the disposal of the growers."[77]

Corona articulated this position through MAPA and CASA mentoring Baca and other Chicano/a activists in the crucial San Diego area. As a grassroots activist organization just miles from the U.S.-Mexico border, MAPA National City organizers witnessed and were called on to address the rising number of harassment and brutality incidents perpetrated by local police, customs officers, and Border Patrol agents against Mexican-origin residents of the area. By early 1972, MAPA National City and the affiliated CASA Justicia collective were working to address incidents that involved Mexican Americans and Mexican immigrants being unduly strip-searched by customs agents and beaten by Border Patrol officers.[78] San Diego Chicano/a activists were developing a conceptualization of the legal violence experienced daily due to immigration enforcement policies that targeted the ethnic Mexican community in particular by formally recording these incidents through testimony and documentation.[79] It was in this context of struggle against state violence and rising anti-immigrant sentiment that a Raza Sí, Migra No contingent of the Chicano movement was mobilized by conceptualizing undocumented Mexican workers and Chicanos as a united *Raza* struggling against *la migra*. This divergent notion of the Chicano relationship with Mexican migrants clashed with that held by Chacón, Chávez, and others in debates over the Assembly Bill 528 that sought employer sanctions against those who hired undocumented immigrants.

AB 528 was signed by Governor Ronald Reagan on November 8, 1971. It made it illegal for an employer to knowingly hire an undocumented immigrant in California *if* it would have an adverse effect on resident workers. The violations would be punishable by a fine between $200 and $500. It was the first law at any level in the United States to impose "employer sanctions" for hiring undocumented immigrants. Its passage influenced U.S. congressman Peter Rodino at the federal level, who held two days of hearings on the state bill and the California experience with undocumented immigration to deliberate possible federal legislation.[80] Employer sanctions would be a key component of proposals for immigration reform issued by President Jimmy Carter in the late 1970s, President Reagan in the early 1980s, and the legislative proposals up to the passage of the Immigration Reform and Control Act of 1986.

During a period of rising unemployment, particularly in California where it had risen from 4.4 percent in 1969 to 7.4 percent by 1971, moderate Republican assemblyman Dixon Arnett argued that "unemployment and welfare problems are increasing due to the hiring of illegal entrants."[81] Arnett's AB 528 appealed to both tax-conscious Republicans in the Assembly who claimed that "illegals" were a drain on welfare and taxpayers, and Democrats who asserted that "illegals" were displacing U.S. workers, driving down wages, and contributing to the even higher unemployment rate among black and Mexican American wage earners. Democrat Peter Chacón was a leading proponent of this latter view.

Chacón voted for the passage of AB 528 in 1971, reasoning that the bill helped the "Chicano" community and "U.S. citizens" more broadly, by positing "illegal aliens" as the major cause of "depressed" wages and "displaced" jobs. He clearly defined "Chicano" along lines of U.S. citizenship status. He argued in a February 1972 editorial that the bill would "prevent wages from being depressed by illegal aliens" and "prevent legal U.S. citizens from being displaced by illegal aliens." He argued further that this bill would assist "Chicanos" because "unemployment among minorities is usually three times the normal rate, in this case, 18 percent." "Many Chicanos in the state," argued Chacón, "are currently being denied work because jobs are going to illegal aliens. Yet the flow of illegal aliens to the state continues unabated."[82]

In addition to arguing that "illegal aliens" displaced Chicanos and other U.S. workers, Chacón also argued that credible organizations such as the UFW also supported the bill. The UFW's support of the Arnett bill convinced many Chicano/a activists to support the measure. Sociologist Kitty Calavita argues that the UFW was not "enthusiastic" about AB 528, but lent "a measure of support" for it.[83] Historian David G. Gutiérrez also describes UFW's support for the bill as "quiet," but outlines their consistent position of perceiving undocumented workers as antagonistic to their efforts. Gutiérrez quotes a Mexican American UFW worker who declared: "I know these people (undocumented workers) want to work. But we can't let them break our strike, in the end we will benefit and they too will benefit. We are suffering for them, they should suffer a little for us."[84] By 1970, the UFW had reached international attention for its efforts and successes in negotiating contracts with the largest grape, citrus, melon, and lettuce growers in the United States. Again, UFW concerns were often considered to be analogous to Mexican American issues. While Calavita and Gutiérrez describe the UFW's support for AB 528 as "quiet" and unenthusiastic, Chacón's editorial indicates his assessment that the Chávez support was especially strong and vigorous. Chacón asserted, "César Chávez and the UFW supported the Arnett bill vigorously during the session and it was partly for this reason that I supported the bill and voted for it."[85]

Chacón also cited support for the bill by statewide representatives of MAPA, the California Rural Legal Assistance—"an organization that has done much for Chicanos and other disadvantaged groups"—and the only other Chicano assemblymember, Alex García.[86] While MAPA statewide president Armando Rodríguez asserted that "MAPA has not taken a position on the Arnett Bill," he gave what Chacón interpreted as support for AB 528 when Rodríguez stated, "Our position was that we generally favored employment for legal aliens and citizens as opposed to employment for illegal aliens."[87] Noting how this bill revealed rifts within MAPA, chairman of the San Diego chapter, Uvalde Martínez Jr., wrote chairperson of the MAPA Southern Region Raul Loya, asking why the San Diego County MAPA administrator and head of the National City chapter, Herman Baca, was protesting the law and putting local assemblymembers "under constant fire." Martínez wrote:

On the 11th of March . . . there was a demonstration denouncing Mr. Chacon in particular. This demonstration had television coverage by the local stations, which later quoted Mr. Baca as being against the measure. He was identified by the local station as being the San Diego County Chairman of MAPA. I am wondering if he knows something I don't. Has MAPA taken a stand for or against ratification of the bill no. AB528 (the Arnett bill)? My impression, as well as the general public in San Diego, judging from the County Administrator's stand; is that MAPA is against the Arnett Bill. I would appreciate any clarification of our policy, concerning this Bill, and clarification referring to public announcements of policy on the local level.[88]

Loya's response revealed further the rifts within MAPA, as he sided with Baca's position. Responding on March 20, 1972, Loya claimed that a resolution was passed opposing AB 528 at the MAPA state executive board meeting in February. The meeting was one member short of reaching quorum, however; hence, MAPA president Armando Rodríguez's wishy-washy assertion that MAPA had not officially taken a position. Loya was clear about his opposition to the bill and support of Baca's protest of Chacón. He exclaimed to Uvalde: "We, as Mapistas, cannot stand complacently idle while our brothers are deported like cattle. We must stop this mass deportation movement or else we'll find history repeating itself as it did during the EXPATRIATION [sic] ERA of the twenties."[89] Loya revealed that he had consulted with CASA in Los Angeles, whose headquarters he had visited, to learn how AB 528 was affecting families. He stated that the law "is tearing the Chicano community apart" and that "we feel so strongly against this law that we are now setting up CASA headquarters in the Imperial Valley and Coachella Valley."[90] Loya, the regional director of MAPA in Southern California clearly perceived the "Chicano community" as being inclusive of undocumented immigrants in his work with CASA and Raza Sí, Migra No contingents within Chicano politics.

Chacón cited support from Assemblymember Alex García of Los Angeles, with whom he wrote another editorial defending their support for the bill as an obligation to "Chicanos."[91] Elected two years before Chacón, as only the third Latino to be elected to the California Assembly in 1968, García also argued that AB 528 would benefit "American citizens" and assist "legal residents get off welfare and into jobs by preventing illegal entrants from being hired in their place."[92] García and Chacón wrote to their Democratic Assembly colleagues concerning a proposal by Assemblymember Bill Brophy that sought to repeal AB 528. Brophy, a Republican, defeated Chicano Democrat Richard Alatorre in a special election in the 49th Assembly District in Los Angeles, where La Raza Unida Party candidate Raul Ruíz gained significant support. Many Democrats, including Chacón, argued that Ruíz caused the defeat of a fellow Chicano because he "took the votes needed by Alatorre to win. . . . One wonders how Chicanos can be duped so easily."[93] García, with Chacón, labeled the Brophy proposal "an anti-Chicano bill which will prevent the hiring of American citizens or resident aliens with lawful status, most of whom are Mexican."[94] This reiterated Chacón's position: "My obligation is not to illegal aliens be they Mexican nationals, Canadians, or anyone else not a citizen. My obligation as the elected representative is to the people in my district, to the American citizen."[95]

Chacón also asserted that Brophy's "dubious motive" for seeking to repeal AB 528 was to take the seat of congressional representative Edward Roybal, the only Mexican American in Congress from California.[96] It is interesting to note (and unnoted by Chácon) that Roybal's position was against AB 528, revealing further differences even between Chicano Democrats. While Roybal did not fully embrace undocumented migrants as "brothers," he saw the law as "discriminatory" and "constitutionally unsound." Roybal actually used the same distinctions as Chácon, García, and other supporters of AB 528 between "Mexican American and Other Spanish Speaking US citizens" and "Illegal Aliens." Yet he used his concern for Mexican American U.S. citizens to posit his position against the bill, arguing that the bill would lead to discrimination against these U.S. citizens. "While aimed at illegal aliens," he asserted, "this law adversely affects the hiring of citizens and legal aliens of Spanish speaking descent."[97]

These leaders sought to influence the very trajectory of the Chicano movement by directing their arguments to movement-themed and community-level newspapers such as *El Chicano, Ideal,* and the newsletter of the Chicano Federation in San Diego. The newsletter worked as a site of debate on AB 528 when it featured MAPA president Armando Rodríguez's perspective in February 1972, Chacón's essay in March, and finally, a perspective from Herman Baca in April of that year.[98]

Baca had criticized the bill at its very beginning when it was proposed in 1971, leading the front against AB 528 in San Diego. His initial critique in 1971 asked: "How do you distinguish an American born Chicano from his brother born in Mexico? In order to be enforced every Chicano will have to prove his citizenship."[99] Referring to the increasingly common occurrences of harassment and disrespect by immigration agents against the ethnic Mexican community that he was confronting as a grassroots activist, Baca argued: "The problem is not black and white. We have people who have been here 10, 20 up to 50 years who have never gotten their citizenship papers because of various reasons—language differences, cultural differences, bureaucratic red tape and an overall general fear of the Immigration Department. We are tired of families being broken up by inhuman and immoral laws."[100] Building on ethnic ties, the shared experience of racial discrimination at the hands of the state, and the struggle to keep families together, Baca articulated notions of Chicano community that were inclusive of undocumented immigrants.

As mentioned in the correspondence between Uvalde Martinez and Raul Loya, Baca led a protest demonstration of about seventy people in front of Chacón's San Diego office where he asserted: "It is obvious that Mr. Chacón cares more about the Democratic party than he does his own people. . . . Mr. Chacón: We do not feel that you can parade as a representative of *Mexican people*, when you destroy their very chances for a better life."[101] Demanding that Chacón rescind his support for AB 528, Baca argued, "It is a known fact the Immigration Department in the United States has been an oppressor of the Mexican people."[102] Questioning Chacón's dedication to the working-class ethnic Mexican communities that he claimed to represent, Baca asserted that AB 528 had led to "thousands of (Chicano) families losing their jobs."[103]

There was ample evidence that this bill did indeed lead to discrimination against ethnic Mexican workers of all citizenship statuses, violating the civil rights of Mexican American citizens as well as scapegoating undocumented workers. Bert Corona commented on the bill: "Tens of thousands of mexicano workers, born here, with documents, have been fired under the pretext of the Dixon Arnett Law. Now the *patrón* [boss] calls all the *mexicano* workers together and says, 'Look, I don't know which one of you is legal or illegal. I want every Mexican worker to show me his birth certificate or his green card.' "[104]According to testimonies during Assembly hearings in 1971 and 1972, just after the law was passed, several long-standing undocumented workers who had gained senior employment status were laid off and replaced with more recently arrived undocumented workers at lower wages. Other workers were taxed by their employers for the risk of being investigated. And as Corona suggested, thousands of Mexicans and Mexican Americans were fired.[105]

Chicano/a immigrant rights activists such as Baca, Corona, and others revealed differing visions of the boundaries of the "Chicano" community. They challenged the exclusion of undocumented Mexican workers from notions of ethnic community and working-class concerns by appealing to the Chicano movement focus on cultural pride to emphasize an indelible connection among all "*mexicano* workers." Corona connected race and class oppression to articulate how citizenship status was used to deter blame away from the "*patrón*."

Supporters of AB 528 failed to engage key contradictions at the heart of the undocumented immigrant debate, chiefly the ways that powerful corporate interests benefited from the cheap labor provided by noncitizen workers and would create provisions to continue to do so. Sociologist Kitty Calavita argues that AB 528 had the effect of neutralizing the effectiveness of the United Farm Workers movement by diverting attention away from employers and onto undocumented workers. Furthermore, the bill became virtually unenforceable due to all the amendments that guaranteed that growers and other businesses were not pressured to prove the status of their workers. The California Conference of Employers Association (CCEA), the California Farm Bureau Federation, the California Agricultural Producers Labor Committee, the National Council of Agricultural Employers, and leaders in the hotel industry immediately saw to it that these loopholes were added to the bill to make it ineffective.[106] In committees that amended the bill, concerns about "harassment" of employers led to removing language that required employers to "reasonably inquire" about their workers' legal status; allowing Social Security cards to be included as proof of legal residency, even though "the Social Security Administration required no information on immigration status in issuing them"; and deleting any reference to those workers with temporary INS work permits who were not necessarily lawful residents.[107] Finally, the Division of Labor Law Enforcement in the California Department of Industrial Relations was charged to enforce the measure. Instead of providing more staffing and resources as requested by the director of this agency, its budget and staff were drastically reduced.[108] Calavita argues that the bill was reduced to a symbolic function, "which reproduced a structure of beliefs concerning the immigrant's role in the economic crisis." "In the process of making the statute acceptable to employers and their representatives," she argues, "the Legislature deleted those provisions which might have made it an effective threat to employers."[109] The law was successful in granting an apparent concession to labor to quell the successful organizing of the UFW without actually doing anything to address the root causes of undocumented migration.[110] Enforcement mechanisms were drastically inept, and employers were therefore licensed to police themselves, were given loopholes, and in effect, were enabled to maintain the status quo of reliance on and exploitation of a transnational undocumented workforce.

Even Chacón and García expressed doubts that businesses would abide by the law. Responding to the testimonies of Bert Corona and Los Angeles Raza Unida Party leader Raul Ruiz, who stated in a California Assembly session that Mexican immigrant and Mexican American workers were being laid off due to the passing of AB 528, Chacón and García countered by expressing doubt that businesses would hold "a high degree of compliance with the Labor Code."[111] They argued: "Mass dislocation [layoffs and deportations of ethnic Mexican workers due to AB 528] such as is alleged assumes a high degree of compliance with the Labor Code by the businesses involved, and/or tough enforcement by the Department of the Labor Code. I doubt whether either of these is a safe assumption."[112] In other words, Chacón and García countered claims that ethnic Mexican workers were being discriminated against as a result of the Arnett bill by arguing that businesses would not enforce the provisions of the bill. Yet in the same memo, they cite an incident in Los Angeles in which "35 men were faced with loss of their job." It seems that, as Calavita argues, a number of businesses were not complying with the bill, while others chose to lay off ethnic Mexican workers of all statuses.

In addition to discounting the assertion that ethnic Mexican workers of all statuses were being laid off, the bill's supporters also discounted the critique that the Arnett bill would lead to increased harassment of mixed-status, mostly ethnic Mexican families. Chacón and García argued: "That the Arnett Law has resulted in broken homes is also unsubstantiated, and further is something which is highly unlikely. The Arnett bill specifically provides that if a person can qualify (not has) for legal residency, he is employable. Under Federal law, even though an individual may have entered illegally at an earlier date, if his children were born here, or if his wife is a legal resident, then he qualifies for legal residency, and therefore would not be put out of a job."[113] This assertion rests on a great deal of faith in the INS and Border Patrol in its ability or desire to discern and carefully follow its intricate protocol to divide "illegal aliens" from legal residents. As argued in chapter 3, Baca, Corona, and the organization CASA were assisting a number of migrants of all statuses who were split from their families, deported under dubious circumstances, and unable to gain legal standing due to the INS's unapproachability and racial presumptions. Chacón and García seemed unaware or unwilling to connect the hostile experiences thousands of CASA migrant members revealed in applying for or proving their legal status to INS officials—much less the outright violence and racial profiling of the Border Patrol that had resulted in harassment, beatings, and worse—to policies that sought to differentiate between "illegal aliens" and legal residents.

These disagreements between Raza Sí, Migra No activists and Chicano politicians in support for AB 528 played out as an open, public debate in many Chicano movement community newspapers and media in California between Baca and Chacón's aforementioned arguments. Going beyond arguing that Chicanos/as should assert a political position against the Arnett bill simply because it was anti-Mexican, Baca outlined how the bill was part of a systematic practice of using race and citizenship status to scapegoat and marginalize racialized and immigrant workers. He argued:

> The state of California is famous for laws such as AB-528 (the Dixon Arnett bill). One only has to check the history books to see the parallel laws that have been passed in the past to solve the unemployment problem. We have had the anti-mining laws, directed against Mexicans as they had discovered gold in the 1850s; the anti-Coolie laws in the 1860s against the Chinese; and the laws prohibiting Japanese and Philipino's [sic] from owning land. In 1932 we had the deportation which, once again, blamed the Chicano for the economic depression that was on hand. In the 1930's we also had the infamous "Okie's law" that prohibited Okie's (Anglos) from coming into California. In 1940 Americans were interned simply because they were of Japanese ancestry. In 1954 it was estimated that over four (4) million Mexicans were deported in "Operation Wetback." . . . Let us not repeat history once more.[114]

Baca facilitated a consideration of subaltern solidarity across borders and racial lines by recalling the state's hand in dividing and subjugating workers by race and citizenship status. Chicano/a immigrant rights activists further argued that the INS routinely turned a blind eye to undocumented workers when growers wanted to exploit their labor. Yet in a moment of economic recession—when "oppressed people" began to voice their discontent—the government sought to scapegoat undocumented workers as "aliens."[115]

By arguing that the Arnett law was a "scapegoat law" aimed at redirecting attention away from "the failure of the system to rectify the causes" of economic recession, Baca offered critical analysis of global capitalist practices.[116] He noted that manufacturing jobs were being exported while unemployment in the United States continued to rise. Addressing Chacón's blame on "illegal aliens" for high unemployment, Baca exclaimed, "The causes of California unemployment is not the so called 'illegal aliens,' who are the victim, but the unscrupulous employers who are allowed to continue their practices of low wages, slave labor conditions, and continual exploitation of Chicanos and other poor people."[117] Engaging Chacón's claim that the Arnett bill would address the much higher rate of unemployment experienced by minorities, Baca attested, "Other causes of unemployment are the War of Viet Nam, technical changes, foreign competition and the unscrupulous businesses who move their businesses to foreign countries to exploit other poor people."[118]

Furthermore, the Arnett law was part of the systematic practice of exploiting laborers. Baca argued, "It is estimated that of the 175,000 Mexicanos who from 1917 to 1930 met the state agricultural needs, only 10% were available in 1936 due to deportation."[119] Baca identified a pattern in which Mexican labor was used by U.S. employers at times of great need and then systematically removed at moments of less need or recession. To this he reinforced the notion that immigration laws that targeted "illegal aliens" are racially motivated and tend not to "distinguish a U.S. born Chicano from his brother across the border." He exclaimed, "The reality is that in order for this law to be enforced, a disenfranchised community with very little political, economic and social resources, will be subjected to further harassment, interrogations, and overall violations of our civil and God-given rights by law enforcement agencies (police, sheriff, D.A. office, etc.) who have shown little sympathy for the rights of Chicanos in the past."[120]

Baca and his allies were battling over the very trajectory of the Chicano movement and confronting the vision held by Chacón and others connected to the liberal state through the Democratic Party to assert an autonomous political trajectory based on the democratic participation of working-class ethnic Mexicans. For Baca and others, ethnic and class solidarities were transnational, and attempts to use juridical citizenship categories enabled the state in its effort to divide poor people and conceal how evolving capitalist practices caused recession and rising unemployment. Thus, the Chacón-Baca debate was but a microcosm of increasingly complex debates internal to Chicano politics in the early to mid-1970s. This played out in the statewide organization of MAPA, a group that from its beginnings was built on a tentative alliance between politician-oriented, Democratic Party activists and grassroots community organizers. The immigration debate would help provoke these two segments within this historic organization to collide once and for all later in 1972, as the next chapter explores.

· · · · · ·

By the mid-1970s, Chávez, Huerta, and the UFW, and Chacón, García, and the Chicano Caucus in the California Legislature had switched their position on employer sanctions and undocumented immigration.[121] As Kitty Calavita puts it: "Not surprisingly this law, which on the surface appeared to be aimed at the employer, in practice put the onus on the employee—both the undocumented and legally resident Mexican-American. . . . Given the distribution of power in these employment relationships, any legislation which focuses on the kind of worker hired will disproportionately and adversely affect workers themselves."[122] Chicano politicians and the UFW soon learned this, but not without the influence of Chicano Raza Sí, Migra No activists in San Diego and throughout California who battled AB 528 vehemently, even as it surfaced rifts in the Chicano movement, organized labor, the Democratic Party, and the U.S. Left. This chapter reveals how these debates over immigration are a window into exploring the limits of liberal solutions to social issues through their proponents' usage of American national boundaries and citizenship categories, and radical imaginings that sought to create solidarities across borders of legal status. Indeed, these radical imaginings reveal democratic spaces of solution making that might be more inclusive of undocumented migrants' perspectives and more insightful on the global political economic roots of such local crises of border policing in San Diego. But even when Chicano/a activists agreed on advocating for undocumented migrants, as explored within the La Raza Unida Party in California in the next chapter, they did not necessarily agree on how to conceive of new immigration policies in the spirit of Chicano self-determination.

5 Delivering the Mexicano Vote

Immigration and La Raza Unida Party

During a visit to Los Angeles in 1973, iconic Chicano movement activist Rodolfo "Corky" Gonzales spoke of a kind of conversion experience he had with regard to undocumented immigration and the U.S.-Mexico border. The Colorado leader of the Crusade for Justice and La Raza Unida Party, Gonzales testified, "Along with many others, I used to think that Mexicans crossing the border were depriving other Mexicans of jobs." He continued: "I also believed that the border should be closed . . . (but) I came to realize that Mexicans who have come here are not replacing any jobs occupied by people on this side of the border. Let's put the Man straight. He is using us to fight and kill each other and become divided."[1] Gonzales's realization was based on an engagement with the contradiction of being the child of an immigrant while supporting border enforcement policies. Gonzales exclaimed, "If I were to say: 'Keep out Mexicans without documents,' then I would be putting a knife into my father's heart. He came from Chihuahua."[2] He also reflected on how the foundational notion of the Chicano movement he had worked so hard to articulate—that Chicanos were a conquered people reclaiming Aztlán, their stolen homeland in the U.S. Southwest—called into question any enforcement of an imperialist border. Gonzales was forced to conclude, "For us to try to prevent Mexicans from coming across to a land which is theirs by historical right is to become part of murderers."[3]

Similarly, Jose Angel Gutiérrez, key leader of La Raza Unida Party in the South Texas town of Crystal City, also showed signs of becoming especially concerned with undocumented immigration earlier that same year. In February 1973, he wrote Herman Baca reminding him about their conversations concerning undocumented workers and requested that Baca establish "a Centro such as CASA in San Antonio."[4] Referring to Baca's participation in a chapter of the immigrant rights service collective Centro de Acción Social Autónoma (CASA) (see chapter 3), Gutiérrez wrote him again in April of the same year, now inquiring whether Baca might host some of his organizers from Texas in San Diego so that they might be trained on how to run a CASA-like service center. Also announcing his plan to attend a "Unity

Rally" in San Diego, Gutiérrez exclaimed, "We must begin an immigration service in Texas."[5]

These two leaders, Gonzales and Gutiérrez, have been remembered as the primary figures who fought out two competing visions of the national La Raza Unida Party: the "Denver Perspective," as one LRUP document puts it, which argued that "we should strive only to develop a revolutionary vanguard party that aims to conduct 'political education campaigns,'" and the "Texas Perspective," which asserts that "the Partido [Party] must strive to win elections and be willing to engage in hardnosed negotiations with non-Partido politicians."[6] These opposing perspectives of an independent vanguard party as opposed to a pragmatic electoral and negotiating mechanism, for good reason, have been the focus on the scholarship that analyzes the historical significance of La Raza Unida Party effort within the Chicano movement. Yet these vignettes reveal how these two leaders of LRUP and the Chicano movement more broadly reveal an important shift toward engaging the (re)emerging immigration question and the broader transnational terrain embedded in this issue, gleaning important new insights from which to understand the debates within LRUP. This chapter will look to, as Gonzales and Gutiérrez did, Chicano leaders in San Diego and broader Southern California, indicating that the work of Herman Baca, MAPA, CASA, and the organizations in the San Diego borderlands that sought to advocate for and engage with undocumented migrants provided significant perspective on how to reorient notions of Chicano self-determination, radical democratic organizing, and the very conception of *La Raza* to articulate a critique of the immigration regime. While LRUP is remembered for its rise and fall with regard to electoral successes and mobilizations that challenged the Democratic Party, it is also important to recognize how this third party also worked as a space to articulate and further analyze the conundrum of the immigration regime as part of its claim to represent a "Chicano" community that increasingly consisted of Mexican immigrants. Deepening an understanding of the struggle to democratize U.S. society beyond creating voters, Chicano/a immigrant rights organizers brought to the LRUP a difficult consideration that not all Chicano/a activists were fully ready to consider—that the immigration regime was a system that churned out "illegal" residents who were in such a precarious position that they were marginalized from sociopolitical processes, ineligible to vote yet intertwined with the community and personal lives of the larger ethnic Mexican community. San Diego movement activists already knew from violent experience that a confrontation with immigration policies was necessary to formulate a truly liberatory politics for Mexicans in the United States and that Democrats, even Chicano Democrats, often stood as barriers to such. They brought that knowledge to the debates that were ongoing within the LRUP from roughly 1971 to 1975.

MAPA Implodes

Defying factions within the organization tied to the Democratic Party, grassroots organizers in MAPA sought to ride the wave of the Chicano movement, specifically using LRUP to gain control of MAPA and work to advance independent Chicano political actions that emphasized grassroots organizing, transnational practices of community that were inclusive of undocumented migrants, and a working-class base.[7] Bert Corona had attempted to forge independent political action within MAPA since its founding, and saw the rise of the Chicano movement and La Raza Unida Party as a way to radicalize the organization. As president of MAPA from 1966 to 1968, Corona led the organization to support the emerging militancy of the larger Chicano movement, as evident in MAPA's endorsement of the land grant struggle of the Alianza in New Mexico, the United Farm Workers' grape boycott, and a walkout of an Equal Employment Opportunity Commission meeting that emerged out of protest of President Johnson's handling of Mexican American affairs.[8] The left-wing shift within MAPA continued under the presidency of Abe Tapia from 1967 to 1971, with the support for the Chicano Moratorium against the Vietnam War in 1970, the MAPA convention endorsement of Chicano third party candidate Ricardo Romo for California governor over Democratic Party leader Jess Unruh in the same year, and a demonstration led by two hundred MAPA organizers in protest against the Democratic Party's failure to redistrict more equitably for Chicanos in 1972.[9] Corona and Tapia's work with the emergent La Raza Unida Party in California represented this continued radicalization of MAPA and created a schism with the bourgeois membership.

In many ways, La Raza Unida Party epitomized the goal of the grassroots political independence that Corona hoped the progressive members of MAPA would forge.[10] After Raza Unida came to fruition in California, Corona issued a manifesto-like appeal to MAPA chapters statewide and the wider ethnic Mexican community entitled *MAPA and La Raza Unida Party: A Program for Chicano Political Action for the 1970s*, which argued that MAPA and other organizations within the ethnic Mexican community should facilitate the launching of La Raza Unida Party. Corona argued, in effect, that MAPA, with its eleven-year history would assist in "delivering the mexicano vote" for the LRUP by continuing its mass registration attempts in the community.

An important component of this strategy, as indicated in Corona's essay, sought to unite the efforts of the Chicano movement in addressing the burgeoning implications of the immigration issue and in this way focus attention on how race and labor exploitation work to oppress ethnic Mexican workers of all citizenship statuses. Corona declared:

> Of special significance in this decade of the 1970's is the growing restlessness, rebelliousness and militancy of Chicanos in the labor unions and the growing resistance of non-documented Mexican people from Mexico to the inhuman and brutal harassment of the Immigration Service, the Border Patrol, and the exploitation by employers. Both of these important factors are indications that the key group in our communities—the workers—is also beginning to move to defend their own and their families' existence. There are estimates in official circles that in California alone, we have more than 300,000 Mexican workers without documents as a permanent part of the labor force. So, the organizing and mobilization for defense of so called "illegal" Mexican workers is a very significant indication of the degree and depth of awareness and movement amongst our people.[11]

Corona was not only attempting to convince Chicano movement activists that undocumented immigrants should be included as a part of the community; he was also arguing that the immigration issue represented an opportunity to more clearly define the movement in class terms. Organizing noncitizen Mexican workers led to "a degree and depth of awareness" beyond a narrow Chicano nationalism or ethnic politics that appealed only to middle-class concerns with gaining access to mainstream institutions. Instead, the position pamphlet sought to address the larger issue of "brutal harassment of the Immigration Service" and its relationship to general economic "exploitation." Indeed, focus on the immigration issue served as a segue into the issues that Corona identified as a central constituency of the Chicano/Mexicano community: workers, that is, "the key group." In this way, Corona argued that the mass mobilization efforts needed to establish La Raza Unida would be supplied by engaging issues that affected community members' everyday lives at its working-class base. Corona called on MAPA, the Brown Berets, unions, and other Chicano groups already with a presence in the barrios and the workplace to mobilize for La Raza Unida. He also noted the historical trajectory calling this forth: "MAPA along with its two predecessor political organizations—ANMA in the 50's and the *Congreso de los Pueblos de Habla Español* of the 30's and 40's—has been a necessary step and element in the struggle for political independence and self-determination of the Chicano people."[12] Indeed, Corona's experience in these historic organizations enabled him to call forth a Mexican American Left tradition that organized on the understanding that "resistance of non-documented Mexican people" and "defense of so-called illegal Mexican workers" was central to organizing La Raza Unida Party in a way that focused on working-class and grassroots concerns. It put forth a vision in which undocumented workers, despite being excluded from citizenship and voting rights, could be accounted for and protected through their inclusion in *La Raza*.

Indeed, this effort would necessitate a clear expansion of the perceived boundaries of the Chicano/a community. Corona exclaimed: "All our raza . . . those born here, those born in Mexico with documents . . . and those that do not have documents, All! We are brothers of blood and peoplehood! We work and pay the same taxes and they even take our children to war from us! Further, we all suffer from the abuse and brutality of the INS and Border Patrol!"[13] Indeed, Corona attempted to capitalize on the prideful reference to Mexican heritage within chicanismo to assert that undocumented Mexican migrants were in fact a part of the community. The legal violence in Southern California by the Border Patrol was evidence of this, just as police brutality had led barrio residents to mobilize as a people. LRUP could be utilized as an autonomous space in which to enact this transnational notion of community and become "A Program for Chicano Political Action."

Herman Baca took Corona's essay to heart and used his resources as a printer to print mass copies of it to present to MAPA chapters throughout the state. Considering himself a mentee of past MAPA presidents Corona and Abe Tapia, Baca also aimed to tilt control of MAPA to the grassroots-based forces once and for all, and solidify community independence from the Democratic Party. When the idea of a La Raza Unida Party arose within MAPA circles, the faction linked to the Democratic Party became deeply opposed to it. After distributing Corona's essay throughout the state in early 1971, Baca ran for MAPA state president at the state convention that summer against Democrat Armando Rodríguez, losing the election by a mere twenty votes. Baca's Democratic opposition accused him of "reverse discrimination" in his advocacy for La Raza Unida in its apparent exclusion of Anglos. Corona's attempt to pass a resolution in support of La Raza Unida Party also failed, but revealed attempts by the grassroots organizers within MAPA to gain control.[14] Members of a rising Chicano bureaucratic class, MAPA's Democratic leadership was vehemently against autonomy and transnational notions of community because it threatened their attachment to the state, sought to unseat their power base, and dislodged the nation-state and juridical citizenship as a means of gaining political power.

In April 1972, the MAPA situation came to a final confrontation as Baca, Corona, and their allies attended the MAPA-sponsored National Chicano Political Caucus in San Jose to mobilize an autonomous shift away from the Democrats and toward La Raza Unida Party. The conference was also hosted by more moderate Mexican American organizations, including the G.I. Forum and LULAC. Baca and Corona's attendance would lead to a confrontation. Baca recalled:

> I remember the caucus was going on. Armando Rodríguez was chairing it and he had the mic. I remember Bert [Corona] walked in and he got a standing ovation. Then somebody from the floor said, "I make a motion that we go on record supporting the Raza Unida Party." That's when all hell broke loose. . . . People started arguing. I ran up there and grabbed the mic (from Rodríguez) and said, "There is a motion on the floor, let's vote on it," and that's when everybody was trying to get the mic from me. They passed the motion and then somebody asked, "What are we doing here at this hotel? Let's go to the barrio." So we wound up in the barrio.[15]

More than half of the caucus joined the LRUP-initiated walkout, held a meeting, and released a number of passed resolutions directed at "all Chicano organizations working for the liberation of Chicanos." It should come as little surprise that the first resolution sought "A drastic overhaul of U.S. immigration policies that affect Mexicans and Latin Americans." This resolution was followed by other internationalist concerns, including an end to the war in Southeast Asia, an end to imperialism in Latin America, an end to U.S. aid to Latin American dictatorships, and strong support for Chicana liberation.[16] Indeed, these LRUP resolutions, initiated in part by Corona's program and facilitated by a Chicano/Mexicano activism at the border, outlined a global analysis of power that emphasized the intersections of a number of struggles.

La Raza Unida Party

The LRUP was a concept that had roots in the struggles against the Equal Employment Opportunity Commission culminating in the 1966 walkout, the gathering of the Chicano Youth Liberation Conference in Denver in 1968, and the application of the party concept in the small town of Crystal City, Texas. Upon its national outgrowth, scholars have developed a failure narrative of the LRUP centered on the competing visions between Gonzales and Gutiérrez, and the party's inability to find electoral success.[17] This lack of success was demonstrated in the party's arrival in California, where the LRUP fell short of winning key voting initiatives such as the incorporation of East Los Angeles and failure to mobilize its constituency to register enough voters to become an official party.[18]

While these assessments are accurate, it is also important to note the lessons gleaned from the San Diego contingent's participation in the LRUP and that chapter's concern about the urgency that the flexing immigration regime signaled in the ethnic Mexican community in the early 1970s. The San Diego chapter did attempt to gain the necessary number of registrants to legitimize the party both locally and statewide. Records from probably 1972 reveal 11 registrars registered 691 people within a span of 17 weeks. Among the most active registrars included men and women such as Gloria Jean Valderrama, Carlos "Charlie" Vásquez, Nick Inzunza, Herman Baca, Norma Mena Cazares, George Baca, and Ricardo Campos. What this reveals is continued engagement with community members in San Diego County, particularly South San Diego. This strategy was a continuation of that of MAPA, but rather than mobilize the Chicano vote to pressure or endorse one of the two major parties, or both, LRUP San Diego sought to register voters to reject both parties. As one flyer that LRUP San Diego shared with the community articulated: " 'El Partido' is being developed to provide meaningful representation for La Raza. In the past, we have been denied this, because of the present Democratic and Republican two-party system, whose representatives have ignored our demands. The fact that our votes helped to place them in Public Office was not taken into consideration."[19] The flyer goes on to make the case for La Raza Unida Party with a reminder that the 3 million people with Spanish surnames in California should proportionally be represented by 12 members of the state Assembly and 6 senators of Mexican descent. They pointed out that in contrast, there were only 2 assemblymen. Another document highlighted the local nature of this underrepresentation, revealing that 250,000 individuals with Spanish surnames lived in San Diego County, but only a single elected official was of Mexican descent.[20]

Again, these were the same claims made under the local MAPA chapter concerning underrepresentation, with a different approach, surely learned through the campaigns Baca and other community organizers experienced to elect Peter Chácon, to fully separate from the Democratic Party. LRUP San Diego seemed to have plenty of volunteers, likely transfers following Baca and Charlie Vásquez out of MAPA and two-party politics. In addition to Baca and Vásquez, Gloria Jean Valderrama, Norma Mena Cazares, and Augie Bareño were LRUP members who also worked on the CASA Justicia staff. LRUP came to replace MAPA for a time at the local level in the politicization front of Chicano movement activism coming out of Baca's leadership, while CASA Justicia continued to service immigrant community members. One member list documented forty-four members of the LRUP.[21] Another listed sixty-six contributors, most of whom donated $5 to $10 once or twice a month.[22] The members paid dues, and one document shows a meager $284 account balance.[23] Person power was indeed the grassroots campaign's strongest resource.

With CASA Justicia operating simultaneously, surely the concerns about repression through the immigration regime were part of the San Diego group's logic of creating self-determination through a Chicano third party. The historiography has emphasized the rift between José Ángel Gutiérrez and Rodolfo "Corky" Gonzales within the national LRUP. The San Diego chapter reflects ways in which the Southern California region more broadly (of which San Diego was a part) attempted to merge both approaches, and in some ways put this synthesis into practice. The chapter undoubtedly was focused on mobilizing a voting base, with the longer term goal of winning elections, as Gutiérrez's position represented. Moreover, its roots in MAPA sought to create a congealed Chicano base that represented the community's interests with regard to negotiating with the two major parties, particularly the Democrats, also reflected Gutiérrez's position.

At the same time, the fact that the San Diego chapter ran few LRUP candidates and focused more on mobilizing a representative base of working-class ethnic Mexicans, as reflected in its registration goals, reveals a consciousness-raising focus that was reflective of Corky Gonzales's position. The immigration and larger police regime that was a central and urgent concern of the San Diego chapter's sociopolitical context greatly shaped this consciousness-raising aspect in which a constituency had to be assembled to create decision-making processes outside of the electoral process to defend and advocate for working-class, undocumented, and other vulnerable members of the community. In this regard, voting was to be a by-product of a mass education effort and consciousness-raising process in order to confront a system that inherently placed a large proportion of the community into an "illegal" status of exclusion, which entailed ineligibility for rights, voting, and citizenship.

As Herman Baca remembers, the San Diego chapter "sidestepped" the divisive rift between the Gutiérrez and Gonzales camps. He recalled:

> Our perspective here was we should get that mandate. In other words, "Let the people decide" [whether to follow Gutiérrez or Gonzales's method]. . . . So we established a figure of [registering] 10,000. [The idea was] "If you're serious as an organizer, well then let's see you produce some fruit here." See because the statewide effort at the time was [registering] 68,000, 1 percent [of the voter population] in order to qualify as a registered, legitimate recognized party. Now, if we couldn't do that with three million [Mexican-origin] people [in California], [register] 65,000, you know, well, what are we talking about? . . . So, I was always of the opinion that it don't matter what politics you're in [the Gutiérrez versus Gonzales positions]. You need a consensus [Laugh] or you're just talking about what you think? And who cares what you think? That's not political, you know, it's an abstract. It's wishful thinking. So we established that we were going to set a goal of [registering] 10,000 [in San Diego County] . . . based on that, [we] kind of sidestepped those two perspectives that existed.[24]

The publishing of ten issues of the San Diego County *La Raza Unida Newsletter* from early 1972 to September of 1973 reveals the LRUP in San Diego functioning as a gathering and community space for a number of struggles coming out of MAPA, CASA, political campaigns, and consciousness-raising dialog about the history of oppression and resistance among Chicano/Mexicano communities, emphasizing especially the battles against the immigration regime. The first issue declared "Victory in San Jose!," detailing the walkout of delegates from the National Chicano Political Caucus, where the San Diego activists joined other Chicano/a organizers in support for La Raza Unida Party and a break from moderates who wanted to stay tied to the Democratic Party. Giving credit to a "Midwest Chicano delegate's caucus," the article explains how this group voiced the "displeasure of the majority of the delegates (at the Caucus) with the obvious direction which the leaders of the official host organizations . . . (M.A.P.A., G.I. Forum, AMAE [Association of Mexican American Educators], and L.U.L.A.C.) had programmed for the participants, particularly in keeping with the dependency upon the Democratic Party as the Chicano community's main hope in politics." This was clearly a denouncement and separation from the middle- and professional-class organizations within the Mexican American community, and a rejection of moderate working-within-the-system politics. The article clearly detailed the Democratic and Republican parties as "opportunistic and racist towards the true and lasting interests of the Chicano community," identifying "La Raza Unida Party as the vehicle for Chicano political action." Reiterating the resolutions calling for an end to the Vietnam War and support for Chicana Liberation, the newsletter went into more detail about its concern with immigration. In this regard, the article articulated how the LRUP supporting delegates sought "Visas for all persons who are in the USA, no more deportations, repeals of the Walter McCarran Act, and a complete overhaul of the Border Patrol and Immigration Service."[25] These resolutions were followed by concerns about ethnic Mexican representation in educational institutions, support for farmworkers, and a "demand that existing law enforcement agencies . . . that have placed Chicanos in second class citizen status be replaced by institutions that are Chicano community controlled," highlighting a political trajectory toward autonomy and self-determination.[26] These articulations of autonomy were asserted with migrants in mind as part of la raza, indicating a working-class orientation within their ethnic politics, as articulated with the prioritized concern with immigration policies, the naming of Bert Corona as head of the San Jose Caucus, "almost unanimous approval" of a framework put forth by the immigrant rights group "CASA Hermandad in Los Angeles as the guiding set of principles for this caucus and thereafter," and a specific call to end all deportations.[27]

The LRUP newsletter in San Diego aimed to educate the community and reflected its concerns with the ways border policing affected its local context. Also in the first issue, an essay on the "Historical Perspective" of Chicanos in California argued that political power was paramount to "Chicanos and Mejicanos" to affirm their interpretation of the Treaty of Guadalupe Hidalgo, which guaranteed "the right of full citizenship to Mejicanos."[28] The use of the word "Mejicano" implied a broader application of the rights guaranteed to not only "Mexicans who chose to stay in the U.S." after the mid-nineteenth-century invasion but also to "so-called 'illegal aliens,'" who were part of "our people." Indeed, they argued that also guaranteed in the treaty was "easy entry into the U.S. of Mejicanos at *any time*."[29] The writers of the LRUP San Diego newsletter took some liberties here in their argument that the treaty provided provisions for easy entry, as there is no mention of migration from Mexico (which could not have been imagined in 1848). However, the writers' main point contended that the treaty's guarantee of rights toward "Mejicanos" should apply to "so-called 'illegal aliens' " as well. Indeed, they recalled how anti-Mexican sentiment following the war led to systematic exclusions and the development of the concept of "illegal aliens" as part of the larger "racist attacks on Chicanos and Mejicanos." The essay argued, "Due to dishonest politicos, ever since then these rights have been totally violated," and racialized exclusions including immigration policies "have become institutionalized through discriminatory laws."[30]

The first issue of the newsletter goes on to articulate this interpretation further in explaining LRUP San Diego's "Areas of Concern" and goal of addressing "the unmet needs of Chicanos and other oppressed minority groups."[31] Numbering four main concerns, the first of course being a rejection of the "Democratic Party—Republican Party" with "essentially no difference . . . because both view us as an exploitable commodity," the second identifies immigration. Again arguing that the Treaty of Guadalupe Hidalgo guaranteed rights of all Mejicanos, including undocumented migrants, LRUP San Diego argued that this was an "open door immigration policy" and called for the "abolishment of the border patrol system." In essence, the argument claimed that the border patrol system violated the treaty, since it denied the "civil rights" guaranteed by the treaty through "undue harassment because they are Mejicanos." They tied this regime of immigration policing agents to "police, sheriffs and other agencies" who discriminate "against our people."[32] This is significant because for Herman Baca and many of the activists involved with LRUP San Diego, this was the first time they offered solutions tied to the treaty and called for abolishment of the border patrol system. Their experience at the border with the overt violence of the Border Patrol and other policing agencies in their own backyard put these concerns at the forefront of their agenda, now centered with the efforts of LRUP San Diego and CASA Justicia, which was engaging with, servicing, and creating leadership among undocumented workers in the San Diego border region. LRUP fell short in many of their electoral goals, but served as a space to develop these radicalized interpretations, analyses, and solutions to the struggle against the deportation regime.

The primacy of the immigration regime issue coming from the local context of San Diego Chicano activism, and the outlook that the LRUP would be the "instrument" through which Raza Sí, Migra No politics would be enacted was further indicated in the newsletter with the publication of Bert Corona's essay, "The Immigration Problem," written in three parts in its first, second, and third issue from early in the year through the July/ August 1972 issue. While much of Corona's analysis has been shared above, one aspect of this essay that is important is how it identifies the vehement debates within Chicano politics over immigration, articulates the position of Raza Sí, Migra No, and identifies LRUP as the site in which to break from the antimigrant politics of some Chicano/a leaders and move forward. In the first issue, for example, Corona begins the essay reflecting on a recent visit to Bay City, Michigan, for a conference where he was speaking about "how they are using the Immigration Service and new immigration laws to exploit mexicano workers."[33] During his visit, he was asked to speak on the issue on television. Upon his arrival to the station, he was told that he would speak thirty minutes later than schedule because another commenter—a professor who was a friend of the station manager—was going to speak before him. Corona remembered:

> Well, who was that *torito* (little bull) they threw at us? That man stood up there for half an hour and tried to sell to the so-called "Mexican Americans" the idea that the greatest threat to their well-being is not the capitalist system, not the corporations, not bad wages, not discrimination, not exploitation. No! You know what it is? A massive horde conglomerated on the other side of the border like hungry wasps, with their teeth bared, descending upon us good "Mexican Americans" to take away our jobs, lower salaries and create problems for our children with diseases and bad living conditions. . . . The problem is our *carnales* (brothers and sisters), who in their poverty come from Mexico to find work. They are the enemy! I said to myself, *hijo de la gata parda* (son of a brown cat). What propaganda![34]

This "propaganda" pitting Mexican Americans against Mexican immigrants was a primary concern in Corona's essay, and by extension, of the LRUP in San Diego. This was the site of an ideological battle outside, and especially, inside Chicano political space. For example, a letter written later that year in December of 1972 to Herman Baca about the LRUP newsletter from a "concerned Chicana" demonstrates how this battle was raging within even Chicano movement circles. The letter lamented:

I fail to understand your great concern for the Mexican Nationals when your first responsibility is to our people here. As to previous experiences in Mexico [*sic*]. They fail to recognize us, as what we are. As far as the Mexican Nationals are concerned we to them are nothing but Pochas or Pochos. I feel a great love for our people, but I don't necessarily like being called a Pocha. . . . What is the great concern for the Nationals? When they wouldn't give two cents for the Chicanos. Please Mr. Baca, don't misunderstand me. I enjoy the Newsletter very much it's just that, I would like to hear more about the Chicanos other than the misfortunes of the Mexican Nationals. I await your answer to my questions in the next newsletter. Thank you for hearing me out!!!

> A CONCERNED CHICANA
> VIVA LA RAZA <u>AQUI</u>!!!!![35]

The San Diego LRUP, through writings articulating an emergent Raza Sí, Migra No politics such as Corona's, were utilizing the third party beyond simply gaining a voting base, but as a site of consciousness-raising at the forefront of pushing forth the internal Chicano movement debate over immigration.

Indeed, Corona's essay goes on to confront liberal Democrats; Chicano/a and union leaders such as César Chávez and the UFW; and Chicano/a differences over the Dixon Arnett bill, as explored in the previous chapter. For example, Corona explained, "Unfortunately, many times the unions, deceived and taken in because they have a little puestecito [little job] over there in the government, say the same things. They support the law advocated by Ted Kennedy and Edmund Muskie that would increase the personnel of la migra [the Border Patrol]. . . . those are amendments that our supposed 'friends'—in the name of protecting the Mexican American worker—are attempting to enact."[36] This comment, again as explored in the previous chapter, revealed the rift within union politics, Chicano activism, and the Left over undocumented workers. More specific to the United Farm Working Organizing Committee, Corona critiqued their position on the Dixon Arnett bill, to demonstrate the LRUP as an autonomous site for struggle on behalf of workers and the Chicano/Mexicano community. He argued, "The Farm Workers thought that by supporting that law they were going to impede the importation of *esquiroles* [scabs] for the purpose of breaking strikes. But the legislature doesn't belong to the Farm Workers.

The legislature is bought and paid for by the corporations, including the *mexicanos* we have there—those they give money to so that they can run as Republicans or Democrats. They're not from La Raza Unida Party."[37]

These analyses and ideas were grounded and applied to the Chicano movement efforts and issues that were ongoing in the San Diego border region community. La Raza Unida Party, CASA Justicia, and remnants of the National City chapter of MAPA operated together in the space of Baca's print shop, Aztec Printers. A large sign that read "CASA Justicia" sat next to "Aztec Printers," highlighting the physical space in which these manifestations of the movement were grounded.[38] The correspondence with the emergence of the LRUP in San Diego with CASA Justicia highlights the focus on immigration as central to the Chicano struggle. The first volume of the LRUP newsletter advertised "CASA Justicia Opens," with a short article in Spanish that explained:

> Those born here, the Chicanos, those that came from the other side
> and already have permanent residence and those who have arrived
> but because of great difficulty have not obtained their visas. . . .
> we are all members of the same people. We are members of the same
> family. . . . United as a hard-working and a poor people, we will leave
> discrimination and oppression. . . . C.A.S.A. is a brotherhood of all
> workers that suffer the tremendous difficulties with visas and problems
> with immigration. . . . if you need help with these related problems
> don't leave without communicating with C.A.S.A. 1839 Highland
> Avenue, National City, California. . . . UNIDOS VENCEREMOS! VIVA
> LA RAZA! PERO VIVA LA RAZA UNIDA! CHICANOS, LOS QUE
> TIENEN VISAS Y LOS QUE NO LAS HAN PODIDO OBTENER!
> [UNITED WE WILL WIN! LONG LIVE THE PEOPLE! BUT LONG
> LIVE A UNITED PEOPLE! CHICANOS, THOSE WHO HAVE VISAS
> AND THOSE THAT CAN NOT OBTAINED ONE!][39]

CASA Justicia's emergence at about the same moment in which the LRUP was created highlights the community space that became centered at the site on Highland Avenue and facilitated through the LRUP newsletter as well as the centrality of immigration to the focus of Chicano community activism in the borderlands.

This community atmosphere was reflected in the description of the many community members involved with the LRUP reflecting, as the above CASA Justicia quote suggests, unity around the notion of family and community.

County director of the LRUP, Herman Baca, always ended each newsletter edition with a personal letter beginning with "Dear La Raza Unida Member." This letter would highlight the community nature of the newsletter with a reminder that it was community-financed and run by volunteers, and calling for donations as well as feedback on whether readers were "critical or favorable." Baca posited in the first issue, "Only by knowing your reactions can we determine the direction of this newsletter."[40] This newsletter would also highlight the latest news concerning other organizations beyond the LRUP and CASA Justicia. For instance, it noted the "Boycott Lettuce" campaign of the UFW from San Diego por La Huelga; the election of a new executive director of the coalitional Chicano Federation, Louie Natividad; the independent candidacy of Ben Moreno for San Diego County supervisor; the campaign to boycott Coors coming out of a mostly Chicano worker struggle in Colorado; local boxing competitions for youth at the neighborhood CASA Salud youth center; and the election of a new board of MAPA-National City.[41] The "Acknowledgment to a Worker" section of each edition created a community atmosphere by highlighting the work for LRUP and other Chicano movement organizations, particularly the actions of Chicanas. For example, Monica Delgadillo graced the first edition of this section, with the writers claiming she was chosen by her fellow workers "out of more than 100" candidates for her work for the LRUP. She was also highlighted for her educational work as a student at California State University, San Diego, where she was studying to become an education counselor, where she "will continue to be an asset to La Raza."[42]

Norma Mena Cazares was also recognized in this section in the second edition, as secretary of CASA Justicia and her instrumental involvement with "registering a large number of the 3,000 La Raza Unida registered people throughout the San Diego area."[43] The news on elections within organizations such as MAPA-National City also revealed that Chicanas were deeply involved in Chicano movement activities in San Diego. The June 1972 elections for officers in MAPA National City revealed that at least three of the seven officer positions were filled by women: Monica Delgadillo as first vice president, Norma Mena Cazares as correspondence secretary, and Gloria Jean Valderrama as treasurer. The MAPA elections the next year in January 1973 revealed that women were still involved, with Gloria Jean Valderrama as first vice president and Norma Mena Cazares continuing as correspondence secretary, but it also may reveal the reality that women rarely gained the top positions as president in this case, or as spokespersons and leaders more generally.

None of the issues feature women as authors of essays or articles espousing analysis, strategy, and critical reflection on the Chicano struggle. Many figureheads, including the aforementioned Bert Corona and Herman Baca, as well as the words of national leaders including César Chávez, José Ángel Gutiérrez, Corky Gonzalez, Reis López Tijerina, and statewide MAPA leaders Armando Rodríguez and Abe Tapia, were looked to for their perspectives and analysis. Chicanas were not featured in the same way. Indeed, a full page of the January/February 1973 edition of the newsletter called "Raza in Action" featured photos of the nation's prominent Chicano leaders. Nine black-and-white photo images sit 3 × 3 on the page, with captions describing the photos such as "Cesar Chavez, United Farm Workers Leader," "Corky Gonzales, Crusade for Justice," and "Jose Angel Gutierrez, National Chairman L.R.U. Party."[44] The only woman pictured and named on the page is "Sra. Ricardo Ortiz," the spouse of Ricardo Chávez Ortiz, a Mexican immigrant who hijacked a commercial airplane to speak of the struggles of being Mexican in the United States. Chávez Ortiz's cause reached the ears of Chicano movement activists, including from the LRUP in San Diego, who wrote, "Ricardo Chavez has become a symbol of our people. . . . His act was not for personal enrichment but for the benefit of poor people and in particular our poor Mexican children."[45] While important in highlighting this particular cause, especially as a Mexican immigrant struggling to find steady work in order to take care of his children and family, it also highlights how the only woman on the page was directly tied to a man in her role as mother and wife. Indeed, the story of Chávez Ortiz reflects this imaginary of "family" in the role of the father-husband as primary breadwinner for his dependents, including his wife and the mother of his children. The last row of pictures in the LRUP newsletter "Raza in Action" page also shows Chicanas, but alongside a picture of young children with protest signs labeled "Tomorrow's Leaders" and an image of protest marchers labeled "Immigration Protest," two Chicanas are featured with the caption "Active Chicanas."[46] That the only images of Chicanas are as the wife of a Chicano hero and as anonymous "Active Chicanas" suggests that the image of the family was hierarchical, sending the message that men were to lead and women and children were to contribute, but follow.

Indeed, as explored in chapter 2, this fits in line with scholarly analysis of gender hierarchies and the notion of *la familia de la Raza* so prominent in Chicano movement imagery and discourse. Another indication of this in the San Diego LRUP newsletter is the prominent usage of the charcoal and pencil portrait called *La Familia* that is featured on the front page alongside the title of the newsletter on all the editions, serving as a kind of logo for the LRUP-San Diego organizations. Critical scholar Richard T. Rodríguez analyzed this image in particular as demonstrative of his larger analysis that the *La Familia* image served to create hierarchal notions of gender and sexuality. *La Familia* by Oaxacan artist Joaquín Chiñas features a man/husband and boy/son looking straight forward and the wife/mother in a rebozo looking to the viewer's right embraced by her husband. The husband's hand, "is massive" says Rodríguez, "it symbolically registers the strength necessary to hold a family together. . . . In many ways it [*La Familia*] functions as an ethnic-specific rendition of the Holy Family upon which Christian and Catholic heteropatriarchal values rest." Indeed, the wife/mother does not look at the viewer and "she does not appear to need women's liberation given the strength she absorbs from within the patriarchal embrace. Alongside her man, her concerns can be addressed only within the space of la familia. Her liberation is possible only through conjugal unification and motherhood."[47]

While this idea of *La Familia* was an important notion that utilized the culturally specific practices of Chicano/Mexicano kinship and community to struggle against very real repression, it is important to consider the ways this notion also facilitated internal hierarchies that contributed to the exclusion of Chicanas and Mexicanas from leadership positons, and participation in decision making. The newsletter also featured several families in its "Worker of the Month" column, revealing the significance of the *La Familia*, concept with all of its contradictions. In the August 1972 edition, for example, an image of "Sr. Y Sra. Armando Arias" is featured above a short article in Spanish calling for Chicano unity and support for LRUP. Highlighting the unity of marriage as featured in the picture, the article asserts, "United [with] our votes we demonstrate to the Democrat and Republican parties the strength from our coming together."[48] The family unit was crucial to this unity. Similarly, the Castañeda family, including spouses Ruben and Olga pictured with their three young children, is highlighted as the Workers of the Month for "possessing a brand of dedication to their people."[49] The article also displays the importance of heteronormative marriage to the Chicano struggle, reminding that "too often, married couples who are active in the movement go unrecognized because of their family obligations." Furthermore, the article goes on to highlight how both Ruben and Olga are contributing to the movement, with Ruben working with the teacher corps program at a local, mostly Chicano, elementary school, and in leadership roles in MAPA, while Olga is employed with La Raza Consortium, a social service organization. The article is sure to point out that Olga is able to contribute to the movement, although she is "deeply involved with her three children," emphasizing the primary role of Chicanas in *La Familia* as mother (it does not emphasize Ruben's parenting role). While acknowledging the struggles of family life and community involvement, and revealing that women's labor is important to the struggle, the concept of family is not prepared to engage in gendered hierarchies and expectations around who should do domestic work such as child-rearing. The gendered and often hierarchical terms of *La Familia* and *la raza* are important to highlight, and suggest that it would take Chicana insurgencies to challenge these notions and practices.

Family was crucial to the immigrant struggle in particular because women and their families were often the victims and survivors of the brutal results of immigration policies on the ground in the San Diego borderlands. As explored in the previous chapters, deportations and acts of violence by police and immigration officials were the material reality that led to calls against "breaking up our families" and Raza Sí, Migra No. The focus on immigration for San Diego LRUP and other movement organizations was centered on the crisis that emerged in the border region where real police and Border Patrol repression affected the lives of ethnic Mexicans families and communities. As examined in chapter 2 in the case of undocumented migrant Martha Elena Parra López, the July 1972 second edition of the LRUP newsletter read alarmingly, "Border Patrolman Accused of Rape."[50] This case in particular would preoccupy the San Diego LRUP newsletter and community activists for several issues, as front pages of the third edition in August of 1972 headlined "Rape Case Ignored," and the December 1972 issue stated, "District Attorney Double Standard on Rape Case."[51]

Reporting on the national LRUP convention, Herman Baca wrote to LRUP members that "threats of deportation" have for years been used to intimidate the Chicano community from voting and participating in politics.[52] By December, the newsletter had given increasing attention to the violence and intimidation emanating from the immigration enforcement policies in reporting on "Mexican Injured by Border Patrolman" and the "Sheriff Indicts Chicanos."[53] Included in the same issue that reported "District Attorney's Double Standard on Rape Case," a reprint of an *El Mexicano* newspaper article discussed how Antolin Gutiérrez Morfín was "intentionally run over" by Border Patrolmen Dennis Boux and Joseph Henning. Gutiérrez Morfín, a thirty-two-year-old man from Michoacán, was attempting to enter the United States with three other men, after which he sustained fractured ribs, an injured spinal column, head contusions, and facial cuts. According to Gutiérrez Morfín, the agents "deliberately" ran over him and after they "finally drove him to the ground and when he tried to get up, he again was run over." Morfín Gutiérrez was attempting to reunite with two sisters and a brother "legally residing in the U.S."[54]

The same issue reveals on the front page that San Diego County Sheriff John Duffy ordered taxicab drivers to "pick up illegal aliens."[55] Calling this action "another slap in the face" received by the Chicano community, the "Duffy Memorandum" was denied for two months by the Sheriff's Department until finally admitting to it after "complaints were received of Chicanos being refused taxi service." This admission by the Sheriff's Department led to a larger community mobilization, which met in November and determined that the "sheriff has placed blanket indictment on the Chicano community" (explored in chapter 6).[56] Acts of harassment, brutality, and violence by both immigration agents and local police, as will be explored more thoroughly in the next chapter, became increasingly central to the San Diego LRUP's understanding of immigration repression as part and parcel of the Chicano liberation struggle. Indeed, this same December 1972 edition of the newsletter also detailed how an ethnic Mexican woman, Mrs. Josephine Jarin, was attacked by a San Diego County Sheriff dog and bitten. An image of Mrs. Jarin's back with four brutal bite marks is featured on the last page of this issue—an issue overflowing with police and Border Patrol violence. The dog-biting incident led to the creation of "an ad-hoc committee to deal with this kind of law abusement [sic]." Baca ended this edition stating, "It is unfortunate that we must bring to light so many abusements [sic] perpetrated against our people by law enforcement agencies . . . to make the Chicano community aware of these racist acts so we can collectively come together to resolve these problems." As legal scholar Ian Haney López argues in his analysis of police violence and the Los Angeles Chicano movement: "Mexican politicization . . . took place in specifically racial terms. Thus perceiving or experiencing police violence made people more likely to think that they were brown . . . race and law constituted each other."[57] Police brutality was "a fact of life" and "routine," and "residents knew it" and constituted their identities and politics as part of the dialectic of race and law.[58] In San Diego, legal violence featured the collective abuse of federal agents licensed to patrol the U.S.-Mexico border and the local police departments in the jurisdictions of San Diego County. The LRUP that emerged out of San Diego County therefore reflected this material experience, but found that due to the co-optive logic of citizenship, other

LRUP activists were not on the same page when it came to Raza Sí, Migra No activism.

"Strikebreakers" and "Communists": Fractures in La Raza Unida Party

Despite the progressive internationalist rhetoric used by many of its members nationwide, LRUP chapters across California fragmented in their attempts to create the Chicano/Mexicano solidarities emerging from the LRUP San Diego and elsewhere. In an April 1972 statewide LRUP meeting in San Jose, a position on the Dixon Arnett employer sanctions bill was tabled in the political workshop, indicating disagreement over the issue.[59] Furthermore, members present at the San Jose meeting voted 14-8 to take "no position on deportations," also revealing vast differences on the issue.[60] Analysis of the subsequent July statewide meeting in Los Angeles—the final California LRUP meeting before heading to the national party convention to be held September 1–4 in El Paso—demonstrated that positions on the immigration question were still unsettled.

This debate on immigration was related to differing ideological approaches to the party's goals and an inability to create a process of facilitating difference and constructive debate. A number of rivalries developed among several factions that led to the marginalization of the San Diego chapter, among others, and the repression of a Raza Sí, Migra No position. The organizers of this conference in Los Angeles included two local chapters, the LRUP Labor Committee and the City Terrace chapter. According to political scientist and participant of the conference Armando Navarro, leaders in these hosting chapters held suspicions about visiting LRUP members associated with MAPA and CASA who might be orchestrating a "takeover."[61] These hosting chapters expressed concern that MAPA- and CASA-affiliated members exerted political approaches that were not authentically radical (and tied to the Democratic Party) in the former and too sectarian and ideological within the latter. The LRUP Labor Committee also held a tense relationship with the Socialist Worker's Party (SWP), whose members were also present. To complicate matters further, Navarro's MAPA-turned-LRUP chapters from San Bernadino and Riverside counties differed with CASA and the "agenda" of Bert Corona as well.[62] San Diego LRUP became caught up within these political rivalries in their association with former MAPA leaders such as Navarro as well as with Corona's CASA.[63]

These tensions surfaced in the labor and deportation workshop at the Los Angeles convention. At first glance, the resolutions passed through this workshop seem to put forth a Chicano/Mexicano position that included undocumented Mexican migrants as fellow ethnic community members and workers. The resolutions also explicitly asserted that "We reject the Dixon Arnett law" because "the law does not penalize the true enemy" and therefore, "we take a position that unites us rather than divides us."[64] This part of the resolution included replacing the term "illegal alien" with "people without documents" and "granting legal protection immediately" and "for an indefinite period" to undocumented workers as "refugees from hunger."[65] It further resolved that all undocumented migrants with current jobs be certified for visas.

Yet in the same set of resolutions, another version of employer sanctions was proposed, one that sought to not only fine employers for hiring undocumented workers as the Dixon Arnett bill proposed but to make it a felony offense for those employers who threatened immigrant workers with deportation, "punishable by a fine of $10,000 or 10 years in prison."[66] Any employer found guilty of such a felony would be required to pay six months' salary to any worker who was deported. Another felony charge of $10,000 and 10 years in prison, the resolution proposed, could be levied at employers who terminated an employee and then hired another employee for the same job at lower wages. The resolutions went on to articulate that after these proposals became law, undocumented migrants would be required to approach immigration authorities within a window of three months to gain access to "begin the processing of visa applications."[67]

This position clashed with stances taken by LRUP San Diego and others influenced by Bert Corona's vision of a united Chicano/Mexicano constituency. Of course this Raza Sí, Migra No contingent saw employer sanctions as indirectly incriminating of migrants and a cause of discrimination against ethnic Mexican workers. During the labor and deportation workshop that proposed and developed these resolutions, the leaders from the Labor Committee reportedly advocated for these positions.[68] CASA member Nacho Uribe and City Terrace LRUP member Pedro Arias were reportedly not allowed to critique the proposal, and according to Navarro in his study of the California LRUP, were threatened with bodily harm. CASA Los Angeles in particular, as well as SWP members and others, vigorously challenged the position put forth by the Labor Committee and "alleged that the Labor Committee's proposal accepted the deportations of undocumented Raza workers."[69] Given the existing positons of Chicano/Mexicano activists on the Dixon Arnett employer sanctions law, criticism likely referred to the ways punishing employers led to discrimination of ethnic Mexican workers and created a stigma on undocumented workers as problematic. The three-month window would only incorporate a select few migrant workers into citizenship and guarantee that the situation would be reproduced indefinitely into the future.

The workshop actually recognized this, admitting that the resolutions were an immediate step that was needed to remove undocumented workers as potential strikebreakers. The resolution stated, "These proposals will not alter the existing immigration structure at all, but they will immediately remove the so-called illegals as potential strike breakers, and low wage marginal workers, as they will not be afraid to unionize and to work on their jobs for fair wages."[70] This reveals the logic of the caucus resolution in that undocumented workers, despite the rhetoric, were not ultimately being conceived as part of the community, but continued to be viewed as outsider "strikebreakers" detrimental to citizen workers, particularly U.S. Chicanos. This appears to be one of the central conflicts dividing the political perspective of the hosting Labor Committee chapter of the LRUP and the opposing view held by CASA, the SWP, and others. While the Labor Committee resolutions proposed to use felony charges to prevent the use of deportation to repress workers' demands and prevent access to a reserve labor pool, Chicano/ Mexicano perspectives suggested that these resolutions recapitulated and reified the citizenship-over-noncitizen hierarchy by continuing to place blame on undocumented workers as "potential strikebreakers" and requiring them to approach the repressive INS to alter their status. Raza Sí, Migra No activists argued that unauthorized workers had long been recruited and employed by U.S. business interests and that the responsibility rested on the state to recognize that legal status had, in many different ways, already been earned. This important debate, however, was thwarted when challengers to the resolution were threatened with bodily harm. As mentioned, Raul Ruíz, moderator of the labor and deportation workshop, commented years later that the host chapter stifled the debate due to concern over a possible takeover by the SWP or CASA (which was associated with the Communist Party).[71]

Further closing of ranks ensued when two Southern California LRUP chapters, San Bernardino-Riverside and Orange County, were not recognized. Several Los Angeles-based LRUP chapters argued that several chapters from the LRUP did not properly register for the convention. Furthermore, these Los Angeles-based chapters, which were dominant in numbers due to the convention's location in the Los Angeles area, accused the LRUP California Southern Region members, including the San Diego chapter as well as San Bernardino-Riverside, of being a threat to "Chicano politics" because they were nonradical MAPA members.[72] Again, Raul Ruiz later explained: "We [the City Terrace chapter, among others] thought that you [Navarro] were Mapistas [MAPA members] disguised as Raza Unida. . . . I think that your allegiance was being questioned. We thought there was some type of conspiracy. This is why we did what we did."[73]

Southern Region members argued that some of the Los Angeles chapters used these techniques to marginalize their insistence on "decentralized" LRUP operations beyond Los Angeles. They asserted that the call for a decentralized LRUP would allow for grassroots organizing that would stay attuned to the needs of working-class Chicano communities. Baca, whose San Diego chapter was recognized only after much debate, joined the unrecognized chapters in a walkout of the meeting. The Southern Region collectively responded to the events of the Los Angeles convention in a manifesto calling for unity and criticizing the "dogmatic cultural nationalism" and "psudo-Marxism [sic] or chest-pounding machismo self-righteous SECTARIANISM" by many LRUP participants. Instead, Carlos Muñoz of the Orange County chapter, along with the rest of the Southern Region, including San Diego, called for a "humanistic nationalism" that would be based on the "human needs of our barrios."[74] Similar to the grassroots approach to organizing that characterized the activism of labor movement veterans such as Bert Corona, the Southern Region sought to avoid ideological and factional squabbles in favor of making the LRUP a viable and attractive mobilizing vehicle for working-class ethnic Mexicans.[75] The Southern Region asserted, "At this stage in the development of our Partido we do not need leaders or spokesman, we need organizers. The kind of organizer dedicated to the tedious and largely unglorified work that goes with organizing local colonias and barrios around the issues Chicanos in those areas relate to and understand."[76] Members of the Southern Region, particularly San Diego activists, understood that this plan of action would of course necessitate a conception of the "Chicano community" to be fluid and embracing of its multigenerational and multiple legal status realties. The accusations of infiltration within California LRUP organizing derailed the process of the democratization of the Chicano movement in favor of consolidating power among a few self-declared ethnic elites who mouthed the nationalist/separatist line. It also shifted its trajectory away from engagement with the transnational community it claimed to represent.

Members of the Southern Region sought to correct this trend by continuing to assert a vision of decentralized local autonomy. To build a mass organization, they insisted, it was necessary to work "from the bottom up." "It is important, therefore," they continued, "that our first battle lines be drawn in the local areas."[77] Concerning the emerging ideological rivalry between Denver, Colorado, LRUP leader Corky Gonzales and South Texas LRUP leader Jose Angel Gutiérrez for the National LRUP chair, the Southern Region argued, "We believe that the local situation must dictate the pragmatic orientation of the Partido."[78] The Denver approach, rooted in the minority status of ethnic Mexicans in that state, sought to focus the LRUP on disseminating revolutionary education campaigns to the Chicano community and working as an independent political force that could pressure local, state, and national decision making. The Texas approach, emergent in a part of South Texas where ethnic Mexicans were a majority and the multilevel structure of local political offices made it possible for ethnic Mexicans to elect their own candidates, emphasized winning elections, gaining official representation, and engaging in hard-line negotiations with non-LRUP politicians. In Southern California, of course, the situation was very different. Although by that time there were numerically more Mexicanos of both nationalities in California than there were in Texas, there were very few places in California where they constituted majorities. This made an effective third-party challenge there much more difficult. As a consequence, the Southern Region argued that through a localized approach to the LRUP that would grant autonomy to particular chapters, the Denver and Texas approaches would not be "mutually exclusive." Instead, decisions about the utility of these two approaches would depend on the local context on a basis that was "critical and independent of those (the Denver or Texas) perspectives."[79] The region asserted further: "Local politics must dictate the tactics to be used in local areas. State policy must be based on the tactics and strategy that are effective in local politics. In other words, until we develop the capability for mass mobilization at the state level, we must operate under a decentralized Partido framework."[80] In this way, the Southern Region envisioned an autonomous local approach to assessing what tactics, strategies, and ideas would apply to their own analysis of their own contexts. This analysis could only be reached, the Southern Region asserted, through "COLLECTIVE LEADERSHIP AS OPPOSED TO INDIVIDUAL LEADERSHIP."[81] Through registering community members to join the LRUP, organizers would be able to assess the local context and the people's concerns. It would also create the base through which to win elections, they argued, and gain legitimacy in the eyes of the Chicano community to put forth successful education campaigns and combine the polarized Denver and Texas perspectives.

The resistance experienced by the Southern Region to ideas concerning local autonomy reveals some of the policing efforts that were prevalent within the LRUP and the wider Chicano movement. Fears of Socialists, Communists, or nonradical MAPA members "infiltrating" what many LRUP activists argued were the "authentic" political interests of the Chicano community were based on continuing reference to a static notion of community at a moment when the fluid and transnational nature of the ethnic Mexican community in the United States was intensifying. As political scientist Christina Beltran asserts, "The struggle for social justice that initially animated Chicano cultural nationalism quickly devolved into debates over cultural authenticity and an emphasis on group unity that led to the demonization and denial of internal disagreement."[82] At a time when activists were engaging the immigration issue to articulate a more fluid understanding of a heterogeneous and ever-changing community, these policing efforts revealed the continued strength of a more reactionary identity politics that tended to obscure the globalized context in which working-class racialized communities in the U.S.-Mexico borderlands were struggling. The energies invested in policing the boundaries of community reveal that important elements of La Raza Unida Party were not prepared to act on the lessons coming from the borderlands. The quick decline of LRUP's fortunes following the party's national convention in 1973 and the continued personal rivalries and animosities dividing Denver's Corky Gonzales and Texas's José Ángel Gutiérrez, and their respective followers, revealed that this innovative third-party project missed an opportunity to engage the concerns emerging from a rapidly shifting demographic reality within the ethnic Mexican communities it claimed to represent.

· · · · · ·

La Raza Unida Party became a local, statewide, and even national *encuentro* through which Raza Sí, Migra No San Diego activists gathered with others to break from what they considered to be bourgeois and anti-immigrant political perspectives, to launch a move toward autonomous Chicano movement organizing that sought self-determination for a definition of *la raza* that centralized the struggles of the undocumented. This vision often differed from the interests of organized labor, the Democratic Party, business elites, and a growing Chicano political class, and for a time, the LRUP emerged as an alternative. These activists soon found that LRUP was plagued with fractures over the immigration issue, among other issues regarding ideology and strategy. Even among a group that surely empathized with and largely perceived undocumented migrants as members of *la raza*, segments within LRUP had very different ideas about what to do about the immigration situation. Even while seemingly advocating for undocumented migrants, many activists with hard-line nationalistic and/or sectarian definitions of community found it difficult to fully incorporate the experience of immigrants into the Chicano movement agenda. This may have stemmed in part from a lack of familiarity with the intense legal violence experienced by working-class ethnic Mexicans that San Diego MAPA, CASA Justicia, and LRUP activists struggled against in the borderlands.

The San Diego LRUP chapter in part also revealed the contradictions and limits of an electoral-based strategy. San Diego LRUP and their allies began to understand that when a large percentage of their community were noncitizens, repressed by deportation policies and public racialized scapegoating, the immigration regime had to be confronted for any semblance of participation in representative democracy to be feasible. While continuing to struggle with a gendered hierarchy in leadership, the LRUP forged a space that forged a politics inclusive of undocumented migrants by using voter registration, the newsletter, and CASA Justicia to not only gain voters but to incorporate and advocate for noncitizen community members as well.

The work of these Raza Sí, Migra No activists in San Diego and wider Southern California made a larger impact on the future evolution of Chicano movement politics because it premised issues that would soon affect community leaders in other regions. For example, although their rivalry over the chairman position of the national La Raza Unida Party indicated that Gutiérrez and Gonzales were two key Chicano movement leaders of the moment, their urgent and shifting positions concerning immigration revealed that they were in the process of coming to terms with the role that noncitizens played in their communities. Their calls for Baca's assistance and Gonzales's shift from an anti-immigrant to proimmigrant position reveals the influence Raza Sí, Migra No politics had in broadening a challenge to the logic of the nation-state, widening Chicano identities across borders, and confronting an (inter)national policing force that targeted ethnic Mexican communities.[83]

Indeed, Gonzales's 1973 conversion speech concluded that the overarching economic structure was the enemy. Arguing that the "economic structure" and the millionaires who used President Nixon as their puppet were the true enemy, Gonzales exclaimed: "This is where the enemy is—the enemy is not our own people! For us to say today, 'No more Mexicans should come in here,' is to be as racist as those who wrote the immigration laws so that people like the Japanese and Chinese, Indians, Blacks and Mexicans could no longer come into this country."[84]

Gonzales's realizations about undocumented immigration revealed the progression of some Chicano/a activists' thinking as they came to see more clearly the entanglement of racism, nationalism, and citizenship status within the practice of the U.S. state as an instrument of global capitalist development. The tie between Gonzales's statement depicting immigration laws as forms of racialized repression and similar statements exerted by Baca, Corona, and other Chicano/Mexicano activists were evidence of how these Southern California activists influenced his thinking on the issue. Similarly, José Ángel Gutiérrez's calls for assistance from Baca to address the need for an immigration service in Texas was evidence that he was engaging what activists in the California borderlands had already been battling: the demographic revolution taking place as unprecedented masses of migrants arrived from Mexico and wider Latin America, and the broadened struggle for liberation in the Chicano/Mexicano community.

The Sheriff Must Be Obsessed with Racism!
The Committee on Chicano Rights Battles Police Violence

· ·

Transforming from a temporary to a permanent organization, the Ad Hoc Committee on Chicano Rights became the Committee on Chicano Rights (CCR) in 1976 after years of harassment and brutality by Border Patrol and Customs Agents. Yet reflecting the interconnection between the deportation regime and local policing, it was struggles against National City and San Diego Police Departments that led to new levels of mobilization that provided the momentum to establish the CCR. When seventeen-year-old Luis "Tato" Rivera was shot in the back and killed by National City Police officer Craig Short in 1975, Chicano/a activists involved in the area MAPA, LRUP, and CASA Justicia organizations had already fought local police for their involvement in identifying, arresting, and delivering to the Border Patrol suspects who were discovered, or profiled, to be undocumented. Rivera was Puerto Rican and therefore like U.S. Chicanos/as, a racialized citizen of the United States. The CCR "Justice for Tato Rivera" struggle facilitated its emergence as an organization that centered on ending the overlapping repression policing unleashed on racialized citizens and racialized immigrants who were subject to intersecting legal violence of both the Border Patrol and local police. This grassroots assessment of how both these policing agencies targeted and systemically brutalized their communities made it quite natural for the CCR to link the experiences of Latinos/as with U.S. citizenship and noncitizens in their collective struggle against repression by policing institutions whether they targeted "criminals" or "illegal aliens." After exhausting Chicano movement organizational units MAPA, CASA, and LRUP, the Ad Hoc Committee on Chicano Rights found that the struggles against state violence, whether emanating from local police or the national Border Patrol, were the actual focal point of their struggles for "Chicano Rights" in the borderlands barrios. Continued onslaught by differing policing tentacles of the state—from the shooting of young Rivera to the continued rogue Border Patrol invasions of ethnic Mexican homes— formed the bases to drop the "Ad Hoc," and become the Committee on Chicano Rights (CCR), a localized independent organization seeking self-determination and battling state violence. The dropping of the "Ad Hoc" signaled the long-term or permanent focus of the CCR on struggling against racialized legal violence.

The Duffy and Hoobler Memorandums

Local police involvement with targeting "illegal aliens" would trigger Herman Baca and the other MAPA-National City/CASA Justicia/La Raza Unida Party San Diego activists to organize the Ad Hoc Committee on Chicano Rights (referred to as the Ad Hoc Committee) to confront the growing siege initiated by local application of anti-immigrant policies in 1971. In a context of a rising number of cases involving harassment and brutality at the hands of INS agents against Mexican Americans and Mexican immigrants, the San Diego County Sheriff John C. Duffy issued a memorandum in September of 1971 that required taxi drivers to assist the department in identifying "aliens." The memorandum proclaimed, "When a taxicab driver picks up a person or groups of persons *whom he feels* may be in this country illegally he should notify his dispatcher via the radio of the situation. . . . The dispatcher will then notify this department who will contact a police agency to stop the taxicab and determine the status of the passengers." It pointed out that the necessity of such a directive was "due to the increasing numbers of aliens entering the country." The memorandum also outlined punishment that drivers risked if they failed to comply with the orders, including a suspension of their taxi-operating permit, indictment as a felony with a $2,000 fine and a five-year prison stint for each alien transported. Evoking both fear and confusion, the memorandum explained, "We do not expect you to call on each individual you transport, but are primarily interested in the large groups of 5 or 6 persons who are obviously, by their mannerisms and dress, illegal entrants into the country."[1]

Activists took note of how local law enforcement policies parroted INS policy and affected the entire ethnic Mexican community in the San Diego borderlands, revealing the stereotype of invading hordes of Mexican immigrants—"large groups of 5 or 6 persons"—that was the basis of the Sherriff's Department order to taxi drivers. Activists responded, as explored in previous chapters, by articulating a common struggle among Mexican immigrants and Mexican Americans. Indeed, the memorandum encouraged racial profiling of ethnic Mexicans in its call to report a person that one *"feels may be in the country illegally."* Baca learned of the memorandum from Ernie Azocar, who came across it as a trustee in the Sweetwater Independent

School District in National City and as liaison to Assemblymember Wadie P. Deddeh of the area 79th District. Soon after, incensed barrio residents began notifying Baca and Chicano/a activists to complain that taxi drivers were refusing service to ethnic Mexicans of all statuses due to fear of incrimination.[2] Baca remembered: "The taxicab drivers, not knowing anything about immigration, and being under threat of penalty, weren't picking up an Mexicanos, any persons of Mexican ancestry. So we started getting complaints from the community that taxicabs were just ignoring them."[3]

Baca soon went on record in *La Raza Unida Party—San Diego Newsletter*, exclaiming, "The sheriff's order has in fact made every cab driver a deputy and an immigration officer . . . causing great injustice to Mexican Nationals and Chicanos."[4] Baca detailed how Duffy's memorandum threatened the two hundred fifty thousand Mexican-origin people in San Diego County due to its racial presumptions. "The Sheriff," Baca exclaimed, "must be obsessed with racism."[5] Baca recalled:

> We had a press conference and lambasted the sheriff's department. The basic argument was that they had no business enforcing federal immigration laws. That was a federal matter. . . . So, like all law enforcement institutions . . . or any institution, they arrogantly chose to discount the complaint saying, you know, it was a problem, and you know, using all the usual, you know, "They were stealing jobs, getting on welfare, medical, hospitals, costing the county money," blah, blah, blah.[6]

Out of this concern, the Ad Hoc Committee brought together a coalition in struggle against an "injustice" shared by "Mexican Nationals and Chicanos." Baca recalled how quickly community members mobilized, "So, we relentlessly went after Duffy. I mean, pickets, demonstrations. I remember, and once again the context of the time . . . getting on the phone one night and saying, 'We're going to have a picket tomorrow in front of the county jail, the San Diego County jail. Spread the word.' And, I remember getting there and there was all these people, you know. There was like five hundred people."[7] The coalition consisted of Chicano movement and more moderate Mexican American organizations in San Diego, including CASA Justicia, MAPA, La Raza Unida Party, the student organization El Movimiento Estudiantil Chicano de Aztlán (MEChA), the G.I. Forum, the Chicano Federation, the Chicano Park Steering Committee, the social service–based Padre Hidalgo Center, the Mexican American Advisory Committee (MAAC), and the Spanish Speaking Political Association.[8] Baca was clear that at this early stage of activism in the Chicano movement in 1971, leaders were still processing how to address the immigration issue. Activists primarily got involved because of the ways Duffy and the Sheriff's Department were targeting and harassing the larger community, particularly when ethnic Mexicans, including those who were United States citizens, were being denied access to taxis.[9]

As Baca recalled, the Ad Hoc Committee mobilized a demonstration in front of the San Diego County Sheriff's office in the County Jail in downtown San Diego just days after the Duffy Memorandum was released.[10] Images of the protest reveal dozens of men and women, many of them appearing to be ethnic Mexican, but also including black and white men and women. They walked in an oval on the sidewalk in front of a building with a sign overhead saying, "San Diego County Sheriff." Another image shows an ethnic Mexican elderly woman with two little girls, the latter two of which hold a sign that reads, "Duffie [sic] You're Indicting Yellow Cab." Another sign on this image is held by a woman and appears to read, "Duffy You Are a Racist." Some other images show signs saying, "Boycott Yellow Cab" and "Cabbies Patrol Border." One picture shows a scaled-back image of a portion of the protesters, consisting of at least forty people marching in front of the sheriff's office alongside the larger building's underpass. Some of the images show sheriff's officers and possibly other officials observing and patrolling the protest.[11] Baca remembered that one particular officer was harassing the protestors. Baca approached the harassing officer and told him, "Hey you SOB. . . . Yeah you, what are you doing harassing our people!?" Baca remembered that the officer got upset, exclaiming, "Hey you can't talk to me like that!" with Baca replying, "Go to hell!" The two men yelled in each other's faces, an image of which reached the front page of the *San Diego Tribune*. Baca recalled that a higher ranking officer intervened in the conflict, and was helpful in sending the harassing officer away.[12] Of course these protests against police provoked more than observation, but surveillance, as one image shows two officials (with a pressed shirt and tie) on top of the roof of a building, one of them observing with binoculars. Furthermore, protests of the Duffy Memorandum were the earliest events recorded by an FBI informant surveying Baca's activism. This event opened Baca's file, marking him as "potentially dangerous because of background, emotional instability or participation in groups engaged in activities inimical to U.S."[13]

There are also images of meetings, presumably organizing the event, one of which shows at least ten individuals seated around a large table, Herman

Baca standing and appearing to facilitate the discussion. Most of the individuals appear to be ethnic Mexican men, with one ethnic Mexican woman in the back listening. Another image, possibly another angle of the same meeting, shows Baca again standing, Charlie Vásquez sitting listening alongside an older man who is next to a young woman. Yet another image shows presumably seven ethnic Mexican men and one ethnic Mexican woman sitting around a table facing one another. This may suggest that while women were heavily present at the protest, consisting of as much as half of the protesters, they were not as well represented at meetings where decisions were made. Abe Tapia, former MAPA statewide president, stands with Baca and an unidentified ethnic Mexican man in one picture. These images of the protest and the meetings reveal a cross section of the community involved in the planning, and the absence of women, and action concerning police units intervening in the rising alarm over "illegal aliens."[14]

Through this campaign and appeals to local, state, and federal officials, the Ad Hoc Committee successfully pressured Sheriff Duffy to rescind the memo. Duffy would issue another memo on January 8, 1973, stating, "Due to the misunderstanding of the memorandum issued by my Department on September 15, 1972, and the apparent misinterpretation of my attempts to clarify it, that memorandum is superseded by the present letter." This letter removed the wording about identifying undocumented immigrants by "mannerisms" and "dress," but continued to insist that those cab drivers "knowingly . . . and with unlawful intent . . . transporting illegal aliens" would face disciplinary measures.[15] Later, Duffy more humbly detailed the information federal officials brought to his attention. "No one but immigration authorities, not even the FBI, has the right to detain, interrogate or arrest illegal aliens," he said. This was due to the fact that immigration was a federal issue strictly up to the Immigration and Naturalization Service to handle. "We do not even have the right to ask them to show their papers," Duffy said.[16] The media attention that the Duffy Memorandum received seems to have influenced other area police departments to back away from the practice of apprehending "illegal aliens." The police chief of nearby Coronado stated: "Until a month ago, our policy was to apprehend illegal aliens and send them over to the Border Patrol. But because of legal interpretations about our authority, we stopped doing so."[17] Other area departments, including La Mesa, El Cajon, and Chula Vista also altered their policies after the Duffy incident. This historical practice, however, would not die easily. In May of 1973, the San Diego Police Department (SDPD) issued a similar policy. The Ad Hoc Committee continued its struggle, now against Chief Ray Hoobler and the SDPD's "Hoobler Memorandum."

San Diego police chief Ray Hoobler interpreted the policies of the Department of Justice quite differently when he reportedly instructed his officers to enforce federal immigration laws against illegal aliens "only when those violations come to the attention of officers when officers are engaged in their routine duties."[18] This memorandum was issued after Hoobler claimed that the Justice Department approved of SDPD policies concerning questioning and detaining suspected "illegal aliens."[19] The U.S. attorney's position asserted, "Provided officers have a reasonable suspicion that the particular individual is eluding examination or inspection by immigration officers, a detention for investigation would be proper."[20] The federal position went on to explain that if a detained individual was determined to be in the country illegally, officers should notify U.S. Immigration Services. Somewhat paradoxically, the position also warned that "local police do not possess the broad authority of immigration officers to apprehend illegal aliens." SDPD legal advisor Gene Gordon argued that "key to the opinion is probable cause."[21] Little was said how such probable cause might be based on racially inscribed codes and profiling.

Acting as director of the Southern Region of the Mexican American Political Association and member of the Ad Hoc Committee, Herman Baca would highlight how Hoobler and the SDPD's interpretation of the policy would unleash racial profiling tactics when he wrote to Mayor Pete Wilson asking if the city council was "willing to assume the responsibility for the violation of the civil and constitutional rights of 250,000 residents of Mexican ancestry in San Diego County?" Baca further inquired whether the city council would be willing to tax its residents for the expenditures required to take on a venture "that will involve massive and unlimited manpower and resources," and be liable for "the civil law suits arising from illegal interrogations, illegal detentions, and false imprisonment of legal residents and citizens of Mexican ancestry."[22]

The next day, May 17, 1973, Chief Hoobler issued another memorandum to "clarify" and "eliminate" any confusion about the SDPD's policy on detaining suspected undocumented immigrations, but Baca interpreted the newest memo as "a reaffirmation to enforce federal laws."[23] Quoting the recent statement by Sheriff John Duffy that "no one but immigration authorities . . . has the right to detail, interrogate or arrest illegal aliens," and referencing the nine area police chiefs who declared a hands-off policy in dealing with immigration law enforcement, Baca suggested, "If this is going to be his [Chief Hoobler's] policy why not issue memos enforcing customs laws, internal revenue laws and other federal laws?"[24] Addressing the Mayor's "failure" to return the initial letter, Baca asked, "Who is making policy and running the city, you or the San Diego Police Department?" After accusing Wilson of not taking the issue seriously, Baca concluded by asserting: "If you and your colleagues are not willing or able to resolve this issue we will be left with no other alternative but to escalate our position. To this course we are committed. Your official position is still awaited."[25]

Baca also expressed a concern in that letter that "Hoobler's practice of issuing memos on illegal aliens to clarify issues can only be viewed by us of the Chicano community as giving this area of law enforcement major priority." "This," he argued, "can only result in the violation of our civil and constitutional rights."[26] Baca's concern would ring true as reports came in concerning harassment and active participation in apprehensions and deportations of Mexican immigrants following Hoobler's memorandum. On June 14, 1973, Father Juan Hurtado, director of the Padre Hidalgo Center in the Logan Heights Barrio in San Diego and member of the Ad Hoc Committee on Chicano Rights, led a press conference expressing that the "church community is greatly disturbed and angered by certain actions undertaken by the San Diego City Police."[27] One of only about three hundred Chicano priests at the time, Father Hurtado as he was known, was involved in key Chicano movement events in San Diego, including support for César Chávez and the UFW in a 1972 campaign in San Diego where Chávez was arrested, in a seminal action with the city government involving the Chicano artist group the Toltecas de Aztlán who founded the Centro Cultural de La Raza, and community organizing efforts that protested zoning and sought community control of social service institutions run by the Catholic Church in Barrio Logan.[28] Father Hurtado reported that soon after Chief Hoobler released his "illegal alien memorandum," police began harassing instructors and students in a church program teaching English as a Second Language (ESL), Driver's Education, and other classes in coordination with the Division of Adult Education of San Diego.[29] Operating in seven locations across the city, classes averaged about twenty to twenty-five students each. One of the ESL teachers, Tony Viana at the Our Lady of Guadalupe church in the Logan Heights barrio, reported that she was interrogated by San Diego police "in a cold and harsh manner" about whether there might be illegal aliens in her class.[30] According to Hurtado, Viana noticed that two students stopped coming to class, and later found out that they were deported to

Mexico. Another one of her students was apprehended by San Diego police, according to Viana, for looking suspicious, and was subsequently deported also.

Dr. Jose Saldivar, director of the Bilingual Education School, noticed the presence of police cars during his visits to evaluate classes at the Our Lady of Guadalupe church and another church in Barrio Logan, Our Lady of Angels. Father Hurtado argued that this police presence had a negative effect on the classes, claiming that student enrollment dropped 50 percent and that the students remaining seemed on edge. "Because of a great deal of confusion and misinformation in the area of immigration, the role police officers play, and the many things that have happened to friends, the students are very terrified of the police," Hurtado's press release reads.[31] Demonstrating the link from the perspective of Mexican immigrants between immigration and local policing, Hurtado explained, "Many students who have had very terrifying experiences with immigration, now have a very negative approach to the police."[32]

To conclude, Hurtado told of a "calculated police raid" that occurred just the day before at yet another church just north of Barrio Logan near Market Street at the Full Gospel Mission Church. The raid, including three officers in two police cars alongside an ambulance, according to Hurtado, "entered the church, stopped the religious service and began looking for brown looking individuals." Up to thirty individuals were asked to exit the church and were subsequently interrogated and asked to reveal their passports. The police questioned the church participants in English, and given that they only spoke Spanish, the questioning ceased and the seven to eight men were arrested.[33] Father Hurtado reported that late in the previous evening before the press conference, he received word that these men were also deported to Mexico. Condemning the ways these incidents revealed how the police violated "a most cherished and fundamental right—freedom to worship without fear and harassment," Father Hurtado and the Ad Hoc Committee demanded that "our elected City Council and Mayor act immediately on this serious matter by communicating to Chief Ray Hoobler all that has been said today, and ask for his resignation."[34]

Herman Baca addressed the San Diego City Council on these issues on the same day as the press conference featuring Father Hurtado, directly demanding that Hoobler be fired when he repeated Father Hurtado's press conference report on the incidents at churches, calling police actions "Gestapo tactics."[35] Chief Hoobler defended the incident at Full Gospel Mission church in a manner that revealed deliberate interworking between SDPD and the Border Patrol, and the execution of a policy that equated "looking illegal" with "suspicious activity." Hoobler justified his officers' actions by arguing that they were simply directed by "a citizen" who saw them as "suspicious." "This check was not initiated by the Police Department but by a citizen who was anxious about suspicious persons," Hoobler explained. What made individuals suspicious to the "citizen" was that they "appeared to be illegal aliens." Hoobler's defense therefore openly acknowledged that his officers acted on this racist presumption. Furthermore, Hoobler explained—as if it was a natural process that—"the seven men were taken into custody and turned over to the Border Patrol as illegal aliens," suggesting the routine nature of such events and an ingrained practice of enforcing immigration policy in cooperation with U.S. immigration authorities.[36] The Ad Hoc Committee would later report that on June 2, 1973, police captured twenty-one undocumented people, and on June 3 another thirty-one were apprehended.[37]

Just after the council meeting, Mayor Wilson also defended the police's actions within the same logic that officers were asked by "informants they consider reliable" to make such investigations and arrests.[38] He sarcastically explained: "It is hardly going out on the street looking for trouble, hardly harassing people. Mr. Baca doesn't really understand the nature of law-enforcement work. . . . Mr. Baca seems to be in search of a cause. Frankly it's a bummer."[39] Baca told the council, revealing the ways police repression reinforced Chicano/Mexicano solidarities: "You have brought us together. You have unified us by assaulting our community—our homes, our churches, our mothers, our fathers. . . . We demand you fire San Diego Police Chief Ray Hoobler!"[40] Despite the mayor and the police chief's defensive posture, the city council did vote unanimously to direct the city manager to issue a report on the matter in two weeks.

Baca and the Ad Hoc Committee would find that by challenging city policing policies, they disrupted Mayor Wilson's practices of patronage that quelled demands from marginalized groups and gained consent from community leaders for his plans to develop the city. Through his "America's Finest City" campaign, Wilson sought to utilize public monies to supplement high-end developers to revitalize downtown and surrounding districts while promising residents that he would contain the urban sprawl most associated with cities such as Los Angeles. As part of these efforts, he sought to clean up and further professionalize the San Diego Police Department to promote the image of "America's Finest City."[41] Baca's public demands to immediately cease policies enacted by SDPD Chief Hoobler in apprehending and delivering "illegal aliens" to the Border Patrol disrupted Wilson's painting of a peaceful, harmonious city free of the urban problems of bigger cities. Furthermore, Baca and the Ad Hoc Committee on Chicano Rights' refusal to concede to Wilson's political patronage further frustrated the mayor.[42]

This would become evident when Mayor Wilson offered a meeting to some of the leaders in the Ad Hoc Committee. After a July 14, 1973, meeting of more than one hundred members of the Ad Hoc Committee, the coalition opted to reject Wilson's invitation to some of its members.[43] In a letter to Wilson, Baca explained as the Ad Hoc Committee chair that the meeting was declined because, "Your correspondence was addressed to individuals and not to the formal structure within the Ad Hoc Committee which is dealing with the Hoobler Memorandum."[44] The letter also detailed that Wilson would need to address the entire Ad Hoc Committee on issues requested of him by the committee. This rejection of Wilson's patronage and of the tactic of meeting with certain individuals instead of the Ad Hoc Committee was met with the mayor's dismay at the individuals he invited to the said meeting.

On July 19, 1973, Wilson responded to the Ad Hoc Committee's refusal by threatening to cut all relations with Chicano Federation director Luis Natividad, one of the Ad Hoc members he invited to meet with, if he continued working with Baca and the committee. The Chicano Federation was a confederation of area organizations that worked for the betterment of the Chicano community. It emerged out of the San Diego County governmental system which provided the bulk of its funding. A parallel Black Federation for the African American community also existed as part of this county level outreach system.[45] Revealing of Wilson's patronage, social critic Mike Davis asserts that the mayor was successful in quashing demands from communities of color by offering token positions and negotiating support from minority leaders.[46] Wilson lamented in a personal letter to Natividad, "Having received no message from you indicating that you could not attend (the meeting with Mexican American leaders), I am compelled to wonder whether your absence was a matter of choice. If so, I regret your decision. And if it was in fact a conscious decision, you should regret it, too, because it was a bad one."[47] Infuriated by a recent showing of a local news program in which Baca appeared to protest the SDPD's policy on apprehending undocumented migrants, Wilson exclaimed to Natividad, "Several Chicano friends have since apologized for Baca's performance and assured me that he was not speaking for the Chicano community. Neither the apology nor the assurance was required. In fact, to any fair-minded viewer it should have been obvious that there was no responsible or representative spokesman, but rather an inept juvenile on an ego trip."[48]

Of concern for Wilson was not only Natividad's failure to attend his meeting but the possibility that he was rejected in preference for participation with the Ad Hoc Committee on Chicano Rights. Wilson was "informed" that Natividad attended an Ad Hoc Committee meeting. To this, Wilson exclaimed: "The thought that you (Natividad) would consciously choose to boycott our meeting in preference for Herman Baca's ridiculous 'leadership' would be truly astounding and very disappointing. I cannot imagine your preferring [a] self-important propaganda to honest communication as a means of solving community problems."[49] Wilson concluded by asking Natividad to inform him if he had, indeed, chosen Baca over him. The stakes were clearly outlined as one or the other. "If I do not hear from you, I must reluctantly assumed [sic] that you feel that Herman's 'leadership' can do more to help San Diego's very important Chicano community than can leadership elected by the people of San Diego," explained Wilson. "And if that is your feeling, I will not expect your participation in any efforts undertaken by me, nor will I trouble you with any further invitations to participate."[50] Clearly Wilson would not speak to or work with anyone working with Baca. What Wilson did not address explicitly, but local activists argued was implicitly evoked, was the Chicano Federation's one-dollar-per-year lease on a building provided by the city of San Diego. Reflecting on Wilson's letter, an Ad Hoc Committee document recalled: "Mayor Pete Wilson memorands [sic] Chicano Federation leader Louie Natividad [to] 'stop working with Herman Baca or lose the Federation's dollar a year lease.' Wilson's ultimatum makes clear a beginning split between activist groups and funded agencies."[51]

Undeterred by Wilson's implied threat of taking the Chicano Federation's one-dollar lease, the Ad Hoc Committee and its allies accused Wilson of assassinating Baca's character to avoid addressing the issue at hand—that the SDPD was illegally apprehending undocumented migrants, and thus harassing the ethnic Mexican community at large. Indeed, some Chicano elected officials came to Baca's defense on July 31, 1973, including a trustee of Southwestern College, Ernie Azocar, who had informed Baca in the first place about the original memorandum issued by Sheriff Duffy. Cosigning a letter defending Baca alongside Azocar were the trustees and board members of area school districts in the South Bay/South San Diego County community, including National School District (National City), Chula Vista

ISD, and San Ysidro ISD, many of whom were elected with the support of Baca's MAPA chapter. They noted in an open letter to Wilson:

> Your attack directed at Mr. Baca, on a personal basis, is seen by many respected individuals as a vendetta on your part to discredit and discolor the issue that we as elected officials and concerned citizens have taken a stand on. Your unprofessional demonstration of petty emotionalism expressed in your letter to several respected individuals about Mr. Baca is far from becoming of the dignity of your position. . . . Your stand on the "alien" issue should not arbitrarily disclude [*sic*] the opinions of the people that it affronts most—the Mexican American. It is our desire that you reconsider your position and listen to what a large segment of our population is trying to advise you of.[52]

The Ad Hoc Committee issued a statement in defense of Baca as well on August 5, 1973, signed off by Carlos Vásquez of CASA Justicia, Gloria Serrano of Trabajadores de La Raza, Victor Martínez of Hermandad Igualdad de Derechos, Frank Metza of Servicios de Inmigracion, Inc., Manuel Osuman of MEChA, Augie Bareño of MAPA, Victor Nieto of MAAC, Luis Natividad of the Chicano Federation, Alberto García of United California Mexican American Associaton, and Albert Puente, vice chairman of the Ad Hoc Committee.[53] They accosted the mayor, asserting, "Your reaction, if not libelous, was at minimum a clear indication of your inability to understand or appreciate the importance to all Chicanos of the problem posed by the continued interference of San Diego Police officers with the freedom of movement of Chicanos in the City of San Diego."[54] Despite Wilson's attempt to depict a harmonious city cleansed of the urban problems of poverty, sprawl, and racial tensions, the Ad Hoc Committee's demand to address an issue fundamentally dealing with "the freedom of movement" of ethnic Mexicans in the city identified a historically embedded social practice of policing racialized laborers.[55] The Ad Hoc Committee assured Wilson that they regarded "Mr. Baca's position with respect to the Hoobler Memorandum as legally correct and meriting of continued support." They concluded by reminding Wilson that his "invitation . . . is considered not essential to the continuance of our efforts to protect our community through all appropriate political or legal channels."[56] Baca also claimed that this type of intimidation was utilized when Wilson wrote similarly "sharp letters" to a total of six Chicano leaders who did not attend meetings requested by the mayor.[57]

Despite the uncompromising persistence of the Ad Hoc Committee and other Mexican American leadership to press the local city elite to alleviate the repression of noncitizens in their community, some groups began to buckle under the pressure displayed by Wilson. According to some activist reflections on these events, social service community organizations receiving funds from the local, state, and federal government began to pull out of the Ad Hoc Committee, including the Chicano Federation, MAAC, and the Padre Hidalgo Center.[58] The Ad Hoc Committee also found that many Chicano organizations would not take a stance on the controversial immigration issue. An organization document recalled this moment: "Among Chicano activists, the immigration issue is thought to be a no win situation. A right-wing mentality among Chicanos allows the undocumented to be seen as job thieves and swelling the welfare lines. The immigration issue proves to be a major test of funded organizations' commitment."[59] What the debate with Wilson reveals is that the call to address border enforcement policies touched a chord among deep-seated interests in the political mainstream. The state had the power to split developing Chicano/Mexicano mobilizations because many Chicano movement organizations, particularly state-funded social service agencies, were dependent on government funds. Furthermore, there was also an ideological battle that became internalized within the activist community, as the Ad Hoc Committee had to contend with the "right-wing mentality among Chicanos" that perceived undocumented workers as "job thieves" who are "swelling the welfare lines."[60]

The Ad Hoc Committee's public criticism of police agencies became particularly concerning for the FBI informant surveying Baca, revealing other forms of repression that influenced fragmentation within the Chicano movement on these issues. Reflecting the internal strife between Baca and the Ad Hoc Committee and those who may have been under the tutelage of Mayor Wilson, the informant reported to the FBI that there was conflict over control of the Chicano Federation and that "Baca was deeply involved with an anti-police fight, whereas the more mature Mexican elements were opposed to the control of local Chicano groups by activists."[61] The informant also noted that "Baca distributed a pamphlet protesting the action of the Chief of Police who allowed his men to stop Mexican Americans and Mexicans who appeared to possibly be illegal aliens." The informant was especially concerned about Baca's ability to use his print shot from where he was "proclaiming police harassment of Chicanos."[62] Indeed, Baca's print shot had played a vital role in mobilizing and informing, alongside his increasing appearance on local television, the ethnic Mexican and larger San

Diego community about the feud and criticism of Duffy, and now the high-profile Mayor Wilson. Indeed, Chief Hoobler and the SDPD engaged in their own form of surveillance when they sent an informant to infiltrate the La Raza Unida Party, which Baca and many in the Ad Hoc Committee were also organizing. Officer Herman V. Iglesias filled out a membership form when presenting himself as Reynaldo A. Chávez, but mistakenly wrote his real name on the form. Baca immediately went to the press, detailing such tactics as "typical of the tactics used by the department to intimidate the community."[63] Chief Hoobler actually admitted to the attempted infiltration, calling it "a one-shot deal" that was necessary "because when people won't talk to us, then we must find other means to gather information."[64] Hoobler's words here ring of Mayor Wilson's outrage over Louis Natividad's decision to decline an invited meeting with ("when people won't talk to us") the mayor and "respectable leaders of the Mexican community."[65] This may reveal Hoobler's close work with Wilson, possibly part of a punishment campaign for refusing the patronage offered by Wilson. Hoobler also claimed that there was a "potential of violence in the community" that made it necessary to infiltrate.[66] It was unclear what this potential was. Ad Hoc Committee members responded by reminding that the real problem stemmed not from activists, but from Mayor Wilson, Chief Hoobler, and the practices of the police department. As Nick Sanchez of the Legal Aid Society reminded, "People are being stopped because their skin is a little darker, they speak Spanish, and their clothes might not be the best."[67]

Baca later spoke to the local media about Ad Hoc Committee efforts to protest the Hoobler Memorandum, arguing that events since its initiation through the summer of 1973 proved it was a racist policy aimed at the entire ethnic Mexican community and that immigration matters were solely under federal jurisdiction. Baca pointed out that "numerous violations of civil and constitutional law have occurred in San Diego County concerning the rights of people of Mexican ancestry" since Chief Hoobler released the memorandum on May 8. Baca elaborated: "Homes, churches and places of employment have been entered under the pretext of searching for 'illegal aliens.' Persons of Mexican descent have been stopped on the street, school children have been interrogated, and persons of Mexican ancestry seeking their legal rights have been abused at the employment offices, at the welfare department, and the San Diego County Hospital. This local memorandum raised many legal, social, and moral questions."[68] He went on to remind that all other police departments in San Diego County had conformed to the understanding put forth previously by the U.S. Justice Department that immigration was a federal issue to be addressed only by the U.S. Congress and the INS.[69]

The stakes were considerably raised in the campaign demanding that Hoobler be fired when parolee Bernardo Gallardo was found shot to death in front of his southeast San Diego home on August 19, 1974. Just days before, Gallardo told Legal Aid Society attorney Richard Walden that SDPD officers Perry R. Bryant and Harold A. Phenix threatened to kill him or have his parole revoked if he did not become an informant for the police department.[70] The Ad Hoc Committee demanded an investigation, reaffirmed their call to fire Hoobler, and sought the creation of a permanent police review commission staffed by community members. While a friend of Gallardo later admitted to accidently killing him, the case signaled for Chicano/a activists the corruption, intimidation, and struggle with the department.[71] These concerns were somewhat validated when Chief Hoobler was forced to resign after it was discovered that he lied to city manager Hugh McKinley about confidential police counseling files that the chief ordered seized and later shredded.[72]

The Ad Hoc Committee, and later its outgrowth, the Committee on Chicano Rights (CCR) formed in 1976, would continue to struggle with the insistence of Mayor Wilson, the new chief William Kolendar, and even Sheriff Duffy again in 1984 to apprehend undocumented residents and enforce deportation policies in league with the Border Patrol and the INS.[73] In part due to the pressure and activism of the Ad Hoc Committee on Chicano Rights, U.S. Attorney General Griffin Bell reiterated the federal government's position on police participation in immigration policy, urging state and local police, "Do not stop and question, detain, arrest, or place an 'immigration hold' on any person not suspected of a crime solely on the ground that they may be deportable aliens."[74] What the Ad Hoc Committee's struggle with the Duffy and Hoobler memorandums revealed, however, was that these seemingly clear instructions were complicated by the way deportation-oriented policies simultaneously required local police to work with the INS if it was inadvertently discovered that a suspect was undocumented. As Attorney General Bell's statement continued, "Upon arresting an individual for a non-immigration criminal violation, notify the Service immediately if it is suspected that the person may be an undocumented alien, so that the service might respond appropriately."[75] The implied instruction to determine whether someone is "suspected" of being undocumented opened up police departments to apply the policy in a way that unleashed intense repression of undocumented residents and the larger ethnic Mexican and

Latino/a community due to the way racialization was embedded in the policy. Therefore, the Ad Hoc Committee's position that "immigration is a federal matter totally a responsibility of the Federal Government" fell short of assessing the ways that immigration policy structurally required police to participate in the deportation regime even as it told police not to arrest individuals solely for being undocumented. The contradictory nature of the Justice Department's position might reveal how elected officials like Pete Wilson could exploit this ambiguity in order to build political capital by targeting undocumented residents in his cleanup campaigns—and his role in what geographer Joseph Nevins calls the ideological "creation of the crisis of immigration"—culminating in his rise to the California governorship in the early 1990s. Furthermore, it may reveal how more recently in the post-911 era, immigration enforcement has created more openings—and even requirements—that request the assistance of local police in apprehensions and deportations.

The creation of the Committee on Chicano Rights, removing the "Ad Hoc" to assert a permanent organization chiefly concerned with forms of state violence such as these struggles with the police, would create a space in which to think further and evolve their position on this structural dilemma. Indeed, the creation of the CCR was in response to yet more police violence, this time when a barrio youth, Luis "Tato" Rivera, was shot in the back and killed by a National City police officer. The persistence of these tragic events ensured that the CCR and area Chicano/a community activists would continue to contemplate, mobilize, and radicalize around the issue of race and state violence in the borderlands.

Justice for Luis "Tato" Rivera!

Racial profiling, harassment, and brutality by police against ethnic Mexicans interlaced the logic of deportation policies with the broader manner in which racialized communities were historically criminalized, patrolled, and all too often, brutalized. For example, in the midst of the battle against the Hoobler Memorandum, nine-year-old Michelle Medina witnessed San Diego County sheriffs beat and arrest family and friends at a birthday party celebration at her cousin's home in north San Diego County on August 11, 1973. "I saw a troop of cops come toward, like a line of army [sic] coming toward the house, and the last thing I saw was the guys and the girls were yelling," said young Michelle. "I heard the sound of the clubs against the people's bodies. My aunt rushed me to the house for me not to see anymore. Then my cousin ran into his house. I saw blood on his shirt. The cops only lying [*sic*] about everything that they said. Don't believe them. I even know they're lying. And I am only nine," Michelle defiantly explained.[76]

In such a context, the work of the Ad Hoc Committee on Chicano Rights quickly transferred to leadership for a community campaign to seek retribution for the National City Police shooting of a Puerto Rican youth, Luis "Tato" Rivera, in 1975. The manner in which barrio residents summoned Baca and the Ad Hoc Committee's assistance, including Tato Rivera's close friends, family and parents, and others revealed the community base that resulted from years of work in MAPA, LRUP, and CASA Justicia in the late 1960s and early 1970s. It also signaled the origins of the CCR as an important organization that emerged due to the random and sustained legal violence they consistently encountered—whether from immigration agents or local police—in their interactions with the ethnic Mexican community in the 1970s San Diego area.

This engagement with racialized state violence developed as Baca and Chicano movement activists gained invaluable experience in their various community-based activities in the working-class suburb of National City. As explored in earlier chapters, Baca's print shop, which was next door to CASA Justicia, served as a central place of community mobilization and political activity from the time Baca first became involved in Chicano movement activities in the late 1960s through MAPA, LRUP, and the Ad Hoc Committee on Chicano Rights. Meetings were held there and organizational planning was fostered as part of the day-to-day operations of the print shop. In this way, Aztec Printing served double duty as Baca's place of work where much of the *movimiento* (movement) literature—flyers, newsletters, brochures, protest signs—were created and as a key site where activists developed and shared their particular visions of a Chicano/Mexicano political future. Located in the centralized business district of National City and surrounded by the residential space of Chicano/Mexicano barrios, "the shop" played an important role in grounding Baca and the Ad Hoc Committee's political activity, exemplifying the goal of building a movement based on the everyday lives of working-class residents.

The Ad Hoc Committee's action in the Rivera case reveals how many community members looked to these activist leaders operating visibly out of the Aztec Printing shop for leadership and guidance on dealing with the many injustices they faced. Only about seven square miles of land, National City sits just five miles south of San Diego city limits along the coast of the San Diego Bay where it extends south. Most of the residential and business zones of the city lie between Interstate 5, which passes north–south as it grips the Pacific coast, and the parallel Interstate 805, which is about two miles east. Within this area, National City Boulevard runs north–south and Highland Avenue runs parallel to it a few blocks eastward. These are the main business, civic, and municipal areas of National City, with Aztec Printing located on 1837 Highland Ave in 1975. To the south is California State Route 54, finished in 1994, stretching east–west along the Sweetwater River, which flows into the San Diego Bay. South of the river is the highly ethnic Mexican populated city of Chula Vista, which extends to the community of San Ysidro, a pene-exclave of the City of San Diego since 1957, which directly reaches the border with Mexico and the city of Tijuana, where I-805 merges with I-5 on the way to the border crossing.[77] The border with Tijuana is about ten miles south of National City. By 1980, the "Hispanic" population in National City would reach 38 percent of the population there and was on the verge of passing the 40 percent "white" population that resided there. In 2010, that breakdown was 63 percent "Hispanic" and 10 percent "white."[78]

Baca reflectively describes National City as a "plantation . . . which dramatized . . . the political-social condition for Chicanos that lived here."[79] With regard to the police in National City, Baca explains the "plantation" analogy: "I've always told people that National City doesn't have a police department. . . . It's got an occupying army." Baca explains the problem is rooted in the fact that the officers do not live in National City. They live in area suburbs, he claims: "They don't cut their grass here. They don't have friends and socialize here. Their wives don't shop here. Their children don't go to school here. They as a family do not go to church here. So, the only thing that they have vested is the almighty paycheck." Baca claims these officers come with attitudes about the large ethnic Mexican population in National City. "We know what they think of National City. Come on. Nasty city, that's what they think. . . . Gang members, illegal aliens, Mexicans," says Baca, "and the bad thing about it is most of those individuals come to work with that attitude."[80] San Diego Chicano movement activist Roberto Martínez, similarly asserts: "Police violence is nothing new in San Diego . . . at the root of the problem is the issue of accountability and oversight. . . . SDPD has the only authority to investigate citizen complaints. . . . the National City Police Department and Chula Vista Police department run close seconds in terms of police violence and lack of oversight."[81]

In this context, Luis "Tato" Rivera was killed by National City officer Craig Short on October 12, 1975. The victim of the sixth shooting by the

National City Police Department (NCPD) in just three years, Rivera, age twenty, was killed six blocks from a reported purse snatching at about 1 A.M. that Sunday morning.[82] The theft occurred outside the recreation hall of St. Anthony Roman Catholic Church as reported by fourteen-year-old Margarita Torres, whose mother, Maria Torres, rented the hall for the evening for a private birthday party. Margarita said two purses were stolen and that they belonged to her sister and a cousin.[83] Witnesses attending the party said they saw a man eating when he suddenly grabbed the two purses and ran out.[84] There was only a three-minute time span between the call to police and the moment Rivera was shot.[85] Police approached Rivera, who was near the scene, and claim that upon confronting him, he ran. Suspected of the theft, Rivera was ordered to freeze by Officer Craig Short as he left the area. As he fled, Rivera was shot once in the back with Short's .357 Magnum. The shot went through his body and exited, hitting a nearby house. Rivera kept running after he was shot, but police caught up with him as he collapsed a few blocks from the church. One witness who lived near the sidewalk where Rivera fell said two ethnic Mexican men, presumably part of the group at the recreation hall in the church who reported the theft, were asked by police if the wounded suspect fit the description of the individual who stole the purses.[86] The two men reportedly said: "No, this is not him. He was taller and skinnier."[87] Rivera was unarmed and dead on arrival at Paradise Valley Hospital.[88] A witness said there was about a three-second time lapse between the order to freeze and the shots.[89] Tato's father, forty-eight-year-old Jesús Rivera, revealed that Rivera had been harassed by National City police before. He also said that witnesses reported that his son did not have the purse he was suspected of stealing, only a necklace around his neck and about ninety-five cents in change. The purses were later found on a lawn nearby the church.[90] Sobbing, Jesús exclaimed: "They got the wrong guy, there has to be an investigation. If they kill your son, you have to be angry. The way he was killed, you have to be angry."[91] Jesús also said that Tato lived with him and his mother, Maria, and was engaged to nineteen-year-old Linda Aragon. The Rivera family moved to National City from Puerto Rico when Luis was a child.[92] National City Police leaders announced a day after the shooting that the officer in the shooting would remain anonymous and stay on full duty as the shooting was to be investigated.[93]

Ad Hoc Committee chairman Herman Baca was in Los Angeles visiting family the weekend the shooting occurred. Baca stated in interviews just following the shooting, "When I returned Monday I found the phones ringing off the hook." The Ad Hoc Committee reportedly received "hundreds of phone calls."[94] Baca also recalled that Monday morning after the shooting, on October 13, Rivera's devastated and angered friends waited for him to arrive at his print shop for another day's work. The youth gave their accounts of the shooting and what occurred. He was asked by the youth to address this issue to bring justice to the situation in the face of the impunity of the police and the larger local power structure. Baca, while sympathetic, replied that he would only act upon the request of the young man's parents. He recalled: "Boom! All the focus came here [to National City]. People came out of the woodwork. . . . I got there that morning. Seventy-five kids were there. 'You've got to say something. You've got to do something' [they said]. I said, 'No, I ain't going to do nothing until the parents request or ask.' So, now that's a Monday morning, okay . . . and so that day was like a hectic day . . . just like it was a dam had burst uphill and . . . the water just came downhill. It's as simple as that." Baca explained that by the afternoon around one hundred to one hundred and fifty people were around his shop, frustrated and infuriated, and asking, "What are we going to do?" "My thing was and always has been that you have to have a mandate," Baca explained. "Don't matter if it's even two persons, but it's a mandate. You're not doing it because that's your opinion or that's your feeling, then it becomes an 'I' thing instead of a 'we' thing. So I said, 'No.' I says, 'Let's call a community meeting, you know, and see what the community wants to do.'"[95]

By that afternoon, Luis's father, Jesus Rivera, said, according to Baca, "do whatever was necessary" to gain justice for his son.[96] The decision by community members, local barrio youth, Rivera's family, and other concerned residents to approach Baca revealed the localized community base gained from earlier activism, and especially his vocal presence in print and local news media. Baca recalled that at the time that he was asked to assist with the Rivera case, following the campaign against Mayor Wilson and Chief Hoobler, there had been a lull in Ad Hoc activity and that he and his close friend Carlos "Charlie" Vásquez were basically, "for the long term," running the organization.[97] That would change drastically with the Justice for Luis "Tato" Rivera campaign. Baca's presence in the community as a small business owner and service provider, and as an activist and facilitator between the media and borderlands ethnic Mexican communities revealed an approach to political mobilization that was locally rooted and engaged with the everyday needs and experiences of the working-class racialized communities.

Following the request given by the Rivera family, Baca and volunteers, especially youth who were friends with Tato, passed out flyers throughout the area community calling for a meeting at the local St. Anthony's Catholic Church.[98] Baca and the Ad Hoc Committee delivered a letter to National City Mayor Kile Morgan inviting him to the meeting as well. "As the top ranking official of National City," the letter wrote, "we feel that the community deserves answers to this tragic incident."[99] The Ad Hoc Committee apparently sent an invitation to the chief of National City police as well, as one news source reported that Baca asked whether any representatives of Mayor Morgan's office or the police department were present, to which no one answered. The meeting took place on Tuesday, October 14, 1973, in the same church where the purse theft took place that led police to pursue and kill young Rivera. Baca recalled that the meeting was "jam-packed" with three hundred to six hundred area residents, along with local press and media.[100] Present was Tato Rivera's father, Jesús, and his fiancée, Linda Aragon.

Many people spoke at the meeting, and a key issue that emerged was how Tato was harassed and threatened by police in the past and how broader community problems with the police were commonplace. Baca was quoted, "A lot of people know this is not the first time the police have acted irresponsibly." Eddie Pérez, a friend of Tato's, stated, "They've [the police] told me 'I'm gonna get you, I'm gonna get you Tato. Honest, they've told me this." Speaking on the broader prevalence of police harassment like this, Tato's fiancée, Linda Aragon, stated: "Pretty soon they're going to get you too. Don't talk, do something . . . I don't want anybody to die."[101]

Through a show of hands or heavy applause, one news source reported, the meeting attendees decided to call for a county grand jury investigation, as requested by Tato's father, Jesús; a federal Civil Rights Commission investigation; an independent investigation by a committee of community residents; and the dismissal of the chief of the NCPD, John F. Leisman. Jesús Rivera spoke at the end of the meeting, thanking the community for attending and exclaiming: "Something has to be done about the killings they are doing here. Next week it will be me or you or him—anyone in the community."[102] It is quite noteworthy that the attendees pointed to quotidian experiences with legal violence and structural analysis at the root of the problem by insisting that this case was part of a larger practice. As legal scholar Ian Haney López asserts in his study of the Chicano movement, "the massive police presence, the constant police brutality, the hostile judges and the crowded jails convinced Mexicans that they were not white."[103] I would add that immigration law enforcement was interlocked with the legal violence that Haney López is describing here, creating the material experiences of race.

Another demand that emerged from the Tuesday meeting was that the city council reveal the name of the officer involved in the shooting. Again, up to that point, officials chose not to release his name to protect the integrity of the investigation. According to Baca, somebody at the meeting remembered that there was a National City Council meeting going on right at that moment. The group, full of outrage, decided to march from the church to city hall to demand that local politicians divulge who killed Tato Rivera and to present the other demands. The compact proximity of National City, in particular the location of St. Anthony's church, where the meeting was, city hall, and the site where Tato was shot located within blocks of each other made marching with large numbers of people feasible. On the way to the city hall, the group stopped at the site where Rivera was killed, viewing the bullet hole that had passed through him and into a nearby house. These physical marks of the violence inflicted on this community reflected the intensifying contestation for space as local residents decided to confront both organs of the state and its policing mechanisms, and in effect, attempted to reclaim their neighborhoods. The group, from one hundred to one hundred fifty people, barged into the city council meeting, surprising the council members as hundreds of local residents, especially youth, packed the room full. Baca remembered: "So all the kids, we just packed that place, man. The kids were behind the city councilmen. They were just surrounded, you know. So I got up there and told them we demanded to know who shot Luis 'Tato' Rivera. 'Well you know, we can't divulge that' [the council said]. 'Well, you better divulge it, because it, because this isn't going away' [answered Baca]."[104] The group also articulated the other demands, to which the city council responded that "it is out of our hands" because it was being investigated by the county district attorney. Baca recalled singling out the only Mexican American member of the city council, Louis Camacho, asking him what his position was. According to Baca, Camacho expressed that as the only Mexican-origin council person, he was sorry, but "his hands were tied."[105]

The anger and participation of Tato's friends in the neighborhood reveal that ethnic Mexican youth were particularly motivated to express their disdain for police treatment of the community. Baca remembered one young man who, after the group left city hall, apologized to Baca for yelling "you f'ing pigs!" and calling the city council "white racists." "I didn't mean, you know, to mess things up back there," the young man said, to which Baca assured him not to worry about it. The young man then pleaded to Baca, asking, "What can I do to help?"[106] Baca recalled that this particular community member was known among barrio residents for having "developed into one of San Diego's prime 'druggists' . . . or 'street pharmacists.'"[107] Baca replied to his desire to help by asking him to sit in the back of the church recreation center where the group was returning and informing the young man: "I'm going to make an appeal for people to help us out with some money. Now, you get back there and you figure out how much money you're going to give us, okay?" Baca remembered that the young man contributed $500. The group raised about $3,000 that evening, and the Ad Hoc Committee was charged with figuring out what to do next.[108] They had the demands, but the group decided to get more community input to make a collective decision about the course of action to be taken up.[109]

The Ad Hoc Committee circulated petitions to the National City community as well as to other areas in the San Diego area to test the degree of support. In a 1976 interview, Baca attributed discontent among the community as related to the "cover up" that National City police and city officials conducted in their decision not to reveal the officer's name or divulge any information.[110] Media coverage revealed witnesses of the shooting event stating the "almost instantaneous" time lapse between the call by Officer Short to "Freeze" and the firing of the shot.[111] These witnesses also revealed how the two men who were part of the party where the purse theft occurred identified that Rivera did not fit the description of the man they saw steal the items. The Ad Hoc Committee also wrote letters to the Grand Jury, the U.S. Attorney General, the federal Civil Rights Commission, and elected officials.[112] This coverage and outreach brought significant publicity to the Justice for Luis "Tato" Rivera campaign.

The publicity also led to threats made against Ad Hoc Committee activists and their families. Baca's brother answered the phone at Aztec Printing around this time and was asked, "Are you Mexican?" When the brother answered yes, the caller warned, "Well, you and every F——[sic] Mexican in that building is going to die." The activists moved forward through such threats, jokingly questioning whether the caller had a special bomb that only kills Mexicans since there were two Anglos in the building at the time the call was made.[113]

After circulating these petitions and community feedback, the Ad Hoc Committee called another meeting on October 19, 1975, about a week after the shooting where about 150 new people showed up concerned about the incident and wanting to join the campaign. Soon after, a demonstration was planned due to the tenseness of the community and campaign members. On October 29, about 1,500 demonstrators again met at St. Anthony's church and marched to city hall. Baca exclaimed to the mayor and council members: "Your action has bordered on total irresponsibility. We accuse you of negligence of your constituted duties. You have shown no leadership. You have passed the buck."[114] The petition signed by about 2,000 people was presented to the council, reissuing the four original demands and adding that not only the officer's name be released but that he be suspended without pay.[115] The council declined to act on such demands, awaiting the ongoing investigation. Baca exclaimed, "They [the city council] have told the police 'if you want to get a vacation, shoot a Mexican,'" referring to the as-of-yet-identified Officer Short being put on paid administrative leave during the grand jury investigation.[116] The marchers were described as "noisy" as they marched the nine blocks from the church to city hall, again stopping to memorialize where Rivera was shot, and setting up in an empty parking lot outside city hall where speeches and chants of "We want justice!" rang out over loud speakers.[117] The march and demonstration was peaceful despite concerns from the city attorney of National City and equal concerns from Chicano/a activists that police would interfere and incite violence that some of them had experienced in the violent Chicano Moratorium march in 1970. Activists instructed the police to get off the streets if they wanted a nonviolent march and the community organizers arranged 125 monitors to assure that the demonstration would be nonviolent.[118]

Before this march, the now much larger member base of the Ad Hoc Committee voted to initiate a recall of the mayor and the city council should they not act on their demands. The idea of a recall was suggested at an earlier meeting by National City resident and former mayoral candidate Ruben Rubio. Since then, the committee had formed a subcommittee to study the details of such an action, and threatened such an action as they confronted the city council again during the October 29 demonstration and march.

The committee moved forward on the recall, especially after Officer Short's name was finally released on November 1, when the grand jury announced its decision not to indict him. With this decision made, District Attorney Edwin Miller decided to charge Officer Short with manslaughter. The Ad Hoc Committee called the grand jury's decision "shameful" and "unacceptable." The jury selection process was criticized when Baca claimed only five Mexican-origin people had served in that body in the last 104 years. They also criticized District Attorney Miller's charge of manslaughter, arguing that the minimum charge should have been murder one. Baca and other activists had criticized Miller before, beginning with his decision in 1971–72 not to charge a Border Patrol agent who sexually assaulted Tijuana resident Martha Elena Parra López (see chapter 2). The Ad Hoc Committee also saw Miller's charge of manslaughter as a "significant victory for the community," crediting the immense pressure the Justice for Luis "Tato" Rivera campaign had put on the district attorney.[119] Jesús Rivera, Tato's father, said of the D.A.'s charge: "I'm very happy over the action taken by the district attorney. . . . I hope justice will be served. If anything I think National City police will think twice before they shoot somebody again."[120]

The campaign had attained an important level of publicity and mobilized concern and solidarity among a number of activists and concerned community members. Beyond the Mexican American/Chicano community, the San Diego County Human Relations Commission, the Union of Pan Asian Communities, the local NAACP (National Association for the Advancement of Colored People), and the National Conference of Christians and Jews were "seriously concerned over the circumstances surrounding the tragic and fatal shooting of Mr. Luis Roberto Rivera and the subsequent lack of disclosure of the facts concerning this incident by National City officials." The commission announced a series of resolutions, including the following: "be it further resolved that this Commission work toward accountability in the development of a citizens' complaint process to assure access and equal treatment."[121] Revealing the kind of pressure he and the city council were under, Mayor Kile Morgan actually invited Baca and the Ad Hoc Committee to give input on the possible creation of a similar commission on human relations in National City and encouraged them to appoint a representative from their organizations to serve. This reveals the pressure the mayor was under due to community protests and outcry. The mayor's engagement with Baca, the Ad Hoc Committee and his willingness to provide resources for a commission demonstrates an attempt to respond to and manage the real pressure the mobilizations placed on local officials.

Indeed, the shooting gained statewide and national attention. U.S. representative Herman Badillo, the first Puerto Rican elected to Congress in 1970, took great interest and expressed concern for the Tato Rivera case. Badillo, the representative of the 21st District in New York, wrote to the United States Attorney General to encourage the Department of Justice to investigate the case, as requested by the Ad Hoc Committee. Stating that after engaging in "communication" with the Ad Hoc Committee, Badillo articulated his belief that the "request has merit" and asked that Attorney General Edward Levi send him a copy of the response to the request.[122]

Badillo, who would be a founding member of the Hispanic Congressional Caucus later in 1976, also sent a letter to the U.S. Commission on Civil Rights Commission urging them to also conduct an investigation of the shooting.[123] Finally, the Congressman informed local officials about his concern, including Mayor Morgan and San Diego County district attorney Edwin Miller.[124] Asking each to keep him updated about the proceedings surrounding the case, Badillo wrote to Miller, "I have been contacted by representatives of the local minority community and I share their concern that a fair and thorough investigation of the matter be undertaken."[125] Mayor Morgan responded to the U.S. representative's request, sending an update just three days following being contact by Badillo.[126] Badillo's correspondence revealed that national actors were aware and involved in the proceedings of Tato's shooting, a testament to the mobilization that the Ad Hoc Committee led with community members and allies.

At the state level, a special hearing was conducted by the California Assembly Criminal Justice Committee discussing what constitutes justifiable lethal force among police officers in direct reference to the Rivera shooting. The hearing was requested by San Diego County assemblymen Peter Chacón and Waddie Deddah. As explored in chapter 4, Chacón and Baca had sparred over opposite positions concerning the Dixon Arnett bill in the early 1970s. Baca, who briefly served as campaign manager in his first campaign, credited Chacón's advocacy for the Justice for Tato Rivera campaign, however, stating, "He made a real attempt to help out on his own, personally and politically. As long as I've known him, he never took such a strong position. He wrote the Grand Jury, the Mayor, and all the city councilmen. He pointed out that he had received many complaints from the Chicano community about police harassment, brutality and impropriety on the city's part. In that regard I think Chacón should be complimented."[127] Chacón had dismissed Chicano/a activist criticism of law enforcement conducting immigration policing just years before, but possibly shifted his tone after several years in which these same activists brought harassment and brutality to light case by case. The state Assembly committee hearing reveals again the success of the Justice for Tato Rivera campaign in gaining broad attention and concern for such issues.

Chacón went further in calling attention to police brutality against communities of color when he wrote to SDPD chief William B. Kolander condemning an August 1975 event that came to light after an investigation on November 14, 1975, when one of his officers claimed he accidently fired his gun when in pursuit of a fourteen-year-old African American youth. The teenage child, who was not injured in the incident, was the son of former NAACP San Diego chapter president and board trustee of the San Diego Community College District, Charles Reid. Officer A. O. Galloway said he pulled his gun when pursuing the teenager, who was riding a motorcycle when he considered firing a warning shot, but chose not to. However, the gun accidently went off, according to Galloway, before he returned it to his holster. Galloway received a formal reprimand, to which the elder Reid expressed criticism of Chief Kolendar, stating, "I am not satisfied with the way the incident has been handled." Writing concerning this incident, and comparing it to the recent shooting of Luis Rivera, Chacón warned Kolendar, "The minority community, Chicanos, Blacks and Asians, are carefully monitoring incidents of this type and do not intend to permit the victimizing of our young people by 'trigger-happy' policemen."[128] Indeed, activists discovered that Officer Short, who was involved in another fatal shooting of an armed suspect just nine months before the Rivera shooting, was nicknamed "Trigger" by his fellow officers.[129]

While the stakes were raised due to local, state, and national conversations ignited by the Ad Hoc Committee's mobilization efforts, this did not lead to a conviction of Officer Short for killing Luis "Tato" Rivera. Craig Short was exonerated by Judge T. Bruce Irendale, who based his ruling, in part, on Short's claim that Rivera could have created a hostage situation if permitted to escape into the residential area. In addition, Irendale corroborated Short's depiction of Rivera, referring to him as "an unpredictable heroin addict with a history of violence." In his testimony, Short claimed that he saw Rivera throw a purse into a yard and that while he was wearing a white shirt—not the yellow shirt the suspect reportedly was wearing—that he saw a yellow fabric in his hands. Short said he knew that Rivera was a "heroin addict" because he was aware that Tato and two other men were recently arrested in an area bar when they were preparing to inject the drug in the restroom. The officer claimed Rivera had to be physically restrained during that arrest. Short also said he received information that Rivera had once pistol-whipped his father with a .38 revolver when he responded to a trouble call in July of 1975. Rivera telephoned the police department the day after the July incident, denying the existence of the gun. Short responded to Rivera's claim by informing him that he should put his hands up if he ever gets stopped by police again. Short admitted that he never found a gun in Rivera's possession in his interactions with him and that he was aware that other police units were on their way to assist him when he decided to shoot Rivera. Judge Irendale used Short's claim that he advised Rivera months earlier to have his hands raised as a means of justifying the shooting. On this basis, Irendale argued, "the die was cast" and to rule otherwise "would set an impossible standard for law enforcement."[130]

A press conference was held on December 4, a day following the exoneration of Officer Short by the Ad Hoc Committee. Speaking for the committee, Baca exclaimed, "First and foremost let me state that it came as no surprise to us of the Chicano community . . . in the past 125 years no policeman has ever been convicted of killing a Chicano."[131] Describing the feelings of "shock," "insult," and "raw anger" coming from the Chicano community, Baca also described the "education" that activists and community members received about "how justice works in San Diego County." Baca asserted: "A Chicano, a Black, a poor working person cannot get justice in San Diego County. This is because there are two court systems, two justice systems in San Diego County, one for the rich and their servants, and one for the people." Questioning Judge Irendale's competency, he also highlighted that key witnesses were not permitted to give testimony in the proceedings, including Joe Harper, who witnessed the two Mexican men tell Short that the dying Rivera did not fit the description of the suspect, and Maria de Jesus Tejada, who witnessed the entire event. The "education" Baca spoke of called for putting the shooting in the context of systemic structural violence and further mobilizing for the recall effort. "We are of the opinion that Short is not an individual act [sic] but an attitude that resides in National City administration."[132] Baca later explained of the Judge's decision, "In going through the process of trying to get justice from the system, the community learned firsthand that it doesn't work."[133]

Recall

The exoneration of Officer Short led the Ad Hoc Committee to further mobilize for the recall of the National City council and mayor. A successful recall would have to gain signatures from 25 percent of registered voters in National City; in 1975, that equaled 1,756 by the end of that year. Baca stated that the committee had already collected 812 signatures in early December of 1975, and sought to mobilize an effort to get the rest of those needed by December 31.[134] The public petition to be signed accosted the National City council and the mayor for "condoning official lawlessness" and failing to "provide representative leadership."[135] In addition to these complaints, the Ad Hoc Committee added several other reasons for the recall, including "bias toward corporate interests in establishing zone regulations," "failure to provide for the safety of our school children," "insensitivity of the multicultural needs of our community," and "failure to provide adequate guidelines and policies for law enforcement officials."[136] The committee soon discovered that of the five city councilpersons, including the mayor, only three were eligible for recall given a rule that those up for reelection within six months were ineligible. Mayor Kile Morgan, Vice-Mayor Mike Dalla, and Councilmember Luther G. Reid were eligible for recall. Reid was known among activists for shooting and killing an unarmed African American youth, one death among the five individuals reportedly killed by NCPD since 1968, when acting as a reserve police officer.[137] Councilmembers Louis Camacho and Ralph Pinson were up for reelection in March 1976, so were ineligible to be recalled. The Ad Hoc Committee decided to run candidates against them. This called for mobilization of community members and activists to collect signatures for the petition throughout the National City community and register voters for support of their candidates in the March election.

The Ad Hoc Committee sought to garner wide "multicultural support" for the recall campaign, given the diversity of National City. In addition to being 38 percent "Hispanic" by 1980, National City was about 13 percent "Asian and Pacific Islander," mostly Filipino, about 9 percent "Black," and 40 percent "White."[138] Baca claimed that "Blacks, Filipinos, Chicanos" made up 52 percent of National City in 1976 and represented the constituency the Ad Hoc Committee sought to organize for the election. Baca elaborated: "We also wanted the support of the Anglo community and in general all concerned citizens. The initial effort for recall was Chicano-based but other ethnic groups quickly compiled their grievances against the established authorities in solidarity with the Chicano effort."[139]

A "Help List" reveals that the Ad Hoc Committee had about eighty individuals on hand to hit the streets to petition and build on voter registration efforts.[140] In addition to support garnered by area Chicano movement activists and the broader ethnic Mexican community, an important link was made when the Nia Cultural Organization, Black Power activists who were former members of Ron Karenga's US organization, came to assist the Ad Hoc Committee.[141] US—a premiere organization of the Black Power movement based in Southern California—sought a cultural revolution, calling for an alternative value system among African-descended people in the United States. The US also became known for the tragic outcomes in its rivalry with the Black Panther Party in Los Angeles in 1969.[142] Former US members, including Ken Msemaji, Fahari Jeffers, and Greg Akili, reorganized into Nia after Karenga was jailed in 1971.[143] Nia, the Swahili word for purpose, became a cadre of Amiri Baraka's national network of the Congress of African Peoples, reflecting ideological developments that combined cultural and anti-capitalist modes of struggle within Black Power activism in the 1970s. The ways struggles against police brutality brought together Chicano/a and black activists is significant in the conservative, militaristic, union-busting context of San Diego.[144] Nia leaders Ken Msemaji, Greg Akili, and Robert Tambuzi appear on the help list, and Baca recalled: "Police brutality was something happening in their community. It was something they could identify with. And they helped out with the recall and the voter registration and the political campaigns."[145]

Racialized structures of police violence would continue to deepen the ties created between the CCR and Nia in the Tato Rivera struggle as would be evidenced when San Diego police killed 21-year-old Tyrone Thomas in 1978. The shooting was similar to Rivera because Thomas was also fleeing as a suspect of burglarly. Thomas ran from the passenger side of a car after being pulled over. When patrolman Frank G. Christenson caught up with Thomas he hit him on the head with his revolver. As Thomas fell to the ground it was reported that the revolver than accidently discharged hitting him in the head and killing him instantly.[146] San Diego African American activists, with Nia leaders, put together a coalition for justice that included Baca and the CCR. Just three years following the Rivera incident, the coalition highlighted the overlapping struggle against police violence. They noted on a meeting agenda, "Throughout America Black and Brown people have been the victims of police killings, beatings, and other forms of brutality. The majority of these incidents are concluded by the police investigating themselves and justifying [sic] their actions. Over the years, murders such as that of Luis Tato Rivera and now Tyrone Thomas, have demonstrated the need for us to come together. We need each other for there is no one else to fill our needs and heal our hurts—but us . . ."[147]

The usage of "Black and Brown" and the reference to the Rivera case reveal the broader links being forged by black and Chicano/a activists. Baca, an official speaker at the justice for Tyrone Thomas community meeting, noted "Justice to the white power structure of this country means just us . . . Nobody can give us justice, we have to fight for it."[148] While Officer Christensen was exonerated, the struggle for Thomas reveals that Nia and the CCR continued to ally with one another to illuminate the ways racialized systems of policing created contexts where black and brown, and in the case of border policing citizen and noncitizen, solidarity was forged. The Rivera struggle and recall attempt was a site in which this generated, as Baca recalled Nia members working "on a daily basis" to "help out with the effort of the recall and registering people and doing the political legwork that had to be done. That issue went on for a good solid year from '75 to '76."[149] Baca describes the recall activists as mostly younger people "of a different generation and a different thinking."[150]

With a deadline on December 31, he recalled the effort to get the 1,756 registered voters required to sign the petition to recall as an "intensive voter drive" centered around the Aztec Printing shop as headquarters. With the money raised from donations from the community and grassroots fundraisers, Baca estimated that the committee raised and spent about $25,000 to fund the entire campaign, and the committee paid organizers to register people to vote and sign the petition. With the time press, the organizers met daily for a time and Baca remembered the camaraderie and atmosphere: "So people used to go out every night [and] get fifty, seventy-five, perhaps a hundred people would be at the shop and they would go out (to petition). And I remember afterwards, we used to have an old, we used to have an old refrigerator there at the old shop . . . and it was always full of beer. . . . Every night, people would come and that's how we used to end the evening or the night. Sit around and talk, drinking beer." Baca recalled the support given by Ruben and Connie Rubio, local owners of the Mexican restaurant "Little Mexico" by donating one hundred and fifty or so rolled "greasy" tacos the people called "the sliders." Sliders and beer would facilitate the collective space and exchange of ideas and experiences. "It was an education for a lot of people," Baca remembered. "They would tell their stories when they would go door to door. And how people would react. Some people would welcome them. Some people would slam the doors on their faces. Some people would accuse them of being communists, you know."[151]

Baca recalled the busy atmosphere of the campaign, and the many people who would come in, including his mentor, Bert Corona, and a Los Angeles contingent; Juan José Peña, La Raza Unida Party leader from New Mexico; and many students and other young people from the area. The Ad Hoc Committee surpassed the required signatures, reaching 1,829, and submitted the petition on New Year's Eve of 1975. A "massive number of people" again arrived at city hall and submitted the petition surrounded by media, and over one hundred of the organizers and supporters celebrated with a house party that evening.[152]

National City officials made the recall process as difficult as possible. Unfortunately for the Ad Hoc Committee, in late January 1976 the city clerk of National City, Ione Campbell, signed off on San Diego County registrar of voters R. T. Denny's determination that only 521 signatures on the petition were valid, while 1,308 were determined invalid because they had the wrong precinct numbers.[153] Ad Hoc Committee activists claimed that at the beginning of the recall campaign, Campbell had given them a misleading precinct map, causing the mistake. The committee filed suit against city officials with a decision to be made in county superior court on March 19.[154]

While the recall was tied up in court, the Ad Hoc Committee organized support for their own candidates and continued to register voters to compete against incumbents Louis Camacho and Ralph Pinson in their March 2 election. The criticism of Camacho in particular was stringent because he was the only Mexican American member of the city council and activists were accusing him of failing to represent the interests of his own community. Baca even claimed that Camacho sided with the rest of the city council so faithfully that he told Justice for Tato Rivera protesters at one point, "If you don't like it, go back to Mexico."[155] Ad Hoc Committee members Jesse Ramírez, former head of the Chicano Federation, and Dr. Oscar Cañedo, instructor at the nearby Southwestern Junior College in Chula Vista, were selected as candidates, urging residents to "Vote for Change!" Ramírez and Cañedo ran together, offering a broad-based platform that, according to their campaign brochure, sought to "Return Honesty and Integrity to the City Government," provide a "Better Quality Police Department," "Eliminate Favoritism towards Business Interests," and "Respond to the Will of the People," among other pledges.[156]

There was concern about systemic repression efforts against the recall and voter registration leading up to the March 2 election. In late February 1976, the Ad Hoc Committee collected several affidavits from their supporters who were visited by two men in white shirts and ties identifying themselves as members of the Deputy Registrar Voters Office. The majority of the stories the residents told in the affidavits described these men investigating households with larger numbers of people living there, as identified in the voter registration rolls. Ruth Rivera, for example, was visited, and was asked who lived in the home and about where her adult children and husband were, and where one of her sons worked. The man told her, "You sure have a house full here." When told by the officials that they were just checking because there were "too many people voting from the same house," Ruth replied, "There are 20 people living in other homes and they can vote." After completing their questioning, the men left.[157]

On other occasions, the officials told people not to vote. Many of the households visited had family members who were mobile, with family connections and work obligations in Tijuana and sometimes Los Angeles. Yet their main address was in their National City homes. The officials took it upon themselves on at least two occasions to inform these residents about who could and who should not vote. After describing who lived in her and her mother's household and that her uncles Manuel and David Ambriz were currently in Tijuana, one resting there from an injury, Alicia Reyes was informed that they could not vote. Alicia explained that Manuel Ambriz lived there with his adult children, her cousins, Victor and Dora, to whom the officials informed her that they could not vote either.[158] One of Alicia's cousins, Gilbert Ambriz, was an Ad Hoc Committee member and was searched and frisked by police when registering residents back in January of 1976.[159] Also, Juana Martínez was told that her four adult children should not vote after she told them that they were living with their father in Tijuana.[160] These kinds of interactions led the Ad Hoc Committee to request federal monitors from the Assistant Attorney General of Civil Rights in the U.S. Department of Justice in the upcoming election.[161]

The incumbents were able to hold off the challengers, including two other candidates who ran, George Waters and Phillip Miligan, with Camacho receiving the most votes of all six candidates at 2,752 and Pinson following with 2,614 out of 10,792 votes. Waters placed third, Cañedo, fourth; Milligan, fifth; and Ramírez, last. The candidates to receive the most and second-most votes were placed in office. But Ad Hoc Committee activists claimed a victory in gaining almost one-quarter of the votes for their candidates in such a short amount of time. Baca exclaimed: "The National City mayor's political machine delivered the block vote for the incumbents. This machine is financially supported by non-resident business people and has been organized for 10 years. In a period of less than three months, supported by only small individual contributions we have successfully organized the support of a large block of voters. This is a significant victory!"[162] Calling this election "round one," the Ad Hoc Committee concentrated its efforts again on the recall.

The Ad Hoc Committee's suit against the city was ruled on March 19 in their favor when Judge Douglas R. Woodworth called the invalidation of more than 1,300 signatures a "bona fide misunderstanding" on the part of Ione Campbell, the city clerk. However, the judge also ruled that the Ad Hoc

Committee had to meet the new year's minimum requirement of 2,704 signatures in 1976, now with 9,616 total registered voters, rather than the 1,756 required based on the 1975 number of registered voters, 7,021.[163] Even though the committee was allowed to fix the invalidated signatures with the wrong precinct numbers, they were still short of the new threshold, at 1,829. They appealed the requirement to abide by the new 1976 threshold, but in July the Fourth District Court of Appeal ruled against the appeal, effectively nullifying the campaign unless the committee decided to start again from scratch.[164]

The Ad Hoc Committee chose to abandon the recall effort, but built on the mobilization that the Justice for Luis "Tato" Rivera had achieved through the local, state, and national spotlight it held over the last nine months. "We are at the point where we must convert the community's emotional response to police brutality into a lasting organization," cried Baca in July of 1976. While the Ad Hoc Committee continued to pressure the local National City government, continued brutality and rising national rhetoric scapegoating "illegal aliens" would continue to lead the cadre out of their neighborhoods and increasingly into the national spotlight with a presidential election approaching.

Craig Short stayed with the National City police force and moved his way up, reaching the role of acting chief of police in 2003 when appointed by the current police chief, who went on medical leave. Short was one of two under consideration for taking up a longer-term position as acting chief pending approval by city officials.[165] Ironically, former Ad Hoc Committee member Luis Natividad sat on the city council that was considering Short's appointment, and Nick Inzunza, the son of Ralph Inzunza, another important Ad Hoc Committee member in the mid-1970s, sat as mayor. Herman Baca spoke out, asserting: "I remember two young men named Luis. One an innocent young man gunned down and ruthlessly killed in 1975, and the other a Chicano activist who used to believe in justice and the will of the people."[166] Soon after, Short's candidacy for chief was rescinded.

From Recall to Repression: The Local and the Global

Aside from exhibiting the community-based nature of the Ad Hoc Committee's activism, the Justice for Luis "Tato" Rivera case revealed how local police repression was interlaced with international policing practices as experienced by the ethnic Mexican community in the San Diego borderlands. Baca and the Ad Hoc Committee on Chicano Rights acted on the

Rivera case, as they had to the law enforcement repression experienced by undocumented immigrants. Whether brutalized by National City Police, San Diego Sheriff's, or Border Patrol agents, the Ad Hoc Committee's inclusion of Chicanos and Mexicanos as part of the same community led to engagement with the simultaneously localized and global ramifications of state violence because it was an issue of expediency as directly experienced by borderlands residents. Cases of cooperation between the Border Patrol and local police abounded in the early to mid-1970s and were a common practice in the San Diego border region. San Diego Chicano/Mexicano activists had struggled against such acts throughout the first half of the 1970s. In January of 1973, for example, Expedito Madrigal signed an affidavit that he and friend Juan Luis Rodríguez were stopped by San Diego Police and interrogated about their citizenship status. Rodríguez informed an Officer Phenix that he was a United States citizen. After "not being satisfied with the explanation given by Mr. Rodriguez," Phenix began questioning Madrigal, who showed him a border-crossing card that was valid for the next seventy-two hours. Phenix decided to detain the two men for four hours until immigration officials arrived. They were released soon after. Critical of these actions, Madrigal, a Tijuana resident, remarked: "The San Diego Police officer made a decision, and with no experience on immigration procedures he arrested and detained Mr. Rodriguez and myself for a period of 4 hours. . . . A San Diego Police Sergeant in charge of that particular shift released us with the usual 'I am sorry this happened, we apologize.' "[167]

The link between local police and border enforcement policies of the INS was particularly experienced by youth. Just as the Rivera case revealed the conflicted relationship between youth of color and local police, Border Patrol agents also maintained a strained relationship with youth. In February 1974, seventeen-year-old Antonio Bustamante and his fourteen-year-old brother, Benjamin, walked home from the local San Ysidro Park where they had just finished playing basketball. A Border Patrolman named Bradshaw noticed them and followed them home. Upon the boys return, the Patrolman proceeded to kick down the door to their home, enter the house, and shut the door. He accused the youth of being "illegal aliens" and allegedly pushed their mother, who was witnessing the event while he used profane language in his accusations. San Diego police officers soon arrived, and with the assistance of the Border Patrol agent, struck the boys and continued to verbally abuse them with accusations of being "illegal." Soon after, however, it was discovered that the boys were United States citizens and the law enforcement agents explained to the boys that it had been a misunderstanding.[168]

These incidents reveal how the intersection of immigration policing forces and local law enforcement at the San Diego borderlands put Chicano/a activists in a position to confront simultaneously local and international practices of repression. For this reason, activists such as Baca simultaneously addressed the interconnected repression at the hands of police, such as the case of Tato Rivera, struggles with Chiefs Duffy and Hoobler, Mayor Wilson, and the Border Patrol. In fact, Chicano/Mexicano activists addressed both issues simultaneously due to the long history of cooperation between local police and the Border Patrol. As these activists saw it, both local and border policing were long-practiced mechanisms for controlling and subordinating the local ethnic Mexican population.

Emergence of the Committee on Chicano Rights

After navigating the fractured political terrain of the mid-1970s and eventually withdrawing from the efforts of MAPA, CASA, and LRUP, the Ad Hoc Committee on Chicano Rights evolved into the Committee on Chicano Rights (CCR) in 1976. It marked a transformation from an ad hoc coalition of participant organizations concerned about engaging immigration and police brutality issues to a coherent member-based grassroots organization. Remembering that many activists from MAPA, CASA Justicia, and LRUP "moved on to social service careers, educational careers, and what have you," Baca describes the group of activists that the Justice for Luis "Tato" Rivera struggle brought in as a "second wave" of Chicano/a youth and activists. Officially founded by a base group of older friends and activists—Baca, Albert García, Carlos "Charlie" Vasquez, Ralph Inzunza, and Albert Puente, the CCR also featured new activists such as student and participant in the Chicano arts movement David Avalos. Avalos remembered getting involved with the Ad Hoc Committee after working with the University of California, San Diego, Chicano student newspaper, *Voz Fronteriza*. He first got involved with the Justice for Luis "Tato" Rivera struggle, and it is interesting to note that he was attracted to the Ad Hoc Committee group because the group had a sense of humor and was located in his home town. Avalos recalled the personal transformation he experienced, beginning with the Justice for Tato Rivera struggle:

I think that here [with the Ad Hoc Committee] is where I began to develop a sense of myself as connected in ways I had never thought of. Developed a sense of myself as operating within a context of history and of society, of politics and economics, of culture and of art. And I began to see that, that what we were doing in this one little town in Southern California around this one case of an individual being killed by a police officer connected us to the entire Chicano Movement. It connected us to the history of Mexico. And it connected us to the black civil rights movement. It connected us to U.S. history. And it connected us to [the fact that] people from around the world at various times in history were faced with these sorts of things. And it was a tremendous feeling. It was a tremendous feeling to feel that I was truly part of history by virtue of doing something in my own home town.[169]

The CCR was established primarily "To secure and protect for all Chicanos (i.e., *Raza*, Mexican American, etc.) and their families, their rights, and privileges vested on them by the Constitution and laws of our Country."[170] This mission statement and bylaws reveal that the CCR was not conceived of as necessarily a radical organization. Its stated purpose, "To foster and perpetuate the basic principles of democracy, i.e., political freedom of the individual and equal social and economic opportunities for all citizens," depicts the organization as a liberal American-based civil rights organization. Indeed, the organization aimed to improve the "political, educational, social and economic conditions of the Chicano community" simply by "encouraging their participation in political, community, and civic affairs."[171] This plan of action to encourage "participation" implied entrance into existing institutions with no mention of engaging in a larger strategy to foment structural change. Even the tones of separatism present in many Chicano movement organizations' notion of Aztlán or cultural connections to Mexico over the United States were not present. Instead, the CCR operated in line with the established constitution of "our Country," implying a more or less traditional American national orientation and plan of action.

As discussed with regard to Baca's activism up to the mid-1970s, however, the notion of a self-determined Chicano community and the conceptualization of the "Chicano" community as a transnational population of racialized citizens and noncitizens shows that the CCR pushed forth questions that ultimately subverted the logic of the liberal state framework. In its transnational conception of community and its focus on emphasizing the differential material experiences of working-class racialized communities, the CCR challenged notions that political borders and liberal state categories of citizenship were encased realities. In this way, the CCR sought to engage with the various tentacles of the U.S. state by insisting on autonomy and a process of community self-determination for Chicanos and Mexicanos. Its very creation was based on addressing the localized context in which ethnic Mexicans, whether U.S. citizens or Mexican migrants, collectively struggled against legal violence in the border region. Its activities emerged from and came more directly to focus on the intermingled repression by the Border Patrol and local police through policies targeting "illegal aliens" and other racialized categories of criminalization. CCR members recalled its foundation as a "reaction to the co-optation of the government funded community organizations by the traditional political apparatus . . . establish(ing) itself as a community-based, non-profit, non-government funded, volunteer membership organization committed to developing social and political awareness in the Chicano/Mexicano/Latino communities."[172] The addition of the term "Latino" may have been a prelude to the expanding notions of identity and community that Chicano/Mexicano activists were exploring as the immigration debate ventured once again outside of the borderlands to the halls of Congress and the popular press in the wider United States, Mexico, and beyond by the late 1970s.

· · · · · ·

Baca and the emergent CCR addressed the intersecting, multiple forms of oppression by local policing and immigration policing by engaging the community at the everyday level, organizing a decision-making process, and engaging in protest, boycott, and consistent demand to varying levels of the U.S. state, from local to federal, for a democratic engagement with the community as the only way to bring justice to these populations. In a context in which a variety of Chicano/Mexicano organizations grappled with the heightening outcry over "illegal aliens" and internal fragmentation, the CCR emerged in the mid-1970s with a solution based in transnational conceptions of "community" that emphasized engagement with the daily experiences of working-class ethnic Mexicans, local autonomy, and collective leadership. As the immigration issue hit national proportions with congressional debates over federal proposals that sought employer sanctions on businesses and increased budgets for the INS throughout the mid-1970s, the election of Jimmy Carter in 1976 solidified the national spotlight on the localized issues that Raza Sí, Migra No activists had engaged through

MAPA, LRUP, CASA Justicia, and the Ad Hoc Committee on Chicano Rights since the first years of the 1970s. The increasing outside repression from police and federal agents, and the arrival of the "illegal alien" debate on the desk of a newly elected president, pushed the deeply fragmented elements of the Chicano/Mexicano population to experiment with new forms of mobilization intended to coalesce around the issue of immigration as part and parcel of the movement for Chicano self-determination. The convergence of these forces during the Carter administration propelled Baca and the CCR to the forefront of (inter)national Chicano/Mexicano mobilizations and established San Diego as an important pole of activism that sought to rectify the contradictions of immigration policy in the late 1970s.

Herman Baca and Bert Corona (Box 54, Folder 10, Herman Baca Papers, Mandeville Special Collections Library, University of California, San Diego).

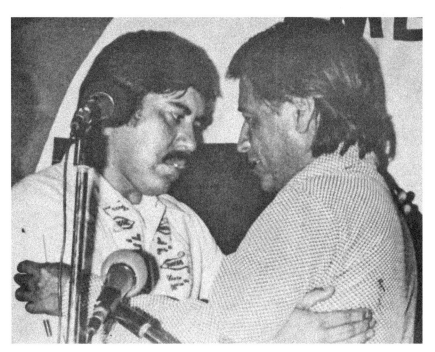

Herman Baca and César Chávez embrace in a moment of agreement at a rally for Proposition 14 on September 17, 1976 (Box 53, Folder 17, Herman Baca Papers, University of California, San Diego).

Norma Mena (Cazares) in front of CASA Justicia and Aztec Printers in National City (Box 53, Folder 9, Herman Baca Papers, Mandeville Special Collections Library, University of California, San Diego).

Organizers register voters for the San Diego La Raza Unida Party. Norma Mena Cazares and Roger Cazares are on the far right (Box 56, Folder 8, Herman Baca Papers, Mandeville Special Collections Library, University of California, San Diego).

A coalition of Chicano/a activists call for the firing of San Diego police chief Ray Hoobler for apprehensions of undocumented residents in the mid-1970s. Carlos Vásquez, representing CASA Justicia, sits third from the left; Herman Baca, representing MAPA, is next to him (Box 55, Folder 9, Herman Baca Papers, Mandeville Special Collections Library, University of California, San Diego).

Protest march against the National City Police killing of Luis "Tato" Rivera, 1976 (Box 59, Folder 1, Herman Baca Papers, Mandeville Special Collections Library, University of California, San Diego).

Ken Msemaji, an unidentified woman, Herman Baca, and Greg Akili at a meeting
to resist the KKK's announcement that they would patrol the border. Msemaji
and Akili of the Nia organization began working with Baca and the CCR
(Committee on Chicano Rights) after the "Justice for Luis 'Tato' Rivera" struggle
and saw intersections with the struggle against the Klan between the black and
Chicano/a communities (Box 60, Folder 12, Herman Baca Papers, Mandeville
Special Collections Library, University of California, San Diego).

Protestor of the KKK's announcement of a border watch program, 1977 (Box 60, Folder 13, Herman Baca Papers, Mandeville Special Collections Library, University of California, San Diego).

A protestor holds a sign designed by Chicana artist Yolanda
López against President Jimmy Carter's immigration
proposal in 1977 (Box 60, Folder 13, Herman Baca Papers,
Mandeville Special Collections Library, University of
California, San Diego).

Rally for the National Protest against the Carter Curtain, 1979. In the front row are the following speakers from left to right: unidentified, Ester Martínez, Armando Navarro, Corky Gonzalez, Herman Baca, Bert Corona, Antonio Rodríguez, and an unidentified man (Box 58, Folder 4, Herman Baca Papers, Mandeville Special Collections Library, University of California, San Diego).

Image from the National Chicano Immigration Conference, San Diego, 1980 (Box 57, Folder 8, Herman Baca Papers, Mandeville Special Collections Library, University of California, San Diego).

Top, Ruben Sandoval testifies to an expert panel of Chicano/a community activists at the National Chicano Immigration Tribunal, 1981. Below, a woman gives her testimony (Box 53, Folder 21, Herman Baca Papers, Mandeville Special Collections Library, University of California, San Diego).

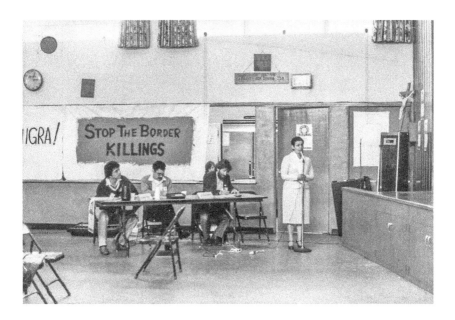

Part III **A Chicano/Mexicano Movement**

Power Concedes Nothing without Demand, 1977–1986

• •

The Carter Curtain, the KKK, and the Chicano Unity March

• •

In the midst of a media frenzy over the Ku Klux Klan's announcement that it would assist the U.S. Border Patrol in apprehending "illegal aliens," CCR chair Herman Baca responded with a warning on a November 1977 afternoon that the "Chicano community" would assert "an immediate response in-kind" to any "interruption of their daily lives."[1] Baca organized a "Unity March" to demonstrate that the Chicano/a community, other communities of color, and their allies refused to be intimidated by the historic terrorist organization. Within a few days, Baca's home was vandalized with messages that read, "WHITE POWER," and "CHICANO GO BACK WHERE YOU CAME FROM (MEXICO)."[2] Undeterred, Baca and the quickly formulated Coalition of Human Rights proceeded with the Unity March and declared that this harassment from a racist organization was only a symptom of the official immigration policy that targeted so-called illegal aliens as a means of subordinating a steady source of cheap laborers.

The KKK border event, alongside federal proposals to further militarize the border, amplified and reinforced an ongoing mobilization among Chicano/Mexicano activists working within working-class ethnic Mexican communities against border enforcement policies. Defense against "interruption of their daily lives" was what Baca and the CCR had struggled for on a daily basis, not only against overtly racist groups such as the KKK, but more commonly against local police and the federal Border Patrol beginning in the late 1960s. Under the call to control the border, Border Patrol agents in conjunction with local police had invaded homes, churches, and schools; jailed, deported, and at times brutalized both Mexican immigrants and Mexican Americans; and daily searched, questioned, and detained border crossers, often under dubious circumstances, throughout the 1970s. By 1977, the CCR in San Diego had already developed processes of local Chicano self-determination through which to address these consistent brutalities and violations of human rights. This practice was locally rooted in engagement with area community members and their experiences with the unassailable effects of border enforcement policies, and other state violations of their rights, in their everyday lives. Therefore, when debate over immigration policies reached the office of newly elected President Jimmy Carter, Baca and others cried out that it was "A Time for Resistance" to intensify and dramatize ongoing contestation between Chicano/Mexicano activists and the state over what sociologist Nestor Rodríguez calls "The Battle for the Border."[3] Rodríguez writes that the battle for the border, as manifested in the "illegal alien" debate, is truly about the maintenance of a method of organizing a global political and economic system that allows the transnational movement of capital while subjugating and policing that of labor. The autonomous migration of third world laborers presents an alternative practice of transnationalism in which workers deemed unfit to be citizens create their own mechanisms of survival that transverse the border, creating transnational communities. These transnational communities can also be political spaces, as Rodríguez notes: "Transnational communities unite with domestic sectors to resist immigration laws, engage in labor struggles and promote multiculturalism."[4] This chapter details this "Battle for the Border" in a border showdown between the Carter administration and Chicano/Mexicano activists in the San Diego borderlands, from 1977 to 1979.

This local and national set of circumstances created the inspiration for one of the most recognized productions of Chicano/a poster art entitled *Who's the Illegal Alien, Pilgrim?* The poster depicts an angry, indigenous man crumbling "immigration plans" in one hand while pointing forcefully forward in a style that evokes the Uncle Sam "We Want You" army recruitment posters. In context, those immigration plans being crushed angrily are President Carter's plans in particular. The artist of the poster, Yolanda López, who was raised in the local Logan Heights barrio, recalled: "And what it (the Carter proposal) did to us as Chicanos and Mexicanos on both sides of the border is we realized that our United States government looked at its citizens, its Mexican American citizens, as the enemy. It looked at the Mexicans as a militaristic enemy. And that scared the devil out of us."[5] With a headdress and jewelry that depicts Aztec or Mayan culture, the man, according to anthropologist Karen Mary Davalos, "suggests that the contemporary fixation on closing the U.S.-Mexico border denies the history of displacement and genocide of indigenous peoples."[6] It is no coincidence that this poster was created in 1978 for the activism headed by the CCR and its struggle against the "Carter Curtain."[7] It epitomized "Chicano/Mexicano" transnational sensibilities that imagined a community of both Mexican immigrants and Mexican Americans. *Who's the Illegal Alien, Pilgrim?* reflected a solidification of ideas created in struggle as Chicanos/Mexicanos refused consent to the attempt by the Carter regime to appropriate "humane" measures on immigration alongside continued militarized solutions that resembled KKK sentiments.[8]

This chapter argues that increasing structural repression exerted by the state through restrictionist policies in the late 1970s led Chicano/Mexicano activists to further extend the boundaries of their communities beyond national borders by exploring connections to Mexican society and experimenting with redefining civil society on transnational ground. It investigates this through analysis of Chicano/Mexicano struggles to link President Jimmy Carter's immigration plan, which would give amnesty to some undocumented immigrants but also further militarize enforcement at the border, with the explicit racism of the KKK in 1977. Indeed, following a demonstration against KKK activity, Baca declared: "On October 29, 1977, the community joined by Chicano leaders from throughout the nation, marched to demonstrate their anger and ran the KKK out of the Chicano community. . . . But the threat posed by the immigration crisis still exists. . . . Fifteen million Chicano/Latino/Mexicanos in the U.S. must now understand that the 'Carter Immigration Proposal' is in fact a loaded gun pointed at our heads."[9] As Baca revealed, immigration policy, the "loaded gun," was pointed not only at Chicanos/as and Mexicanos/as but at the wider diaspora of Latin American migrant communities as "Chicano/Mexicano" became "Chicano/Mexicano/Latino." Using the term "Latino" acknowledged that the racialization process exerted by border enforcement affected not only Mexicans but also other migrant communities from the Americas residing in different parts of the United States. The nationalization of the immigration crisis through President Carter's proposal and the international media headlines of a resurgent KKK seeking to deport "illegal aliens" put Chicano/Mexicano activists in a position to consider their relationships to other Latino/a communities beyond the Southwest and Mexican America. This is investigated by analyzing a series of Chicano/Mexicano mobilizations against the "Carter Curtain," culminating in a 1979 national march against President Carter's immigration proposal in San Diego. Refusal by U.S. state actors to address Chicano/Mexicano concerns alongside further terror and brutality exerted on Latino/a border crossers throughout the late 1970s led activists to consider the Mexican government and wider Mexican society as an alternative means through which they could struggle. Their worlds were expanding and their relations with other Latinos/as as part of a global movement interconnected with Mexico and wider Latin American were explored in reaction to the global forces of capital that brought migrants to the border and led apparatuses of the U.S. state to respond with repression.

The Carter Curtain and the KKK

With large support from Mexican Americans in his election, President Carter was expected to present a more humane immigration policy, responding to the increasing civil rights concerns expressed by leading Latino/a leaders. Carter nodded to such concerns by nominating Leonel J. Castillo, a Mexican American politician and former Chicano movement organizer in Houston, Texas, for director of the INS in March 1977.[10] The rise of an activist identified as the head of an important Chicano movement organization to become the leader of the INS is an important entry point into the ways Carter and the Democratic Party attempted to incorporate concerns among Chicano/a and Mexican American activists on human rights abuses within immigration policies.[11]

Carter's nomination of Castillo as commissioner of the INS represented a departure from the past, more militarized, vision of the preceding Republican-appointed INS leader and former Marine Corp commandant Leonard F. Chapman. For example, a *Los Angeles Times* article entitled "Nominee Fits Carter's Mold" highlights Castillo's disagreement with Chapman over the latter's figure of twelve to fourteen million undocumented immigrants in the country, indicating that the estimate was "too high" because "many who had been counted had crossed the border previously."[12] Describing Castillo as a "liberal" and "fiscal conservative" with a "downhome manner" and "personal involvement with public politics," the article identifies his humane position on amnesty. Castillo is quoted: "Hopefully, I want to enforce the law with a little more sensitivity and humanity. . . . I want to visit detention centers and maybe sleep in one or two of them."[13] Castillo, who spoke Spanish, also asserted that the immigration service had been unduly insensitive to Mexican immigrants.[14] Castillo met with Chicano/ Mexicano leaders, including Baca and Corona in San Diego, to get grassroots feedback on immigration issues.

After President Carter allowed commercial farmers in the border town of Presidio, Texas, to access Mexican immigrant workers in June 1977, the cordialities between Baca and Commissioner Castillo ended.[15] Baca used the media buzz over the Presidio event to outline the key contradictions and concerns the CCR held after almost a decade of struggle against border policing within border ethnic Mexican communities. He argued in a letter to

President Carter that "your administration is attempting to have it both ways. On the one hand without any regards to the unemployed, your administration (through the INS) continues to perpetuate the status quo by bringing in cheap foreign labor and allowing U.S. business to exploit it. While on the other hand, the INS advocates that 'illegal aliens' must be kept out of the United States at the cost of hundreds of millions of taxpayers' dollars because supposedly they are stealing jobs and causing unemployment." Baca called these two practices "a Dr. Jekyll and Mr. Hyde contradiction . . . [symbolizing] a hypocritical approach by your administration in failing to solve the immigration problem which is currently before you."[16] Targeting the new Mexican American INS commissioner, Baca claimed Castillo acted as a "coyote" (smuggler) for agribusiness. Beginning with the CCR, many Chicano/a activists nicknamed the commissioner Leonel "Coyote" Castillo.[17]

The announcement of Carter's immigration plan on August 4, 1977, all but confirmed the suspicions of the CCR and other Chicano/a and Mexican American organizations.[18] The president described "this problem" as follows: "Millions of undocumented aliens have illegally immigrated to the United States. They have breached our nation's immigration laws, displaced many American citizens from jobs, and placed an increased financial burden on many states and local governments."[19] Carter's plan proposed to escalate border enforcement manpower and technology, place sanctions on employers who hired undocumented workers, grant amnesty to some undocumented immigrants depending on how long they had been in the United States, instate a temporary worker program, and build a wall at the border in San Diego and El Paso.[20] Carter's immigration plan was the culmination of congressional debates over immigration policy that had occurred throughout much of the decade. For instance, employer sanctions in the proposal simply reflected legislation that the CCR and Chicano/Mexicano activists had struggled against in California in the early 1970s. The Dixon Arnett bill, and later the proposed Rodino bill at the federal level, sought to sanction employers who hired undocumented immigrants. The parts of the proposal to build a wall at the most crossed border sites and to increase the technology and manpower of the Border Patrol reveal how employer sanctions legislation was based on and had evolved into identifying "illegal aliens," not employers, as the primary culprit in the criminalized act of entering the United States without documentation.

Chicano/Mexicano activists such as the CCR jousted with the president over his proposal's concentration on targeting "illegal aliens," asserting the experiences of borderland ethnic Mexican communities for the past decade. They argued that any law enforcement solution to the immigration issue would have the effect of discriminating against Latinos/as of all statuses and reinforce, rather than deter, the ability of businesses to continue to access cheap noncitizen laborers. The CCR rearticulated its stance on employer sanctions, arguing: "We don't oppose punishing employers. We oppose punishing our people. The result of the proposal would be that punishment by discrimination at the hands of employers who will simply refuse to hire any person of Mexican or Latin ancestry."[21] By 1977, CCR activists had become all too familiar with the ways Mexican Americans as well as Mexican immigrants were affected by attempts to deport "illegal aliens" due to the racial presumptions of border enforcement policies. Chicano/Mexicano activists such as the CCR jumped on the proposal to build a wall between the United States and Mexico—which they labeled the "Carter Curtain"—as a symbol of racism that epitomized the often-violent effects that border militarization had had on ethnic Mexican communities in the borderlands.

Chicano/Mexicano activists argued that the proposal not only exacerbated the ethnic Mexican community's problems with the Border Patrol by further militarizing it but also reinforced a system of noncitizen labor exploitation. Baca reminded that "the Border Patrol has worked with business interests," illustrating a picture of deportation as a means of labor control. In a letter to President Carter responding to his proposal, Baca exclaimed, "Your administration (through the INS) continues to perpetuate the status quo by bringing in cheap labor and allowing U.S. businesses to exploit it."[22] The guest worker provisions of the proposal were described as a slave-like program that would create a "captive labor force that will work hard, cheap and scared."[23] Baca argued that the provisions of the proposal would allow temporary workers to stay to work and require them to pay taxes. Yet they would not have access to citizenship, voting, or public services, and would therefore be subject to taxation without representation. To dramatize how border enforcement policies enabled a system of noncitizen labor exploitation, Chicano/Mexicano activists used analogies with slavery, asserting that undocumented workers were routinely denied access to legal standing so that that they could not defend themselves and be relegated to performing cheap labor.

Yet Carter's proposal was the first to include amnesty provisions that would acknowledge the presence of millions of undocumented persons and give them the opportunity to become U.S. citizens. For this reason, Carter's plan was considered liberal in its mixing of amnesty and enforcement mechanisms, a trend that has shaped the immigration debate ever since. Chicano/Mexicano activists asserted that their definition of "amnesty" was starkly different than Carter's. Activists had made arguments for a form of amnesty that would develop a pathway to citizenship with minimal requirements. From Chicano/Mexicano perspectives, undocumented workers had already become society members and were owed access to citizenship due to the labor and taxes they had contributed. In this context, Baca labeled Carter's definition of amnesty a "false promise." He argued that the proposal did not really recommend "amnesty" but puts forth a long list of requirements that would lead to an "adjustment of status" for migrants who entered before 1970. Baca explained that in contrast to "amnesty," an "adjustment of status" was a device that was already part of immigration law that determined particular qualifications so that a select number of immigrants could become citizens. Border Patrol apprehension data suggests that undocumented migration had incrementally increased throughout most of the 1970s, reaching just under one million in 1977.[24] The majority of undocumented migrants had arrived in the past two years, therefore ensuring that only a small percentage of them would benefit from Carter's policy and its "amnesty" for migrants who entered before 1970.[25] Baca also argued that the INS had a seven-year waiting list for citizenship papers, guaranteeing that "it will take years before anyone will benefit."[26]

Debates between Chicano/Mexicano activists and proponents of the Carter Plan would intensify when a few months following Carter's proposed crackdown on "undocumented aliens," leaders of the infamous Ku Klux Klan held a press conference at the San Ysidro–Tijuana Border Station to announce their intent to start a Border Watch Program. David Duke, the KKK's national leader, told reporters that the illegal alien problem "is changing the fabric of American life" due to the "rising flow of color . . . washing over our borders."[27] Duke went on to argue that the border should be sealed off, that it should be illegal for employers to hire undocumented workers, and that if he had the power, he would deport every "illegal" present in the United States. The KKK planned to begin a patrolling program on the U.S.-Mexico border from Texas to California.[28] Klan members would work to spot undocumented migrants and report sightings to the Border Patrol via C.B. radios. The Klan patrollers would apprehend migrants in some cases and would also be armed where legal. Accompanied by a small entourage wearing T-shirts with "white power" written on them, Duke was also given a tour of border facilities by INS officials.[29]

The CCR led a Chicano/Mexicano effort to not only decry the presence of the notoriously racist organization but to intensify its engagement with the U.S. state and further mobilize Latinos/as and allies to put forth alternative interpretations of border enforcement policies. Local Latino/a community members and activists in San Diego perceived this announcement as a direct threat to their well-being and safety. Phone calls poured into Baca's workplace, with community members expressing their concern about the presence of such a racist and notorious group in relation to the repercussions of the heated immigration debate.[30] According to Baca, these community members perceived the KKK as an invading force "trying to do (to us) what they did to blacks in the South."[31] Indeed, San Diego African American leaders were also appalled, including members of the Nia Cultural Organizations, who had worked with the CCR on police brutality cases (see chapter 6), and the first African American city councilman, Leon Williams, who witnessed a cross burning from his Southeast San Diego home the night after the KKK press conference.[32] Nia again came to the CCR's aid several months following the struggle for slain Puerto Rican youth Luis "Tato" Rivera in 1975, which ended with an attempt to recall the National City Council in 1976. In a context in which the infamous KKK was involved with local policing, structures of racialized law enforcement again brought the black and Chicano/a struggle together. Furthermore, these struggles created spaces in which Chicano/a activists explored their relationship to and overlapping histories with African American communities in regard to racialized terror and policing in dialog with Black Power activists. Within a couple of days after the KKK press conference, the CCR held their own press conference, where Baca asserted: "We are here to state, today, that Chicano communities, from the United States, will not tolerate or meekly submit to terrorist harassments, intimidations, or interruption of their daily lives. Let it be made clear, right now, least [sic] any of these individuals have the mistaken idea that Chicanos are going to submit passively; that any action taken by these groups against our people will call forth an immediate response in kind."[33]

Already aware of the many cases of legal violence inflicted on ethnic Mexican individuals of all citizenship statuses in San Diego at the hands of Border Patrol and local police in search of "illegal aliens," the KKK's explicit announcement to apprehend "Mexican-looking individuals," enabled Baca to demonstrate the experience of racialization of Chicano/a communities to a wider world, highlighting a shared struggle of undocumented migrants and U.S. Latinos/as. The CCR would link this dramatic experience of racialization to the more common practices of border enforcement policies and the proposed "Carter Curtain."

Soon after his speech, Baca was appointed head of the quickly formulated Coalition for Human Rights, an alliance of Chicano/a, African American, and other concerned activists from San Diego and wider Southern California. As revealed in a photo of one of the coalition's meeting (see figure 5) Nia leaders Greg Akili and Ken Msemaji emerged as key leaders revealing the overlapping struggle and acts of solidarity that continued to be structured by San Diego's racially charged atmosphere.[34] Furthermore, Baca recalled the coalition's meeting: "After the press conference we decided that . . . this tour, this action (and) this seed being planted by this right-wing racist, terrorist-type group—was a result of the policy that continued the manipulation and exploitation of Mexican labor that was affecting our community, our efforts at enfranchisement. So we decided we were going to confront it. So we called for a march."[35]

Further harassment would polarize the situation. While working at his print shop to organize the march, Baca's spouse Nadyne phoned him on the morning of October 21 to inform him that racist messages had been spray painted on his home reading, "Chicano, go back where you came from (Mexico)" and "White Power."[36] Baca had not noticed it having left early in the morning when it was still dark. It was retaliation from KKK members or sympathizers to the march called by the CCR and the Coalition. Uneasy about the situation, Baca sent his family to Los Angeles to stay with relatives until the march had commenced. For the next several nights, a number of Baca's compatriots stayed to protect him at his home, patrolling the area with rifles. After several nights of patrolling, the group decided to send Baca to stay at one of their homes, so they could get rest in preparation for the upcoming march.[37]

The vandalism against the Baca family was just one instance in a surge of Klan activity in the tense San Diego area. An accidental shooting of a known Klansmen had occurred at an East County bar when the manager attempted to break up a fight on October 20. Furthermore, two other homes were inscribed with the letters "KKK" in Southeast San Diego, home to many of the area's black and Latino/a residents on October 20, in addition to the cross burning reported by Councilman Leon Williams on October 18.[38] In such an environment, communities of color and their allies were especially compelled to forge a response to the increased white supremacist activity and the threatening environment. The San Diego police chief reported that he was prepared for violence when the Klan's border watch program was to commence on October 22.[39] Coupled with the upcoming Chicano-led protest march, a media spotlight was pointed at San Diego to observe whether tensions might boil over.

The coalition proclaimed that the KKK harassment of the Chicano community was a by-product of federal immigration policy and it was therefore the responsibility of President Carter himself to alleviate the situation. Baca referred to the tacit approval of the Klan activity by the Border Patrol to make his point. This "tacit approval" referred to the tour given to the KKK by INS officials. INS official James O'Keefe participated in the tour, and while he responded to the media that he discouraged KKK involvement, he also exclaimed, "As far as receiving information from them, we welcome information from any citizen. . . . We would respond—if we have the manpower."[40] Chicano/a leaders argued that this invitation by INS officials, by giving a tour and affirming that the border patrol would act on KKK reports, was proof of the absurdity and racial hysteria that surrounded the immigration debate.

Indeed, Baca declared: "We charge the Carter Administration with failure to produce an effective immigration policy which is just, reasonable and humane. We hold Lionel Castillo, Commissioner of the INS to blame for the current situation for his failure and inability to control the operations of the INS, Border Patrol, or its' officials in the field. Finally, we hold accountable the local police, politicians and media, who through their manipulation of a serious issue have contributed to the present hysteria surrounding the undocumented alien issue."[41] Out of such an assessment, Baca and the coalition demanded that President Carter immediately remove the INS officers that allowed the tour, that a congressional investigation be conducted on the whole border situation, that the Carter administration meet with Chicano/a community leaders, and that the administration further require that the INS disavowal support of extremist, racist groups.[42]

The Unity March was held a week after the start of the KKK Border Watch program in protest of the presence of the Klan at the border and the implied cooperation displayed by the Carter administration. Area Chicano/a, African American, and progressive forces were joined by national Chicano movement leaders in the protest march that would launch a national campaign against the Carter immigration plan. Estimates of the protest participants ran from three hundred to one thousand.[43] During the March and rally, protesters would make their views clear. Chicano movement veteran Corky Gonzales proclaimed that the border patrol is to Chicanos what the

KKK was to African Americans in the South. He exclaimed at the protest rally: "La Migra is just as guilty, just as racist as the KKK. They are twins dressed in different uniforms who mistreat, terrorize and brutalize our people." Longtime labor organizer and Baca's mentor, Bert Corona, referred to the KKK as "right-wing terrorists . . . who are a pimple on the body of a decaying system." The Carter plan embodied the "decaying system," argued Corona, and attempted to pass "systematic and legalized racism" as comprehensive reform.[44] The explicit racism of the Klan made it quite easy for Chicano/a activists to link it with the implicit racism of the Carter plan.

As Baca's speech vowing "an immediate response in-kind" to Klan harassment on the Chicano/a community revealed, the threat of random violence led activists to stabilize the situation using their own faculties. Hysteria over the immigration crisis and the repeated neglect from various state actors to address the violence emanating from the Border Patrol led to a breakdown of "law and order" as Baca put it, creating the conditions for dialog between Chicano/Mexicano activists and apparatuses of the U.S. state to deteriorate. This led to further mobilization and reliance on autonomous action based on the expanding notion of a Chicano/Mexicano community. As Baca remarked at the Unity March, "On October 29, 1977 the community joined by Chicano/a leaders from throughout the nation, marched to demonstrate their anger and ran the KKK out of the Chicano community. . . . But the threat posed by the immigration crisis still exists. . . . Fifteen million Chicano/Latino/Mexicanos in the U.S. must now understand that the 'Carter Immigration Proposal' is in fact a loaded gun pointed at our heads."[45] Indeed, by highlighting the embarrassing media display in which INS officials accommodated the KKK border watch program, these activists took advantage of such a link to make explicit to a broader constituency the subtle racial assumptions that underpinned current Border Patrol practices and President Carter's proposed immigration bill.

In these ways, the CCR asserted a self-determined response based on the everyday experience and operation of the transnational Chicano/Mexicano community in the borderlands. The call to defend against "interruptions of (the Chicano community's) daily lives" intensified activist constructions of community political practice based on transnational processes of everyday life within ethnic Mexican communities independent from the hegemonic gaze of capital and the state. The years of structural violence on racialized borderland communities and the ascension of the immigration issue to the national level facilitated further enactment of autonomous community action in a transnational context. This can be demonstrated further in Baca's speech concerning the KKK in which he highlights the last seven years, through three presidential administrations:

> We have spoken out for the creation of a just, humane and responsible immigration policy. We have repeatedly condemned the militarization of the border. We have decried, repeatedly, the human degradation, brutalities, harassments, rapings [*sic*], and killings that have occurred on these borders. We have repeatedly condemned the use of the local police, border task force, and sheriff deputies, in carrying out INS/Border Patrol functions. These actions have only served to solidify the violent nature of proposed solutions.[46]

Baca described the response to their demands: "The continued insistence of attempting to resolve the undocumented worker problem through the policies of 'Control and Containment,' implemented by PARA MILITARY FORCES and DOCTRINES has led to its inevitable conclusion. The breakdown of law and order."[47]

Inverting notions of "law and order" assumed to be caused by criminalized populations to criticize the destabilizing actions of policing agencies and the state, Baca recounted the years spent dialoging about, pleading for, and demanding from various levels of the government an end to militarized solutions to undocumented migration. These types of solutions were based on a definition of the problem as migrants' malicious entrance into the United States and subsequent displacement of Americans. President Carter, again, described undocumented migrants as criminals who "breached our nation's immigration laws," "displaced many Americans from jobs," and became a "burden" on local governments. On this basis, a military solution was imagined as necessary over a willingness to fully acknowledge grassroots Chicano/a demands.[48] Despite activist calls for the alleviation of state violence, President Carter's solutions sounded eerily similar to KKK Grand Dragon David Duke's concerns about the "rising flow of color washing over our borders." In both cases, the migrants themselves were deemed the problem. Their act of crossing was further criminalized and deemed a threat to "American citizens" conjuring centuries-old patterns of defining U.S. citizenship as white by depicting migration as criminalized—and directly or indirectly, racially different from the majority population.[49] Therefore, solutions called for keeping noncitizens out, by force. Baca's speech echoed that Chicano/Mexicano cries for justice from systematic state violence had not been answered and revealed a significant shift in their strategy by beginning the process of contemplating solutions outside the United States in relation to the transnational space of the U.S.-Mexico borderlands.[50] Unity March participant and San Antonio Chicano/Mexicano activist Mario Cantu expressed this sensibility when he asserted, "The involvement of the Chicano movement in an issue which has international ramifications is a crucial step in understanding that basic denial of human rights of Mexicanos from Mexico is also a basic denial of Chicano human rights in the U.S. That the Chicano movement can move away from purely local concerns to one that involves the basic human rights of people from other countries, clearly signals a new era for the Chicano movement."[51]

President Carter's initial immigration policy proposal failed to advance into legislation, leading him to establish the U.S. Select Commission on Immigration and Refugee Policy in October 1978. This "blue-ribbon" commission was set to study and make recommendations to the president and Congress on "appropriate" measures to the immigration problem. The commission, headed by the president of Notre Dame University, Father Theodore Hesburgh, for the most part reaffirmed and legitimized Carter's initial plan of action in its 1981 report calling for "enhanced boundary enforcement efforts" as "a necessary precondition for the implementation of a legalization program" to avoid, according to the report, "inducement of further illegal immigration."[52] The commission's legitimizing effects ensured that the struggle against Carter Curtain–like policies would continue beyond his administration.

Stop the Carter Curtain!

Staying on the offensive, the CCR and its allies, including elder unionist Bert Corona, now head of the National Immigration Coalition in Los Angeles and Denver-based Chicano movement icon Rodolfo "Corky" Gonzales, extended their notion of the Chicano/Mexicano community to enact transnational responses to the immigration crisis that engaged not only the U.S. state but the Mexican state as well. President Carter was set to meet with Mexican president Jose López Portillo, chiefly with regards to oil in Mexico, in Mexico City from February 14–16, 1979. Chicano/Mexicano activists would take this opportunity to continue their protests against the Carter Curtain, but more important, consider their relationship with the Mexican government as an assertion of self-determination and a strategy for the alleviation of brutality. The meeting with López Portillo in the context of heightened hysteria over "illegal immigration" created a situation in which the CCR and

Chicano/Mexicano activists considered the role of the Mexican state in the exploitation of undocumented migrants. Activists perceived the increase of oil production in Mexico as giving unprecedented leverage to the Mexican state in negotiations with the United States. In this way, Chicano/Mexicano activists sought to pressure the Mexican government to include humane address of the immigration issue as part of trade negotiations.

Chicano relations with Mexico were complex. As discussed in earlier chapters, the Chicano movement emerged in a context in which a largely American-born Mexican-origin contingent of activists used the notion of "Aztlán" to emphasize a strategy of engaging U.S. society as an indigenous people that, although emphasizing pride in Mexican culture, implicitly separated them from Mexico and immigrants. At the same time, emphasis on Mexican cultural identity and reckoning with the U.S. conquest of Northern Mexico made wider communes with Mexico and the wider Americas possible. While some Chicano movement activists did engage the Mexican state, most notably Jose Angel Gutiérrez as representative of La Raza Unida Party in South Texas, others, such as CASA leaders Mario Cantú and Antonio Rodríguez, led vehement critiques of the Mexican government following the 1968 massacres of the student movements at Tlatelolco.[53] Gutiérrez and Raza Unida's interaction with Mexico demonstrated a pragmatic approach that perceived the Mexican government as an ally, a source of financial and political support, and a pathway to asserting Chicano self-determination in the global arena. On the other hand, Baca recalls his ally Mario Cantú's mobilization of demonstrations against Mexico's government during President Luis Echeverría's visits to the United States and his vehement abhorrence of the Mexican state, which was demonstrated when Cantú apparently "attempted to physically kick" the president during a protest.[54] This represented a contingent of Chicano/a activists vehemently critical of the Mexican state's dirty war against subversives in the 1960 and 1970s. Although a supporter of Cantú, Baca was less concerned about a stringent critique of Mexico, as indicated by his bewilderment about Cantú's "deep, deep hatred" for the PRI (Partido Revolucionario Institucional; Institutional Revolutionary Party), Mexico's dictatorial political party, "for some reason."[55] This did not prevent Baca from criticizing Mexico and the PRI as described below, but it indicated that he approached the Mexican state with an expectation that they would act on behalf of ethnic Mexicans in the United States. This appears to be pragmatic and strategic, as bringing the Mexican government, media, and civil society into the hotly debated immigration topic offered the opportunity to exert pressure on U.S. and Mexican politicians during a time when the United States and Mexico engaged one another concerning new oil reserves in the Mexican states of Tabasco, Campeche, and elsewhere by the late 1970s.[56]

Chicano/Mexicano activists interceded in U.S.-Mexico negotiations when the CCR released a press release in January 1979 announcing a national protest march coinciding with the meeting of Carter and Portillo. A central issue was the brutalities experienced by Mexicans in the United States, best symbolized by the proposed construction of a border fence—the "Carter Curtain" in San Diego/Tijuana and El Paso/Juárez. Activists protested the "Vietnam like militarization of the United States-Mexican border" that had led to "massive violations of human and constitutional rights by the Border Patrol on the Chicano community."[57] A spokesperson for the CCR stated, "Any agreement reached in Mexico City, will ultimately have an effect on the social, economic, and political future of the Chicano community in the United States."[58] Leaders Gonzales, Corona, and Baca explained the significance of this march in a television interview, calling attention to the contradiction of U.S. economic desires to cross the border into Mexico while construction of a wall was proposed to keep Mexican workers out. Chicano movement veteran from Colorado, Corky Gonzales, explained:

> The main purpose of the march today is to protest the cactus curtain of the fence that is being put up in Tijuana barrios . . . to the violation of human rights of people *sin documentos* [without documents] and Chicano people who are citizens of this country . . . to Carter who is going to meet with Portillo to take care to recognize the human rights of our people both here and those who cross what we call the imaginary frontier. I feel that Carter's purpose for the meeting with Portillo has more to do with high finances and profits in dealing with the purchase of oil and natural gas.[59]

Gonzales's comments reveal a critical approach to the hegemonic foreign policy of the United States and an implicit call to Mexico to recognize and act on the interconnected situation between Mexican Americans and Mexicans in the United States. Baca would contribute to the interview by calling attention to the larger structural forces that immigration policy was failing to address. He explained, "What we are saying is that all the solutions [to the immigration debate] have been adverse to the victim . . . like let's get more border patrol, let's get more military . . . rather than dealing with the causes of the whole immigration issue, which are political, social and economic in nature."[60] In an attempt to not only inform the American public but the Mexican public about the transnational implications of the Carter Curtain and immigration policy, Corona explained further:

> We view the building of this new fence and the increased and stepped up militarization of the entire U.S. and Mexico Border as very symbolic in the sense and within the context of the hostile action not only against the Mexican people in Mexico and the Mexican nation but against all Mexican and Latino people in the U.S. That hostility has been expressed historically in lower wages being paid to the Mexican and Latino workers who perform the same work as Anglo and other workers, [and] lower social and living conditions. . . . When they put a border facing Latin America like they are intending to put here it [sic] merely symbolizes, emphasizes and enforces the racist and the chauvinistic discriminatory treatment that our people have suffered and lived through in the U.S.[61]

Corona's statement reveals the strategy being taken up among Chicano/ Mexicano activists with regard to addressing both the U.S. and Mexican states in the immigration issue. They continued to criticize the racism and disregard demonstrated by U.S. officials' disappointing responses to their complaints concerning legal violence and the immigration regime and appealed to the Mexican government and society as fellow Mexicanos living in a hostile environment that needed alleviation. This would enable the utilization of the Mexican state as a tool in addressing the immigration system's brutalization of ethnic Mexican communities by intervening in the desire by these two states to reach a new economic agreement on oil.

Corona closed the interview by emphasizing the Chicano movement goal of reckoning with the legacy of conquest that had relegated Mexicans in the United States to second-class citizenship and further led to the creation of a system in which Mexican noncitizen labor was continually exploited and subjugated. He exclaimed, "This used to be Mexico and this is the reality that has to be understood by 220,000,000 Americans as well." Corona continued: "The only way to stop the exploitation of workers on this side of the border is to give them all the rights that those of us who are born here have. The right to . . . not be deported, the right to unify economies, the right to organize into unions."[62] Corona conceptualized a vision of citizenship that acknowledged the already unified economies of the United States and Mexico that would recognize migrant workers as legitimate society members. This vision was expressed to both U.S. and Mexican audiences.

This call to bind the destinies of ethnic Mexicans in the United States and Mexicanos/as in Mexico was initiated by Baca a week earlier. Baca had traveled to the Hotel Palacio Azteca in nearby Tijuana to appeal to the Mexican press and wider Mexican society "a message from the 16 million Chicanos/Latinos residing in the United States." Like Corona's attempt to connect the identities of Mexicans in Mexico with Chicanos/as in the United States through a shared experience of repression under the U.S. government, Baca asked, that "the Mexican people join us in stopping the construction of that most odious symbol of racism, discrimination, and bigotry. . . . the Carter Curtain." Aside from tying together the plight of the Mexican and ethnic Mexicans in the United States through a shared culture that was to be degraded by a fence between the two nations, Baca also argued that this was a "test" that would determine future U.S. social and economic dominance of Mexico. Baca attempted to convince Mexicanos/as that their interests were tied up with the fate of undocumented workers. At stake, Baca argued, was whether the entirety of Mexican society would be subject to exploitation by the United States in the same manner as undocumented Mexicano/a migrants. "The fence is a test," Baca exclaimed, "If we Chicanos and Mexicanos fail . . . [it will be] a clear signal to American policy makers that the United States can proceed without concern with the continued abuse and exploitation of the Chicano in the United States, and the exploitation of Mexico's resources (undocumented workers and oil) without fear."[63] Binding U.S. Chicanos, undocumented migrants, and Mexicanos/as in Mexico together was not simply bloodlines, but the shared struggle against the effects of U.S. imperialism and the rule of capital. In this way, not only were the voices of the undocumented added to the immigration debate but working-class and poor members of a developing nation were called upon to voice their discontent with the policies of an imperial power within the world system.

In this mobilization, Chicano/Mexicanos imagined a transnational method of addressing the immigration crisis by mobilizing working-class participants in the overlapping economies of these two nations to express their concerns and demands to both the Mexican and U.S. governments. This widening of activities through consideration of appealing to the Mexican government and civic society reveals how Chicano/Mexicano activists began to consider transnational solutions to the immigration crisis. This emerged through engagement with the shifting realities of their local community. By reconceptualizing their community as consisting of both new migrants and multigenerational racialized citizens, continued border enforcement repression led them to extend the Chicano movement critique of U.S. imperialism. They asserted that the legacies of anti-Mexican sentiment not only justified the erecting of "capricious borders" after the U.S. conquest of Northern Mexico, creating Mexican American second-class citizens one hundred fifty years ago, but continued to be utilized to develop immigration laws that facilitated a system of labor exploitation that disciplined migrants and racialized ethnic Mexican communities. Chicano/Mexicano activists called on the Mexican nation itself to assist in the battle of its people struggling against racism and exploitation in the United States—both with the recent arrival of Mexicano/a migrants and as part of the long-struggle of Chicanos/as. This was an assertion of autonomy in that Chicano/Mexicano activists and community members opted to appeal to the Mexican government in response to the inability or unwillingness of the U.S. state to address their demands to end brutality. Having conceived of their community as a transnational space, and noting the interest between the U.S. presidency and the Mexican government to negotiate a new petroleum trade policy, they recognized new paths of struggle and were not limited to the mechanisms of one nation-state.

Yet while these ideas and assertions of transnational autonomy floated about after the release of the Carter proposal and KKK fiasco, it was still unclear what these activists wanted beyond addressing and alleviating harassment and brutality, and an end to militarization of the border. The National March Against the Militarization of the Border and the Carter Curtain in 1979 sought to bring attention to the brutal results of militarized immigration policies to the U.S., Mexican, and wider public, but what did Chicano/Mexicano activists expect to accomplish from these tactics? Indeed, significant questions abounded. For one, what was expected of the Mexican government? Activist strategists hoped that Mexico would help call for an end to militarized border policies as contingent on a petroleum deal with the United States, but was this wishful thinking? What was Mexico's role in the undocumented immigration issue? And was Mexico's petroleum industry strong enough to make such demands against what the activists themselves recognized as powerful and vested corporate interests that wanted century-old access to cheap migrant labor?[64]

These questions were left open, as the purpose of the National March was to again bring attention to the brutal results of border enforcement policies. The march was put together to assert a "united front" by the "Chicano community" to show "opposition" to the Carter Plan, the proposed wall, militarization, and violations of human rights.[65] While it did not put forth concrete solutions to the problem, the action convened a national dialog among Chicano/Mexicano and grassroots immigrant rights activists over the vexing problem of immigration policy in a broader transnational context. It widened the playing field to consider the role that the Mexican people and government might play in their attempts to alleviate the brutality at the border. It also suggested, again, that President Carter and other U.S. officials meet with the "communities most affected" by immigration policy. President Carter actually invited the San Diego Chicano Federation, which Baca and the CCR had worked with, to meet with him as part of a larger meeting with "Hispanic leaders" for insight in preparation of the meeting with López Portillo the following week.[66] After a community meeting, the Federation refused to meet with Carter on the grounds that he continued to support construction of a fence at the border and their doubt "that he will seriously consider any input that will not coincide with his present policy."[67] They instead invited Carter to meet "directly with the people" to discuss the effects of immigration policy on border communities at the National Protest March. These two ideas—one that considered the transnational scope of struggle through engagement with Mexico and the other that insisted that ethnic Mexican communities at the border were entitled to a voice in discussions of immigration policy due to their experiences of racialization and brutality—built the foundation for further action as a transnational autonomous entity based in Latino/a borderlands communities. Furthermore, more violence would prompt Chicano/Mexicano activists to not only call for alleviation of brutality but for collective, independent contemplation on and solid solutions to this crisis at the border.

· · · · · ·

The first year in which Carter and the first Mexican American INS commissioner Leonel Castillo were in office premised a longer fight that the CCR and its allies would engage in for the rest of Carter's administration and beyond. Within this struggle, the CCR assisted in cultivating a position on immigration that refused the attempt by Democratic Party elites to combine their human rights concerns within the same package as continued law enforcement and other coercive measures. Law enforcement solutions, the CCR argued, were based on a system of subordinating immigration statuses that put migrants in a rightless state. San Diego activist and artist Yolanda López depicted these notions within *Who's the Illegal Alien, Pilgrim?*, and while she recalls a reluctance by the CCR to use the poster more pointedly, in years to come it became recognized and used within Chicano/a activist circles for its assertive message questioning the very premise of the immigration regime—what moral authority does the U.S. state have to say who is supposed to be here in a settler colonial context?[68] López has recovered other posters she created that depict the Carter plan as the coming home of the militarization used in wars abroad. Several of these posters depict barbed wire, representing the oppression of the immigration regime through the presence of a war zone—indeed, Chicano/a activists described San Diego as the "Vietnam of the Southwest." López's poster asking, "Is brown skin a criminal act?" depicts this sentiment and places a young Brown woman and child among the barbed wire, bomb smoke, and helicopters depicted in many of her posters. This poster art therefore visually depicted the solidification of what the CCR and other Chicano/Mexicano activists were articulating during the Carter struggles: that warlike conditions are inherently opposed to notions of a humane policy. Appointing a brown man as head of an organization that enforces a policy that targets brown people for expulsion did not alleviate this situation, they declared, nor did coupling human rights concerns with further militarization and the maintenance of subordinated noncitizen categories.

The presence of the racist KKK a few months later further sensationalized the issue. Undoubtedly, the proposal and the KKK presence engendered further racialization of ethnic Mexicans, and more broadly, Latinos/as in the United States via discourse on immigration that divided citizen from noncitizen by deploying race, whether implicitly or explicitly. As Omi and Winant's valuable concept of racial formation continues to remind, racialization is a process that is repackaged and redeployed in new contexts.[69]

But more poignantly, this chapter not only reviewed how these events further deployed race to perform national sovereignty without disrupting the ebbs and flows of global capitalism but also asserted that these events amplified and reinforced an ongoing mobilization among Chicano/Mexicano activists. In this difficult context, Chicano/Mexicano activists experimented with extending the boundaries of their solidarity across racial lines and beyond national borders, exploring connections to Mexican society and redefining civil society on transnational ground. Furthermore, Chicano/Mexicano activists were compelled to create independent analyses and processes in which to contemplate, disseminate, and collectively forge solutions to the immigration process in reaction to the inability or unwillingness of liberal nation-state actors to respond to their demands. This created the space in which the CCR learned to convene grassroots Chicano/

Mexicano and broader Latino/a activists from across the country to collectively contemplate solutions and voice their frustrations to a transnational audience. Building on these developments, Chicano/Mexicano activists led by the CCR would enact notions of self-determination to exert alternative forms of belonging that challenged not only the U.S. state but the Mexican state for its collusion with the system of immigrant exploitation.

8 Abolishment of the INS/Border Patrol

The Chicano National Immigration Conference and Tribunal

Evoking the words of a formerly enslaved abolitionist, the CCR defined the goals of the Chicano National Immigration Tribunal. On April 11, 1981, the CCR reconvened a number of the one thousand grassroots activists who had participated in the National Chicano Immigration Conference about a year earlier to hear the voices of several survivors of *migra* brutality and remember those who did not survive the abuse of a militarized immigration policy. More than fifty cases of harassment and brutality by Border Patrol agents, customs officers, and local police enforcing policies that targeted "illegal aliens" were presented at the tribunal proceedings. The cases were recorded, supported by archival evidence and collected to create a more than one thousand–page document that was presented to the administrations of Presidents Ronald Reagan and Jose López Portillo in Washington, D.C., and Mexico City, respectively. Quoting nineteenth-century abolitionist Frederick Douglass's observation that "Power concedes nothing without demand. It never did and it never will . . . the limits of tyrants are prescribed by the endurance of those whom they oppress," the CCR introduced a document, but more important, initiated a radically democratic process that demonstrated an alternative practice of social membership, calling for the abolition of the "slave-like" immigration regime and organizing a transnational community that defied the logic of the nation-state by revealing its collusion with capital.[1] The tribunal emphasized the voice of the survivors of brutal yet routine episodes of violence perpetrated by border enforcement agents, creating a process in which transnational residents of a racialized community, whether documented or undocumented, held these actions accountable and facilitated collective analysis and articulation of solutions to the immigration issue. With regard to the violence shared by survivors, the description and analysis of the testimonies put forth at the tribunal and wider coalition of "Chicano/Mexicano/Latino" activists' usage of these testaments deserve forewarning of their graphic descriptions of brutality.[2] Activists revealed the details of these incidents out of a process in which leaders were often called on to struggle for justice by community and family members, particularly in cases involving death, or where survivors themselves came forth to voice their own insistence on justice and called on community leaders for solidarity and action. By revealing these details and testimonies, activists sought to render the U.S. and Mexican states accountable for their collusion with and practice of a racialized system of labor exploitation—to reveal the brutal face and realities that these so-called policies subjected ethnic Mexicans and Latinos/as to in the borderlands and, increasingly, beyond.

In this way, the Chicano Tribunal epitomized an assertion of self-determination that is best captured in activist scholar Gustavo Esteva's analysis in "The Meaning and Scope of the Struggle for Autonomy." The tribunal, and the conference preceding it, asserted the "capacity and liberty" for transnational working-class Latino/a communities to "determine their identity and their ways of life and government in their own spaces . . . and forms of communion with the society at large."[3] The "society at large" was widened to include the binational space of the United States and Mexico—a civic society that defied the boundaries between the two nations. They also asserted a refusal to abide by the hierarchical construction of citizen over noncitizen and stamped their demand to dialog with the U.S. and Mexican states as an autonomous transnational Chicano/Mexicano and wider Latino/a community.

Quoting the formerly enslaved orator Frederick Douglass was more than a convenience; it revealed a deeply intertwined relationship between what scholars have referred to as abolition democracy and struggles for Chicano self-determination and immigrant rights. Abolition democracy characterizes radical mobilizations that seek a complete uprooting of systems of racialized labor exploitation, most recently discussed in relationship to the prison industrial complex.[4] Chicano/Mexicano/Latino activists at the Chicano National Immigration Conference in 1980 asserted an abolitionist stance against deportation-oriented immigration policies when they proclaimed solutions that sought "the abolishment of the INS/Border Patrol . . . of the militarization policy between the U.S./Mexico as a solution to the immigration issue . . . [and] on all quotas on immigration from countries where the USA has political, economic and military domination."[5] As historian Gaye Theresa Johnson asserts, "The twofold demand for the full spectrum of human rights, as well as white historical accountability, illumines a long-shared philosophy among Blacks and Browns in the United States about the nature of their rights as human beings."[6] Identifying this "long-shared philosophy" with "abolition democracy," Johnson defines this perspective as "a radical political perspective that demanded freedom in its entirety—nothing less than the material realization of all the rights supplied to elite whites."[7] Deepening this tie between black and brown movements within the Chicano struggle for immigrant rights was discourse that analogized the historical practice of slavery with the plight of undocumented migrants and the policing mechanism that ethnic Mexicans and Latinos/as were subjected to in the regime of deportation-oriented policies. These analogies became deeply embedded in the discourse used by the Committee on Chicano Rights' lead spokesperson, Herman Baca, and other leaders of this mobilization, including Bert Corona, Corky Gonzales, and others. Tied to a Mexican American political tradition that identified and called for solidarity with Black Freedom movements, the discourse and symbolism of "slavery" worked to call attention to the crisis of immigration.[8] While this rhetorical strategy risked underplaying the degree to which the humanity of enslaved peoples in the slavery system of the nineteenth century was denied, labeling the issues emerging out of deportation-oriented immigration policies "the slave issue of the twentieth century" enabled activists to identify these issues not as a policy in need of reform, but as a system of racialized labor exploitation in need of abolition. Like enslaved peoples, activists argued that undocumented migrants had no legal standing and this enabled employers to exploit them and increase their profit margins— what Baca called the United States' long history of "addiction to free or cheap labor."[9] In this way, activists tied notions and practices of abolition democracy with the struggle for Chicano self-determination and immigrant rights.

Highlighting two events organized by the CCR in San Diego, the National Chicano Immigration Conference and Memorial March in 1980 and the National Chicano Immigration Tribunal in 1981, this chapter explores how in the wider Chicano/a struggle for immigrant rights, Chicano/a activists developed an autonomous response to the immigration crisis by conceiving of themselves as a transnational community. Chicano/a demonstrations against President Jimmy Carter's immigration plan in the late 1970s mobilized a network of grassroots Chicano/a and immigrant organizations across the United States and the borderlands. In what would be Carter's last year in office, the CCR organized the Chicano National Immigration Conference and Memorial March in May of 1980. Following several tragic encounters between mostly ethnic Mexican border crossers and INS agents in 1979, culminating in the death of two children, the CCR organized the conference to not only protest these tragedies but to collectively put forth solutions from the perspective of working-class ethnic Mexican and Latino/a communities. These grassroots Chicano/a activists convened in San Diego to lead a concerted effort to not only highlight the oppressive results that border militarization had had on their communities but also to demand that their own practices of community and belonging that disrupted hierarchical divisions between citizens and noncitizens be acknowledged. This practice of transnational social membership was demonstrated further through the National Chicano Immigration Tribunal almost a year later in April of 1981. On the basis of what these activists began to refer to as "Chicano/Mexicano/Latino" communities, they asserted a right to self-determine their own identities and processes of solution making in between but in dialog with both the U.S. and Mexican states. The Chicano Tribunal provided the perspectives of working-class, transnational Chicano/Mexicano/Latino communities on immigration policies and demanded from both nations an end to the brutalities as part of a systematic practice that they had endured the past decade.

La Frontera en Sangre—The Bloody Border

CCR member and artist David Avalos put together a pamphlet that through sketches, collage, and commentary depicted the violent nature of border enforcement policies by recording a number of incidents that occurred following the National Protest March against President Jimmy Carter's immigration policy proposal in 1979. Entitled *La Frontera en Sangre* (The bloody border), on the cover is a sketch of two migrants handcuffed together and on their knees. Both are Mexican men; one is being shot in the chest, blood spilling out of him, by a standing Border Patrol agent, while the other looks on in terror. The two men are on a line indicating the U.S.-Mexico border. Behind them on the ground it reads "Mexico." The agent is standing, in uniform and hat, emotionless. Behind the migrants in the background are the words "Human Rights? Racism! Due Process? Bigotry! Summary Trial and Execution? Brotherhood? Justice! Inhuman! Disgusting!"[10] Avalos's sketch depicts a real event, the killing of twenty-four-year-old Efren Reyes on March 17, 1979, by a Border Patrol agent. He was handcuffed to twenty-two-year-old Benito Rincon, who was also shot by the agent but survived, in San Ysidro on the U.S. side of the border at San Diego-Tijuana. For Avalos, the sketch of the real event depicted the violence and brutality of militarized border enforcement that the National Protest March was meant to bring attention to. It also demonstrated CCR chair Herman Baca's words that he had previously exclaimed arguing that militarized policies would lead to an "inevitable conclusion: the total breakdown of law and order."[11] A string of incidents in 1979 in which migrants, including children, were brutalized and even killed at the border confirmed the CCR and their allies' main concerns that their communities were under siege due to state-sponsored attempts to enforce the border between the United States and Mexico.

Just three days after the shooting of Reyes and Rincon, a four-year-old boy, Mario Alberto Canedo, died waiting to receive treatment for a heart condition at the Border Station in Tijuana. The event occurred when the boy was rushed from his home just outside Tijuana by his aunt, Guadalupe Astorga. Mario was recovering from heart surgery, having been released from University Hospital in San Diego just days earlier. After he began coughing up blood, Astorga and another relative drove him to the border with hopes of reaching University Hospital to address the matter.[12] Without a multiple-entry visa, the boy and his aunt had to wait for clearance to cross the border for medical attention. Astorga later recalled, "I asked them to give me attention, and they didn't pay any attention to me."[13] She arrived at the border and informed a Mexican police officer that the child was sick. The police officer went to the front of the border station to inform the U.S. officer that the child was sick. Astorga showed the U.S. officer the child and was directed to secondary inspection with a yellow tag, which could indicate anything from an emergency to further searching needed. She waited in this line for what she reported as "a long time."[14] Becoming desperate, she exited her car and went to the front of the line to plead with U.S. Border Patrol officers to let them through. Despite her desperate pleas of "Emergencia! Emergencia!" (Emergency! Emergency!), an officer reportedly told her: "I don't care. You go down there so they can check your identification." Customs agents then asked her to wait before crossing the U.S.-Mexico border. After spending about thirty minutes pleading at the border-crossing station, Astorga let out a "blood-curtailing scream" as the boy gasped his last breath in her arms. An ambulance arrived moments too late.[15]

A few months later, an incident involving another child, an eighteen-month-old baby, would further infuriate Chicano/a activists. Manolo Alberto, a Tijuana resident and U.S. citizen born in Los Angeles, died of starvation three days after being denied entrance into the United States for treatment. The woman who brought the baby into the border checkpoint, a family friend named Lupe Alonzo, called the border inspectors "cruel and callous."[16] A customs inspector reported that upon entrance of Alonzo and

Alberto at the border checkpoint, "the baby was in third stage malnutrition, when the body starts consuming its organs to sustain itself."[17] Despite the baby's appearance, the primary customs inspector, thinking there might be narcotics in the car, instructed Alonzo to go to the secondary inspection area. This shifted the decision-making responsibilities from customs to immigration officers on whether to allow Alonzo and Alberto entrance into the United States. Alonzo presented the child's birth certificate to the officer, who reportedly said, "I can tell he's Mexican without looking at the birth certificate."[18] This aggression by the border agent revealed what ethnic Mexican border crossers had complained about for at least the past decade: the wider practice by immigration officers of approaching border crossers, as Alonzo put it, "angrily to catch them off guard" and intimidate them. Alonzo was denied entrance and sent back to Mexico with Alberto. The baby died at a Tijuana hospital three days later.[19]

Baca recalled the event involving the eighteen-month-old baby, Manolo. He said: "I particularly remember that case because they finally let them (the boy and family friend) cross a day or so after we raised holy hell about it. So finally they let him across to be buried."[20] As Baca's eyes filled with tears, he recollected: "And I had never seen a coffin for a baby. It was like a shoebox. And I'll always remember looking at his little face and I just kept saying, 'Why? Why?' You know, he didn't have anything to do with this. And you know that just teed me off to no end. It just made me angrier."[21] These events tragically demonstrated the silencing of undocumented voices in debates over immigration. Baca's emotional reaction to become angrier might indicate a wider sentiment experienced by Chicano/a activists and members of the ethnic Mexican community struggling against brutalities at the border. This structural repression ignited resistance to it, further motivating imaginings of alternative practices and an end to the terror interceding in the daily lives of working-class borderlands communities. Indeed, the CCR led efforts to address these issues and used the increasing national media coverage on deaths and brutalities at the border to call further attention to the violence they had struggled against for at least a decade.

Indeed, the emotional residue demonstrated by Baca's response and encapsulated in the community mourning and rage over the deaths of young Manolo and Mario might be conceptualized as a refusal to accept Border Patrol violence as routine, particularly if we consider the human costs of these policies indicated in Baca's tears and Guadalupe Astorga's "blood-curtailing scream" over the death of her nephew in her arms. As social theorist John Holloway observes from the Zapatista struggle: "When we write or when we read [about struggle], it is easy to forget that the beginning is not the word, but the scream. Faced with the mutilation of human lives by capitalism, a scream of sadness, a scream of horror, a scream of anger, a scream of refusal: NO."[22] Astorga's scream of terror, anger, and despair over young Mario's death marked another starting point for reflection and resistance to the dehumanizing effects embedded within immigration policy. Immigration policy here is the particular effect of globalizing capitalism and its alliance with the state at the U.S.-Mexico borderlands: a system that marks some people as "illegal" as a means of creating a disposable workforce. So we might take Astorga's scream as not simply a scream of rage—an expression of despair—but as a refusal to accept the reality that a police force must inflict a system that targets "illegal" people, and in so doing, decides who stays and goes, and in some cases, who lives or dies. Astorga's and others' retelling of her story created a counterpublic, alternative social world where her voice counted—a world that Chicano/a activists attempted to further build.

In between the incidents of the shooting of Rincon and Reyes in March and the death of Alberto in June of 1979, nineteen-year-old Guillermo Lozano, seventeen-year-old Ismael Villa, and Martin Olmos (age unknown) were injured when shot by Border Patrol officers from helicopters in San Ysidro. Earlier in the year, thirty-year-old Margarito Balderos had been shot twice in the back after surrendering to Border Patrol in San Ysidro. Late in the previous year, twenty-one-year-old Abel Reyes Silva had been shot in the back by a Border Patrol officer at the border in Tijuana and a pregnant woman, Maria Contreras, died of a heart attack while being interrogated by border officials in Progreso, Texas.[23] These brutal incidents were recorded in Avalos's *La Frontera en Sangre* pamphlet, calling for further mobilization.

These events further demonstrated the unwillingness of U.S. state actors to respond meaningfully to Chicano/a demands. The CCR and other Chicano/Mexicano activists had kept tabs on these events and were further propelled to insist on action to alleviate an increasingly undeniable situation of violence and injustice. The death of eighteen-month-old Alberto, a U.S. citizen and a baby, seemed to mark a tipping point for activists involved in battling the brutalities of immigration for the past decade. As had been the case since the early 1970s, events of violence against women and children were particularly disturbing to activists, enabling a strong case for attention to these situations by depicting the Border Patrol and larger immigration deportation policies as invasive and destructive to the most vulnerable members of society and disruptive of family unification.[24] Indeed, the CCR marked the death of the baby who was a U.S. citizen by asserting a commitment to alleviate the situation: "A U.S. citizen born resident of Mexico, Mario Alberto was a seriously ill baby who desperately needed special medical treatment. Though properly documented, Mario Alberto was barred from entry into the United States and died days later in Tijuana. It is to the end of this kind of immigration tragedy and to stopping all other acts of violence and discrimination against our people, that the CCR has dedicated itself to."[25] This assertion maintained the CCR as an authority and leader on the issue of immigration due to its involvement with these situations and its location at the site of so many of the brutalities at the San Diego borderlands.

Competing Notions of Democratic Practice

The CCR sought to engage the U.S. state for immediate alleviation of these brutal incidents by again calling for a formal dialog between the communities that were affected by this violence and government officials. Activists did, again, catch the attention of U.S. congressman Edward Roybal, who as head of the Treasury subcommittee, which encompassed investigation of U.S. Customs services, headed a hearing on the deaths of the two children in the San Diego-Tijuana borderlands. The CCR activists had a preceding relationship with Roybal, who held a hearing in 1972 around a string of border violence and harassment incidents. Responding to yet another string of brutal incidents, Roybal held the hearing at a U.S. Customs station in San Diego in 1979, where Alonzo and Astorga testified about the horrific events that led to the deaths of young Mario and Manolo. Roybal and San Diego area congressman Lionel Van Deerlin concluded that something had to be done about the situation, but reminded activists that the hearing was only to gather facts.[26] A historic figure due to being the first Mexican American U.S. congressman elected from California in the twentieth century, Roybal was challenged by Baca at the hearings to bring more urgency to the issue and begin a dialog with borderlands Chicano/Mexicano communities. Baca questioned the planning and structure of the meeting and doubted that there would be any meaningful results because "case after case [has been] dismissed with a see-no-evil, hear-no-evil, speak-no-evil attitude."[27] Baca criticized the location of the hearings at the port-of-entry customs offices, exclaiming that it was "like investigating the wolf in the wolf's den."[28] The CCR had sought out a public hearing for much of the decade, where larger discontents with the INS and immigration policy could be confronted by Chicano/Mexicano leaders and community members. In fact, it was revealed that plans to hold the hearing at an elementary school in a mostly ethnic Mexican community were shelved due to concerns with safety. Furthermore, governmental responses had tended to compartmentalize and bureaucratize issues of brutality, as Roybal's Treasury subcommittee only held jurisdiction over U.S. Customs, not the INS, which was the target of central blame by activists for the deaths of the two children and wider systemic violations of human rights. Baca challenged Roybal at the hearing, exclaiming: "We know the primary cause of the deaths of these two children was the INS, so what are we investigating? We have waited 7 years, we believe these hearings should have been open."[29] Roybal shot back: "What surprises me more than anything is your lack of gratitude. You (Baca) have the nerve to stand there for local consumption and say what you did. The truth of the matter is that I'm the only one who helped you. What you want Mr. Baca is a demonstration, a big show, and you're getting it." Baca responded, "Mr. Congressman, we want solutions."[30]

The seven-year span Baca referred to revealed the failure of the hearings by Roybal and the mechanisms of the U.S. state in 1972 to aptly address the brutality at the border—brutalities had remained, if not multiplied, by 1979. Congressman Roybal experienced the brunt of Chicano/Mexicano activist frustrations over further death and violence and another denial of their demands for a public meeting that would facilitate dialog between their communities and U.S. officials to address Border Patrol and INS legal violence. Baca's confrontation with Roybal, and more readily the CCR's leading role in confronting these atrocities, reaffirmed an attempt to demand dialog with the U.S. state (and as discussed later, the Mexican state) on the terms of autonomous working-class ethnic Mexican and Latino/a communities. Indeed, Baca's declaration to a U.S. state actor that "we want solutions" acknowledged the inability of state actors to create solutions, or even meet and speak on equal footing with Chicano/Mexicano community leaders in ethnic Mexican communities.

What this exchange reveals is a political approach that was diametrically opposed to democratic practice: acting as a state representative and enacting a formal process of liberal representative democracy, Roybal revealed its hierarchical arrangement in his desire for gratitude as "the only one who helped you." While Roybal had been critical of and concerned about the brutalities, the practice of arranging official hearings where some victims were invited to "gather facts" rather than create solutions or collectively analyze the facts and make collective decisions was severely limiting. Baca and the CCR imagined a decision-making process that would include every-day community members, the migrants who were brutalized, and other members of the ethnic Mexican community who were all too aware of the hostile relations with law enforcement within daily life in the border region. The revelation of these contested practices of democracy shifted Chicano/Mexicano strategies of engaging the U.S. state to engaging other grassroots activists and Latino/a community members. The CCR would seek to practice Chicano/Mexicano autonomy and self-determination by enacting their own forms of radical democratic practice. Baca and the CCR called for Chicano/Mexicano grassroots activists to convene in San Diego to col-lectively define solutions to border enforcement policies. Baca explained: "It is our position that all of the past and present proposals which have or are being advocated by policy-makers have failed to resolve the immigra-tion issue. Any new and positive changes are going to have to be defined by us, the Chicano community."[31]

The Chicano National Immigration Conference and Memorial March, May 23–25, 1980

While a number of scholars have noted how Chicano movement attempts to forge unity led to a number of gains alongside internal fractures that de-veloped out of competing definitions of "Chicano" authenticity, the National Chicano Immigration Conference offers intriguing analysis of strategies of building ethnic community in that Chicano identity was conceived of in a transnational manner, and that as part of this conception, differences within the community were acknowledged and contemplated upon. The confer-ence considered key structures that produced differences in citizenship status, time of arrival from Mexico, and national affiliation, thereby acknowl-edging the heterogeneity within the "Chicano/Mexicano" community. Its emphasis on a grappling with internal differences and initiating a collec-tive process seeking to give voice to the most vulnerable among them in terms of legal status suggested processes of autonomy that worked through differences rather than deducing them.

Workshops on the particular plights of incarceration of the undocu-mented, women and immigration, and organized labor reflected a concern with different groups within the community in terms of citizenship status, gender, and class. The focus on internal difference and its transnational scope enabled the possibility of a more inclusive and expansive notion of "self-determination" as something forged through recognition of both differences and shared repression, and shared struggle against that racialization. This notion of "self-determination" by a community imagined as transnational created the context in which local autonomy could facilitate representation of racialized citizens and migrant noncitizens in the globalizing constructs of capitalist development that encouraged migration.

The conference brought a broad spectrum of activists representing about two hundred organizations from throughout California, including San Diego, Los Angeles, San Jose, Oakland, San Francisco, and Santa Barbara; from Texas, including San Antonio, Houston, and El Paso; from Colorado, including Denver and Pueblo; and from Chicago and Tijuana. It brought together well-known Chicano movement and Mexican American organizations, including chapters of the Brown Berets, MEChA, the Crusade for Justice, and the Chicano Moratorium Coalition, as well as local chapters of LULAC, the G.I. Forum, and the Mexican American Legal Defense and Education Fund (MALDEF). Also participating were a number of grassroots social service organizations (i.e., the Vecinos de Casa Familiar [Neighbors of Family House], San Diego; Escuela de la Gente [The People's School], Van Nuys, CA; and Centro de Inmigracion Pro-Comunidad [Pro-community Center of Immigration, Santa Barbara); religious institutions (i.e., Hispanic Community Lutheran Ministry, Tucson; Acción Católica Juvenil [Catholic Youth Action], Los Angeles; and the Archdiocesan Latin American Committee, Chicago); emergent immigrant rights groups (i.e., Coalition for Immigrant Rights, Houston, and the National Center for Immigrant Rights, Los Angeles); artist collectives (i.e., El Teatro de la Esperanza [Theater of Hope], Santa Barbara; El Movimiento Artistico Chicano [The Chicano Artist Movement], Chicago; and El Centro Cultural de la Gente [Cultural Center of the People], San Jose); labor unions (i.e., United Auto Workers #165, Los Angeles, and the United Domestic Workers of America, San Diego); and legal aid societies (i.e., El Paso Legal Assistance Society; Legal Aid Society Orange County; and Civil Rights Litigation Center, San Antonio). Also included were a small number of non-Latino activists of color, including the Union of Democratic Filipinos; the former head of the Black Power organization Nia, Ken Msemaji; and American Indian movement leader Dennis Banks. Other prominent speakers and participants included Bert Corona; Corky Gonzales; Soledad "Chole" Alatorre; Ruben Bonilla, national chairman of LULAC;

Lupe Saldana, national chair of the American G.I. Forum; and Professor Rodolfo Acuña.[32] It was estimated that about 1,000 individuals participated in the conference, representing about 200 organizations, while about 4,000 participated in the memorial march the following day.[33]

Baca greeted these participants in the conference in what one report noted as "an hour-long, applause-punctuated speech" by framing the ensuing dialog around contemplation of the root causes of "illegal immigration" that tied the global scope of capitalist practices, U.S. neoimperialism, and exploitation of labor to the subordination of the Latino/a population in the United States.[34] Veteran activist Bert Corona and Corky Gonzales reinforced these analyses in their introductory speeches. Gonzales noted the futility of relying on the U.S. state and the need for autonomous action. These ideas echoed Baca's call for an alternative perspective on immigration outside of the mainstream aspects of the "illegal alien" debate that were framed around enforcement on the one hand and mixed enforcement/ amnesty provisions on the other. These ideas were further unpacked in a more thorough analysis in a speech Baca gave a week earlier. In this speech, Baca situated a Chicano position on immigration outside of the dominant framework that posited a "historically racist, chauvinist view" on the one hand and the "liberal view" on the other.[35] Baca explained that solutions that relied on enforcement and mass deportation as a solution were analogous to the racist views held by the Ku Klux Klan or Nazis, "who view any non-whites as a problem." "The second perspective," he argued, "is more dangerous" because "confused" and "good willed liberals" simply sought to "call for re-shuffling without getting to the causes of the problem."[36] This was more dangerous, Baca argued, because "if put into practice, it would sanctify exploitation" since proposals such as that presented by President Carter called for amnesty alongside more "repressive legislation," including further militarization and guest worker programs. Baca explained that the liberal perspective failed to recognize the U.S. "domination of Mexico" that created the context in which Mexican workers are forced to migrate to the United States for economic survival and are subsequently exploited as noncitizens, or, as the Carter proposal also suggests, as part of a temporary guest worker program. This situation in which amnesty would be packaged alongside a formalization of the importation and exploitation of Mexican workers is what made the liberal perspective so dangerous according to Baca. Again, tying this situation to other societal practices of racial subordination and racialized labor exploitation, Baca argued, "It would create an apartheid system in the Southwest if these guest worker plans were put into effect because you need a tremendous enforcement system."[37]

Baca argued further that guest worker programs would discipline labor organizing as the Bracero Program of the mid-century did, "creating a strictly defined lower-economic class."[38] For this reason, the CCR defined the immigration issue as the "slave issue of the 20th century," and argued that "these same attitudes led to the ultimate degradation of chattel slavery in this country's history. If things continue we will reach the same point again."[39] Evoking slavery and the apartheid system most closely associated with South Africa enabled Baca to identify the problems emanating from immigration as systematic, that is, part of a structural practice of racialized labor exploitation that was not in need of reform but abolition.

This understanding of the structural framework of deportation-oriented immigration policy revealed the embedded relationship between black and brown freedom movements. Recalling his experiences, Baca noted the similarities between the slave system and the practice of border enforcement within immigration policy. He reflected, "Really when you take the immigration issue and the Afro-American experience there's a deep parallel. . . . The so called illegal alien immigration issue has been structured also to provide cheap labor so they could be easily exploited at will and the whole mechanism, just like in the slave system, ensured that people have no right to defend themselves."[40] Baca's understanding of this historic relationship between the African American and Mexican American communities developed not only out of a Chicano/a struggle against the system of border enforcement but in actual work with black activists in the San Diego borderlands, particularly the Nia Cultural Organization.

As explored in chapters 6 and 7, the CCR formulated a working relationship with Nia in the context of struggle against police violence in the extrajudicial shootings of Luis "Tato" Rivera and Tyrone Thomas, and to confront the overlapping threat of white supremacist vigilantes and border policing in the event of KKK support of the Border Patrol in 1977. The politics of solidarity between the CCR and Nia contextualizes Baca's discourse on slavery, racial segregation, and apartheid as part of a shared struggle between Chicano/a and black activists rooted locally, but with transnational implications.

Indeed, in the late 1970s Nia and the Black Federation of San Diego, also headed by Nia organizer Vernon Sukumu, participated in the call for international pressure against apartheid in South Africa by exposing local San Diego ties to it.[41] Early in 1978, a coalition of chiefly African American organizations, but also the CCR, charged the city and county of San Diego with investing in corporations doing business in apartheid South Africa. "San Diego money is being used to prop up a racist regime," said Greg Akili of Nia.[42] Demanding complete disinvestments, the coalition forced the local government to explain these dubious connections. After much debate and deliberation, the County Board of Supervisors was able to maintain its ties to U.S. corporations in South Africa by requesting that companies sign onto Reverend Leon Sullivan's principles for investment in South Africa, which guaranteed the fair treatment and equal pay of South African workers, non-segregation in the work place, increase in the number of blacks in management and investment in black communities to improve day-to-day life among other commitments.[43] Yet Nia and the coalition argued that the monitoring of U.S. companies and their subsidiaries in South Africa was impossible, due chiefly to South African law, which did not allow outside observing. Furthermore, they argued that the signatories of the principles did not address the basic policy of apartheid and subtly supported its maintenance.[44] Engagement with apartheid by black organizations and the CCR revealed the international scope that these groups had taken and the ways in which the black and Chicano/a activist community broadened their horizons to engage undocumented immigration from Latin America for the latter and apartheid on the African continent for the former. Indeed, while Nia ceased around 1979, former member Ken Msemaji was present at the Chicano/a conference. Possibly indicating further shifts towards structural issues around race and labor, Msemaji came representing the local chapter of the United Domestic Workers of America union. Importantly, "apartheid" became a key part of the discourse in the Chicano/a struggle for immigrant rights, as evidenced in many of Baca's speeches. The construction of a white supremacist system, dominated by a white minority over a majority indigenous population resonated with the historical narrative of the Chicano/a struggle against Euro-American invaders and the projected increase of the ethnic Mexican population.

This dialog between Nia and the CCR also produced dynamic positions taken by Black Power activists on immigration. This had culminated for Nia by April of 1978 as the CCR and broader Chicano/a activism began the struggle against the Carter Curtain. At that time, Nia leader Ken Msemaji issued a clear position stating, "Herman Baca and the Committee on Chicano Rights represents our interest and concerns regarding the immigration issue and the Carter Immigration Plan."[45] This general public statement reminded that "Nia is predominately a Black Organization working primarily in the black community in San Diego" and identified broader African American support throughout California by highlighting matching positions taken by "Most of the Black Elected Officials in California including Lt. Governor Mervyn Dymally."[46] Nia's diasporic and internationalist definition of black identity enabled an analysis of immigration as a racial system that also affected black migrants. Msemaji concluded the statement by saying, "We are extremely concerned about our brothers and sisters from the West Indies, Panama and Haiti etc. Who constantly are having their human rights violated by immigration officials."[47]

Nia's position on immigration was further elaborated in their yearly Malcolm X commemoration march when in 1978 the theme was "Jobs are a right—not a priviledge."[48] A year after they focused on the theme of South African apartheid, the focus on full employment articulated a concern for high unemployment among African Americans and other workers of color while maintaining solidarity with migrant workers. Nia and their allies reversed the rhetoric on the immigration debate, pointing out that it was U.S. businesses that crossed the border into Mexico and other third world nations, and left thousands out of work in the United States. Featuring celebrities and noted activists including white progressives Jane Fonda and Tom Hayden, AIM leader Dennis Banks and the UFW's Dolores Huerta, Fonda represented this sentiment well in a speech. She asserted "U.S. multinational corporations . . . are the real illegal aliens. The firms exploit low wages and lack of union protection there and help create poor economic conditions that send Mexican workers north for jobs."[49] At a time of recession when calls for stricter border enforcement were reaching alarming levels, Nia promoted in solidarity and partnership with groups such as the CCR, that the real issue was not immigrants, but economic shifts that resulted in a lack of jobs for working people and especially communities of color.

Engaging these discourses with a global scope and across different communities' struggles against racial oppression, the CCR sought to begin Chicano/a contemplation of solutions that addressed the root problems tied up in the collusion between first world nation-states and global capitalists and imperialist ventures into the third world. Baca argued that the U.S. government was obligated to let working-class Latin Americans and others migrate to the United States because "they've let Chase Manhattan run amuck in the third world."[50] This justified the solution of granting immediate amnesty to any noncitizen "person or dependent . . . even if he came in 1 second ago."[51] Citing that for every one dollar invested in Mexico, seven dollars is taken out, Baca declared that immediate legal standing was necessary because migration was simply a symptom of the larger cause of global capitalism and U.S. imperialism. He argued further that to accomplish this "third way" of addressing the immigration crisis, it was necessary to put "political power in the hands of those most affected by the immigration issue—the Chicano/Mexicano/Latino community."[52] It is in this logic that the CCR framed the dialog among grassroots activists at the National Chicano Immigration Conference.

The grassroots approach for the conference that sought to organize working-class Latino/a communities was evident in its organization. In contrast to the hearings conducted by Congressman Roybal, the conference was held at St. Rita's Catholic Church in a working-class, largely ethnic Mexican area of San Diego. Furthermore, as a Catholic parish, it reflected the conscious effort of the conference organizers to hold the event in a preexisting institution within the local working-class ethnic Mexican community. The conference was affordable, costing ten dollars for registration that included meals, entertainment, and information about recent CCR struggles over immigration, including *La Frontera en Sangre* booklet created by CCR member David Avalos. Free lodging was also provided upon request.[53]

Working-class Mexicano/a cultural practices were also evident in the proceedings of the conference. In this way, cultural identity was forged to promote a transnational, autonomous, and working-class politics, and to enact a form of self-determination based on the everyday cultural idioms of Chicano/Mexicano communities. For example, before the opening speeches, an invocation was conducted by Sister Sarah Murietta of the Padre Hidalgo Center. Chicano/a *teatros* [theater groups] provided music and entertainment that galvanized the conference themes of unity, community, and political solidarity, with undocumented immigrants as part of a Chicano/Mexicano community. For example, Chicano poet Jose Antonio Burciaga performed, as well as the San Diego-based Latin folk and rock musical group Los Alacranes Mojados.[54] Mariachis set the mood in the mornings before the conference meetings and in the evenings after them. Pan dulce (Mexican sweet bread) was served for breakfast, and on the last day of the conference before the March, the tradition of serving menudo (tripe and hominy stew) on Sunday morning convened participants following a Catholic mass performed by Bishop Gilbert Chávez. These cultural practices surrounded and reinforced the conference themes of celebrating Mexicano/a culture and uniting as one people through shared ethnic ties across boundaries of nationality and citizenship status.

For example, Teatro de la Esperanza, a Santa Barbara-based theatre troupe, performed the play *Victima*, culminating the theme of unity and political solidarity across national lines and citizenship status. The play began by proclaiming, "The Chicano is a victim of a subtle and complex form of oppression, which because of particular racial and historical factors differs from traditional forms yet results in the same end; the exploitation of one group, for the benefit of another."[55] The play then followed the life of Amparo, a girl from Mexico forced to flee the violence of the Mexican Revolution in 1913 to the United States. In Scene 2 entitled, "The First Deportations–1921," Amparo meets Julian at a dance where they escape a deportation raid by "the skin of their teeth." Amparo and Julian marry and have a son, Samuelito. In the midst of the Depression and the repatriation of Mexicanos/as back to Mexico, Amparo loses Samuelito while being deported by train. Samuelito is then adopted by Mexican American parents, goes by the name "Sam," becomes a war veteran, and joins the Border Patrol, moving up the ranks. Soon after, Sam's long-lost brother and sister migrate to the United States for opportunity, leaving Amparo and Julian, who is sick, behind. After Julian passes away, Amparo has no choice but to migrate to the United States to be with her children there. At the climax of the play, Sam raids a factory strike and detains his long-lost family. As he unknowingly interrogates his own mother, he figures out who she is but denies it, ultimately deporting her. The final scene has Sam's inner turmoil manifest in a nightmare. The play ends with a rendition of the Chilean folk song "El Pueblo Unido, [The United People]" signaling the need to recognize the familial, ethnic, and political links between undocumented Mexican migrants and Mexican Americans. In the context of the conference, this play expressed key themes that sought to extend a political agenda based on a shared reality among Mexican immigrants and Mexican Americans that had long fragmented ethnic Mexican politics in the United States. This notion of identity was not based on blood lines but was reflective of the material realities that Chicano/Mexicano activists in San Diego had engaged for decades, namely, that state repression affected the everyday life and aspirations of ethnic Mexicans and Latinos/as of all citizenship statuses. The inclusion of "Latino" that had developed in recent years as activists began identifying the community as "Chicano/Mexicano/Latino" might indicate new notions of solidarity that would include wider Latin Americans in this experience, as the play ended with a Chilean protest song, possibly paying homage to the struggles in that nation against the U.S. imperialism demonstrated in the CIA-orchestrated coup of Socialist president Salvador

Allende earlier in the 1970s. The shared repression experienced by this transnational community is what the conference set out to more fully define by providing autonomous working-class Latino/a solutions to the immigration process outside of the carrot-and-stick "liberal" official policy proposals that combined a limited amnesty with further militarization and temporary worker "slave" programs.

Indeed, the workshops convened to call for the complete dismantling of border enforcement and deportation mechanisms, the right of laborers to cross borders and have the same basic rights as citizens, and a binational and international collaboration that was inclusive of the independent voice of Chicano/Mexicano/Latino communities. The "Border Violence" workshop, convened by Baca, Ruben Sandoval, and Albert García, called for the abolishment of the INS/Border Patrol and an end to the binational policy of militarization at the border as a solution to migration between Mexico and the United States. The Border Violence workshop's resolutions revealed how Chicano/Mexicano activists now perceived the roots of border violence in a transnational context, put in place not only by the policies consistently exerted by the U.S. state but approved by the Mexican state as well.

The latter assertion reveals that these grassroots activists not only blamed the U.S. state for border violence but held the organs and leadership of the Mexican state responsible as well. Leading up to the conference, the CCR and other Chicano/Mexicano activists had engaged President Jose López Portillo in his talks with President Carter about Mexico's growing oil industry to little avail. In 1980, the CCR proposed that President López Portillo act by creating a bilateral commission to address ongoing struggles in San Diego to stop the detention and alleged deportation of children without their parents.[56] Lack of response from the Mexican state led to more critical appraisals by Chicano/Mexicano activists. Baca asserted the more critical approach to the Mexican state when he argued: "Mexico, because of its situation, has never defended the Chicano like it should. . . . Concerning the immigration issue for example, we see the Chicano Movement in complete contradiction with forces in Mexico. While the Chicano is against temporary worker programs, the PRI is for them. . . . There is a great difference between the Mexican people and the PRI."[57] Baca's comments reveal that many activists had become critical of the Mexican government in its apparent unwillingness or inability to address the abuses within border enforcement policies. This led the CCR to continue to consider transnational alliances, but with the "Mexican people" rather than the ruling PRI members, whom Baca cited as "reactionary forces in power."[58] Instead, the CCR sought to locate "progressive forces (in Mexico) that are doing the same thing we are trying to do."[59] Indeed, the call for the National Chicano Immigration Conference and Memorial March by the CCR to be held in May 1980 marked a positioning in which Chicano/Mexicano activists sought to collectively develop solutions to the immigration crisis on their own by calling forth community organizations from across the United States and the U.S.-Mexico border region in San Diego. This process of collective consideration revealed the expression of Chicano self-determination based on the notion of the community as a transnational entity independent from but wedged in between and engaged in autonomous dialog with the United States and Mexican states on the immigration issue.

This act brought full circle the transnational definitions of community that Chicano/Mexicano activists in San Diego had developed in battle against Border Patrol legal violence for almost a decade. Baca asserted how a fluid definition of community facilitated sustained independent resistance to systems of border enforcement. He noted: "Chicano to me means change . . . but instead of being anti-Mexicano as some have tried to project it [the Chicano movement and identity], it was really an effort of trying to learn about being a Mexicano. We never said we weren't Mexicano. At the same time, we needed to make Mexico aware of our situation over which we had no control—and make clear we would have to be respected for our efforts."[60] Indeed, Baca made clear that relations with Mexico were just as problematic for "Chicanos" as with the United States. Because Mexico was unwilling to assist Chicano/Mexicano activists and transnational ethnic Mexican communities in the United States with repression from border enforcement policies, Baca argued, "The Chicano was forced to look inward and understand that if we wanted respect, we would have to fight for it, if we wanted change we would have to make it ourselves."[61]

Here Baca outlines well the structural constraints that actually created the conditions in which a significant number of working-class ethnic Mexican community organizations would conceptualize their community as autonomous entities in between the hegemonic rule of both the United States and Mexican states. This assertion revealed the inability of both states to facilitate the demands of its peoples due to their alignment with the interests of transnational capital. Baca stated that the inability of the two national governments to end the violence placed on ethnic Mexican and Latino/a communities and forcing "the Chicano" to "look inward" ultimately was "a positive thing because it has reinforced us (Mexican Americans and

Mexican nationals) as one people and I see a linking up somewhere in the future based on that understanding and that respect."[62]

The "Chicano/Mexicano Perspective" workshop reflected this transnational analysis of power by proposing solutions that crossed borders. Reckoning with the U.S. conquest of the Southwest, the Chicano/Mexicano Perspective workshop participants led by Corky Gonzales asserted, "That this conference go on record as demanding unconditional residency for all people with all rights and privileges of indigenous people as provided for in the Treaty of Guadalupe Hidalgo."[63] Following the extended notion of the "Chicano/Mexicano" community as an entity that preexisted in what became the U.S. Southwest, the participants recontextualized the Treaty of Guadalupe Hidalgo, which guaranteed that the citizenship rights of the Mexican inhabitants of the Southwest following the U.S.-Mexican War be extended to contemporary migrants from Mexico. This epitomized the extension of Chicano movement goals of rectifying the long history of Mexican subjugation in the United States in an era of increasing globalization and migration by making official the interlaced and unequal social, political, and economic ties between the United States and Mexico.

The assertion of Chicano/Mexicano historical rights to roam the U.S.-Mexico border region did not prevent the conference from looking beyond the wider issue of migration from the global south to the north. In fact, the class analysis of labor exploitation as a key part of immigration policy facilitated the assertion of a type of class identity that intersected and existed alongside an ethno-racial community membership. Indeed, the second resolution of the Chicano/Mexicano workshop stated, "That this conference go on record as abolishing all quotas on immigration from countries where the USA has political, economic, and military domination."[64] This resolution reflected Baca's earlier assertions that U.S. society owes global south migrants the opportunity to migrate because U.S. policymakers have "allowed Chase Manhattan to run amuck in the third world." Due to analysis of the immigration issue as not solely an attack on Chicanos but more widely a manifestation of capital power and control of third world and working-class peoples more broadly, the conference was able to transcend narrow nationalist solutions.

This sentiment was reinforced by resolutions from the "Economics, Labor, and Foreign Worker Program" workshop facilitated by veteran labor activist Bert Corona and Nick Hernandez. This workshop went on record for "supporting an Open-Border for immigrant workers and a Closed-border for multinational corporations."[65] This analysis of power as emanating not just from an ambiguous racism but primarily from multinational corporations enabled a solution that considered the global scope of inequality and its reproduction through a system of globalization that allowed the free movement of capital but policed that of labor. The rejection of any guest worker programs, defined as "twentieth century slavery," reflected this sentiment further.[66]

While the conference expressed broad notions of inclusivity in its analysis of race and class oppression, it failed to report on the "Women and Immigration" workshop in its final proceedings and resolutions, thus neglecting to consider the powerful ways in which patriarchy and heteronormativity shaped global systems of power. While other workshops were not reported on, including the workshops on media and legislation, it may be reflective of the consistent problem that the Chicano movement had with regard to gender and the masculinized space of political leadership. While the Chicano Immigration Conference and the wider Chicano movement addressed and contemplated the experience of a group often subordinated within their community, noncitizens, Chicano critiques of border policing were based largely on the ways in which it broke up the nuclear family. This construction of Chicano ties through a celebration of families reinforced the domesticated positions of women as wives and mothers, limiting the ability of feminist concerns and female leadership to reach a matter of significance. Veteran labor activist Soledad "Chole" Alatorre, along with Adela Serrano, Ann Legrada, and Maria Montes, were supposed to have led the workshop, but no evidence reveals its resolutions or even whether the workshop took place. More important, the conference participants and its leaders decided not to publish the resolutions if in fact the workshop did occur.[67] The conference proceedings and resolution missed the opportunity to explore and grapple with the ways women's issues and discourses of gender, sexuality, and family limited the inclusion of the many identities existent within the ethnic Mexican community.

The conference did extend notions of identity and solidarity across national boundaries through engaging Mexican civil society. Several newspapers, particularly in the Mexican press in Tijuana and wider Baja California, printed the resolutions of the workshops at the conference. Baca held a press conference in Tijuana days before the conference, charging that the U.S. press did not report the problems of Mexican Americans due to its racist history.[68] Furthermore, the "Labor, Economics and Foreign Worker Program" workshop resolved that it supported the demands made at an

International Immigration Conference held a month earlier in Mexico City, revealing solidarities with groups in Mexico advocating for undocumented migrant workers.[69] The Chicano/Mexicano Perspective workshop demanded that the Mexican government support progressive groups in Mexico and Chicano groups in their struggle for human rights and demand compliance with the Treaty of Guadalupe Hidalgo. This was based on the "fact" that, "somos un pueblo sin fronteras" (we are a people without borders) and therefore "the struggle for immigrant rights is part and parcel of the struggle for Chicano/Mexicano rights to self-determination."[70] This pronouncement of transnational citizenship enabled these activists to assert a community identity that sought autonomy from, but compliance with, both the U.S. and Mexican states.

The effects of the National Chicano Conference on Immigration on Mexican activists and wider society are difficult to measure. Mexican activists' participation in the conference was minimal, as only one immigrant rights group from Tijuana was found to attend. Yet the Mexican media, particularly that in Tijuana and wider Baja California, churned out story after story on the conference and other Chicano movement activities that focused on immigration. San Diego Chicano/a activists had become especially familiar with the Tijuana press through the years due to their proximity to the border. Baca recalled: "The U.S. media, even in our own backyard in San Diego would not cover our issues. So we came to find that the Tijuana media would eat stuff on racism up, send it to Mexico City and it would come full circle back to the U.S. press."[71] Indeed, in planning the conference, a CCR meeting noted this strategy for getting media coverage when it was stated that activists "have learned that the best way to get attention in Washington is through Mexico." They noted further that "through the last 10 years they (Chicano/a activists in San Diego) have been able to educate the media to the immigration situation and have encouraged investigative reporting as opposed to the previous bylines doled out by the INS."[72] Baca argued that going through Mexico and back to the U.S. press pressured the San Diego press to finally take note of their activities, concerns, and demands.[73]

Later in 1981, engagement with Mexican society brought several CCR members and wider Chicano/Mexicano activists, including Bert Corona, to an academic conference called the First Symposium on Immigration at the Autonomous University of Sinaloa in Culiacán, Sinaloa, Mexico.[74] This conference highlighted the growing transnational activity that San Diego and wider Chicano/Mexicano activists were engaging in regarding hysteria over "illegal aliens." Baca used the conference for more exposure to the violence exerted on the ethnic Mexican community in San Diego and throughout the U.S., and to spread the word about the solutions that Chicano/a grassroots organizations proposed at the National Chicano Immigration Conference. Indeed, at a press conference in Culiacan, CCR activists noted that the Chicano Immigration Conference participants had elected that they report on recent violations committed at the U.S. Mexico border to the Culiacán symposium "for the purpose of demanding an end to the abuses that occur daily to Mexicanos/Chicanos in the United States."[75] Cited were the cases of four-year-old Mario Canedo, the shooting of Efren Reyes and Benito Rincon while handcuffed, as well as the February 1979 shooting of Margarito Fernandez and the May 1979 shooting of Martin Zarate and Ricardo Real, both sixteen years of age, by the Border Patrol.[76] These interactions in Mexico reveal how Chicano/Mexicano participants in the National Chicano Immigration Conference sought to enact transnational forms of community and coalition by disseminating information about the abuses experienced by Mexican and other Latino/a migrants due to border enforcement.

The Culiacán symposium also shows how the CCR and wider Chicano/Mexicano movement sought to expose the experiences and give voice to undocumented migrants themselves. A key resolution from the National Chicano Immigration Conference that outlined future activities for the CCR was the appointment of a representative of the conference participants to "present the most degrading violations of human rights to international Human Rights Organizations with the understanding that the long range solutions be in our people's self-determination."[77] By documenting and presenting the experiences and voices of noncitizens and racialized citizens abused by the Border Patrol and wider immigration policy, the conference participants sought to redefine notions of who was qualified to participate in the process of creating immigration policy. This insurgent notion of social membership countered the rules of citizenship within the nation-state to include undocumented migrants residing in or working in the U.S.-Mexico borderlands. This alternative social membership also refused to abide by national boundaries between the United States and Mexico, redrawing its social geography to include the transnational space of the United States and Mexico. To enact this notion of belonging, the Chicano Immigration Conference opted to hold a tribunal, officially giving time and space to those abused by border enforcement and immigration policies and enacting an autonomous process of solving the immigration crisis.

The Chicano National Immigration Tribunal, April 11, 1981

Noting that Frederick Douglass was "oppressed by a policy similar to today's immigration policy," the CCR analogized the plight of Chicano/Mexicano/Latino working-class communities with the African American struggle against slavery when remembering the words of "a man born into slavery who rose above his chains and outlined clearly what we must do to end our oppression."[78] Quoting Douglass, the CCR introduced a document that encapsulated a notion of transnational belonging and democratic practice that challenged that of the nation-state and immigration policy in the service of capital. Activists argued that the failure for U.S. state officials (and Mexico, for that matter) to respond to the brutality and violence perpetrated against migrants and U.S. Latinos/as revealed the role that race played in decision-making processes within liberal democracy. Furthermore, they argued that maintaining an official policy that racially profiled Latinos/as, whether noncitizens or citizens of the United States, worked to keep their communities subordinated. This was at the service of capital, ultimately, in that it maintained a cheap subordinated workforce that was also disposable and lacked rights. The fallout of this racialized subordination in service of a hierarchical labor system made Latinos/as vulnerable to violence due to the law enforcement mechanism deemed necessary to immigration policy. While differences among ethnic Mexican and Latino/a community members, in particular legal status, but also gender and class, led to varying and differing degrees of legal violence, this created a shared experience that activists sought to unite around. Indeed, the tribunal revealed the testimonies of a number of non-Mexican Latinos/as, citizens, noncitizens, men, women, children, and allies.

The tribunal, coupled with the resolutions from the Chicano immigration conference a year earlier, came at an important moment to challenge and contrast with the U.S. Select Commission on Immigration and Refugee Policy, which issued its final report on March 1, 1981. This commission, created by President Carter, came to reinforce his immigration policy proposal that failed to advance into legislation. Its bipartisan makeup and leadership under an educational and religious leader, Father Theodore Hesburgh, gave it an air of legitimacy and compromise, establishing what geographer Joseph Nevins asserts was "the basis for subsequent debate and legislation regarding immigration control."[79] Outlasting President Carter's administration, it created the foundation for subsequent debate on immigration policy under the new administration of Republican president Ronald Reagan. Contrasting with this official report and study, the Chicano Immigration Tribunal revealed an on-the-ground purview of the stakes of immigration policy, particularly the ways "enforcement," as recommended by the commission, affected the lives and physical bodies of ethnic Mexicans in the borderlands.

The tribunal was planned as a result of the National Chicano Immigration Conference proceedings almost a year earlier. It convened at Our Lady of Angels Catholic Church in the neighborhood of Logan Heights, the heart of the ethnic Mexican community in San Diego.[80] The tribunal was conducted in the hall of the church, and was welcoming to the community and anyone willing to observe the testimonials. Its stated goals included to "Give those who have been victimized by the INS/Border Patrol a forum to present testimony and cases to a panel of distinguished national leaders. . . . Nationally document the massive violations of human rights against undocumented persons . . . and also the violations of civil and constitutional rights of the 20 million Chicanos/Latinos in the U.S. by the INS/Border Patrol . . . and Draft a Chicano position paper based on the documented cases . . . to be presented to President Reagan and Portillo."[81] The panel of national leaders included Professor Rudy Acuña from California State University, Northridge; Chicano movement icon Corky Gonzales of Colorado; Lupe Sanchez, leader of the Arizona Farmworkers; Jose "Pepe" Medina, the former CASA member in the early 1970s who facilitated drafting the Undocumented Immigrant Bill of Rights in Mexico City; and Herman Baca. The panel included only a few leaders from outside of the Southwest, Ernesto Chacón from Wisconsin and Juan Solis from the Legal Center for Immigrants in Illinois, and only two women, Sister Sara Murrieta of the local Padre Hidalgo social services and Margo Cowan of the Manzo Project in Arizona.[82]

Seventeen testimonials recalled more than fifty cases at the event where survivors, relatives of the abused, and observers familiar with particular cases of brutality presented the details of how border enforcement policies affected Latino/a migrants and citizens throughout the United States and the binational borderlands. These cases were arranged into eight different categories, including denial of medical services, use of deadly force by law enforcement officials, abuse of children, inflicting unnecessary physical violence, systematic violations of human rights, and raids of community and workplace by INS/Border Patrol agencies.[83]

These incidents revealed the many dimensions through which border enforcement policies affected Latinos/as in the United States and in the borderlands. In addition to the violent incidents noted in David Avalos's pamphlet, *La Frontera en Sangre*, the Chicano Tribunal put forth dozens of additional testimonies. Again, these testimonies deserve forewarning of their graphic content and brutality. Activists sought to reveal the face of the suffering involved with deportation-oriented immigration policies, and survivors and observers came forth to tell their stories. For example, the testimony began with former Border Patrol officer Frederick Drew, who recalled the cruelty and brutalities that he witnessed when in this position in 1966. He recalled beatings, shootings, and other cruel and callous behavior among agents, and in Mexican territory witnessed an agent rape a woman. An African American, Drew showed vehement concern for the issue, for he had testified about many of these incidents in 1972.

More examples included a February 1980 event when Border Patrol agents in Jim Hogg County, Texas, shot at a truck while in pursuit of undocumented migrants, resulting in a crash that killed two people and injured eleven. In Arizona, three undocumented persons, Manuel García, Elezar Ruelas, and Bernabe Herrera, were tortured and hanged due to the vigilantism of the Hanigan family. These were among the most dramatic incidents in which physical violence and death resulted from hysteria over "illegal aliens."[84]

The tribunal also reported that deportations disrupted families and lives of migrants. One undocumented Mexican worker was deported to Guatemala because INS agents thought he looked Guatemalan. Frank Amaro from the Mexican American National Organization (MANO) in Los Angeles testified about the more than three hundred cases from 1971 to 1979 in which his organization had assisted children separated from their parents due to deportation. He noted that a number of the families were never reunited. MANO sought to keep these children from entering the foster system because it made reunification with their families more difficult. Elvia Murphy Davalos was forcibly separated from her husband when INS agents detained and stripped-searched her. They were visiting from Tijuana on a legitimate temporary visa to visit Disney Land. These practices also affected U.S. citizens of Latino/a ancestry. At least two Puerto Rican men, and therefore U.S. citizens, reported that they were routinely being harassed and detained by INS officers. Several U.S. citizens were detained, harassed, and at times deported.[85] One of the men, Luis Arquer, claimed he was pulled over and asked for his immigration papers on at least two separate occasions by West Chicago police officers. In both cases he explained he was Puerto Rican and a United States citizen. One officer accused him of speeding, the other of failing to use his turn signal, yet neither wrote Arquer a ticket after he revealed he was a citizen. Arquer chose to use another route to get to work and avoid West Chicago. Arquer ended his declaration written for the tribunal asserting, "The West Chicago Police Department is involved in the practice of routinely detaining, interrogating and harassing Latinos to inquire about their immigration status. Consequently, I am involved in a class action lawsuit challenging their racist harassment of Chicano/Latino people."[86] Harassment by border officials across the country influenced a shared Latino/a identity around the experience of being racialized and profiled as "illegal aliens" by law enforcement agents and others.

In the finalized document of the tribunal proceedings, newspaper coverage and additional archival evidence was added to a summary of the testimony for each case. The tribunal proceedings document noted that these cases "represent nothing but the tip of the iceberg of immigration abuses."[87] Furthermore, the tribunal leaders argued, "The enclosed documentation proves beyond a shadow of a doubt that these rights violations which have been perpetrated under the color of the law, are widespread and commonplace."[88] The racialized experiences of the Latino/a community, both noncitizens and citizens, had been systematically erased. The tribunal document worked as a collective demand for a ceasing of this erasure, demanding recognition of their alternative notion of self-determination, community formation, and social membership.

The tribunal demanded to not only end the abuse of their communities but through the very act of proceeding with an independent tribunal, called for the right to exist as a transnational community. The Chicano Tribunal in this way enacted a democratizing project that enabled participation in the affairs of both societies. Rather than exist at the infrapolitical level, Chicano/Mexicano and now—Chicano/Mexicano/Latino—communities sought to engage with and therein demand recognition from the apparatuses of the U.S. and Mexican governments. This was made clear in the one thousand–page documented created out of the tribunal as it was addressed to new president Ronald Reagan and President Jose López Portillo. A letter to both presidents appeared in the first few pages of the document "formally request(ing) a response to the enclosed documents outlining specific cases of violations of human, civil, and constitutional rights of persons of Mexicano/Latino ancestry by the INS/Border Patrol and other law enforcement agencies."[89] Addressed by Baca acting as the appointed representative of the proceedings of the National Chicano Immigration Conference and the Chicano National Immigration Tribunal, the letter reminded the two presidents that the escalation of violence due to border enforcement polices "has been totally ignore by both United States and Mexican policy-makers," and therefore required an intervention by "Chicano/Mexicano/Latino" communities in the continuing binational talks concerning petroleum trade and immigration. For this reason, Chicano/Mexicano leaders demanded an immediate end to violence from the everyday practice of border enforcement, the establishment of a binational commission with substantive dialog with communities in "areas most affected by immigration abuses," and an inclusion of the abuses documented in the tribunal summary in any future talks on immigration policy. Noting the transnational space in which their communities exist, Baca asserted, "It is our position that the social, economic, and political interdependency between [the] United States and Mexico demands that these actions be taken immediately."[90]

The tribunal document concluded with recommendations asserted by Chicano/Mexicano activists that reiterated the need to abolish the INS/Border Patrol, cease all deportation mechanisms, and ensure the protection of the human and civil rights of undocumented migrants. A list of the resolutions from the National Chicano Immigration Conference along with a "Bill of Rights for the Undocumented Worker" asserted these recommendations to the two administrations. Developed at the First International Conference for the Full Rights of Undocumented Workers in Mexico City a year before, the Bill of Rights asserted thirteen decrees. Included in these decrees were that every immigrant worker have the right to establish legal residency by demonstrating a status as a wage earner and taxpayer, the right to all constitutional rights afforded citizens, the right to be reunited with family, access to labor rights, the right to bilingual education and bilingual legal proceedings, the right to vote in the federal elections of her or his country of origin, and the right to vote in local and state elections of the nation resided in.[91] In these ways, Chicano/Mexicano activists asserted through the tribunal document a reconfiguration of the nation-states' bounded management of rights to take into consideration the transnational operation of capitalism from the perspective of migrant laborers and racialized citizens.

· · · · · ·

Continued repression and violence exerted by border enforcement policies in the San Diego borderlands facilitated Chicano/Mexicano assertions of autonomy in a transnational context. The National Chicano Immigration Conference and National Chicano Immigration Tribunal in 1980 and 1981 were the culmination of mobilizing efforts that expressed already practiced modes of social, cultural, and economic survival. Despite harassment, and at times, violent repression, Mexican and other Latino/a working-class migrants continued to challenge en masse an arrangement of globalization that impoverished their homelands and attempted to police their movement. Chicano/a activists formulated a process of ethnic community through which the intersecting political needs of racialized citizens and noncitizens were considered and acted upon. The Chicano Tribunal, therefore, not only sought redress from the U.S. and Mexican states; it demanded the recognition of already existing Latino/a transnational community processes of survival and solutions. In so doing, insurgent notions of social membership and radically democratic practice were expressed and enacted that redrew a civil society that more readily acknowledged the shared political, social, and economic realities in the U.S.-Mexico borderlands. Furthermore, it gave voice to racialized laborers and residents of all statuses, many of whom were deemed otherwise "illegal," enacting a practice of global interconnection built through the experiences of the most degraded among us.

Conclusion

The Long Walk for Rights

· ·

When I began research for this book in 2006, some of the largest demonstrations in the history of the United States occurred when millions of migrants and their children—the largest group by far being Mexican, Central American, and other groups from Latin America—took to the streets to protest legislation that would make undocumented status a felony. From March to May, "Mega Marchas" (Mega Marches) took place and more than one million people marched in Los Angeles while tens of thousands protested in San Diego, including hundreds of students walking out of high schools to historic Chicano Park and at least fifty thousand marching downtown, the largest in the city's history.[1] At the latter march, I recall observing the crowd don a huge, makeshift flag with a Mexican eagle eating a snake, and behind it red, white, and blue stripes, as the participants roared. It seemed that ethnic Mexican communities were imagining new identities and new sociopolitical realities, stamping their cultural worldview as Mexican but engaging and demanding rights from social institutions in the United States. This was widely based on an assertion of earned rights through the foundational labor they provided in the U.S. economy. Commentary on the historic 2006 marches even suggested that an emergent notion of belonging—or at least assertions that suggested them—were expressed by noncitizen protesters who demanded immediate legal standing, noting their rights of belonging in U.S. society without disconnecting with their home societies, and asserting these demands independently from existing discourse on solutions to the immigration crisis.[2] Out of this moment emerged a new immigrant rights struggle, particularly the Dream movement, in which young people pressured mechanisms of the state to grant legal standing and a path to citizenship to at least some of the over ten million undocumented people residing in the United States. This pressure was most legible in President Barack Obama's executive order of Deferred Action for Childhood Arrivals (DACA) in 2012, which granted temporary status for some migrant youth.

A decade later as I completed this book, billionaire Donald Trump was elected president of the United States in 2016 in part on his promises to build a wall at the U.S.-Mexico border and somehow force the Mexican government to pay for it. Insisting that Mexico does not "send its best" to the United States, Trump aroused especially white middle- and working-class voters by accessing a deeply embedded trope regarding Mexican criminality, exemplified when he said during the campaign: "They're bringing drugs. They're bringing crime. They're rapists. And some I assume are good people."[3] As I write, Trump just issued a series of executive orders to build a wall at the U.S.-Mexico border, to withhold federal money from sanctuary cities, to increase the number of Border Patrol and ICE agents, and to implement a temporary ban on seven majority-Muslim nations. Herman Baca commented on the Trump phenomenon, calling it "Hitler-fascist" and claiming that it revealed the "white supremacy" of the Republican Party with its appeals to anti-Mexican sentiment embedded in the immigration issue, thus using "Chicanos/Latinos . . . as the piñata for his campaign." It is important to note that Baca reiterated what he calls "a Chicano perspective" on immigration—that "to deport 11 million (mostly Mexican) 'illegal' aliens . . . is a contrivance (as all deportations have been) to keep Mexican workers in a rightless state and 60 million Chicanos/Latinos disenfranchised."[4] Baca points to the Trump phenomenon as a repeat of history, and as one of demographics—an expression of white anxiety concerning "a historical population shift in the U.S. that by 2041 white Americans will become the nation's minority population and lose power!"[5]

Of equal concern to Baca is how the Trump phenomenon reveals the "little to no political power" that "Chicanos/Latinos" possess even when reaching record demographic proportions, with about sixty million people making up 17 percent of the population. For Baca, a "massive political resistance" among ethnic Mexicans and other Latinos/as is necessary to survive the "same historical oppression and violation of our rights" that will surely come otherwise as "Trump gets his hands on every law enforcement agency in the U.S."[6] Baca criticizes a political class of Mexican American and U.S. Latino/a commentators ("His/Her 'Panics'") who repeatedly plead to the community to vote for "the lesser of two evils" and "the best of the worst." Baca asks of these leaders: "If we are 60 million, why do we act like we are only 7 million? Politically, the only solution I see to end the above is our people's own political self-determination."[7]

Baca's commentary demonstrates his continued insistence on reminders that the racial oppression experienced by the Chicano/Latino community via immigration policies is rooted in structural inequality and class concerns.

In a similar comment on the Arizona "show-me-your-papers" laws, he also explained that "our community" needs to understand that "the 'immigration problem' is systemic and historical (since the end of the U.S./Mexico War) and, like the Afro-American slave system (early 1600 to mid-1800), was created because of this country's economic historical addiction to FREE and CHEAP labor."[8] Baca explained further, "The existing immigration system is a labor issue and exists because Mexican workers are in a rightless condition."[9] In other words, immigration policies that employ law enforcement and militarized solutions do not reflect an attempt to repair a broken system but actually further equip a more than century-year-old labor system by empowering police forces to further manage and control a noncitizen and racialized workforce.

Baca's analysis of the current moment and on anti-immigrant laws such as those in Arizona reveals how this book's explorations of ethnic autonomy as a vehicle through which to address the structural class inequalities embedded within immigration policies in a globalizing political economy continues to hold relevance. Baca's call to organize as a people makes sense if we take Omi and Winant's assertion that racialization projects, such as immigration policy, are often rearticulated by the targeted racialized group to assert forms of resistance.[10] Indeed, ethnic Mexicans and other Latinos/as from the Congreso of the 1930s to the CCR in the 1980s organized as a people to resist a system that targeted, harassed, brutalized, and ultimately excluded them from any meaningful/actual experiences of citizenship. But if we also note that ethnic and racial identities and mobilizations can and do elide class and labor concerns, then we find the significance of the history of Chicano/Mexicano mobilizations within Baca's assertion that the Latino/a community needs to organize with the understanding that the immigration system is by and large a "labor issue." If we recall how mainstream media outlets often cover the immigration debate—framing it as a "Latino" issue—we see that this effectively empties the debate of any real class and labor content, as well as its relationship to other racialized and working-class sectors of society. Therefore, the notion that it is not simply about the rights of Latinos/as but more fully about the continued existence of systems of labor exploitation leads us to key questions concerning how to address situations such as the Trump phenomenon. Trump's presidency is based on an age-old U.S. tradition of calling for working-class white people to unite with white elites against their fellow workers of color as he promises to crack down on movements such as Black Lives Matter, #NotOneMore immigrant rights struggles, movements against Islamophobia, and connections with Palestine and indigenous resistance at Standing Rock.

The resolutions and testimonies of the National Chicano Immigration Conference and Tribunal epitomized an alternative practice of belonging that was expressed through a transnational ethnic community and consciously sought to mobilize independently from yet in dialog with the state. This practice of an insurgent belonging not only sought the conferring of rights for a particular ethnic community but expressed class concerns and structural critiques through engagement with racialized labor regimes and oppression. Chicano/Mexicano activists argued that their particular experience of oppression was tied to a global system that enabled capital to access noncitizen laborers and transverse the globe while subjugating laborers to border enforcement mechanisms. They argued that "crises" over "illegal aliens" were constructed by elites to divide people with similar ethnic and class ties. In this way, Chicano/Mexicano activism addressed wider labor and class issues through mobilization as an ethnic community.

In light of more recent developments calling for more militarization and deportations, it's worth reflecting on the trajectory of the CCR's activism as organizers faced a major obstacle in passage of the pivotal Immigration Reform and Control Act (IRCA) of 1986. The IRCA successfully fragmented Chicano/Mexicano mobilizations by appeasing some activists through the granting of a limited amnesty while others continued to seek out the complete demilitarization of immigration policy. The abolitionist position on the deportation regime asserted through the voices of the oppressed who survived the sheer terror and state violence that enforced such a regime emerged at a moment when the federal government debated and created a new policy to appease some of the human rights–oriented groups such as the CCR, while maintaining its foundation as a system of labor exploitation and militarization. As the Chicano/a struggle against the deportation regime consistently revealed, it was Democrats and Republicans, liberals and conservatives, and capital and the state that converged to maintain this system. The "flexibility of capital" in the neoliberal age created a circumstance in which certain concessions could be gained and at least create some refuge for the vulnerable positionality undocumented workers and families found themselves in, fomenting debate and fragmentation in the Raza Sí, Migra No movement. This emerged as President Reagan and a bipartisan committee in Congress sought to address the emergent national debate on immigration in the 1980s.

Simpson-Mazzoli and Other Bills

In large part emerging from the arguments made by President Jimmy Carter's proposal, and those of the bipartisan U.S. Select Commission on Immigration and Refugee Policy, Republican Alan Simpson and Democrat Romano Mazzolli introduced an immigration bill that emerged as the proposal with the most potential to be passed by the fall of 1983. Reflecting the Select Commission's recommendation of increased resources for border policing and interior enforcement targeting undocumented migrants, employer sanctions, and an amnesty program, the CCR and other Chicano/a and immigrant rights advocates continued to battle the enforcement provisions and limited inclusion of undocumented migrants who would qualify for the amnesty provisions.

Indeed, in his signature fashion, Herman Baca exclaimed to the press that the Simpson-Mazzoli bill was "the most racist piece of legislation since the U.S.-Mexican War of 1846."[11] Of particular concern for the CCR was the Simpson-Mazzoli proposal to initiate a "South African National I.D. card"—referring to the bill's recommendation to issue national identification cards—alongside continued critiques of plans to increase the number of Border Patrol agents and initiate a "Bracero-type" guest worker program.[12] To oppose this, the CCR announced that it would sponsor a "Walk for Rights" in San Diego, whose participants would march from San Diego seventeen miles to the U.S.-Mexico border in San Ysidro. The march would "send the U.S. Congress a message that the Simpson/Mazzoli Plan is unacceptable and that it will be opposed by the Chicano community even though it may pass."[13] Furthermore, the CCR sought to "urge the Chicano community to oppose any candidate (Democrat or Republican) that supports passage of the Simpson/Mazzoli bill" and "present an alternative solution."[14] The CCR continued to assert this "alternative" "Chicano/Mexicano perspective" on immigration—which sought abolishment of the INS—in the midst of growing legislative proposals that sought a mix of further militarization and a limited amnesty.[15]

The CCR's resistance to Simpson-Mazzoli was part of a national coalition it helped create that included Chicano/a and Latino/a activists and advocacy organizations that had coalesced around criticism of restrictionist aspects of immigration legislation since the Carter plan was announced in the late 1970s. This political position, as David G. Gutiérrez has asserted, evolved into "a remarkable new consensus on the immigration controversy among

Mexican American and Chicano political activists," including mainline national organizations such as the Congressional Hispanic Caucus, the National Council of La Raza (NCLR), the Mexican American Legal Defense and Education Fund (MALDEF), and organizations that historically supported restrictionist immigration policies such as the League of United Latin American Citizens (LULAC) and the American G.I. Forum. LULAC and the G.I. Forum shifted their positions on immigration during the "broad-based process of reassessment" that groups such as the CCR in the Chicano movement began in the 1970s.[16] This continued to be the case as these middle-of-the road organizations maintained the coalition that emerged from the Carter plan years in their opposition to the restrictionist elements of the Simpson-Mazzoli bill, particularly the autocratic proposal to require national identification cards. The United Farm Workers and the American G.I. Forum, however, initially supported the bill and had to be pressured to change their position, while the Congressional Hispanic Caucus (CHC) relied on criticism from one or two of its members to consolidate opposition to the bill only by the end of the 1981–82 congressional session, indicating the fragility of such a coalition.[17] This fragility of this coalition was also demonstrated in divide over Congressman Roybal's attempt to propose an alternative bill—the CCR criticized its acceptance of law enforcement and, later, employer sanction provisions while the CHC could not reach consensus on the provisions on amnesty and temporary labor recruitment.[18]

The broader coalition's impetus to unite around a Raza Sí, Migra No sentiment emerged, of course, from Chicano movement organizations such as the Committee on Chicano Rights in San Diego, among a wider network of Chicano/a radicals. It is important to note that Chole Alatorre and Bert Corona organized the National Coalition for Fair Immigration Law and Practices in an effort to coalesce these Raza Sí, Migra No activists at the national level, based on their work within a revitalized Hermandad Mexicana network that resembled the CASAs of the early 1970s.[19] This kind of activism also influenced many non-Chicano/a organizations to develop critical positions and join the coalition against the Simpson-Mazzolli bill, including the American Civil Liberties Union, the American Immigrant Lawyers Association, the U.S. Catholic Conference, and others.[20] Many of the grassroots organizations present at the National Chicano Immigration Conference and the subsequent tribunal also continued their criticisms.

The Walk for Rights was endorsed by national organizations, including MALDEF and MEChA, local chapters of the National Lawyers Guild, MAPA, the American G.I. Forum, local student groups as well as the Organización

Femenil Nacional (Women's National Organization), Unión del Barrio, the Centro Cultural de la Raza [Cultural Center of the People], and the Padre Hidalgo Center.[21] The seventeen mile march began in San Diego at Our Lady of Guadalupe Church in the Logan Heights Barrio; there were stops at St. Jude's Church in Shelltown, St. Anthony's in National City, Our Lady of Guadalupe in Otay, and Our Lady of Mount Carmel in San Ysidro, where there was a rally, and finally, it was completed at the U.S.-Mexico international border.[22] The CCR claimed that three thousand people participated in the march.[23]

The march was an important action to resist the emerging trajectory toward what Chicano/a activists called the "carrot-and-stick" approach to immigration policy, which sought a mix of further militarization with a limited amnesty. It also represented the last mass march the CCR successfully organized, in part because Baca began to see the demonstrations as ineffective. Baca remembered coming to this realization at the Walk for Rights march: "When we were marching along the border I saw and heard some of Border Patrolmen mocking the march. It was then [that] I decided to never return or repeat such a march in a non-violent fashion."[24] Baca's frustration signaled the weight of powerful interests reflected in the bipartisan discourse on federal proposals such as the Simpson-Mazzolli bill, which insisted on solutions that embedded law enforcement as an inherent part of any "comprehensive" immigration policy. It also signaled the emerging decline of the CCR's influence, as it indicated a shift away from one of the most powerful abilities of the organization in its now fifteen-year struggle against the immigration regime—the ability to mobilize hundreds if not thousands of Chicano/a community activists and their allies in the important border region. Furthermore, although the Walk for Rights action criticized particular aspects of the proposal, there is only sparse indication that the CCR continued to assert explicitly the important call for INS and Border Patrol abolition, an idea that was supported by the several thousand participants of the National Chicano Immigration Conference just two years earlier and held the potential to articulate an alternative solution. Nonetheless, the action was an important part of national criticism that stopped the bill from being passed in the fall of 1983.

IRCA

While the Simpson-Mazzoli proposal was ultimately defeated in the House, its basic premises were redirected and negotiated in the Simpson-Rodino bill in 1986. Appeasing a number of interests such as loosening employer responsibility for verifying the authenticity of employee documents, allowing agricultural workers who had worked for more than ninety days temporary residency, and expanding some of the amnesty provisions, the bill became known as the Immigration Reform and Control Act (IRCA) of 1986.[25] In addition to the agricultural lobbyists' and other capitalists' interests in an immigrant workforce, some of these concessions convinced Chicano/Latino civil rights advocates to support the bill as well. Bert Corona remembered that the shift to include more undocumented people in the amnesty provisions by pushing back the cutoff date to include those who had entered before 1982, rather than 1980 according to the previous proposals, led to fragmentation at the national level as the NCLR, UFW, and five members of the CHC threw their support behind the bill.[26] He explained: "By 1986, our coalition had fallen apart. It had been hard to maintain momentum. . . . This new (amnesty) date still excluded thousands, but some in our coalition, such as church groups and the National Council of La Raza, believed that this was better than nothing. . . . We lost by a few votes."[27] While many Chicano/a and Latino/a activists celebrated or sought to work with the amnesty programs IRCA initiated, the CCR held firm on its position that it was impossible to work with the INS/Border Patrol because it was an inherently anti-Mexican entity. "If the blacks were gaining amnesty, would they trust the KKK?" asked Baca. "Would the Jews trust the Gestapo?"[28]

IRCA created a path to citizenship for immigrants who entered without documents and lived continuously in the United States on or before January 1, 1982. One year after temporary residency status, these migrants could gain permanent legal residency. The law also implemented employer sanctions, a provision CCR and other Chicano/Mexicano activists fought against since it became a California state law in 1972. The bill also ordered increasing Border Patrol agents by 50 percent for each of the next two years, and allocated $422 million for 1987 and $419 million for 1988 to implement enforcement of immigration laws. IRCA also denied legal immigrants access to federal benefits for five years, made available $1 billion a year to aid states with larger undocumented populations, and created a "Seasonal Agricultural Workers Program." The program would give temporary legal status to farmworkers who had worked in the United States continuously for at least ninety days. Finally, the bill modified the H-2 temporary worker program. While this guest worker program already existed, IRCA streamlined the application and review process, and relieved employers of housing responsibilities.[29]

The CCR criticized the "carrot-and-stick" policies of IRCA, as it had previous proposals, arguing that the new law is "labor legislation posing as immigration reform."[30] Referring to the streamlining of the H-2 temporary worker program within the bill, Baca maintained that Congress "legislated slavery" through the estimated three hundred fifty thousand or more Mexican migrant workers who would be recruited. He noted the contradiction that the bill was both supposed to stop undocumented migration of workers and import guest workers at the same time. Baca highlighted that this workforce was gifted to the "secondary labor sector of the U.S. economy, i.e. agri-business, hotels, motels, restaurants, garment industry, etc." Baca also criticized the claim that IRCA would stop undocumented migration because it failed to address its root causes, namely, U.S. imperialism and global inequality. "Persons flee their native land," exclaimed Baca, due to the "economic rape of Mexico and other Latin American countries by America's trans-national corporations with the cooperation of the host countries [sic] right-wing industrial oligarchies." Revealing the influence of arriving Central American refugees escaping regimes supported by U.S. foreign policy initiatives, Baca concluded that political refugees would continue to arrive "because of this country's support for oppressive Right Wing [sic] rulers."[31] Indeed, it was the continued arrival of more undocumented migrants that would serve as the basis for an available labor source for the aforementioned industries. One moderate think-tank study reports on IRCA retrospectively, "Given the diminishing number of U.S. workers available or interested in meeting jobs in the fast-growing service, construction, and other lower skilled sectors, foreign workers filled the gap; and in the absence of legal avenues to enter the labor market, workers and employers took the easier path available to them."[32] The undocumented population, at about 4 million in 1986, did drop to 2.5 million in 1989, but then rose to 6.2 million by 1996, peaking at 12.2 million by 2007.[33]

The CCR was especially critical of the amnesty provisions as well, calling them a "false amnesty," just as they did earlier proposals but also pointing to the problem that Mexican migrants were supposed to approach what they considered an inherently anti-Mexican entity: the INS/Border Patrol. This harkens to the call to abolish this bureaucracy. The initial critique of the amnesty provision was that proof of residency would be needed, and what qualified as proof would be at the discretion of the very entity that had perpetrated the legal violence that the CCR had battled against for more than a decade before. Referring also to the requirement that residency be continuous to qualify, Baca rhetorically questioned, "Who is the person(s) that will determine proof of continuous residents? The most corrupt, incompetent, racist agency in the entire U.S., the Immigration and Naturalization Service, the same leopard with the same old stripes."[34]

Indeed, acting on the call to abolish the INS, the CCR demanded in a December 1986 press release and a letter to the Speaker of the U.S. House of Representatives, Jim Wright, that a new agency be created to administer the amnesty provisions of IRCA. Prompting Congress to address the history of racialization, Baca exclaimed in a letter to the Speaker of the House, "After working with the immigration issue for the last 16 years that [sic] because of the sordid history & the inherent administrative incompetency of the INS, that this agency will not be able to administer the new amnesty legislation in a fair, just and humane manner to persons of Mexican ancestry."[35] Noting a history of the INS targeting ethnic Mexicans, Baca listed the problematic and tragic policy decisions, including the Bracero Program, Operation Wetback of 1954, past deportations, and continued threats of deportation by the Border Patrol.[36] The request was addressed after being referred to Representative Jack Brooks, chair of the Committee on Government Operations, in January 1987. As elected officials had done many times in past requests to address these issues, the request was passed off to other elected officials, this time the Reagan administration. "You may be assured," Brooks dismissively explained, "that should the Administration propose legislation to create a new agency . . . it will be carefully considered."[37] Nonetheless, the CCR continued its critical analysis insisting on historical accountability of the INS in the amnesty provision.

As the INS implemented IRCA, the CCR criticized the employer sanctions part of the bill, claiming it would "serve as a prerequisite for a police state apparatus" when it required all employers "from small business to corporations" to verify citizenship status.[38] The CCR also accused the INS of greed when it announced a $185 charge to apply for amnesty. "Having the undocumented pay for the Simpson/Rodino amnesty program," insisted Baca, "is like having the black slaves pay for the Civil War in 1865 that supposedly set them free."[39] Calling again for the creation of a new agency, it was this rhetoric that identified the deportation regime as a system deeply embedded in racialized hierarchies similar to past racial systems such as slavery and conquest that continued to serve as the basis for criticism of the IRCA bill. This refusal to work in any way with the INS would lead, however, to conflict with other perspectives that saw the amnesty provision as a pragmatic opportunity to mobilize more community members and future voters. Furthermore, with a step away from organizing marches and creating mobilizations that could collectively back up Baca and the CCR's critiques, and during a period when many Chicano/a, "Hispanic," and Latino/a organizations became preoccupied with the amnesty process, the abolitionist assertions of the National Chicano Immigration Conference and Tribunal just a few years before began to recede.

The Legacy of the CCR/Raza Sí, Migra No

Not only did the process of passing IRCA reveal the fragmentation of a coalition of Chicano/a and Latino/a advocates but its implementation demonstrated the ways the state truly intervened in the culmination of Raza Si, Migra No mobilizations. The CCR's critiques, and even outright call, that migrants *not* pursue the process leading to amnesty available through IRCA, led to criticism and an implicit breaking of ties with Bert Corona and the Hermandad Mexicana. Breaking with his political mentor, the one who "infused the Chicano Movement" with the immigration issue, Baca argued that anyone working to get funds from the INS/Border Patrol to conduct classes and outreach for migrants and assist them in gaining citizenship status through IRCA was consorting with the very entity they had been fighting against for all those years. In Baca's opinion, at this moment: "The movement lost its principal spokesperson, which was Bert Corona. You have the spectacle of the person who had taught so many of us that the INS and the Border Patrol were the Gestapo of the Mexican people now taking money from this organization. It didn't make no political sense."[40]

Corona and the Hermandad Mexicana in Los Angeles took the opportunity to receive funds from the amnesty provision of IRCA to assist undocumented immigrants in achieving the language and civic requirements that would make them eligible for legal status and, eventually, citizenship. In his oral history, Corona claimed the Hermandad assisted about one hundred sixty thousand undocumented residents in the years following the implementation of IRCA from the late 1980s to 1992. This was a pragmatic approach to the new post-IRCA reality and a direct way of providing for the undocumented constituency served by the Hermandad. According to Corona, in addition to gaining citizenship, the classes helped individuals obtain job-related skills such as literacy, high school diplomas, and methods of surviving economic shifts that could make their already exploitative jobs obsolete.[41]

Baca's critique that these classes served an assimilative and co-opting mechanism is countered by Corona's reflections on how the Hermandad was conducting classes through the radical pedagogy of critical theorist Paulo

Freire. Baca stressed: "The classes were on how to be good U.S. citizens. Not classes, you know, to go out and organize. I guess it was supposed to happen by osmosis." Yet Corona paints a picture of a dialectical process in which students and teachers learned from one another, developing critical knowledge and reflection on the way power had created their conditions historically, and even, contrary to Baca's pessimism, on how to organize. Corona, fully aware of the severe problems within IRCA, explained: "We stress [in the classes] that history is being continually made by people, by the masses of people who struggle to correct injustices and to improve the quality of life for their families. We don't believe that civics . . . can and should be learned only from memorizing pamphlets and books. We feel that in order to learn civics, people must be involved in the civics process."[42] Corona gave examples of students visiting Sacramento and Washington, D.C., as part of the class advocating and lobbying for more funds for their classes.[43]

This study concludes by exploring the contestation between Baca and his mentor Corona's approach to amnesty during IRCA not to make a claim for who was correct, but rather to consider how the shift toward preoccupation with amnesty occurred within immigration and Chicano/Latino rights struggles in recent years, the reasons for the decline of the CCR and its influence, and the ways the CCR continued to evoke a vision that sought to create a world without deportation. Corona's description of how the Hermandad utilized classes, funds, and programs offered by the amnesty provisions of IRCA contests Baca's notion that participation in this process could only reinforce the hegemony of the deportation regime. To the contrary, Corona's description seems to subvert the hegemonic goals of such a program by creating yet another interface between undocumented residents and the racialized U.S. citizens with whom they shared community. The space could be used to provide a precarious population with immediate relief from the fear of being deported, skills to gain necessities for their families, and agency through political engagement and critical learning.

By the late 1980s, the CCR had no constituency to be accountable to the way the Hermandad did, which explains in part the different trajectory. The Hermandad, in the manner that the CASAs did a decade before, was made up of a collective of undocumented families and workers. The amnesty provisions therefore offered the opportunity to provide for the needs of the Hermandad's base. The CCR, with its loose style of calling for mobilizations at particular moments, and its move away from providing for the needs of the undocumented since the closing of CASA Justicia, was not answerable to the dire circumstances so many working-class undocumented migrants were in. Without leadership and engagement in the day-to-day lives of undocumented workers and families, a victim-narrative often limited opportunities to tap into immigrant networks of surivial and resistance. And again, the CCR's decision in the 1983 march to no longer mobilize such demonstrations because they were ineffective also cut off ties and engagement with its community. Without mobilization efforts such as those in the past—registration drives, electoral mobilizations, demonstrations, and protests—the CCR became what its predecessors initially were—a small group of friends and families that grew up together in the National City barrios and congealed around the charismatic leadership of Herman Baca.

As with many organizations built around charismatic leadership, the CCR suffered from an inability to mentor and produce new leadership from its ranks. While undoubtedly many activists cut their teeth and learned invaluable lessons about organizing and analyzing social issues from the CCR, there was no mechanism to hone in on that leadership to contribute to the future development of the CCR and maintain a base. Again, this became apparent by 1986 when the CCR's mobilization efforts were reduced to Baca's commentary within differing media outlets. The parting of ways with young leaders who formed the Unión del Barrio—Ernesto Bustillos, Jeff Garcilazo, Howard Holman, and others who were leaders of the CCR during its struggle against the Carter Curtain and the National Chicano Immigration Conference and Tribunal in 1980–81—reveals this reality. While the Unión remembers its parting of ways as cordial and maintains the utmost respect for Baca and the CCR as part of their origin narrative, it also demonstrates the inability for the CCR to grow with younger activists with new energy and ideas as the Unión went on to become, and continues to be, a key leader in radical Chicano/a struggles in San Diego and beyond.[44] As activist, artist, and participant in CCR actions in the late 1970s Yolanda López put it, "Herman was the originator of it [the CCR], the policy maker, the creative thinker about it and all the other men were like satellites."[45]

As López's comments allude to, this practice of leadership had a very gendered dimension to it. As this study reveals, Chicana and Mexicana activists and community members formed an important part of the activities the CCR and its predecessor organizations conducted. They were present, and often made up at least half of the participants at demonstrations, protest actions, and registration drives, and provided services to community members and engaged in other actions. Women such as Martha Elena Parra López, Guadalupe Astorga, Lupe Alonzo, Linda Aragon, and many others spoke out against the violence perpetrated by police, the Border Patrol, and customs agents to hold them accountable to the particular way this violence targeted women's bodies or to highlight the injustice done to their loved ones. Organizers and activists such as Norma Mena Cazares, Gloria Jean Valderrama, Nadine Baca, and many mothers, sisters, wives, and women whose labor assisted everything from door-to-door petition signing to hosting out-of-town guests, providing food, and organizing gatherings for the many events and actions, served as the backbone to community action and the history of struggle this book documents.

It was rare, however, that Chicanas and Mexicanas were part of the decision-making processes or ascended into leadership positions. It took women such as Norma Mena Cazares, who had "no issue telling them (the men) they are full of it" to challenge the "domineering" tendencies of many of the men who backed up Baca's opinions to get into key leadership and decision-making roles.[46] As Yolanda López remembers, "I love Herman a lot . . . for his courage and not being afraid to call out individuals and institutions for their racism and classism, but yes . . . he is the alpha-male."[47] In what López describes as a "familial"-based organization such as the CCR, gender roles often played out in ways that assumed men to be in leadership and women in the background doing domestic or administrative labor. As a girlfriend to one of the men in the CCR's inner circle, López remembered: "I was a girlfriend. I was not seen as, I think . . . anything other than that. . . . We [Chicanas] were not part of the leadership. We were not consulted about what to do or what was going on. Rarely were we even included in conversations about what was going on in San Diego and the power structure and National City. . . . I was interested in it (CCR actions) intellectually. And I was interested in it as far as being a citizen. You know, as an activist. But that part was not recognized. We were seen as the girlfriend and everything the girlfriend does. Or [as responsible for what] a wife does in that situation."[48] These patriarchal practices, often left unexamined by the CCR leadership, highlighted the undiscovered potential to hone further leadership skills and contributions that were available among activists with feminized identities specifically, but also among youth, the undocumented, and others more broadly. In contrast, Bert Corona's description of a Freirean approach to the classes for the IRCA amnesty programs sought to empower new leadership.

The decline of CCR activism can also be linked to the ways the corporate nonprofit sector and government entities directly or indirectly suppressed organizations that insisted on a self-funded, volunteer-based organization. The CCR sought to ensure that state and corporate influence would be avoided, in line with maintaining its goal and practice of Chicano self-determination, and its decline reveals the serious challenges of this radical practice. As this type of organization, resources, both human and financial, were difficult to come by as many former members moved on to work in the nonprofit sector, government, education, and other endeavors. Furthermore, repression from FBI surveillance, police infiltration, official corruption, and biased media depictions of Baca and the CCR as crazed radicals definitely had its effects. By 1986 and afterward, the CCR—and MAPA, CASA Justicia, La Raza Unida Party, and the Ad Hoc Committee before it— always operated with a core of individuals around Baca, but had attracted and mobilized community members and activists around particular causes at particular moments, in large part to battle the state violence emanating, relentlessly, on the ethnic Mexican community in the border region. While these issues of legal violence continued to occur after 1986, that community members and activists did not rally around organizations such as the CCR in the same way might be connected to the presence of, attraction to, and preoccupation with state-funded organizations that benefited from the more than $10 million allocated from the INS to organizations claiming to serve the ethnic Mexican and wider Latino/a community. Furthermore, the decline of grassroots activism indicated the rise of a Latino/a political class that would come to manage the ethnic politics of immigration. In this regard, Baca's critique of Corona and the Hermandad reveals important ways in which the amnesty provisions of IRCA co-opted social movement forces that could have focused on uprooting the deportation regime. While Corona's explanation of the classes and programs highlights the nuance not captured by Baca's stringent critique, it also reveals that much of the energy of these students became focused on requesting more government funding for the extension of amnesty provisions. For instance, Corona described using the classes to politicize students but emphasizes their lobbying for "more funds for the amnesty classes." He also describes how the Hermandad was "trying to get federal and state resources to establish job training." Although Corona had a thorough analysis of the limits of the amnesty provisions, the focus on government funding and an expansion of amnesty provides a glimpse into how IRCA unleashed co-optive forces that reoriented immigrant rights activism toward focusing on amnesty rather than constructing the systematic critique that Raza Si, Migra No Chicano activism presented in the years leading up to 1986.

In a 1987 *La Prensa* interview titled "Amnesty One Year Later," Baca highlighted how the amnesty allocations for church and social service groups, the fees undocumented families were forced to pay for the application process, and charges by lawyers and other "advocates" who did the paperwork for these families were estimated to make $5 to $7 million off of the undocumented residents. Furthermore, the eligibility requirements for amnesty were, according to Baca, designed to minimize the number of undocumented residents that gained citizenship. As reports have established, fully half of the undocumented residents in the country were excluded by the 1982 cutoff date. Comparing the red tape and difficult requirements to the historical suppression of African American voters through poll taxes and literacy tests, Baca exclaimed, "At the very beginning questions were raised about what was the real intent of the Act especially when you consider all the conditions that were made to apply for amnesty."[49] Indeed, reports revealed that as many as two million undocumented residents were excluded by the cutoff date, while about five hundred thousand who were eligible did not apply. This has been attributed to a failure of the law to prioritize family unification, a short amount of time given to plan its implementation, the short twelve-month period to apply, the fees required, and the failure to implement effective forms of outreach.[50]

As the CCR's Chicano perspective would put it, this exclusion is of design, as the premise for anyone needing amnesty is admitting that they have indeed committed a criminal act. Baca warned: "We now have to live with the stigma that the law attaches to persons of Mexican ancestry which is one of being criminals . . . people dealing outside the law in spite of the fact that they are enticed here by the secondary labor market. This concept of Mexicans being criminals by extension is applied to all of Mexican ancestry."[51] This echoes the expanding criminalization of migrants and other people of color that would occur throughout the 1990s. As critical scholar Lisa Cacho asserts: "Criminalization can operate through instituting laws that cannot be followed. People subjected to laws based on their (il)legal status—'illegal aliens,' 'gang members,' 'terrorist suspects'—are unable to comply with the 'rule of law' because U.S. law targets their being and their bodies, not their behavior. They are denied not only the illusion of authorship but even the possibility of compliance."[52] And herein is where Baca and the CCR's work and critical perspective on activists who engaged in the amnesty provisions and state-funded services continues to be important. Baca asserted that out of IRCA, "amnesty became the predominate project within that [immigration] issue that had been a foremost priority type issue that affected our entire being. I'm talking about 'our being,' meaning all persons of Mexican ancestry, that this, that instead of addressing the root causes, now people were doing the mechanical, you know, really rationalizing it, in my opinion, just simple rationalization."[53] In this regard, the legacy of the CCR is crucial to understanding the history of struggle against the deportation regime, as focus on this organization and its predecessors shatters the narrow terms of the immigration debate. The CCR reveals a radical tradition of ideas that understood immigration policy as a system of racialized labor management, and in such a context any law enforcement aspect to it meant legal and physical violence on the ethnic Mexican and Latino/a community. As a system with exploitiative, violent and racialized roots, they argued, it was in need of abolishment.

Specifically in the context of the 1986 IRCA act, participating in the amnesty provisions, whether intentional or not, proved to shift the debate toward the need for more amnesty, leading many activists to concede to the naturalization of law enforcement solutions as inherently part of any solution to the immigration crisis. This makes Baca and the CCR's critique of Corona and the Hermandad specifically, and the co-optive framing of the immigration debate around amnesty more broadly, crucially significant. As political scientist Alfonso Gonzales argues, in the decade or so historical evolution of the immigration debate leading up to the 2006 Mega Marchas, "Immigration reformers . . . are structurally locked into a game of perpetual compromise . . . which often forces them to accept the established terms of the debate over migration control. . . . They reach a consensus . . . that preserves the social reproduction of the global capitalist system and the institutionality of the homeland security state as a necessary and nonnegotiable part of any US migration control strategy."[54] The history of the CCR reveals that the origins of such "perpetual compromise" were in many ways initiated in the IRCA Act of 1986. More important, it reveals a longer history of struggle against and refusal to adhere to this type of compromise, the ways solidarity was built between Chicanos/as and Mexicanos/as in a context of legal violence, and the attempt to implement a position that imagined the abolishment of the deportation regime.

Notes

Introduction

1. Herman Baca, interview by author, August 2, 2006.

2. A note on ethno-racial terminology: The book uses the term "ethnic Mexican" to refer to people of Mexican heritage regardless of their nationality (U.S. or Mexican) or citizenship status (U.S. citizen or immigrant). I use the term "Mexican American" to refer to U.S.-born or naturalized citizens of the United States who are of Mexican heritage. I use the term "Chicano" and "Chicana" in reference to individuals who identified with the "Chicano movement" and "Chicano/a" to describe the women and men who engaged collectively in activism extending from this historically situated movement. In reference to the politics, activism, and thought of the Chicano movement, I use "Chicano" in part to signify the gendered hierarchies that were usually implied within that historical context as well as to emphasize the actual language used by participants in that historical moment. Ramón Gutiérrez's assertion in "Community, Patriarchy and Individualism" outlines a context where "although the movement persistently had advocated the self-actualization of all Chicanos, Chicanos still actually meant males" (47). I use the term "Mexicano/a" or Mexican immigrant to refer to Mexican immigrants from Mexico who are in the United States. I use "Chicano/Mexicano" when referring to a political identity that sought solidarity and identification between Mexican Americans and Mexican immigrants. I use the term "Latino/a" in reference to people in the United States who are of Latin American cultural heritage. Ethno-racial identity and terminology is always a contentious and ongoing process, and therefore cannot be used without some degree of fluidity and limitations. I use primarily Stuart Hall's theoretical work, as exhibited, for example, in "Old and New Identities, Old and New Ethnicities" and the concept of "racial formation" as developed by Michael Omi and Howard Winant in *Racial Formation in the United States*.

3. Herman Baca, interview by author, August 2, 2006.

4. In *Impossible Subjects: Illegal Aliens and the Making of Modern American*, historian Mae Ngai asserts that the Immigration Act of 1924 initiated a "regime of immigration restriction" through its comprehensive restructuring of immigration policy and numerical quota systems that "established first time numerical limits on immigration and a global racial and national hierarchy" and its articulation of "a new sense of territoriality, which was marked by unprecedented awareness and state surveillance of the nation's contiguous land borders" (3). In "The Deportation Regime," anthropologist Nicolas De Genova conceives of a "deportation regime" in

relation to a more "elementary" problem of "human freedom of movement" (33). De Genova situates the use of a "deportation regime" in the post-9/11/2001 moment to emphasize that "deportation has achieved a remarkable and renewed prominence" through the concerns about counterterrorism and Homeland Security (35). I find the term useful for describing the regime Ngai identifies being initiated in 1924 in its centering of deportations/deportability, law enforcement/policing, and the targeting of so-called illegal people. Deportation policies within the Homeland Security state, while vastly different in historical context and shear political power and massive investment in border security post-9/11 compared to the Border Patrol's meager emergence in the 1920s, are therefore part of the same historical development based on legally invented "illegal" subjects that are deportable and enacting policing powers to deploy racial systems, new senses of territoriality, and more concentrated state surveillance systems. For this reason, I use the terms "immigration regime" and "deportation regime" interchangeably when referring to the post-1924 era.

5. Corona, *Bert Corona Speaks*, 19.

6. Herman Baca, interview by author, August 2, 2006.

7. On "racial capitalism," see Robinson, *Black Marxism*, 9–28.

8. On abolition as a politics and analytical concept in the United States, see Du Bois, *Black Reconstruction in America*; Davis, *Abolition Democracy*; Lipsitz, "Abolition Democracy and Global Justice"; Johnson, *Spaces of Conflict, Sounds of Solidarity*, 7–9; and, tying abolition to the current immigrant rights movement, Lytle Hernández, "Amnesty or Abolition."

9. "Resolutions Passed at the Chicano National Immigration Conference," May 24, 1980, Folder 12, Box 41, HBP.

10. Works this study referenced to conceptualize San Diego–Tijuana as a complex border region, includes, Alvarez, *Familia*; Griswold del Castillo, *Chicano San Diego*; Herzog, especially, *Where North Meets South*; Davis, Mayhew, and Miller, *Under the Perfect Sun*; and Nevins, *Operation Gatekeeper*.

11. By "transnational" I am referring to migrant subjectivity as inherently border crossing, the system of militarized border enforcement at the U.S.-Mexico border as a binational project tied to larger global political economic shifts, and the transformative expansion of analysis and activism that tied local struggle to fluctuating global capitalist schemes by U.S. Chicano/a activists who engaged with the immigration crisis as a central community issue. Furthermore, I use the term "transnational" to refer to the agency of migrants who traversed the boundaries between two nations and put U.S. Chicano/a activists in a position to consider the wider ramifications of ethnic politics in the U.S.-Mexico borderlands. See Rodríguez, "The Battle for the Border"; Gutiérrez and Hondagneu-Sotelo, "Introduction: Nation and Migration"; and Briggs, McCormick, and Way, "Transnationalism: A Category of Analysis."

12. On hegemony, see Gramsci, *Selections from the Prison Notebooks*, and Hall, "Gramsci's Relevance for the Study of Race and Ethnicity."

13. Alatorre, "Plight of Immigrant Workers in the U.S.," n.d., 1976, Box 29, BCP.

14. This perspective builds on the work of the working-class Chicana/Latina feminisms of labor activists such as Luisa Moreno and Emma Tenayuca. For scholarship that documents this, see, for example, Ruiz, *Cannery Women, Cannery Lives*; Vargas, "Tejana Radical"; and Schmidt Camacho, *Migrant Imaginaries*. See also del Castillo, *Between Borders*; Torres, *Chicana without Apology*; Davis, *Women, Race and Class*; Anzaldúa and Moraga, *This Bridge Called My Back*; Anzaldúa, *Borderlands/ La Frontera*; Pérez, *The Decolonial Imaginary*; Lorde, *Sister Outsider*; and hooks, *Ain't I a Woman*. Most relevant for this study are the critiques of movement activism by Chicanas and queer Chicanas and Chicanos as documented in the work of Alma M. García, *Chicana Feminist Thought*; Ruiz, "La Nueva Chicana"; Espinoza, "Revolutionary Sisters"; Rodríguez, *Next of Kin*; and Blackwell, *Chicana Power!*.

15. For recent writing on the Chicano movement, see Araiza; *To March for Others*; Bebout, *Mythohistorical Interventions*; Behnken, *Fighting Their Own Battles*; Blackwell, *Chicana Power!*; Chávez, *Mi Raza Primero!*; Flores, *Grounds for Dreaming*; Matthew García, *From the Jaws of Victory*; García, *The Chicano Generation, The Chicano Movement*, and *Blowout!*; Gomez, *The Revolutionary Imaginations of Greater Mexico*; Krochmal, *Blue Texas*; Mantler; *Power to the Poor*; Mariscal, *Brown-Eyed Children of the Sun*; Haney López, *Racism on Trial*; Montejano, *Quixote's Soldiers*; and Oropeza, *Raza Sí! Guerra No!*. A classic book on the Chicano movement remains Muñoz, *Youth, Identity, Power*.

16. Herman Baca, interview by author, August 2, 2006.

17. Robinson, *Black Marxism*, 26.

18. While not extensive, works of influence on indigenous histories, expansion, and the process of capitalist development include, Brown, *Bury My Heart at Wounded Knee*; Ned Blackhawk, *Violence over the Land*; Usener, *Indians, Settlers and Slaves in a Frontier Exchange Economy*; Miles, *The Ties That Bind*; Saunt, *A New Order of Things*. Influences on slavery and capitalism include Williams, *Slavery and Capitalism*; Du Bois, *Black Reconstruction in America*; and Robinson, *Black Marxism*. On colonialism, race, and capitalist development, see Lowe, *The Intimacies of Four Continents*. On conceptual bases of settler colonialism see, Patrick Wolfe, "Settler Colonialism and the Elimination of the Native."

19. Saxton, *The Rise of the White Republic*. See also Frye Jacobson, *Whiteness of a Different Color*.

20. See Du Bois, *Black Reconstruction*, 17–32; Roediger, *The Wages of Whiteness*; Ignatiev, *How the Irish Became White*; Frye Jacobson, *Whiteness of a Different Color*. On the social formation of the white working class in juxtaposition to Mexicans, see Streeby, *American Sensations*.

21. Blackhawk, *Violence over the Land*; Almaguer, *Racial Faultlines*; Montejano, *Anglos and Mexicans in the Making of Texas*; Gonzalez, *Refusing the Favor*; Barrera, *Race and Class in the Southwest*; Pérez, *The Decolonial Imaginary*.

22. Lee, *At America's Gates*; Ngai, "The Architecture of Race in American Immigration Law" and *Impossible Subjects*; Almaguer, *Racial Faultlines*; Shah, *Contagious Divides*; Yung, *Unbound Feet*. For a guiding assertion of the significance of

Asian exclusion to U.S. immigration and cultural politics, see the introduction to Lowe, *Immigrants Acts.*

23. The Naturalization Act of 1790 restricts citizenship to "any alien, being a free white person." In 1868, the Fourteenth Amendment expanded eligibility to persons of African descent, but still undetermined were those who were neither white nor black. The Immigration Act of 1965 fully removed the overt usage of white identity as a determinant to eligibility while keeping the regime of illegality in place.

24. Jung, *Coolies and Cane.*

25. Camarrillo, *Chicanos in a Changing Society.*

26. Ngai, *Impossible Subjects.*

27. Ibid., *Subjects*, 91.

28. Balderrama and Rodríguez, *Decade of Betrayal*, 183. Of course, these were not all forced removals and systemic deportations; many were fully voluntary, whereas others were heavily influenced or coerced to "volunteer" to repatriate. Nonetheless, the impetus for the program was that people of Mexican origin in particular should leave to give jobs to "Americans." Also, the majority of U.S. citizens repatriated were children.

29. For the evolution of Chicano/a thinking on the issue of Mexican immigration and the significance of Mexican immigrants to the Chicano movement, see Flores, "Post-Bracero Undocumented Mexican Immigration and Political Recomposition"; David G. Gutiérrez, "Sin Fronteras?," *Walls and Mirrors*, 179–206, and "Globalization, Labor Migration and the Demographic Revolution"; Mario T. García, *Memories of Chicano History*, 286–320; Ernesto Chávez, "¡Mi Raza Primero!," 61–79; Pulido, *Black, Brown, Yellow and Left*, 124–133; Schmidt Camacho, *Migrant Imaginaries*, 152–193; and Patiño, " 'All I Want Is That He Be Punished,' " 21–46.

30. On the concept of *encuentros*, or encounters, as gatherings to create alternative arrangements to forms of oppression, colonialism, and capitalism, see Zapatista Army of National Liberation, "First Declaration of La Realidad for Humanity and Against Neoliberalism."

31. Referencing Matt García's explanation, the United Farm Workers, or UFW, is the organization's most popularly known name. The union became the United Farm Workers Organizing Committee (UFWOC) in August 1966 after the merger of the National Farm Workers Association (NFWA) and the Agricultural Workers Organizing Committee (AWOC). The AFL-CIO granted the UFWOC an independent charter to the UFW in February 1972 and the name was formally adopted in September 1973. For simplicity, I use UFW unless it becomes necessary to make distinctions with its other iterations. Matt García, *From the Jaws of Victory*, 299n1.

32. On the politics of history making and a "decolonial," or *curandera*, method of reading the archives, see Levins Morales, *Medicine Stories*, 1–56, and Pérez, *The Decolonial Imaginary.*

33. Clandestine Revolutionary Indigenous Committee—General Command of the Zapatista Army of National Liberation, "Sixth Declaration of the Selva Lacondona."

Chapter One

1. Larralde, "El Congreso in San Diego," 17.
2. Ibid.
3. See Mario T. García, *Memories of Chicano History.*
4. Tenayuca and Brooks, "The Mexican Question in the Southwest."
5. Moreno, "Caravans of Sorrow: Noncitizen Americans of the Southwest," 122.
6. Laura Pulido and David Lloyd explain that there were "two waves of settlers in the southwestern United States." The first wave came from Spanish imperial and Mexican state colonization efforts to Hispanicize indigenous people. A complicated process, these colonizing efforts featured many "settlers of color" who were indigenous, Afro-descendent, and/or identified in mixed race categories including mestizo/a and mulato/a. Therefore, Spanish-speaking and Mexican-origin people comprised a settler force that later became subject to the settler colonialism of the United States in the conquest of northern Mexico and the colonization of Mexican-origin and indigenous peoples in the region. See Lloyd and Pulido, "In the Long Shadow of the Settler," 797. For a provocative assessment of the problematic logic within claims to Mexican indigeneity among Mexican American writers of this generation in the 1930s and 1940s, see Olguín, "Caballeros and Indians." On indigenous peoples of present-day San Diego, especially the Kumeyaay, see Griswold del Castillo, "Natives and Settlers: The Mestizo Heritage," and Viejas Band of Kumeyaay Indians, *Viejas History Booklet.* The Viejas Band of Kumeeyaay reference the work of Florence Connelly Shipek.
7. See, for example, Clark, *Mexican Labor in the United States*; Slayden, "Some Observations on the Mexican Immigrant"; Taylor, *Mexican Labor in the United States* and *An American-Mexican Frontier*; and Gamio, *Mexican Immigration to the United States* and *The Life Story of the Mexican Immigrant.*
8. For insightful discussions of the intricacies of intraethnic relations in the first half of the twentieth century, see Galarza, "Mexicans in the Southwest: A Culture in Process"; McWilliams, *North from Mexico*; Gómez-Quiñones, "Piedras contra la luna, México en Aztlán y Aztlán en México," and "Notes on the Interpretation of the Relations between the Mexican Community in the United States and Mexico"; Paredes, *With a Pistol in His Hands*; Márquez, *LULAC*; and David G. Gutiérrez, *Walls and Mirrors.*
9. Gutiérrez, *Walls and Mirrors.*
10. Ngai, *Impossible Subjects.*
11. On communities of color, the CIO, and the Communist Party, see, Ruiz, *Cannery Women, Cannery Lives*; Kelley, *Hammer and Hoe*; and Vargas, *Labor Rights Are Civil Rights.*
12. On Congreso, see García, *Mexican Americans*; Ruiz, *Cannery Women, Cannery Lives*; Gutiérrez, *Walls and Mirrors*; Sánchez, *Becoming Mexican American*, 227–52; Larralde, "El Congreso in San Diego"; Vargas, *Labor Rights Are Civil Rights*; Schmidt Camacho, *Migrant Imaginaries*, 37–40; and Johnson, *Spaces of Conflict, Sounds of Solidarity*, 1–47.

13. Balderrama and Rodríguez, *Decade of Betrayal.*

14. First National Congress of the Mexican and Spanish American Peoples of the United States, *Digest of Proceedings*, April 1939 (public domain).

15. Ibid.

16. Ibid.

17. Ibid.

18. Gutiérrez, *Walls and Mirrors*, 115–16. The League of United Latin American Citizens (LULAC) best represents a middle-class Mexican American organization whose members at the time favored differentiating themselves from Mexican immigrants.

19. Sánchez, *Becoming Mexican American*, 245.

20. On El Congreso's struggles against gender oppression, see ibid., 227–28. On women activists in the San Diego Congreso, see Larralde, "El Congreso in San Diego," 22, and Larralde, "Roberto Galvan," 155–56.

21. "Adopted by the Second Convention of the Spanish Speaking People's Congress of California, Dec. 9 and 10, 1939," Ernesto Galarza Papers, as quoted in Sánchez, *Becoming Mexican American*, 248.

22. First National Congress of the Mexican and Spanish American Peoples of the United States, *Digest of Proceedings*. See also Gutiérrez, *Walls and Mirrors*, 115–16, and Sánchez, *Becoming Mexican American*, 209–10.

23. Sánchez argues, "The upsurge in Chicano political activity that occurred in the 1930s and early 1940s, however, involved at its core an attempt by the children of the immigrant generation and those who arrived in the United States as youngsters to integrate themselves into American society." While I do not disagree with this assertion, I would add that this activity, particularly that of advocacy for noncitizens, profoundly reshaped, at least momentarily, notions of integration with American society by conceiving of belonging beyond the realm of the nation-state. See Sánchez, *Becoming Mexican American*, 249–52.

24. García, *Mexican Americans*, 150. Quote taken from the ethnic Mexican community newspaper *La Opinion*, April 26, 1939, 1.

25. García, *Memories of Chicano History*, 115.

26. García, *Mexican Americans*, 150.

27. Larralde, "El Congreso in San Diego," 20. "Coyote" refers to a human smuggler who provides services to assist migrants in illicitly crossing the U.S.-Mexico border.

28. Bert Corona, interview by Carlos M. Larralde, April 25, 1980. Quoted in Carlos M. Larralde, "El Congreso in San Diego," 19.

29. Lowe, *Immigrant Acts*, 13.

30. Larralde, "El Congreso in San Diego," 20.

31. Carey McWilliams, interview by Carlos M. Larralde, June 12, 1979. Quoted in Larralde, "El Congreso in San Diego," 20.

32. Larralde and Griswold del Castillo, "Luisa Moreno," 3.

33. Ibid., 5. For analysis of the broader successes and history of Moreno and the UCAPAWA, see Ruiz, *Cannery Women, Cannery Lives.*

34. Ruiz, *Cannery Women, Cannery Lives*, 81. Ruiz cites *UCAPAWA News*, July 1939, May–June 1940, and January 15, 1942, as the source to detail the activities of Local 61.

35. Moreno, "Caravans of Sorrow: Noncitizen Americans of the Southwest," 122.

36. Larralde, "Roberto Galvan," 156.

37. Ibid., 156–57.

38. Larralde, "Roberto Galvan," 157. Larralde notes that the African American newspaper *The California Eagle*, based in Los Angeles, was a rare exception in reporting on the prevalence of KKK violence at the border.

39. Sánchez, *Becoming Mexican American*, 248–49. Sánchez reminds us that the American Communist Party aligned against Nazism when Germany invaded Russian territory in 1942.

40. Sánchez, *Becoming Mexican American*, 249. The popular front strategy also sought to legitimize the American Communist Party in its unity with mainstream political efforts against Nazism. For the problems faced especially by workers of color due to the popular front strategy used by the American Communist Party, see Ruiz, *Cannery Women, Cannery Lives*, and Kelley, *Hammer and Hoe*. These authors essentially argue that the popular front strategy limited the autonomy that had facilitated workers of color and women into successful CIO mobilizations.

41. Luisa Moreno, interview by Carlos M. Larralde, April 17, 1971. Referenced in Jacobo and Griswold del Castillo, "World War II and the Emerging Civil Rights Struggle," 98.

42. Larralde and Griswold del Castillo, "Luisa Moreno," 6; Beck and Williams, *California*, 395–96.

43. Larralde, "Roberto Galvan," 156.

44. Larralde and Griswold del Castillo, "Luisa Moreno," 6.

45. Larralde, "El Congreso in San Diego," 24.

46. Larralde, "Roberto Galvan," 161.

47. Larralde, "El Congreso in San Diego," 22.

48. Ibid., 20.

49. The zoot suit for young men consisted of drape pants that ballooned out at the knee and were closely tapered at the ankle, an oversized jacket and often a broad-rimmed hat with a watch chain hanging from the pocket. Young women often crafted their own zoot style with short skirts, heavy makeup and the same fingertip jacket. Propogated by youth of color, and often challenging of prevailing norms of racial segregation, gender and sexual boundaries, and occupation of space in wartime urban settings, authorities were often threatened and expressed concerned about the phenomenon.

50. On recent scholarship on the zoot-suiters, the Sleepy Lagoon incident, and the Zoot Suit Riots, see Alvarez, *The Power of the Zoot*; Escobedo, *From Coveralls to Zoot Suits*; Ramirez, *The Woman in the Zoot Suit*; and Pagan, *Murder at Sleepy Lagoon*.

51. Gutiérrez, *Walls and Mirrors*, 125–26.

52. Larralde and Griswold del Castillo, "Luisa Moreno," 7.

53. Ibid., 4.

54. Ibid., 4.

55. Ibid., 5.

56. Ibid., 6.

57. Ibid., 5.

58. Ibid., 7.

59. Ibid., 9.

60. David G. Gutiérrez, *Walls and Mirrors*, 125. Edward Escobar also argues that the zoot conflicts were a watershed moment in which the Los Angeles Police Department more thoroughly tied people of Mexican origin with criminality. See Edward Escobar, *Race, Police and the Making of a Political Identity*.

61. Gutiérrez, *Walls and Mirrors*, 128.

62. The Internal Security Act of 1950.

63. The first Red Scare occurred roughly between 1917 and 1920 in reaction to the Bolshevik revolution in Russia.

64. For how these developments affected ethnic Mexican politics in particular, see Gutiérrez, *Walls and Mirrors*, 161–68.

65. On the purges inflicted on the labor movement in the Cold War era, see Buhle, *Taking Care of Business*.

66. Larralde and Griswold del Castillo, "Luisa Moreno," 9.

67. Ibid.

68. Ibid., 11.

69. Ibid., 10.

70. García, *Memories of Chicano History*, 119.

71. Ibid.

72. Larralde, "Roberto Galvan," 169.

73. Ibid., 167.

74. U.S. House of Representatives, Committee on Un-American Activities, *Investigation of Communist Activities in the State of California, Hearing Before the Committee on Un-American Activities*, 83rd Cong. (April 21, 1954).

75. See Gutiérrez, *Walls and Mirrors*, 152–78; García, *Memories of Chicano History*, 169–92. Little scholarly attention has been given to La Hermandad Mexicana. Sparse information appears in Larralde and Griswold del Castillo, "San Diego's Ku Klux Klan," 8, and García, *Memories of Chicano History*, 290–95. Similarly, little attention has been paid to the political practices of various chapters of MAPA in California and its relationship to immigration and noncitizens. Brief mention appears in Brilliant, *The Color of America Has Changed*; Gutíerrez, *Walls and Mirrors*, 181; García, *Memories of Chicano History*, 200–201; and Navarro, *La Raza Unida Party*, 148–50.

76. Reston, "How Trump's Deportation Plan Failed 62 Years Ago," and Lytle Hernández, *Migra!*, 171–95.

77. Statistics recorded and compiled by Kelley Lytle Hernandez, *Migra!*, 122–23.

78. Gutiérrez, *Walls and Mirrors*, 141–42.

79. García, *Memories of Chicano History*, 184.

80. Rodríguez, "The Battle for the Border."

81. Hernández, *Migra!*, 191–95.

82. Chávez, *¡Mi Raza Primero!*, 17–18.

83. García, *Memories of Chicano History*.

84. Ibid., 192.

85. Ibid., 186.

86. Ibid., 182.

87. Ibid., 183–84.

88. Ibid., 181.

89. Larralde, "Roberto Galvan," 164.

90. Ibid., 169.

91. García, *Memories of Chicano History*, 290–91.

92. Larralde, "El Congreso in San Diego," 27.

93. Hermandad Mexican Nacional, Document, August 1951. In *Hermandad Mexicana: 25th Anniversary: Un Daño Contra Uno es un Daño Contra Todos*, program bulletin, 1971, HBP; also found in Box 29, BCP.

94. Ibid.

95. Ibid.

96. García, *Memories of Chicano History*, 241.

97. Ibid., 241–42.

98. Ibid., 199–200.

99. Johnson, *Spaces of Conflict, Sounds of Solidarity*, 4–5.

Chapter Two

1. Affidavit of Martha Elena Parra López, June 7, 1972, Box 6, Folder 1, HBP.

2. "Border Patrolman Accused of Rape," *San Diego County La Raza Unida Party Newsletter*, July 2, 1972, Box 14, Folder 8, HBP.

3. Torgerson and Del Olmo, "Tension Grows in Battle of 'Chain Link Curtain.'" *Los Angeles Times*, July 30, 1972, B3.

4. Ibid.

5. "Border Patrolman Accused of Rape," July 2, 1972, Box 14, Folder 8, HBP.

6. Torgerson and Del Olmo, "Tension Grows in Battle of 'Chain Link Curtain.'"

7. On this historic link between local police and federal border patrolling, see "'Hands-Off' Policy on Aliens Aired: Only Immigration Authorities May Hold Suspects, Lawmen Told," April 26, 1973, Box 22, Folder 3, HBP.

8. Affidavit of Martha Elena Parra López, June 7, 1972, Box 6, Folder 1, HBP.

9. According to sociologist Paula A. Bar, scholarly definitions of sexual harassment describe conduct that is "unwelcomed or unsolicited, is sexual in nature, and is deliberate or repeated," including verbal comments, gestures, and physical contact. Legal scholar Catharine MacKinnon's definition highlights how sexual harassment

occurs "in the context of a relationship of unequal power." See Bar, "Perceptions of Sexual Harassment," 461, and MacKinnon, *Sexual Harassment of Working Women*, 27. For a useful review of more recent scholarship on sexual harassment, see Uggen and Blackstone, "Sexual Harassment as a Gendered Expression of Power," 65–68.

10. Affidavit of Martha Elena Parra López, June 7, 1972, Box 6, Folder 1, HBP.

11. Ibid.

12. To make alien removal more efficient, the U.S. Immigration Service initiated voluntary departures in 1927 to avoid hearings and detention. This process has been expanded at different times since and continues to be a key part of expulsions at the U.S.-Mexico border. See Ngai, *Impossible Subjects*, 60; Lytle Hernández, *Migra!*, 76, 80; and Transactional Access Records Clearinghouse, "Controlling the Borders."

13. Affidavit of Martha Elena Parra López, June 7, 1972, Box 6, Folder 1, HBP.

14. Ibid.; "Border Patrolman Accused of Rape," July 2, 1972, Box 14, Folder 8, HBP.

15. Torgerson and Del Olmo, "Tension Grows in Battle of 'Chain Link Curtain.'"

16. Ibid.

17. Affidavit of Martha Elena Parra López, June 7, 1972, Box 6, Folder 1, HBP.

18. Ibid.

19. Torgerson and Del Olmo, "Tension Grows in Battle of 'Chain Link Curtain.'"

20. Affidavit of Martha Elena Parra López, June 7, 1972, Box 6, Folder 1, HBP. Sylvanna M. Falcón asserts that the power conferred to Border Patrol agents in a context with little or no supervision enables incidents of sexual violence, harassment, and intimidation. See Falcón, "Rape as a Weapon of War."

21. Affidavit of Martha Elena Parra López, June 7, 1972, Box 6, Folder 1, HBP.

22. Ibid.

23. "Border Patrolman Accused of Rape," July 2, 1972, HBP; Affidavit of Martha Elena Parra López, June 7, 1972, Box 6, Folder 1, HBP.

24. Harassment and violence are defined within Ian Haney López's notion of "legal violence." Haney López asserts: "The massive police presence, the constant police brutality, the hostile judges, and the crowded jails convinced Chicanos they were brown. 'Law' for Chicanos . . . means the police and the courts, and legal violence refers principally to the physical force these institutions wield. Law carried out on the street—as opposed to law on the books." In a similar way, U.S. Customs and Border Patrol officers, as well as other mechanisms of immigration law, consistently enacted both psychic and physical violence on Mexicans and Mexican Americans in the border region. See Haney López, *Racism on Trial*, 9.

25. David G. Gutiérrez, "Sin Fronteras?"; Pew Hispanic Center, "Mexican Immigrants in the United States, 2008."

26. The director of the immigrant service organization CASA Justicia, Carlos "Charlie" Vásquez, claims that about three hundred women came forth in early 1972 with complaints of being strip-searched. Carlos Vásquez, interview by author, September 7, 2006.

27. Pew Hispanic Center, "Mexican Immigrants in the United States, 2008."

28. According to the U.S. Census Bureau, the Mexican-origin population was approximately 1.7 million in 1960, 4.5 million in 1970, and 8.7 million in 1980. The Census reported that the Mexican-origin population was 28.3 million in 2006.

29. Gutiérrez, "Sin Fronteras?."

30. See Gutiérrez, "Globalization, Labor Migration, and the Demographic Revolution," and Sassen, "America's Immigration 'Problem.'"

31. Sassen, "U.S. Immigration Policy Toward Mexico in a Global Economy."

32. Sassen, "America's Immigration 'Problem.'"

33. Gutiérrez, "Globalization, Labor Migration, and the Demographic Revolution," and Sassen, "U.S. Immigration Policy Toward Mexico in a Global Economy."

34. Acuña, *Anything but Mexican*, 114. See also Ngai, *Impossible Subjects*, 261. In 1976, the U.S. Congress imposed a 20,000-person quota on immigration from Mexico, exacerbating the shift from legal to illegal migration. Furthermore, this 1976 act closed loopholes that allowed the children of undocumented migrants born in the United States to legalize their status.

35. Gutiérrez, *Walls and Mirrors*, 152–78.

36. Ibid.

37. Hondagneu-Sotelo, *Gendered Transitions*.

38. Prieto, *Beautiful Flowers of the Maquiladora*; Schmidt Camacho, *Migrant Imaginaries*.

39. Pessar, "Engendering Migration Studies"; Sassen, "U.S. Immigration Policy Toward Mexico in a Global Economy"; Schmidt Camacho, *Migrant Imaginaries*, 232–53.

40. Pessar, "Engendering Migration Studies," 580.

41. Espiritu, *Asian American Women and Men*.

42. Joseph Nevins asserts, "The end of the 1960s/early 1970s saw the emergence of a conservative-led war—with the Nixon administration at the helm—on crime and illicit drug use, one that often pointed the finger at Mexico for being a source of the illicit commodities." See Nevins, *Operation Gatekeeper and Beyond*, 78.

43. Chávez, "A Glass Half-Empty."

44. Nevins, *Operation Gatekeeper and Beyond*, 77–78.

45. Torgerson and Del Olmo, "Tension Grows in Battle of 'Chain Link Curtain.'"

46. Cockcroft, "The Story of Chicano Park"; Delgado, "A Turning Point"; Mulford and Barrera, "Chicano Park," https://www.youtube.com/watch?v=hXwZLo8hrp4; Ortiz, "'¡Sí, Se Puede!'"; Mariscal, *Brown-Eyed Children of the Sun*, 210–46.

47. For notions of San Diego as an actual borderland geographic space in which territorial boundaries are divided, crossed, and policed, see Nevins, *Operation Gatekeeper and Beyond*. On this notion of border and borderlands as a specific geographic site, I refer to Alvarez, "The Mexican-U.S. Border," and McC. Heyman and Campbell, "Recent Research on the U.S.-Mexico Border." Conceiving of the ways in which territorial borders shape social relations beyond the actual border, see Lubhéid, *Entry Denied*.

48. Flores, "Post-Bracero Undocumented Mexican Immigration and Political Re-composition"; Gutiérrez, "Sin Fronteras?"; and Schmidt Camacho, *Migrant Imaginaries*, 152–93.

49. Herman Baca, interview by author, September 13, 2006. On this rift, see also veteran activist Bert Corona's analysis in Mario T. García, *Memories of Chicano History*, and Gutiérrez, *Walls and Mirrors*, 179–205.

50. Herman Baca, interview by author, September 13, 2006.

51. Viesca, translation of the column "Aqui Estamos!," Box 17, Folder 8, HBP.

52. Jean Crowder, "Congressmen Hear Minorities," *National City Star-News*, April 30, 1972.

53. Ibid.

54. Ibid.

55. Ibid.

56. Vic Villalpando to Herman Baca et al., February 15, 1972, Box 6, Folder 3, HBP, and Crowder, "Congressmen Hear Minorities."

57. Villalpando to Herman Baca et al., February 15, 1972, Box 6, Folder 3, HBP.

58. "60 Persons Claim Brutality by U.S. Border Officials."

59. Villalpando to Baca et al., February 15, 1972, Box 6, Folder 3, HBP.

60. Carlos Vásquez, interview by author, September 7, 2006.

61. *Roberta Baca v. Vernon Hann, 1972–73*, Box 3, Folder 16, HBP.

62. "Statement Taken from Mrs. Roberta Baca on January 20, 1972 at 1:00 P.M.," Box 3, Folder 16, HBP.

63. Ibid.

64. Chávez, "A Glass Half-Empty," 178.

65. Ibid, 175.

66. Herman Baca to Congressman Lionel Van Deerlin, March 20, 1972, Box 13, Folder 7, HBP.

67. On *la familia de la Raza* see Schmidt Camacho, *Migrant Imaginaries*, 165–78 and Rodríguez, *Next of Kin*, 26–27.

68. "Immigration and Customs Hearing," Flyer, Box 3, Folder 16, HBP.

69. Roybal, "Some Strange Customs at the Border," *Los Angeles Times*, June 19, 1972.

70. Diaz, "Las Revisiones en la Frontera un Atentado Contra la Dignidad," Box 17, Folder 8, HBP. Translated from "Al grito 'Chicano Power,' y 'Raza sí, Migra no,' el grupo de norteamericanos de ascendencia mexicana, caminaban en un gran óvalo afuera de la Corte Federal, con pancartas y leyendas que repudiaban la actitud de los agentes de aduana y migración."

71. Ibid.

72. "Picket Picket Picket," Flyer, Box 3, Folder 16, HBP.

73. For border militarization as low-intensity warfare, see Dunn, *The Militarization of the U.S.-Mexico Border*. On sexual assault by officers as an inevitable consequence, see Falcón, "Rape as a Weapon of War." See also Lubhéid, *Entry Denied*. The more recent incidents of rape at the border, as explored by Falcon and Luibhéid,

reveal the more systematic documentation of these occurrences as organizations such as Human Rights Watch and Amnesty International, government entities such as the Office for the Inspector General, the American Friends Service Committee, media outlets, and grassroots community organizations have recorded these incidents since the 1980s, unlike during the 1970s and earlier.

74. Ramón Gutiérrez, "Community, Patriarchy and Individualism." In conceptualizing family, gender, and heteropatriarchy within the Chicano movement, I also refer to the work of Scmidt Camacho, *Migrant Imaginaries*, 165–78; Rodríguez, *Next of Kin*; and Blackwell, *Chicana Power*.

75. On the domestic roles expected of Chicanas in the movement as embodied in the concept of *la familia de la Raza* or race as family, see Schmidt Camacho, *Migrant Imaginaries*, 169.

76. "Border Patrolman Accused of Rape," July 2, 1972, Box 14, Folder 8, HBP.

77. I am influenced by the Chicana feminist writings in response to sexism in the Chicano movement that explore the complexities of ethnic nationalism's tendency to mobilize as a people against racism without addressing patriarchy and other social hierarchies internal to the Latino/a community. See for example, Alma García, *Chicana Feminist Thought*.

78. "Border Patrolman Accused of Rape," July 2, 1972, Box 14, Folder 8, HBP.

79. Ibid.

80. Ibid.

81. Conceiving of gender as a major modality through which a racialized community was imagined on transnational ground is related to the notion articulated by Stuart Hall that "race is the modality through which class is lived." See Hall, "Race, Articulation and Societies Structured in Dominance."

82. Albert García to Congressman Lionel Van Deerlin, November 24, 1972, Folder 19, Box 20, HBP. On Miller's alliance with MAPA for his election, see Herman Baca, interview by author, August 2, 2006.

83. Evelle J. Younger to Albert García and Robert R. López, May 4, 1973, Box 20, Folder 19, HBP.

84. "Delay Irks Roybal in Rape Prosecution." *Los Angeles Times*, August 27, 1972.

85. "Border Patrolman Accused of Rape," July 2, 1972, Box 14, Folder 8, HBP; Affidavit of Martha Elena Parra López, June 7, 1972, Box 6, Folder 1, HBP.

86. Albert García to Senator Allan Cranston, April 4, 1974, Box 17, Folder 8, HBP.

87. *Migra* is a colloquial term used among Mexicans, Mexican Americans, and other Latinos/as as a derogatory reference to the Border Patrol or other border officials. Embedded within this term is the collective understanding that border officials are anti-Mexican and anti-Latino/a.

88. *Compañera* translates into English as "companion" or "comrade," meaning a close friend that one struggles alongside with.

89. On the Chicana feminist movement developing simultaneously but seemingly out of dialog with the transnational Chicano/a activism discussed here, see Alma García, *Chicana Feminist Thought*, and Blackwell, *Chicana Power*.

Chapter Three

1. David G. Gutiérrez, *Walls and Mirrors*.

2. Augie Bareño, interview by author, July 27, 2012.

3. C.A.S.A.-Hermandad General de Trabajadores San Diego correspondence to all other CASA Centros, February 10, 1975, Box 22, Folder 6, CC.

4. For work on CASA, see Pulido, *Black, Brown, Yellow and Left*; Ernesto Chávez, *¡Mi Raza Primero!*; Gómez-Quiñones, *Chicano Politics*; Marisela Chávez, " 'We Lived and Breathed and Worked the Movement' "; Mario T. García, *Memories of Chicano History*; Gutiérrez, "CASA in the Chicano Movement" and *Walls and Mirrors*, 179–205.

5. Soledad Alatorre to Aileen Eaton, July 26, 1974, Box 14, Folder 1, BCP.

6. Augie Bareño, e-mail message to author, August 26, 2012.

7. Ibid.

8. Pulido, *Black, Brown, Yellow and Left*, 117.

9. García, *Memories of Chicano History*, 287.

10. Carlos "Charlie" Vásquez and Herman Baca, interview by author, July 27, 2012.

11. Ibid.

12. Ibid.

13. Ibid.

14. "Our History," http://www.maacproject.org/main/about-us/our-history/. MAAC later became the Metropolitan Area Advisory Committee.

15. Roger Cazares and Norma Mena Cazares, interview by author, January 28, 2017.

16. Carlos "Charlie" Vásquez, interview by author, September 7, 2006.

17. Here I am considering political theorist Engin F. Isin's contention that a citizenship regime has been created that emphasizes a hierarchical circumstance for citizens and ever-present noncitizens in Western democracies, and that noncitizen challenges to this hierarchal structure entail a subversive form of "being political." See Isin, *Being Political*.

18. Carlos "Charlie" Vásquez, interview by author, September 7, 2006.

19. Carlos "Charlie" Vásquez and Herman Baca, interview by author, July 27, 2012; Carlos "Charlie" Vásquez, interview by author, September 7, 2006; Norma Mena Cazares and Roger Cazares, interview by author, July 20, 2012. *Carnitas* are a cut of pork that is often grilled at gatherings in Mexican communities. *Tardeadas* were events with food and often music and other festivities utilized by community organizations to raise money for a cause.

20. Carlos "Charlie" Vásquez, interview by author, September 7, 2006.

21. Norma Mena Cazares and Roger Cazares, interview by author, July 20, 2012.

22. Alvaro Camargo to Bert Corona, June 4, 1973, Box 14, Folder 1, BCP.

23. Ibid.

24. Mercedes Alba to Bert Corona, November 18, 1972, Box 3, Folder 1, BCP.

25. Asunción Esparza Vera to CASA, June 10, 1974, Box 3, Folder 1, BCP.

26. Manuel Monterrosa Urías, CASA to American Consulate, Tijuana, B.C., Mexico, July 28, 1972, et al., Box 31, Folder 7, BCP.

27. Manuel Monterrosa Urías, CASA to American Consulate, Monterrey, Mexico, August 4, 1972, Box 31, Folder 7, CC.

28. Maria Luisa Sánchez Portilla, CASA to American Consulate, San Salvador, El Salvador, July 27, 1972; Affadavit of Adolfo Lanuza Cruz and others in American Consulate Letters, Box 31, Folder 7, CC; Jose Antonio Orellano Martínez, San Salvador, El Salvador, to Soledad Alatorre, Los Angeles, May 20, 1974, and others in "Letters," Box 3, Folder 2, BCP.

29. American Consulate Letters, Box 31, Folder 7, CC; Letters, Box 3, Folder 2, BCP.

30. Carlos "Charlie" Vásquez, interview by author, September 7, 2006; Carlos "Charlie" Vásquez and Herman Baca, interview by author, July 27, 2012.

31. Carlos "Charlie" Vásquez and Herman Baca, interview by author, July 27, 2012.

32. Luis A. Aguilar to Bert Corona, June 16, 1973, Box 3, Folder 2, CC, and Luis A. Aguilar to Director of Organizing Committees against Deportations, June 16, 1973, Box 3, Folder 2, CC.

33. Carlos "Charlie" Vásquez and Herman Baca, interview by author, July 27, 2012.

34. Federal Bureau of Investigation notes on surveillance of Herman Baca, quoted in Committee on Chicano Rights, Inc. and Herman Baca vs. The United States Department of Justice, 1978–1982, p. 3, Box 11, Folder 8, HBP.

35. Carlos "Charlie" Vásquez and Herman Baca, interview by author, July 27, 2012.

36. Herman Baca, interview by author, August 14, 2006.

37. Carlos "Charlie" Vásquez, interview by author, September 7, 2006.

38. Ibid.

39. Carlos "Charlie" Vásquez, interview by author, September 7, 2006.

40. Norma Mena Cazares and Roger Cazares, interview by author, September 8, 2006.

41. Chávez, "We Lived and Breathed and Worked the Movement."

42. Gloria Jean Valderrama Nieto, interview by author, July 27, 2012.

43. Norma Mena Cazares and Roger Cazares, interview by author, February 1, 2016.

44. Ibid.

45. Bert Corona, *Bert Corona Speaks*, 19.

46. Augie Bareño, interview by author, July 27, 2012.

47. Pulido, *Black, Brown, Yellow and Left*; Chávez, *¡Mi Raza Primero!*; Gómez-Quiñones, *Chicano Politics*, 150–52; García, *Memories of Chicano History*; Gutiérrez, "CASA in the Chicano Movement."

48. Gutiérrez, "CASA in the Chicano Movement," 13.

49. The primary organizations these younger activists came from included the Committee to Free Los Tres and CASA Carnalismo. It is also important to note that

the Rodríguez family was politically involved in the student movement in Mexico. The student movement was heavily repressed, culminating in the Tlatelolco Massacre in 1968. See García, *Memories of Chicano History*, and Pulido, *Black, Brown, Yellow and Left*.

50. García, *Memories of Chicano History*, 310.

51. Ibid.

52. Ibid., 310–11.

53. "The Committee for Chicano Rights, Organizational History, July 21–22, 1979," Folder 6, Box 12, HBP.

54. For Corona's recollection of the break, see García, *Memories of Chicano History*, 308–15.

55. "The Committee for Chicano Rights, Organizational History, July 21–22, 1979," Folder 6, Box 12, HBP.

56. David G. Gutiérrez writes that the San Diego, San Jose, and Greeley Colorado chapters of CASA "strongly dissented to CASA's new stance as a revolutionary vanguard" after a series of national meetings that concluded in July 1975. The Los Angeles chapter's position as a revolutionary vanguard was agreed upon by a majority of the chapters, leading to the official withdrawal of the San Diego and San Jose chapters from the national organization. The Greeley chapter withdrew six months later. See Gutiérrez, "CASA in the Chicano Movement," 15.

57. C.A.S.A. San Diego to National CASA, February 10, 1975, Box 22, Folder 6, CC.

58. Baca's relationship to class struggle and Marxism was complex. As a protégé of Corona, Baca referred to the exploitation of Mexican labor as the central goal of U.S. immigration policy. In this way, he highlighted how race and citizenship status justified the exploitation of labor and divided workers, particularly those of Mexican descent, along the lines of citizenship status. In these assertions, connections to Marxism and class analysis are apparent. Yet Baca also displayed reluctance to use Marxist concepts too explicitly or discuss the possibility of developing a class consciousness among the ethnic Mexican community. Instead, he often opted to evaluate the political consciousness of the ethnic Mexican community in terms of "self-determination." In this way, Baca was much more pragmatic in his opinion that this system of labor exploitation he was encountering, in the guise of immigration policy, must be addressed and obliterated in order for the ethnic Mexican community to be in any position to discuss its political trajectory. Baca thus tended to look at the "Chicano community" as a nation within a nation, similar to the internal colony model exerted by U.S. third world proponents within the black, brown, and yellow power movement. Little was said explicitly about how this "nation" should confront its internal class struggles except for statements that the exploitation of Mexican labor by U.S. businesses was detrimental. Baca's unyielding support for Corona's ideas about centralizing the experience of the Mexicano/a worker and allying it with other workers seemed to imply, however, that he sought to move forward politically based on an intersecting ethno-racial and class experience.

59. See "Internal Document, National Organization," Correspondence from CASA San Diego to National CASA, Box 22, Folder 6, CC.

60. Pulido, *Black, Brown, Yellow and Left*, 5.

61. "Internal Document, National Organization," Correspondence from CASA San Diego to National CASA, Box 22, Folder 6, CC.

62. C.A.S.A. San Diego to National CASA, February 10, 1975, San Diego Nucleo, Box 22, Folder 6, CASA papers.

63. Norma Mena Cazares and Roger Cazares, interview by author, January 28, 2017.

64. Carlos "Charlie" Vásquez and Herman Baca, interview by author, July 27, 2012.

65. Jacobo Rodríguez to Herman Baca, March 15, 1975, Box 6, Folder 4, HBP.

66. "Report on San Diego 2/22/76," Juan Gutiérrez, CASA San Diego to CASA Los Angeles, Box 22, Folder 6, CC.

67. Ibid.

68. Juan Gutiérrez to CASA L.A., "Reporte Semanal de San Diego July 26, 1976," Box 22, Folder 6, CC.

69. Ibid.

70. Juan Gutiérrez to CASA L.A., "Reporte de San Diego, 9/13/76," Box 22, Folder 6, CC.

71. Ibid.

72. Ibid.

73. Ibid.

74. Ibid.

75. Carlos "Charlie" Vásquez and Herman Baca, interview by author, July 27, 2013.

Chapter Four

1. Herman Baca, interview by author, August 28, 2006.

2. I am using the terms "Chicano Democrat" strategically here to show that many newly elected Mexican-origin officials identified with and utilized the ethnic mobilization of the Chicano movement. In contrast to the debates between, for example, Chicano movement activist Jose Angel Gutiérrez and Mexican American congressman Henry B. Gonzales in Texas. The usage of "Chicano" versus "Mexican American" symbolized the rift between movement activists and more conservative members of the ethnic Mexican community that subscribed to assimiliation as a tactic of addressing discrimination. Gonzales disassociated himself from the movement due to his perception that its adherents were proponents of "racism in reverse" in their emphasis on Chicano identity. Many newly elected ethnic Mexican officials identified with and participated in manifestations of the Chicano movement and used the term "Chicano" and the ethnic-based politics associated with it. My discussions of assemblymen Peter Chacón of San Diego and Alex García in this section

are cases in point. This understanding reveals yet another strand among a myriad of identity postulations with various class, gender, and national connotations that Chicano movement strategy evolved into and that were rigorously debated and contested. On the Gutiérrez/González debate, see David G. Gutiérrez, *Walls and Mirrors*, 186–87.

3. Calavita, *California's "Employer Sanctions."*

4. Brilliant, *The Color of America Has Changed*, 167.

5. Mario T. García, *Memories of Chicano History*, 196.

6. Ibid., 197–205.

7. Gerald Horne, *Fire This Time*, 12; Vargas, *Labor Rights Are Civil Rights*, 271.

8. Pitti, *The Devil in Silicon Valley*, 149; see also Ernesto Chávez, *¡Mi Raza Primero!*, 12.

9. See also Gutiérrez, *Walls and Mirrors*, 161–68.

10. Vargas, *Labor Rights Are Civil Rights*, 271.

11. On the influence of Cuba and other decolonial or anti-imperialist movements in the global south on the Chicano movement, see, for example, Mariscal, *Brown-Eyed Children of the Sun*; Lipsitz, "Not Just Another Social Movement"; Oropeza, *¡Raza Si! ¡Guerra No!*; and Gómez, *The Revolutionary Imaginations of Greater Mexico*.

12. García, *Memories of Chicano History*, 203.

13. Gutiérrez, *Walls and Mirrors*, 181.

14. Mariscal, *Brown-Eyed Children of the Sun*, 7.

15. Foley, "Becoming Hispanic."

16. García, *Memories of Chicano History*, 198–99.

17. Referencing Matt García's explanation, the United Farm Workers, or UFW, is the organization's most popularly known name. The union became the United Farm Workers Organizing Committee (UFWOC) in August 1966 after the merger of the National Farm Workers Association (NFWA) and the Agricultural Workers Organizing Committee (AWOC). The AFL-CIO granted the UFWOC an independent charter to the UFW in February 1972 and the name was formally adopted in September 1973. For simplicity, I use UFW unless it becomes necessary to make distinctions with its other iterations. Matt García, *From the Jaws of Victory*, 299n1.

18. Quoted in Brilliant, *The Color of America Has Changed*, 187.

19. Ibid.

20. For an example in San Bernadino and Riverside County, California, see Navarro, *La Raza Unida Party*, 108–25, and a brief discussion of MAPA in San Diego and Los Angeles under Baca and Corona, 137–38.

21. Herman Baca to U.S. Civil Rights Commission, Appendix B, "1968 Estimate of the Chicano Population in San Diego County," Box 13, Folder 5, HBP.

22. Herman Baca, interview by author, August 2, 2006.

23. Ibid. Dennis Chávez was a U.S. senator from New Mexico from 1935 to 1962. He was the first Latino/a U.S. senator to serve an elected term.

24. Rosales, *Chicano!*, 6, 14, 16. See also Gonzales-Berry and Maciel, *Contested Homeland*.

25. "Biography and Herman Baca Timeline, Register of the Herman Baca Papers," HBP.

26. Herman Baca, interview by author, August 2, 2006.

27. Augie Bareño, interview by author, July 27, 2012.

28. See Blackwell, *Chicana Power!*, 71. For direct accounts by Chicana activists on their experiences in Chicano movement activism and struggles with sexism, and early reflection and analyses on the connections between struggles against race and class oppression and struggles against patriarchy, see Alma García, *Chicana Feminist Thought*.

29. Blackwell, *Chicana Power!*, 99.

30. Ibid., 71.

31. For insights into Chicana experiences in the San Diego Chicano Movement in the university and artistic collectives see Laura E. García, Sandra M. Gutiérrez, and Felica Nuñez, *Teatro Chicana*.

32. Augie Bareño, interview by author, July 27, 2012.

33. Herman Baca, interview by author, August 2, 2006.

34. Ortiz, "'¡Sí, Se Puede!,'" 130–31.

35. Mariscal, *Brown-Eyed Children of the Sun*.

36. Norma Mena Cazares and Roger Cazares, interview by author, July 20, 2012.

37. Teatro Campesino emerged from the farmworkers' struggles led by the United Farm Workers (UFW), particularly to raise awareness among workers and the larger public about the grape strike and boycott from 1965–1970. It was the cultural front of the movement, founded by Luis Valdez who was a student and UFW member at the time, the group utilized Mexican cultural traditions to dramatize the struggle against farm bosses, strikebreakers, and others, often from the back of flatbed trucks in the fields. See Yolanda Broyles-González, *Teatro Campesino*.

38. Herman Baca, interview by author, August 2, 2006.

39. Excellent analyses of the articulation of a brown, nonwhite identity by Chicano movement activists include Haney López, *Racism on Trial*, and San Miguel, "*Brown, Not White*."

40. Chávez, *¡Mi Raza Primero!*

41. First National Chicano Youth Liberation Youth Conference, *Plan de Aztlán*.

42. MEChA was created within the *Plan de Santa Barbara*, which was written by the Chicano Coordinating Council on Higher Education and adopted at a symposium at the University of California, Santa Barbara, in April 1969. See Muñoz, *Youth, Identity, Power*.

43. Navarro, *La Raza Unida Party*, 108–34.

44. Hermandad Mexicana Founding Document, 195, Box 29, BCP.

45. García, *Memories of Chicano History*, 290–91.

46. Herman Baca, interview with author, August 2, 2006.

47. Breirer, "Pete Chacón, 89, Assemblyman, Leading Voice in Bilingual Education," *San Diego Union-Tribune*, January 3, 2015; Perry, "Peter Chacón Dies at 89," *Los Angeles Times*, January 19, 2015.

48. Breirer, "Pete Chacón, 89, Assemblyman, Leading Voice in Bilingual Education," *San Diego Union-Tribune*, January 3, 2015.

49. California State Archives, "Biography," http://www.oac.cdlib.org/findaid /ark:/13030/c8x34z2x/entire_text/.

50. Herman Baca, interview by author, August 2, 2006.

51. "Our History," http://www.maacproject.org/main/about-us/our-history/. MAAC later became the Metropolitan Area Advisory Committee.

52. Herman Baca, interview by author, August 2, 2006. On the traditionally Democratic constituency of the 79th district, see Clance, "County GOP Lists Aid to Candidates," *San Diego Union*, August 4, 1970.

53. Herman Baca, interview by author, August 2, 2006.

54. Ibid.

55. "Mills, Boney Outlays Put at $41,266," *San Diego Union*, July 7, 1970.

56. Herman Baca, interview by author, August 2, 2006.

57. Ibid.

58. Ibid.

59. On Marie C. Widman, see "San Diego Democratic Chief Quits," *Los Angeles Times*, January 15, 1970. On George Koulaxes, see "Koulaxes-Chacón Contest Neckand-Neck in 79th," *San Diego Union*, June 3, 1970, and Greek Orthodox Ladies Philoptochos Society, Anthousa Chapter, "2013 Atousa Award," http://anthousa.org /Anthousa_Award.html.

60. *San Diego Union*, June 1, 1970, A-11.

61. Herman Baca, interview by author, August 2, 2006.

62. *San Diego Union*, June 1, 1970, A-11.

63. Herman Baca, interview by author, August 2, 2006.

64. "Koulaxes-Chacón Contest Neck-and-Neck in 79th," *San Diego Union*, June 3, 1970; "Computer Fails, Halts Count," *San Diego Union*, June 4, 1970, A2; "2 Key Races Settled by Computer Tally," *San Diego Union*, June 5, 1970.

65. Herman Baca, interview by author, August 2, 2006.

66. Applegate, "Some People in This Town Don't Like Herman Baca and He Doesn't Care." *Reader: San Diego's Weekly*, Vol. 8 No. 24, (June 21, 1979): 9.

67. Herman Baca, interview by author, August 2, 2006. See also Bareño, "¡Cuando tu vas, yo ya vengo; Or, This Ain't Our 1st Rodeo!," *La Prensa San Diego*, September 18, 2009. Bareño, a participant, writes, "An educator, Pete Chacón was elected to the California Assembly in November of 1970. . . . His primary campaign manager was Herman Baca who brought many volunteers from MAPA and various community groups, to the process, ending in an unexpected victory for Chacón. The mainstream democratic interest subsequently took charge of the general election campaign against Republican Tom Hom and Chacón was elected."

68. "Hom Backs Bill to Limit Busing," *San Diego Union*, June 25, 1970, B-4; "Dinner at VFW Hall Will Honor Chacón," *San Diego Union*, August 11, 1970, B-5; "'Rally Day' Keeps Unruh on Move," *San Diego Union*, August 23, 1970; "New Course Urged for Democrats," *San Diego Union*, October 6, 1970, B-9; "Chacón Criticizes Hom's

Record," *San Diego Union*, October 8, 1970; Chet Dinnel, "Assemblyman Assails Hom's Voting Record," *San Diego Union*, October 11, 1970, B-3; "McGovern Says Nation Eyeing 79th," *San Diego Union*, October 22, 1970, B-9; "Candidates Clash in Roundup Here," *San Diego Union*, October 26, 1970.

69. "Candidates Clash in Roundup Here," *San Diego Union*, October 26, 1970; "Big Turnout Seen at Polls Tuesday," *San Diego Union*, November 1, 1970; "Let's Be Fair! Democrats Not Responsible for Hom Indictments," *San Diego Union*, November 2, 1970, B-6.

70. Charles Ross, "Legislative Shift Upsets GOP's Plan," *San Diego Union*, November 5, 1970, 1.

71. Isidro Ortiz, " '¡Sí, Se Puede!,' " 136.

72. California State Archives, "Biography," http://www.oac.cdlib.org/findaid /ark:/13030/c8x34z2x/entire_text/.

73. Herman Baca, interview by author, August 2, 2006.

74. Gutiérrez, *Walls and Mirrors*, 197–99. See also Matthew García, *From the Jaws of Victory*; Pawell, *The Crusades of Cesar Chavez* and *A Union of Their Dreams*; and Flores, *Grounds for Dreaming*.

75. U.S. Customs and Border Protection, "U.S. Border Patrol Fiscal Year Southwest Border Sector Apprehensions (FY 1960-FY 2014)," http://www.cbp.gov/sites /default/files/documents/BP%20Southwest%20Border%20Sector%20Apps%20 FY1960%20-%20FY2014_0.pdf.

76. Gutiérrez, *Walls and Mirrors*, 197–99.

77. Ibid., 287.

78. Vic Villalpando to Herman Baca et al., February 15, 1972, Box 6, Folder 3, HBP; José T. Viesca, translation of the column "Aqui Estamos!," *National City Star-News*, July 30, 1970, Box 17, Folder 8, HBP; Roberta Baca v. Vernon Hann, 1972–73, Box 3, Folder 16, HBP; Vic Villalpando to Herman Baca et al., February 15, 1972, Box 6, Folder 3, HBP; and Crowder, "Congressmen Hear Minorities," *National City Star-News*, April 30, 1972.

79. Vic Villalpando to Herman Baca et al., February 15, 1972, Box 6, Folder 3, HBP. See also chapters 2 and 3.

80. Calavita, *California's "Employer Sanctions,"* 4.

81. Quoted in ibid., 26, 49. It climbed to 9.2 percent by 1976.

82. Peter R. Chacón, "Statement on the Illegal Alien Law—What's Good and What's Bad about It?," Box 22, Folder 1, HBP. See also *Chicano Federation Newsletter* 2, no. 3 (March 1972), Box 22, Folder 1, HBP.

83. Calavita, California's "Employer Sanctions," 30.

84. Gutiérrez, *Walls and Mirrors*, 197.

85. Peter Chacón, "Statement on the Illegal Alien Law—What's Good and What's Bad about It?," Box 22, Folder 1, HBP.

86. Ibid.

87. Armando Rodríguez, "What Is MAPA's Position?," *La Voz de MAPA*, February 1972, Box 2, Folder 30, HBP.

88. Uvaldo Martínez, Jr., to Raul Loya, March 1972, Box 13, Folder 5, HBP.

89. Raul Loya to Uvaldo Martínez, March 20, 1972, Box 22, Folder 1, HBP.

90. Ibid.

91. Peter Chacón, "Statement on the Illegal Alien Law—What's Good and What's Bad about It?," Box 22, Folder 1, HBP.

92. "Brophy Bill Regarding Employment of Illegal Aliens," Memorandum from Alex García and Peter Chacón to Democratic Assemblymen, February 16, 1972, Box 22, Folder 1, HBP. The first two Latinos elected to the California Assembly in the modern era were Phil Soto (1962–66), a Democrat from La Puente in Los Angeles County, and John Moreno (1962–64), a Democrat from Los Angeles.

93. Peter Chacón, "Statement on the Illegal Alien Law—What's Good and What's Bad about It?," Box 22, Folder 1, HBP.

94. "Brophy Bill Regarding Employment of Illegal Aliens," Memorandum from Alex Garcia and Peter Chacón to Democratic Assemblymen, February 16, 1972, Box 22, Folder 1, HBP.

95. Peter Chacón, "Statement on the Illegal Alien Law—What's Good and What's Bad about It?," Box 22, Folder 1, HBP.

96. Ibid.

97. "Press Statement of Congressman Edward Roybal," February 14, 1972, Box 22, Folder 1, HBP.

98. Chácon, "Guest Editorial Law 538," *El Chicano*, March 15, 1972; Corona, "The Immigration Problem," *Ideal*, July 27, 1972.

99. "Picket AB 528," Press Release, March 11, 1971, Box 13, Folder 7, HBP.

100. Ibid.

101. Nancy Ray, "Chicano Picket Chacón's Offices: Assemblyman's Vote Favoring Ban on Jobs for Illegal Aliens Assailed," *San Diego Union*, February 11, 1972.

102. Ibid.

103. Ibid.

104. Bert Corona, *Bert Corona Speaks*, 19.

105. Calavita, *California's "Employer Sanctions,"* 49.

106. Ibid., 33–35.

107. Ibid., 34–40.

108. Ibid., 41–42.

109. Ibid., 52.

110. Other labor organizations and unions that supported AB 528 are indicated by letters from the California Teamsters to Peter Chácon, February 12, 1972, and the United Rubber, Cork, Linoleum, and Plastic Workers of American to Peter Chácon, February 18, 1972, Box 22, Folder 1, HBP.

111. "Brophy Bill Regarding Employment of Illegal Aliens," Memorandum from Alex García and Peter Chacón to Democratic Assemblymen, February 16, 1972, Box 22, Folder 1, HBP.

112. Ibid.

113. Ibid.

114. Herman Baca to Assemblyman Peter R. Chacón, March 3, 1972, Box 13, Folder 7, HBP.

115. Ibid.

116. Herman Baca, "Chicanos Protest Illegal Alien Law," *Chicano Federation Newsletter* 2, no. 4 (April 1972), Box 22, Folder 1, HBP.

117. Ibid.

118. Ibid.

119. Herman Baca, "Chicanos Protest Illegal Alien Law," *Chicano Federation Newsletter* 2, no. 4 (April 1972), Box 22, Folder 1, HBP.

120. Ibid.

121. Kitty Calavita, *California's "Employer Sanctions,"* 50. On Chavez's shift in position, see Gutiérrez, *Walls and Mirrors*, 196–99.

122. Kitty Calavita, *California's "Employer Sanctions,"* 50.

Chapter Five

1. "Corky Gonzales Speaks: Corky Gonzales Spoke at La Placita for Los Tres," *La Raza Unida-San Diego County Newsletter* 9 (April/May 1973), Box 14, Folder 8, HBP.

2. Ibid.

3. Ibid.

4. Jose Angel Gutiérrez to Herman Baca, February 23, 1973, Box 14, Folder 13, HBP.

5. Ibid.

6. La Raza Unida Party Organizing Committees Southern Region to La Raza Unida Party Organizers State of California, August 21, 1972, Box 26, Folder 6, CC.

7. On La Raza Unida Party, see Ignacio García, *United We Win*; Navarro, *La Raza Unida Party*; and Santillan, *La Raza Unida*.

8. Navarro, *Mexicano Political Experience in Occupied Aztlán*, 359–60.

9. Ibid.; on MAPA support for Ricardo Romo, see Santillan, *La Raza Unida*, 36–37.

10. Mario T. García, *Memories of Chicano History*, 200–201. Corona says of MAPA, "My own position, and that of many others, was that we had been rejected by the Democratic Party in previous electoral efforts. We needed therefore to build an independent electoral machine, one that could engage in progressive politics without having to compromise with the Democrats—or with the Republicans, for that matter. I also believed that MAPA should not remain strictly an electoral organization but that it should involve itself in the various issues affecting the Mexican communities" García, 200.

11. *MAPA and La Raza Unida Party: A Program for Chicano Political Action for the 1970s*, Box 14, Folder 4, HBP.

12. Ibid.

13. Ibid. My translation from: "Toda nuestra raza. . . . Los nacidos aquí, los nacidos en Mexico que tienen documentos. . . . y los que no tienen documentos, Todos!

Somos hermanos de sangre y raza! Todos trabajamos y pagamos los mismos impuestos y nos llevan a nuestros hijos a las guerras por parejo! Ademas, todos sufrimos por los abusos y brutalidad de la emigración y el Border Patrol!"

14. Navarro, *La Raza Unida Party*.

15. Herman Baca, interview by Navarro, May 31, 1997. Quoted in Navarro, *La Raza Unida Party*, 149.

16. Navarro, *La Raza Unida Party*, 149.

17. García, *United We Win*; Navarro, *La Raza Unida Party*; Santillan, *La Raza Unida*.

18. García, *United We Win*; Navarro, *La Raza Unida Party*; Santillan, *La Raza Unida*; Muñoz and Barrera, "La Raza Unida Party and the Chicano Student Movement in California"; and Ernesto Chávez, *¡Mi Raza Primero!*.

19. "Registrese El Partido De La Raza Unida," Box 15, Folder 10, HBP.

20. "Si no votamos no valemos," Box 15, Folder 10, HBP.

21. Phone Number List, Box 14, Folder 11, HBP.

22. "La Raza Unida Contributions," Box 14, Folder 11, HBP.

23. Past Due List, Box 14, Folder 11, HBP.

24. Herman Baca, interview by author, August 14, 2006.

25. "Victory in San Jose!," *San Diego County La Raza Unida Party Newsletter* 1, no. 1 (1972), Box 14, Folder 8, HBP.

26. Ibid.

27. Ibid.

28. "A Historical Perspective: The Chicano in California Politics," *San Diego County La Raza Unida Party Newsletter* 1, no. 1 (1972), Box 14, Folder 8, HBP.

29. Ibid.

30. Ibid.

31. "Areas of Concern," *San Diego County La Raza Unida Party Newsletter* 1, no. 1 (1972), Box 14, Folder 8, HBP.

32. Ibid.

33. Corona, "The Immigration Problem," *San Diego County La Raza Unida Party Newsletter* 1, no. 1 (1972), Box 14, Folder 8, HBP.

34. Ibid.

35. "A Concerned Chicana" to Herman Baca, December 17, 1972, Box 13, Folder 5, HBP.

36. Corona, "The Immigration Problem," *San Diego County La Raza Unida Party Newsletter* 1, no. 1 (1972), Box 14, Folder 8, HBP.

37. Corona, "The Immigration Problem," *San Diego County La Raza Unida Party Newsletter*, no. 2 (August 1972), Box 14, Folder 8, HBP.

38. See image of Norma Mena Cazares in front of CASA Justicia and Aztec Printers, Box 52, Folder 5, HBP.

39. Translated from "Los nacidos aqui, los Chicanos, los que vienen del otro lado y que ya son residentes permanentes, y los que han venido pero por las dificultades tan grandes todavia no tienen sus visas . . . todos somos miembros de la misma

Raza. Somos miembros de cada familia. . . . C.A.S.A. es una hermandad de todos los trabajadores que sufren las tremendas dificultades por la visa y demas problemas de la imigracion. . . . Si necesita ayuda con problemas relacionados no deje de comunicarse con C.A.S.A." *San Diego County La Raza Unida Party Newsletter* 1, no. 1 (1972), Box 14, Folder 8, HBP.

40. Ibid.

41. *San Diego County La Raza Unida Party Newsletter* 1, no. 2 (July 1972), Box 14, Folder 8, HBP.

42. *San Diego County La Raza Unida Party Newsletter* 1, no. 1 (1972), Box 14, Folder 8, HBP.

43. *San Diego County La Raza Unida Party Newsletter* 1, no. 2 (July 1972), Box 14, Folder 8, HBP.

44. *San Diego County La Raza Unida Party Newsletter* 1, no. 8 (January/February 1973), Box 14, Folder 8, HBP.

45. *San Diego County La Raza Unida Party Newsletter* 1, no. 1 (1972), Box 14, Folder 8, HBP.

46. *San Diego County La Raza Unida Party Newsletter* 1, no. 8 (January/February 1973), Box 14, Folder 8, HBP.

47. Rodríguez, *Next of Kin*, 33–34.

48. *San Diego County La Raza Unida Party Newsletter*, no. 3 (August 1972), Box 14, Folder 8, HBP.

49. *San Diego County La Raza Unida Party Newsletter*, no. 3 (August 1972), Box 14, Folder 8, HBP.

50. *San Diego County La Raza Unida Party Newsletter*, no. 2 (July 1972), Box 14, Folder 8, HBP.

51. *San Diego County La Raza Unida Party Newsletter*, no. 3 (August 1972), and no. 7 (December 1972), Box 14, Folder 8, HBP.

52. *San Diego County La Raza Unida Party Newsletter*, no. 5 (October 1972), Box 14, Folder 8, HBP.

53. *San Diego County La Raza Unida Party Newsletter*, no. 7 (December 1972), Box 14, Folder 8, HBP.

54. Ibid.

55. *San Diego County La Raza Unida Party Newsletter*, no. 7 (December 1972), Box 14, Folder 8, HBP.

56. Ibid.

57. Haney López, *Racism on Trial*, 153.

58. Ibid., 154.

59. La Raza Unida State Party Convention, Reports on Committees, "Resolutions Passed in Political Workshop," San Jose, April 8–9, 1972, Box 26, Folder 6, CC.

60. La Raza Unida State Party Convention, Reports on Committees, "Resolutions Passed in Labor and Deportations Workshop," San Jose, April 8–9, 1972, Box 26, Folder 6, CC.

61. Navarro, *La Raza Unida Party*, 151.

62. Interview of Armando Navarro, California State Archives State Government Oral History Program, UCLA Center for Oral History Research, August 3, 1989, http://oralhistory.library.ucla.edu/viewItem.do?ark=21198/zz0o0s2fhs&title=TAPE%20NUMBER:%20II,%20Side%20One%20(August%203,%201989). Relatedly, former Labor Committee leader Jimmy Franco, Sr., writes that Navarro led "members of the then Mexican American Political Association (MAPA) chapters from San Benardino and Riverside counties" and "created a number of phony and unknown LRUP chapters" engaging in "unprincipled red-baiting of CASA and Bert Corona" revealing deep seated differences, accusations, and conflict. See Franco, "La Raza Unida Party of California," http://www.latinopov.com/blog/?p=6280, posted September 28, 2012.

63. It is important to note that the LRUP Labor Committee became the Maoist August Twenty-ninth Movement (ATM) in 1974. ATM would argue that Chicanos in the U.S. constituted a separate Chicano Nation separate from Mexico, due to the particular struggles of Mexicans in the U.S. since the Mexican American War. This position contrasted with CASA's idea that Mexicans in the U.S. and in Mexico were one people. These positions formed the basis of disagreement over the Mexican immigrant question. See Pulido, *Black, Brown, Yellow and Left*, 131–33.

64. La Raza Unida Party State of California Resolutions, Los Angeles, July 1–2, 1972, CC.

65. Ibid.

66. Ibid.

67. Ibid.

68. Navarro, *La Raza Unida Party*, 152.

69. Ibid.

70. Ibid.

71. Ibid.

72. La Raza Unida Party Organizing Committees Southern Region to La Raza Unida Party Organizers State of California, August 21, 1972, Box 26, Folder 6, CC. See also Carlos Muñoz, interview by Nick García, February 5 and 12, 2003.

73. Navarro, *La Raza Unida Party*, 152.

74. La Raza Unida Party Organizing Committees Southern Region to La Raza Unida Party Organizers State of California, August 21, 1972, Box 26, Folder 6, CC.

75. Indeed, Baca had printed hundreds of copies of Corona's manifesto, "MAPA and La Raza Unida Party" in 1971. Corona called for mass canvassing as a way of engaging the ethnic Mexican community. He exclaimed, "The effects of all this type of work are only truly reaped if we repeatedly and constantly carry out the canvassing, caravanning, etc. Sporadic and once-in-a-while mobilizing is not fruitful nor effective. We must saturate our barrios—our people's minds this summer—with the reasons and urgency to establish La Raza Unida Party." He identified this grassroots organizing as tied to the trade union movements of the past, including that of the Congreso del Pueblo que Habla Español and la Asociacion Nacional Mexico-Americano (ANMA) of the 1930s and 1950s, respectively. "MAPA and La Raza

Unida Party: A Program for Chicano Political Action for the 1970s," Box 14, Folder 4, HBP.

76. La Raza Unida Party Organizing Committees Southern Region to La Raza Unida Party Organizers State of California, August 21, 1972, Box 26, Folder 6, HBP.

77. Ibid.

78. Ibid.

79. Ibid.

80. Ibid.

81. Ibid.

82. Beltrán, "Patrolling Borders," 599.

83. It is noted that the Mexican state also participated in these policing efforts as will be further explored in the evolution of Chicano/Mexicano mobilizations for the rest of the 1970s. For an excellent example of cross-border analysis of border policing, see Hernández, "The Crimes and Consequences of Illegal Immigration," 421–44.

84. "Corky Gonzales Speaks: Corky Gonzales Spoke at La Placita for Los Tres," *La Raza Unida-San Diego County Newsletter* 9 (April/May 1973), Box 14, Folder 8, HBP.

Chapter Six

1. San Diego County Sheriff's Department, "Sheriff John Duffy Memorandum," September 15, 1972, Box 22, Folder 3, HBP.

2. Herman Baca, interview by author, August 2, 2006.

3. Ibid.

4. "Sheriff Indicts Chicanos, Community Demands Apology," *La Raza Unida Party—San Diego Newsletter*, no. 7 (December 1972), Box 14, Folder 8, HBP.

5. Ibid.

6. Herman Baca, interview by author, August 2, 2006.

7. Ibid.

8. "The Committee for Chicano Rights, Organizational History, July 21–22, 1979," Box 12, Folder 6, HBP.

9. Herman Baca, interview by author, August 2, 2006.

10. "The Committee for Chicano Rights, Organizational History, July 21–22, 1979," Box 12, Folder 6, HBP. See also "Herman Baca Timeline," Description of the Herman Baca Papers, HBP.

11. "Yellow Cab Company," Memo Protest Photographs, Box 54, Folder 14, HBP.

12. Herman Baca, interview by author, August 2, 2006.

13. Clarence M. Kelley, Director of the Federal Bureau of Investigation, letter re: Herman Baca File 157-5120, Box 3, Folder 3, HBP; "Herman Baca—Extremist Matter—Spanish American," FBI Report, p. 9, Box 3, Folder 3, HBP.

14. "Yellow Cab Company," Memo Protest Photographs, Box 54, Folder 14, HBP.

15. John F. Duffy, San Diego County Sheriff's Department, Correspondence "To All Taxi Cab Drivers," January 8, 1973, Box 22, Folder 3, HBP. Duffy cited U.S. Legal Code 1324 as a reason to enforce.

16. "'Hands-Off' Policy on Aliens Aired," *San Diego Union*, April 26, 1973.

17. Ibid.

18. "Mayor Rejects Chicano Demand to Fire Hoobler," *San Diego Evening Tribune*, June 15, 1973.

19. "Right of Police to Detain, Quiz Aliens Backed," *San Diego Union*, May 15, 1973.

20. Ibid.

21. Ibid.

22. Herman Baca to Mayor Pete Wilson, May 16, 1973, Box 10, Folder 29, HBP.

23. Herman Baca to Mayor Peter Wilson, May 22, 1973, Box 10, Folder 29, HBP.

24. Ibid.

25. Ibid.

26. Ibid.

27. Rev. Juan Hurtado, "Ad Hoc Committee on Chicano Rights, Press Conference at Chicano Federation," June 14, 1973, Box 10, Folder 29, HBP.

28. "We Remember," Herman Baca Eulogy for Juan Hurtado, October 28, 1996; "Obituary Father Juan Hurtado, October 25, 1996," Box 24, Folder 5, HBP. See also Sánchez, "Juan Hurtado, 65, Was Ex-Priest Whose Efforts Supported Latino Causes," *San Diego Union*, October 28, 1996.

29. Rev. Juan Hurtado, "Ad Hoc Committee on Chicano Rights, Press Conference at Chicano Federation," June 14, 1973, Box 10, Folder 29, HBP.

30. Ibid.

31. Ibid.

32. Ibid.

33. Baca claimed that thirty people were questioned and seven were arrested. Father Hurtado recalled that seven to eight men were arrested. See "Mayor Rejects Chicano Demand to Fire Hoobler," *San Diego Evening Tribune*, June 15, 1973, and Rev. Juan Hurtado, "Ad Hoc Committee on Chicano Rights, Press Conference at Chicano Federation," June 14, 1973, Box 10, Folder 29, HBP.

34. Rev. Juan Hurtado, "Ad Hoc Committee on Chicano Rights, Press Conference at Chicano Federation," June 14, 1973, Box 10, Folder 29, HBP.

35. "Mayor Rejects Chicano Demand to Fire Hoobler," *San Diego Evening Tribune*, June 15, 1973.

36. Ibid.

37. "Chicanos Threatened Class Action Law Suit," *National City Star-News*, July 29, 1973.

38. "Mayor Rejects Chicano Demand to Fire Hoobler," *San Diego Evening Tribune*, June 15, 1973.

39. Ibid.

40. Ibid.

41. On Wilson's mayoral terms and political ascendancy, see Davis, "The Next Little Dollar," 103–8.

42. Ibid.

43. "Chicano Committee Rejects Meeting with Mayor Wilson," *Viewpoint*, July 18, 1973.

44. Herman Baca to Mayor Pete Wilson, July 14, 1973, Box 10, Folder 29, HBP.

45. Martínez, "The Border and Human Rights," 224.

46. Mike Davis argues that Wilson successfully placated minority communities by offering token positions within the city government and negotiated with minority leaders in order to keep the peace and proceed with his development plans. For instance, Davis claims that African American councilman Leon Williams consented to support Wilson's downtown development scheme in exchange for the political clout to hone new black leaders, thus creating what Davis calls the "Williams Machine." See Davis, "The Next Little Dollar," 103–8.

47. Pete Wilson to Louis Natividad, July 19, 1973, Box 6, Folder 4, HBP.

48. Ibid.

49. Ibid.

50. Ibid.

51. "The Committee for Chicano Rights, Organizational History, July 21–22, 1979," Box 12, Folder 6, HBP.

52. Robert W. Baker, Benjamin Moreno, Ernest Azhocar, Oscar Canedo, Al Y. Casillas, and Ray Parra to Peter Wilson, July 31, 1973, Box 6, Folder 4, HBP. See also "Chicano School Trustees Ask Wilson to Reconsider," *National City Star News*, August 5, 1973.

53. Ad Hoc Committee on Chicano Rights to Pete Wilson, August 5, 1973, Box 6, Folder 4, HBP.

54. Ibid.

55. See chapter 1 for the history of vigilantism and policing the ethnic Mexican community in San Diego. For the history of labor control and vagrancy laws in the Mexican American context, see Montejano, *Anglos and Mexicans in the Making of Texas*, and Escobar, *Race, Police, and the Making of a Political Identity*. For San Diego, see Griswold del Castillo, "From Revolution to Economic Depression." For Mexican Americans and the KKK in San Diego and Southern California, see Larralde and Castillo, "San Diego's Ku Klux Klan."

56. Ad Hoc Committee on Chicano Rights to Pete Wilson, August 5, 1973, Box 6, Folder 4, HBP.

57. "Chicanos Threaten Class Action Suit," *National City Star-News*, July 29, 1973.

58. "The Committee for Chicano Rights, Organizational History, July 21–22, 1979," Folder 6, Box 12, HBP.

59. Ibid.

60. Ibid.

61. "Herman Baca—Extremist Matter—Spanish American," FBI Report, p. 9, Box 3, Folder 3, HBP.

62. Ibid.

63. "Hoobler Confirms Club's Claim of Police Infiltration-Attempt," *San Diego Evening Tribune*, July 27, 1973.

64. Ibid.

65. Pete Wilson to Louis Natividad, July 19, 1973, Box 6, Folder 4, HBP.

66. "Hoobler Confirms Club's Claim of Police Infiltration-Attempt," *San Diego Evening Tribune*, July 27, 1973.

67. Ibid.

68. Herman Baca, Ad Hoc Committee on Chicano Rights to William Roth, October 1, 1973, Box 6, Folder 4, HBP.

69. Ibid.

70. "Chicano Groups Demand Probes, Hoobler Firing," *San Diego Evening Tribune*, August 27, 1974.

71. "SD Police Chief Resigns," *National City Star-News*, September 11, 1975.

72. Ibid.; Lagies and Ziegas, "Chief Hoobler Quits Force," *San Diego Evening Tribune*, September 10, 1975.

73. Herman Baca writes correspondence to William French Smith, United States Attorney General, January 18, 1984, Box 22, Folder 3, HBP.

74. United States Department of Justice, Press Release, June 3, 1978, Box 22, Folder 3, HBP.

75. Ibid.

76. "North Co. Sherriffs Riot," *San Diego County La Raza Unida Newsletter*, no. 10 (September 1973), Box 14, Folder 8, HBP.

77. Chula Vista was about 47 percent "Spanish-origin" in 1980. The 2010 United States Census reported 58 percent was "Hispanic or Latino." San Ysidro was 93 percent "Hispanic/Latino" according to San Diego Association of Governments (SANDAG) in 2011.

78. "National City," SANDAG, San Diego's Regional Planning Agency.

79. Herman Baca, interview by author, August 14, 2006.

80. Ibid.

81. Roberto Martínez, "The Border and Human Rights," 240.

82. Paz, "Tato Rivera Killing," *Voz Fronteriza* 1, no. 1 (January 5, 1976); Avalos, Robledo, and Torres, "Recall in National City," *Voz Fronteriza* 1, no. 2 (February 2, 1976).

83. Himaka, "Manslaughter Charged in S. Bay Police Slaying," *San Diego Union*, November 1, 1975.

84. Funabiki, "Policeman in Shooting Still on Duty," *San Diego Union*, October 14, 1975.

85. Himaka, "Manslaughter Charged in S. Bay Police Slaying."

86. Funabiki, "Policeman in Shooting Still on Duty."

87. Ibid.

88. Paz, "Tato Rivera Killing"; Avalos, Robledo, and Torres, "Recall in National City."

89. Paz, "Tato Rivera Killing."

90. Funabiki, "Policeman in Shooting Still on Duty."

91. Ibid.

92. There was a sizeable number of Puerto Ricans in California, about forty-seven thousand in 1970, the vast majority of whom lived in Los Angeles and the San Francisco-Oakland area. Even in these cities with larger Puerto Rican populations than San Diego, there were no distinct enclaves or neighborhoods, possibly reflecting the Rivera family's experience living in a primarily ethnic Mexican barrio. Puerto Ricans made up 0.25 percent of the California population and about 2 percent of the Latino/a population in 1970, and suffered similar socioeconomic repression as ethnic Mexicans, African Americans, Puerto Ricans in other parts of the United States, and other communities of color. There was an important increase in Puerto Rican migration to California between 1960 and 1970. When asked if the Puerto Rican Luis Rivera was a Chicano, Baca reportedly answered, "This is not a racial issue but a human rights issue." See Funabiki, "Policeman in Shooting Still on Duty"; United States Commission on Civil Rights, Western Regional Office, *Puerto Ricans in California*; and Funabiki, "In National City Police Chief Ouster Demanded," *San Diego Union*, October 15, 1975.

93. John Funabiki, "Policeman in Shooting Still on Duty."

94. Avalos, Robledo, and Torres, "Recall in National City"; Funabiki, "In National City Police Chief Ouster Demanded."

95. Herman Baca, interview by author, August 10, 2006.

96. Avalos, Robledo, and Torres, "Recall in National City."

97. Herman Baca, interview by author, August 10, 2006.

98. Ibid.

99. Herman Baca to Mayor Kile Morgan, October 14, 1975, Box 29, Folder 7, HBP.

100. Avalos, Robledo, and Torres, "Recall in National City."

101. Funabiki, "In National City Police Chief Ouster Demanded."

102. Ibid.

103. Haney López, *Racism on Trial*, 9.

104. Ibid.

105. Avalos, Robledo, and Torres, "Recall in National City."

106. Herman Baca, interview by author, August 10, 2006.

107. Ibid.

108. Ibid.

109. Avalos, Robledo, and Torres, "Recall in National City."

110. Ibid.

111. Funabiki, "Policeman in Shooting Still on Duty."

112. Avalos, Robledo, and Torres, "Recall in National City."

113. Ibid.

114. Funibiki, "Council Recall Bid Hinted in Slaying," *San Diego Union*, October 29, 1975.

115. Avalos, Robledo, and Torres, "Recall in National City."

116. Funibiki, "Council Recall Bid Hinted in Slaying."

117. Ibid.; Avalos, Robledo, and Torres, "Recall in National City."

118. Avalos, Robledo, and Torres, "Recall in National City."

119. Ibid.

120. Himaka, "Manslaughter Charged in S. Bay Police Slaying."

121. Betty Pengelley to Herman Baca, November 13, 1975, Box 33, Folder 14, HBP.

122. Herman Badillo to the Honorable Edward Levi, November 11, 1975, Box 33, Folder 14, HBP.

123. Herman Badillo to John Bugs, U.S. Commission on Civil Rights, November 13, 1975, Box 33, Folder 14, HBP.

124. Heman Badillo to the Honorable Edwin Miller, November 13, 1975, Box 33, Folder 14, HBP, and Herman Badillo to Mayor Kile Morgan, November 13, 1975, Box 33, Folder 14, HBP.

125. Heman Badillo to the Honorable Edwin Miller, November 13, 1975, Box 33, Folder 14, HBP.

126. Mayor Kile Morgan to Congressman Herman Badillo, November 17, 1975, Box 33, Folder 14, HBP.

127. Avalos, Robledo, and Torres, "Recall in National City."

128. Peter H. Chacón to William B. Kolendar, November 17, 1975, Box 33, Folder 14, HBP.

129. On the previous shooting, see Himaka, "Manslaughter Charged in S. Bay Police Slaying"; the nickname was mentioned in Herman Baca, interview by author, August 10, 2006.

130. Ott, "Judge Says Action Was 'Justifiable,'" *San Diego Union*, December 4, 1975.

131. Ad Hoc Committee on Chicano Rights, Immediate Press Release, December 4, 1975, Box 33, Folder 14, HBP.

132. See Ad Hoc Committee on Chicano Rights, Immediate Press Release, December 4, 1975, Box 33, Folder 14, HBP, and Scaglione, "Judge Probe," *San Diego Union*, December 5, 1975.

133. Ibid.

134. Scaglione, "Judge Probe," *San Diego Union*, December 5, 1975.

135. Avalos, Robledo, and Torres, "Recall in National City."

136. Herman Baca, Consuelo Rubio, Jesse Ramirez, and Oscar Canedo, "Notice of Intention to Circulate Petition for Recall of Kile Morgan from the Office of Councilman of the City of National City California," *National City Star-News*, November 16, 1975.

137. Avalos, Robledo, and Torres, "Recall in National City"; Ad Hoc Committee on Chicano Rights, Immediate Press Release, December 4, 1975, Box 33, Folder 14, HBP.

138. "National City: City Overview," SANDAG, San Diego's Regional Planning Agency.

139. Avalos, Robledo, and Torres, "Recall in National City."

140. "Help List," Box 29, Folder 7, HBP.

141. Brown, *Fighting for US*, 128–29.

142. Brown, *Fighting for US*.

143. Scot Brown describes the post–1975 Nia Cultural Organization as a former "cadre of CAP (Congress of African Peoples)." See Brown, *Fighting for US*, 128–29.

144. For the history of Ron Karenga and US, see Brown, *Fighting for US*.

145. Herman Baca, interview by author, February 27, 2009.

146. Ed Sylvester, "D.A. Won't File Charges on Policeman in Fatal Scuffle," *Los Angeles Times*, June 13, 1978; "NAACP Asks Probe of S.D. Shooting," *San Diego Union*.

147. "Gathering of the Community," Flyer, July 12, 1978, Box 38, Folder 4, HBP.

148. Notes on community gathering, Box 38, Folder 4, HBP.

149. Herman Baca, interview by author, March 6, 2009.

150. Herman Baca, interview by author, August 2, 2010.

151. Ibid.

152. Ibid.

153. "Certificate to Recall Position," January 26, 1976, Box 29, Folder 7, HBP.

154. Avalos, "Round One in National City," *Voz Fronteriza* 1, no. 3 (March 8, 1976).

155. Herman Baca, interview by author, August 10, 2006.

156. "Vote for Change! Cañedo Ramirez | N.C. Council," Brochure, Box 64, Folder 3, HBP.

157. Ruth Rivera, "Affidavit of Sworn Statement," February 24, 1976, Box 29, Folder 7, HBP.

158. Angelina Reyes, "Affidavit of Sworn Statement," February 24, 1976, Box 29, Folder 7, HBP.

159. Gilbert Ambriz, "Affidavit of Sworn Statement," No Date, Box 29, Folder 7, HBP.

160. Juana Martínez, "Affidavit of Sworn Statement," February 24, 1976, Box 29, Folder 7, HBP.

161. Herman Baca to Stanley Pottinger, February 26, 1976, Box 29, Folder 7, HBP.

162. Avalos, "Round One in National City."

163. Avalos, Robledo, and Torres, "Recall in National City."

164. Avalos, "A.H.C. Continues Organizing Effort," *Voz Fronteriza*, July 1976.

165. David Avalos to Herman Baca, e-mail correspondence, July 14, 2003, Box 33, Folder 14. In the email Avalos reprints a section of an article from the *San Diego Union-Tribune*, July 12, 2003.

166. David Avalos to Herman Baca, e-mail correspondence, July 14, 2003, Box 33, Folder 14, HBP.

167. Expedito Madrigal Affidavit, July 16, 1973, Box 6, Folder 4, HBP.

168. Albert R. García to Kimball H. Moore, March 4, 1974, Box 6, Folder 4, HBP.

169. David Avalos, interview by Margarita Nieto at the Southern California Research Center in San Diego, CA, Smithsonian Archives of American Art, June 16 and July 5, 1988.

170. Articles of Incorporation of Committee on Chicano Rights, Inc., November 24, 1976, Box 6, Folder 1, HBP.

171. Ibid.

172. Register of the Herman Baca Papers, Biography, HBP.

Chapter Seven

1. "Unity March," *La Prensa*, November 10, 1977.

2. Dietrich, "4 Incidents Probed; Letters 'KKK' Found," *San Diego Evening Tribune*, October 22, 1977. The graffiti did include the parentheses "(Mexico)."

3. Rodríguez, "The Battle for the Border," 17–21.

4. Ibid.

5. Yolanda López, interview by author, June 2, 2016.

6. Davalos, *Yolanda M. López*, 5.

7. Ibid., 54.

8. For a discussion of López's poster within the context of Chicano Movement struggle against immigration policies, see Davalos, *Yolanda M. López*, 53 and 55.

9. "Unity March," *La Prensa*, November 10, 1977.

10. San Miguel, *Brown Not White*.

11. Quoted in Applegate, "Some People in This Town Don't Like Herman Baca and He Doesn't Care," *San Diego Reader*, June 21, 1979.

12. Nicolas C. Criss, "Immigration Nominee Fits Carter Mold," *Los Angeles Times*, April 8, 1977.

13. Ibid.

14. Ibid.

15. John Crewdson, "Mexican Pickers Helping Growers Buy a Little More Time," *New York Times*, June 26, 1977 (reprinted in the *Chicago Tribune*, August 5, 1977); Associated Press, "U.S. Allowing Mexicans to Aid in Onion Harvest," *Washington Post*, June 22, 1977, A9; "A Return to the Bracero System?," *Los Angeles Times*, June 24, 1977, E6.

16. Ibid.

17. "Double Talk in Texas," *CCR Newsletter* 1, no. 1 (September 1977), Box 10, Folder 23.

18. Historian David G. Gutiérrez argues that the Carter immigration proposal provoked a "remarkable" shift among ideologically diverse Mexican American organizations by the late 1970s, which now "expressed solidarity with undocumented migrants." "This position solidified," states Gutiérrez, "when President Jimmy Carter announced his immigration reform package in summer 1977." See David G. Gutiérrez, "Sin Fronteras?"

19. Ibid.

20. Ibid.

21. "CCR Interview," *El Gallo* 9, no. 5 (August–October 1977), 6. See Box 1, Folder 1, HBP.

22. Herman Baca to President Jimmy Carter, July 6, 1977, Box 7, Folder 1, HBP.

23. "CCR Interview," *El Gallo* 9, no. 5 (August–October 1977), 6. See Box 1, Folder 1, HBP.

24. Figure cited in Gutiérrez, "Sin Fronteras?," 10.

25. Mexican immigrants in the United States numbered 454,000 in 1950, hit 760,000 by 1970, and by 1980 would reach about 2.2 million. Pew Hispanic Center, *Mexican Immigrants in the United States, 2008*. On political-economic factors for this growth, see David G. Gutiérrez, "Globalization, Labor Migration and the Demographic Revolution," 62–63, and Sassen, "America's Immigration 'Problem.'"

26. "CCR Interview," *El Gallo* 9, no. 5 (August–October 1977), 6. See Box 1, Folder 1, HBP.

27. *San Diego Evening Tribune*, October 17, 1977; Standefer, *San Diego Union*, October 17, 1977; Standefer, *San Diego Union*, October 18, 1977; "Newspaper Clippings, 1977, October–December, Ku Klux Klan," Box 68, Folder 3, HBP.

28. The Ku Klux Klan has a long history of policing ethnic Mexicans at the U.S.-Mexico border and Southern California. See Larralde and Griswold del Castillo, "San Diego's Ku Klux Klan."

29. Ibid.

30. Herman Baca, interview by author, August 23, 2006.

31. Ibid.

32. See Standefer, *San Diego Union*, October 18, 1977, and "Unity March," *La Prensa*, November 10, 1977.

33. Herman Baca, Committee on Chicano Rights, Press Release, October 20, 1977, Box 41, Folder 12, HBP.

34. Photo of Herman Baca, Greg Akili, Ken Msemaji and unidentified woman at Coalition for Human Rights meeting, circa Novemeber 1977, Box 60, Folder 12, HBP.

35. Herman Baca, interview by author, August 23, 2006.

36. Dietrich, "4 Incidents Probed; Letters 'KKK' Found," *San Diego Evening Tribune*, October 22, 1978.

37. Herman Baca, interview by author, August 23, 2006.

38. Standefer, "'No Retaliation' Klan Says of Fight," *San Diego Union*, October 21, 1977.

39. Standefer, *San Diego Union*, October 18, 1977.

40. Ibid.

41. "Chicanos List Demands to Carter Administration," *Chicano Federation of San Diego County, Inc. Newsletter* 7, no. 9 (November 1977), Box 61, Folder 5, HBP.

42. Ibid.

43. "Unity March," *La Prensa*, November 10, 1977.

44. Ibid.

45. Ibid.

46. Ibid.

47. Ibid.

48. Jimmy Carter, "Undocumented Aliens Message to Congress," August 4, 1977, Woolley and Peters, The American Presidency Project (online), http://www.presidency.ucsb.edu/ws/?pid=7923.

49. For analysis of the interconnection between immigration systems of control and its hand in shaping the boundaries of authentic U.S. citizenship, see Lowe, *Immigrant Acts*, 1–36. For the construction of U.S. citizenship in relation to the creation of the Border Patrol and the "illegal alien," see Ngai, *Impossible Subjects*, 7. Ngai asserts that the construction of the "illegal alien" "produced 'alien citizens'—Asian Americans and Mexican Americans born in the United States with formal U.S. citizenship but who remained alien in the eyes of the nation."

50. Herman Baca, Committee on Chicano Rights, Press Release, October 20, 1977, Box 41, Folder 12, HBP.

51. Ibid.

52. Nevins, *Operation Gatekeeper and Beyond*, 81–82; Briggs, "Report of the Select Commission on Immigration and Refugee Policy: A Critique."

53. In the early 1970s, Mexican president Luis Echeverria provided Jose Angel Gutiérrez with funds to provide scholarships to Mexican American students through the Becas para Aztlán program, as well as funds for other activities of La Raza Unida Party. For an excellent overview of Chicano movement positions on Mexico, see Gómez, *The Revolutionary Imaginations of Greater Mexico*, 40–66. See also Armando Navarro, *La Raza Unida Party*, 254–56. Other scholarly works that consider relations between Chicanos/as and Mexico are Gómez-Quiñones, "Piedras contra la luna, México en Aztlán y Aztlán en México," 494–527, and "Notes on the Interpretation of the Relations between the Mexican Community in the United States and Mexico"; and Schmidt Camacho, *Migrant Imaginaries*, 152–93.

54. Herman Baca, interview by author, August 23, 2006.

55. Ibid.

56. Grayson, "The Mexican Oil Boom."

57. Committee on Chicano Rights Press Release, January 22, 1979, Box 18, Folder 11, HBP.

58. Ibid.

59. Maria Velasquez, KCST-TV, interview of Herman Baca, Corky Gonzales, Bert Corona et al., "Undocumented Mexican Visitors Program," February 11, 1979, Box 1, Folder 11, HBP.

60. Ibid.

61. Ibid.

62. Ibid.

63. Committee on Chicano Rights, Press Release, Tijuana, B.C., Mexico, February 3, 1979, Box 18, Folder 11, HBP.

64. Indeed, Mexico's oil boom was debt-financed, helping to bring petroleum prices down, dropping Mexican revenues and resulting in a major economic crisis in the 1980s. Therefore, Chicano/a activists hopes that the Mexican state would have the power to influence, and even demand, adjustments to U.S. immigration policy via U.S. state leaders were based on a weak foundation. Mexico's economic crisis in the 1980s would facilitate the neoliberalization of its economic policies as new leadership turned away from the nationalist-based policies of the

postrevolutionary PRI toward projects of economic globalization, culminating in the North American Free Trade Agreement (NAFTA) in 1994. Reina, Servín, and Tutino, "Introduction: Crises, Reforms, and Revolutions in Mexicano, Past and Present," 4–5.

65. Committee on Chicano Rights Invitation Letter to Participation in National Protest March, February 11, 1979, Box 18, Folder 11, HBP.

66. Richard Hernandez, Deputy Assistant to President Jimmy Carter to Emma Creel, Director of the Chicano Federation, February 6, 1979, Box 18, Folder 11, HBP. For a recent reflection on this event, see Gonzalez, "Emma Creel-Vargas: Chicano Federation Chairwoman Was a Tireless Activist," *San Diego Union-Tribune*, December 30, 2009.

67. Chicano Federation Press Release, February 1979, Box 18, Folder 11, HBP.

68. Yolanda López, interview by author, June 2, 2016. See also Karen Mary Davalos, *Yolanda M. López*, 52–57.

69. Omi and Winant, *Racial Formation in the United States*.

Chapter Eight

1. "Summary from the Chicano National Immigration Tribunal 1981," "Statement of Purpose," Box 43, Folder 1, HBP.

2. "Chicano/Mexican/Latino" was one of the emergent self-identifying terms that the document writers emerging out of these gatherings used, as will be discussed later in the chapter. See "Resolutions Passed at the Chicano National Immigration Conference," May 24, 1980, Box 41, Folder 12, HBP, and "Summary from the Chicano National Immigration Tribunal 1981," Box 43, Folder 1, HBP.

3. Esteva, "The Meaning and Scope of the Struggle for Autonomy."

4. Du Bois, *Black Reconstruction in America*; Davis, *Abolition Democracy*; Lipsitz, "Abolition Democracy and Global Justice"; Johnson, *Spaces of Conflict, Sounds of Solidarity*; and Lytle Hernández, "Amnesty or Abolition."

5. "Resolutions Passed at the Chicano National Immigration Conference," May 24, 1980, Box 41, Folder 12, HBP.

6. Johnson, *Spaces of Conflict, Sounds of Solidarity*, 8.

7. Ibid., 7–9. Johnson more specifically notes the relationship between Mexican American struggles in the Congress of Spanish-Speaking People and the tenets of "abolition democracy," particularly the activism of Luisa Moreno and the Congress's insistence "that whites accept blame for the racial and ethnic stratification that had evolved in the Southwest." As noted in chapter 1, in the 1930s the Congress of Spanish-Speaking People and Mexican American labor activism premised important aspects of the activism of the CCR.

8. Gaye Theresa Johnson identifies how the Mexican American Left in the 1930s, 1940s, and 1950s revealed ties with and support for African American freedom struggles. See Johnson, *Spaces of Conflict, Sounds of Solidarity*.

9. Herman Baca, interview by author, March 6, 2009.

10. David Avalos, *La Frontera en Sangre*, Committee on Chicano Rights, 1980, Box 43, Folder 1, HBP; see also Box 106, Folder 6, CCLRA.

11. "Unity March," *La Prensa*, November 10, 1977.

12. *Los Angeles Times*, March 23, 1979.

13. Golum, "Two Deaths at Border Probed," *National City Star News*, 1979.

14. Ibid.

15. Ibid

16. "Officials Called Cruel in Barring Ill Child at Border," *New York Times*, June 21, 1979.

17. Golum, "Two Deaths at Border Probed."

18. Ibid.

19. Ibid.

20. Herman Baca, interview by author, September 2006.

21. Ibid.

22. Holloway, *Change the World without Taking Power*, 1.

23. David Avalos, *La Frontera en Sangre*, Committee on Chicano Rights, 1980, Box 43, Folder 1, HBP.

24. See chapter 2 for analysis of how notions of the "family" worked as a basis on which border enforcement policies were critiqued as disruptive of families by splitting them up. See also Rodríguez, *Next of Kin*.

25. David Avalos, *La Frontera en Sangre*, Committee on Chicano Rights, 1980, Box 43, Folder 1, HBP.

26. Golum, "Two Deaths at Border Probed."

27. *El Tiempo Chicano*, 1979. See Box 42, Folder 1, HBP.

28. Ibid.

29. Ibid.

30. Ibid

31. Herman Baca to Danny Villanueva, April 10, 1980, Box 41, Folder 12, HBP.

32. Committee on Chicano Rights List of Participants in the National Chicano Immigration Conference and Memorial March, 1980, Box 41, Folder 13, HBP.

33. "The Slave Issue of the 20th Century: 1,000 Attend National Immigration Conference," *Unity*, June 6, 1980, Box 42, Folder 1, HBP; "Herman Baca Timeline," Finding Aid, HBP.

34. "Chicanos Hear Warning on 'Legal Slavery,'" *San Diego Union*, May 25, 1980, Box 42, Folder 1, HBP.

35. Herman Baca Speech, May 12, 1980, Box 41, Folder 13, HBP.

36. Ibid.

37. Ibid.

38. Ibid.

39. Ibid.

40. Herman Baca, interview by author, March 6, 2009.

41. On the activism of Nia, the Black Federation and the broader internationalist dimensions of the Black Freedom Movement in San Diego and Southern California

see forthcoming from Mychal Matsemela-Ali Odom, *From Southern California to Southern Africa*.

42. *San Diego Union*, March 14, 1978.

43. Leon Sullivan, "The Sullivan Principles."

44. Black Federation of San Diego to Herman Baca et al., January 31, 1979, Box 17, Folder 5, HBP. By 1984, Sullivan himself asserted similar concerns that Nia held when he reminded that "The principles were never intended to be a camouflage for corporations to hide behind." He argued further, "More enforcement is needed." He testified before congressional committees that "the full compliance with the Sullivan Principles of all American companies with operations in the Republic of South Africa should be made mandatory by the United States government, and backed up with embargos, tax penalites, sanctions, loss of government contracts and any other effective means." See Sullivan, "The Sullivan Principles and Change in South Africa," *Africa Report*, May–June 1984.

45. Ken Msemaji to "Whom it may concern," April 5, 1978, Box 30, Folder 6, HBP.

46. Ibid.

47. Ibid.

48. "Jobs are a right—not a priviledge." Photograph. Box 56, Folder 10, HBP.

49. Ed Sylvester, "Fonda Stirs San Diego Job Rally: Actress Denounces Multinational Corporations," *Los Angeles Times*, May 20, 1978.

50. Ken Msemaji to "Whom it may concern," April 5, 1978, Box 30, Folder 6, HBP.

51. Ibid.

52. Ibid.

53. "Registration Form with Agenda and Confirmed Speakers for Conference and March," Box 41, Folder 12, HBP. Also part of the conference packet was a brochure put out by the AFL-CIO titled *The Multinational Corporation: A Modern Day Dinosaur That Eats the Jobs of American Workers*, National Chicano Immigration Conference: A Time for Resistance Packet, May 23, 1980, Box 42, Folder 1, HBP.

54. "The Conference Agenda," National Chicano Immigration Conference, 1980, Box 106, Folder 6, CCLRA; "A Time for Resistance, Organized by CCR, Tentative Agenda," Flyer, Box 41, Folder 12, HBP.

55. El Teatro de la Esperanza, Summary of *La Victima*, Box 106, Folder 6, CCLRA.

56. Herman Baca to President Jose Lopez Portillo, February 28, 1980, Box 41, Folder 12, HBP.

57. "Interview: Herman Baca of the Committee on Chicano Rights," *El Foro Del Pueblo* 1, no. 3 (May 1980).

58. Ibid.

59. Ibid.

60. Ibid.

61. Ibid.

62. Ibid.

63. "Resolutions Passed at the National Chicano Immigration Conference," May 24, 1980, Box 43, Folder 1, HBP.

64. Ibid.

65. Ibid.

66. Ibid.

67. Ibid.

68. "Asegura Un Lider Chicano: La Prensa Americana Ha Sido Racista y Discrimatoria," *El Heraldo de Baja California*, May 19, 1980. See Box 42, Folder 1, HBP. The Mexican newspapers, *ABC*, *Voz de Pueblo*, *El Mexicano*, and *Zeta* reported on the conference and listed at least some of the resolutions. See Box 42, Folder 1, HBP.

69. The complete resolution reads, "That this conference go on record as supporting the demands presented at the International Immigration Conference in Mexico City held on April 28, 1980." See Box 43, Folder 1, HBP.

70. "Resolutions Passed at the National Chicano Immigration Conference," May 24, 1980, Box 43, Folder 1, HBP.

71. Herman Baca, interview by author, August 23, 2006.

72. "Committee on Chicano Rights Community Meeting," February 27, 1980, Box 106, Folder 6, CCLRA

73. Herman Baca, interview by author, August 23, 2006.

74. Baca's mentor, Bert Corona, was involved with the Autonomous University of Sinaloa the previous year and its conference on amnesty. It is interesting to note that the conference's theme of amnesty mostly referred to amnesty for political prisoners who protested the Díaz Ordaz regime in 1968 and Corona inserted amnesty for undocumented migrants to the United States with his participation acting as professor in the Chicano Studies Department at California State University, Los Angeles. It is likely, therefore, that CCR member participation in the 1980 symposium was also related to the connections Corona had already established. See "Conferencia Culicán, Mexico," Box 30, Folders 13 and 14, BCP.

75. Committee on Chicano Rights, "Informe a la Prensa, Culican, Sinaloa," June 16, 1980, Box 41, Folder 12, HBP.

76. Ibid.

77. "Resolutions Passed at the National Chicano Immigration Conference," May 24, 1980, Box 43, Folder 1, HBP.

78. "Summary from the Chicano National Immigration Tribunal 1981," "Statement of Purpose," Box 43, Folder 1, HBP.

79. Nevins, *Operation Gatekeeper and Beyond*, 82.

80. "Ya Basta! Chicano National Tribunal," Flyer, Box 44, Folder 4, HBP.

81. "Statement of Purpose," Box 44, Folder 4, HBP.

82. "Chicano National Immigration Tribunal," Flyer and Cover Page, Box 44, Folder 4, HBP.

83. "Summary from the Chicano National Immigration Tribunal 1981," Table of Contents, Box 43, Folder 1, HBP.

84. "Summary from the Chicano National Immigration Tribunal 1981," Letter to President Ronald Reagan and Jose Lopez Portillo, Box 43, Folder 1, HBP.

85. Ibid.

86. "Declaration of Luis Arquer." "Summary of the Chicano National Immigration Tribunal," April 11, 1981, Box 43, Folder 1, HBP.

87. Ibid.

88. Ibid.

89. "Summary from the Chicano National Immigration Tribunal 1981," Letter to President Ronald Reagan and Jose Lopez Portillo, Box 43, Folder 1, HBP.

90. Ibid.

91. "Summary from the Chicano National Immigration Tribunal 1981," "Bill of Rights for the Undocumented Workers," Box 43, Folder 1, HBP.

Conclusion

1. On the Los Angles Mega Marchas, see Alfonso Gonzales, *Reform without Justice*, 48–74. On San Diego, see Berenstein, "50,000 Throng Downtown in Immigrant Rights March," *San Diego Union-Tribute*, April 10, 2006. Raymond Beltran of *La Prensa* cites 100,000 at this march; see Beltran, "Entering 2007, We End a Dramatically Active Year," *La Prensa-San Diego*, December 29, 2006.

2. See David G. Gutiérrez, "Citizens, Noncitizens and the Shell-Game of Immigration Policy Reform: A Response to Dan Tichenor."

3. Ye He Lee, "Donald Trump's False Comments Connecting Mexican Immigrants and Crime," *Washington Post*, July 8, 2015.

4. Herman Baca, "Pa' pendejo no se estudia! A Historical Chicano Perspective," *San Diego Free Press*, May 25, 2016.

5. Ibid.

6. Herman Baca, "What Will Happen to Us? A Chicano Perspective on the Trump Presidency," *San Diego Free Press*, January 18, 2017.

7. Herman Baca, "Pa' pendejo no se estudia!"

8. Committee on Chicano Rights Press Release, "Boycott Arizona," April 23, 2010.

9. Ibid. Words in boldface are reflective of the actual text.

10. Omi and Winant, *Racial Formation in the United States.*

11. Committee on Chicano Rights, "For Immediate Press Release," August 17, 1983, Box 12, Folder 15, HBP.

12. Herman Baca to potential funder, circa August 1983, Box 12, Folder 15, HBP.

13. Ibid.

14. Ibid.

15. "Resolutions Passed at the National Chicano Immigration Conference," May 24, 1980, Box 43, Folder 1, HBP.

16. David G. Gutiérrez, *Walls and Mirrors*, 180.

17. Navarro, *Mexicano Political Experience in Occupied Aztlán*, 444; Sierra, "In Search of National Power," 140–41. For a national analysis of Chicano/Latino politics and struggle among Latino/a elected officials and national organizations see Christine Marie Sierra, "In Search of National Power."

18. Sierra, "In Search of National Power," 142–43. Congressman Roybal proposed two bills, the first seeking to eliminate employer sanctions from the bill in the 97th Congress, the second in the 99th Congress, to include it as a concession.

19. Mario T. García, *Memories of Chicano History*, 316; Herman Baca, interview by author, September 13, 2006.

20. García, *Memories of Chicano History*, 316.

21. Joaquin G. Avila, MALDEF to Herman Baca, August 19, 1983, Box 12, Folder 15, HBP; Committee on Chicano Rights, "For Immediate Press Release," August 17, 1983, Box 12, Folder 15, HBP.

22. Committee on Chicano Rights, Inc., Things You Can Do," Flyer, August 17, 1983, Box 12, Folder 16, HBP.

23. "Biography," Finding Aid, HBP.

24. Quoted in Navarro, *Mexicano Political Experience in Occupied Aztlán*, 442.

25. Nevins, *Operation Gatekeeper and Beyond*, 83; García, *Memories of Chicano History*, 317.

26. Sierra, "In Search of National Power," 146–47.

27. García, *Memories of Chicano History*, 316–17.

28. Cordova, "Immigration Bill Will Fail, Activist Says," *Fresno Bee*, December 8, 1986.

29. White House Office of the Press Secretary, "The Signing of the S. 1200, The Immigration Reform and Control Act of 1986," November 6, 1986, Box 36, Folder 3, HBP.

30. *La Prensa* Board of Directors interview Herman Baca, CCR, *La Prensa*, circa 1986, Box 36, Folder 3, HBP.

31. Ibid.

32. Chisti and Kamasaki, *IRCA in Retrospect: Guideposts to Today's Immigration Reform*.

33. Ibid.

34. *La Prensa* Board of Directors interview Herman Baca, CCR, *La Prensa*, circa 1986, Box 36, Folder 3, HBP.

35. Herman Baca to Jim Wright, December 9, 1986, Box 36, Folder 3, HBP; CCR, "For Immediate Press Release," December 11, 1986, Box 36, Folder 3, HBP.

36. Ibid.

37. Representative James Brooks to Herman Baca, January 12, 1987, Box 36, Folder 3, HBP.

38. CCR, "For Immediate Press Release," January 22, 1987, Box 36, Folder 3, HBP.

39. CCR, "For Immediate Press Release," March 17, 1987, Box 36, Folder 3, HBP.

40. Herman Baca, interview by author, September 13, 2006, Session 11.

41. García, *Memories of Chicano History*, 318–20.

42. Ibid., 319.

43. Ibid., 319–20.

44. Unión del Barrio, "UdB History—1981–1983," http://uniondelbarrio.org/main/?page_id=202.

45. Yolanda López, interview by author, June 3, 2016.

46. Norma Mena Cazares, interview by author, February 1, 2016.

47. Yolanda López, interview by author, June 3, 2016.

48. Ibid.

49. Muñoz, "Amnesty One Year Later," April 28, 1988, *La Prensa San Diego.*

50. Chisti and Kamasaki, *IRCA in Retrospect: Guideposts to Today's Immigration Reform*

51. Muñoz, "Amnesty One Year Later."

52. Cacho, *Social Death*, 6.

53. Herman Baca, interview by author, September 13, 2006.

54. Gonzales, *Reform without Justice*, 9–11.

Bibliography

Manuscript Collections

La Jolla, CA
  Mandeville Special Collections Library, University of California, San Diego.
    Herman Baca Papers (HBP)
Palo Alto, CA
  Stanford University Special Collections Library
    Bert Corona Papers (BCP)
    CASA Collection (CC)
Santa Barbara, CA
    Donald C. Davidson Library, Department of Special Collections, University
      of California, Santa Barbara
    Centro Cultural de La Raza Archives (CCLRA)

Government Documents

United States Commission on Civil Rights, Western Regional Office. *Puerto Ricans in California*. Baltimore, MD: Thurgood Marshall Law Library, University of Maryland School of Law, January 1980.

Reports, Pamphlets, and Other Documents

Chisti, Muzaffaar, and Charles Kamasaki. *IRCA in Retrospect: Guideposts to Today's Immigration Reform*. Migration Policy Institute Issue Brief, No. 9, January 2014.

First National Chicano Youth Liberation Youth Conference. *Plan de Aztlán*, 1969.

First National Congress of the Mexican and Spanish American Peoples of the United States. *Digest of Proceedings*, April 1939.

Hermandad Mexicana Nacional. Founding Document. August, 1951. In *Hermandad Mexicana: 25th Anniversary: Un Daño Contra Uno es un Daño Contra Todos*. Program bulletin, 1971.

Pew Hispanic Center. *Mexican Immigrants in the United States, 2008*. Washington, DC, 2008.

Newspapers

ABC (Monterrey, N.L., Mex.)
El Chicano (Colton, CA)
El Gallo (Denver, CO)
El Heraldo de Baja California (Tijuana, B.C., Mex.)
El Mexicano (Tijuana, B.C., Mex.)
El Tiempo Chicano (National City, CA)
Fresno Bee
Ideal
La Prensa (San Diego, CA)
La Raza Unida Party San Diego County Newsletter

Los Angeles Times
National City Star-News
New Africa
San Diego Evening Tribune
San Diego Union
San Diego Union-Tribune
Voz de Pueblo
Voz Fronteriza (La Jolla, CA)
Washington Post
Zeta (Tijuana, B.C., Mex.)

Oral Histories by Author (in Mandeville Special Collections Library, University of California, San Diego)

Herman Baca, August 2, 2006, San Diego, CA.
——, August 14, 2006, National City, CA.
——, August 23, 2006, National City, CA.
——, August 28, 2006, La Jolla, CA.
——, August 30, 2006, La Jolla, CA.
——, September, unknown date, La Jolla, CA.
——, September 13, 2006, La Jolla, CA.
Norma Mena Cazares and Roger Cazares, September 8, 2006, Chula Vista, CA.
Carlos "Charlie" Vásquez, September 7, 2006, San Diego, CA.

Oral Histories by Author (in Author's Possession)

Herman Baca and Carlos "Charlie" Vásquez, July 27, 2013, National City, CA.
Augie Bareño, July 27, 2012, San Diego, CA.
Norma Mena Cazares and Roger Cazares, July 20, 2012, Chula Vista, CA.
——, February 1, 2016, Chula Vista, CA.
——, January 28, 2017, by telephone.
Yolanda López, June 2, 2016, by telephone.
Olivia Puentes Reynolds and Norma Mena Cazares, March 12, 2016, Chula Vista, CA.
Gloria Jean Valderrama Nieto, July 27, 2012, National City, CA.

Oral Histories by Others

Avalos, David, interviewed by Margarita Nieto, June 16 and July 5, 1988, San Diego, CA. Smithsonian Institution, Archives for American Art. https://www.aaa.si.edu /collections/oralhistories/transcripts/avalos88. Accessed August 15, 2016.
Muñoz, Carlos, interviewed by Nick García, February 5 and 12, 2003, Berkeley, CA. The Bancroft Library, University of California, Berkeley.

http://digitalassets.lib.berkeley.edu/roho/ucb/text/munoz_carlos_2014.pdf.
  Accessed January 31, 2017.
Navarro, Armando, interviewed by Carlos Vásquez, August 3 and December 21,
  1989. UCLA Oral History Program, for the California State Archives State
  Government Oral History Program. http://oralhistory.library.ucla.edu
  /viewFile.do?itemId=30149&fileSeq=4&xsl=http://oralhistory.library.ucla.edu
  /xslt/local/tei/xml/tei/stylesheet/xhtml2/tei.xsl#div00001. Accessed
  January 31, 2017.

Internet-Accessed Documents

Baca, Herman. "Pa' pendejo no se estudia! A Historical Chicano Perspective." *San
  Diego Free Press*, May 25, 2016. http://sandiegofreepress.org/2016/05/a-chicano
  -response-to-donald-trump/. Accessed August 15, 2016.
——. "What Will Happen to Us? A Chicano Perspective on the Trump Presidency."
  San Diego Free Press, January 18, 2017. http://sandiegofreepress.org/2017/01
  /chicano-perspective-trump-presidency/. Accessed January 31, 2017.
California State Archives. "Biography." Inventory of the Peter Chacón Papers,
  Sacramento, CA. http://www.oac.cdlib.org/findaid/ark:/13030/c8x34z2x
  /entire_text/. Accessed May 5, 2016.
Carter, Jimmy. "Undocumented Aliens Message to Congress." August 4, 1977. The
  American Presidency Project, John Woolley and Gerhard Peters. Santa
  Barbara, CA: University of California. http://www.presidency.ucsb.edu/ws
  /?pid=7923. Accessed November 23, 2010.
Clandestine Revolutionary Indigenous Committee—General Command of the
  Zapatista Army of National Liberation. "Sixth Declaration of the Selva
  Lacondona." June 2005. http://enlacezapatista.ezln.org.mx/sdsl-en/. Accessed
  January 18, 2017.
Franco, Jimmy. "La Raza Unida Party of California." *Latinopov.com Blog*.
  http://www.latinopov.com/blog/?p=6280, posted September 28, 2012.
  Accessed July 31, 2016.
Greek Orthodox Ladies Philoptochos Society, Anthousa Chapter. "2013 Atousa
  Award." http://anthousa.org/Anthousa_Award.html. Accessed July 27, 2015.
Metropolitan Area Advisory Committee (MAAC). "Our History." http://www
  .maacproject.org/main/about-us/our-history/. Accessed August 11, 2015.
Mulford, Marilyn and Mario Barrera. "Chicano Park." documentary. https://www
  .youtube.com/watch?v=hXwZLo8hrp4. Accessed February 11, 2014.
Reston, Maeve. "How Trump's Deportation Plan Failed 62 Years Ago." CNN Politics
  CNN Politics, January 19, 2016. http://www.cnn.com/2016/01/19/politics
  /donald-trump-deportation-mexico-eisenhower/#. Accessed August 13, 2016.
SANDAG (San Diego Association of Governments). "Chula Vista." http://www
  .sandag.org/resources/demographics_and_other_data/demographics/fastfacts
  /chul.htm. Accessed July 28, 2016.

———. "National City." http://www.sandag.org/resources/demographics_and _other_data/demographics/fastfacts/nati.htm. Accessed July 28, 2016.

———. "San Ysidro." http://datasurfer.sandag.org/download/sandag_census_2000 _cpa_san-ysidro.pdf. Accessed July 28, 2016.

Sullivan, Leon. "The Sullivan Principles." www.marshall.edu/revleonsullivan /principles.htm. Accessed June 8, 2017.

———. "The Sullivan Principles and Change in South African." *African Report*, May–June 1984. http://digitalcollections.library.cmu.edu/awweb/awarchive ?type=file&item=494984.

Transactional Access Records Clearinghouse. "Controlling the Borders." Syracuse, NY: University of Syracuse. http://trac.syr.edu/immigration/reports/141/. Accessed February 28, 2013.

Unión del Barrio. "UdB History—1981–1983." http://uniondelbarrio.org/main /?page_id=202. Accessed August 13, 2016.

U.S. Congress. House. Investigation of Communist Activities in the State of California. *Hearing Before the Committee on Un-American Activities.* 83rd Congress, 2nd Session, April 21, 1954. https://archive.org/details /investigationofc00708unit. Accessed May 1, 2013.

U.S. Customs and Border Protection. "U.S. Border Patrol Fiscal Year Southwest Border Sector Apprehensions (FY 1960-FY 2014)." http://www.cbp.gov/sites /default/files/documents/BP%20Southwest%20Border%20Sector%20 Apps%20FY1960%20-%20FY2014_0.pdf. Accessed November 4, 2012.

Viejas Band of Kumeyaay Indians. *Viejas History Booklet.* 2014. http:// viejasbandofkumeyaay.org/wp-content/uploads/2014/10/ViejasHistoryBooklet .pdf. Accessed January 26, 2017.

Zapatista Army of National Liberation. "First Declaration of La Realidad for Humanity and against Neoliberalism." 1996. http://flag.blackened.net/revolt /mexico/ezln/ezlnwa.html. Accessed January 7, 2017.

Published Articles and Books

Acuña, Rodolfo. *Anything but Mexican: Chicanos in Contemporary Los Angeles.* New York: Verso Press, 1994.

Almaguer, Tomas. *Racial Faultlines: The Historical Origins of White Supremacy in California.* Berkeley: University of California Press, 1994.

Alvarez, Luis. *The Power of the Zoot: Youth Culture and Resistance during World War II.* Berkeley: University of California Press, 2008.

Alvarez, Robert R., Jr. *Familia: Migration and Adaptation in Baja and Alta California, 1800–1975.* Berkeley: University of California Press, 1987.

———. "The Mexican-U.S. Border: The Making of an Anthropology of Borderlands." *Annual Review of Anthropology* 24 (1995): 447–70.

Anzaldúa, Gloria. *Borderlands/La Frontera: The New Mestiza.* San Francisco: Spinsters/Aunt Lute Press, 1987.

Anzaldúa, Gloria, and Cherrie Moraga, eds. *This Bridge Called My Back: Writings by Radical Women of Color.* New York: Kitchen Table/Women of Color Press, 1981.

Araiza, Lauren. *To March for Others: The Black Freedom Struggle and the United Farm Workers.* Philadelphia: University of Pennsylvania Press, 2013.

Balderrama, Francisco, and Raymond Rodríguez. *Decade of Betrayal: Mexican Repatriation in the 1930s.* Albuquerque: University of New Mexico Press, 1995.

Bar, Paula A. "Perceptions of Sexual Harassment." *Sociological Inquiry* 63, no. 4 (October 1993): 460–70.

Barrera, Mario. *Beyond Aztlán: Ethnic Autonomy in a Comparative Perspective.* Notre Dame, IN: University of Notre Dame Press, 1990.

——. *Race and Class in the Southwest: A Theory of Racial Inequality.* Notre Dame, IN: University of Notre Dame Press, 1979.

Bebout, Lee. *Mythohistorical Interventions: The Chicano Movement and its Legacies.* Minneapolis: University of Minnesota Press, 2011.

Beck, Warren A., and David A. Williams. *California: A History of the Golden State.* New York: Doubleday, 1972.

Behnken, Brian. *Fighting Their Own Battles: Mexican Americans, African Americans, and the Struggle for Civil Rights in Texas.* Chapel Hill: University of North Carolina Press, 2011.

Beltrán, Cristina. "Patrolling Borders: Hybrids, Hierarchies and the Challenge of Mestizaje." *Political Research Quarterly* 57, no. 4 (December 2004): 596–607.

Blackhawk, Ned. *Violence over the Land: Indians and Empires in the Early American West.* Cambridge, MA: Harvard University Press, 2006.

Blackwell, Maylei. *¡Chicana Power! Contested Histories of Feminism in the Chicano Movement.* Austin: University of Texas Press, 2011.

Briggs, Laura, Gladys McCormick, and J. T. Way. "Transnationalism: A Category of Analysis," *American Quarterly* 60, no. 3 (2008): 625–48.

Briggs, Vernon M. "Report on the Select Commission on Immigration and Refugee Policy: A Critique." *Texas Business Review* 56, no. 1 (January–February 1982): 11–15.

Brilliant, Mark. *The Color of America Has Changed: How Racial Diversity Shaped Civil Rights Reform in California, 1941–1978.* New York: Oxford University Press, 2010.

Brown, Dee. *Bury My Heart at Wounded Knee: An Indian History of the American West.* 1971. Reprint, New York: Picador, 2007.

Brown, Scot Brown. *Fighting for US: Maulana Karenga, the US organization, and Black Cultural Nationalism.* New York: New York University Press, 2003.

Broyles-González, Yolanda. *Teatro Campesino: Theater in the Chicano Movement.* Austin: University of Texas Press, 1994.

Buhle, Paul. *Taking Care of Business: Samuel Gompers, George Meany, Lane Kirkland and the Tragedy of American Labor.* New York: Monthly Review Press, 1999.

Cacho, Lisa. *Social Death: Racialized Rightlessness and the Criminalization of the Unprotected.* New York: New York University Press, 2012.

Calavita, Kitty. *California's "Employer Sanctions": The Case of the Disappearing Law*. Research Report Series 39. La Jolla, CA: Center for U.S.-Mexican Studies, University of California, San Diego, 1982.

Camarrillo, Albert. *Chicanos in a Changing Society: From Mexican Pueblos to American Barrios in Santa Barbara and Southern California, 1848–1930*. 1979. Reprint, Dallas: Southern Methodist University Press, 2005.

Chávez, Ernesto. *¡Mi Raza Primero! (My People First!) Nationalism, Identity and Insurgency in the Chicano Movement in Los Angeles, 1966–1978*. Berkeley: University of California Press, 2012.

Chávez, Leo R. "A Glass Half-Empty: Latina Reproduction and Public Discourse." *Human Organization* 63, no. 2 (Summer 2004): 173–88.

Chávez, Marisela. " 'We Lived and Breathed and Worked the Movement': The Contradictions and Rewards of Chicana/Mexicana Activism in El Centro de Acción Social Autónomo-Hermandad General de Trabajadores (CASA-HGT), Los Angeles, 1975–1978." In *Las Obreras: Chicana Politics of Work and Family*, edited by Vicki L. Ruiz, 83–105. Los Angeles: UCLA Chicano Studies Research Center Publications, 2000.

Clark, Victor S. *Mexican Labor in the United States*. Washington, DC: U.S. Bureau of Labor Statistics, 1908.

Cockcroft, Eva Sperling. "The Story of Chicano Park." *Aztlán* 15 (Spring 1984): 79–103.

Corona, Bert. *Bert Corona Speaks on La Raza Unida Party and the "Illegal Alien" Scare*. New York: Pathfinder Press, 1972.

Davalos, Karen Mary. *Yolanda M. López*. Los Angeles: University of California, Los Angeles Chicano Studies Research Center Press, 2008.

Davis, Angela. *Abolition Democracy: Beyond Empire, Prisons and Torture*. New York: Seven Stories Press, 2006.

———. *Women, Race and Class*. New York: Vintage Press, 1981.

Davis, Mike. "The Next Little Dollar: The Private Governments of San Diego." In *Under the Perfect Sun: The San Diego Tourists Never See*, edited by Mike Davis, Kelly Mayhew, and Jim Miller, 17–144. New York: New Press, 2005.

De Genova, Nicolas. "The Deportation Regime: Sovereignty, Space and the Freedom of Movement." In *The Deportation Regime: Sovereignty, Space and the Freedom of Movement*, edited by Nicolas De Genova and Nathalie Peutz, 33–65. Durham, NC: Duke University Press, 2010.

del Castillo, Adelaida, ed. *Between Borders: Essays on Mexicana/Chicana History*. Encino, CA: Floricanto Press, 1990.

Delgado, Kevin. "A Turning Point: The Conception and Realization of Chicano Park." *Journal of San Diego History* 44, no. 1 (Winter 1998).

Du Bois, W. E. B. *Black Reconstruction in America*. 1935. Reprint, New York: Russel & Russel, 1956.

Dunn, Tim. *The Mililtarization of the U.S.-Mexico Border, 1978–1992: Low-Intensity Conflict Doctrine Comes Home*. Austin: University of Texas Press, 1995.

Escobar, Edward. *Race, Police and the Making of a Political Identity: Mexican Americans and the Los Angeles Police Department, 1900–1945*. Berkeley: University of California Press, 1999.

Escobedo, Elizabeth R. *From Coveralls to Zoot Suits: The Lives of Mexican American Women on the World War II Homefront*. Chapel Hill: University of North Carolina Press, 2013.

Espinoza, Dionne. "'Revolutionary Sisters' Women's Solidarity and Collective Identification among Chicana Brown Berets in East Los Angeles, 1967–1970." *Aztlán* 26, no. 1 (Spring 2001): 17–58.

Espiritu, Yen Le Espiritu. *Asian American Women and Men*. Thousand Oaks, CA: Sage Press, 1997.

Esteva, Gustavo. "The Meaning and Scope of the Struggle for Autonomy." *Latin American Perspectives* 28, no. 2 (March 2001): 120–48.

Falcón, Sylvanna. "Rape as a Weapon of War: Militarized Rape at the U.S.-Mexico Border," *Social Justice* 28, no. 2 (2001): 31–50.

Flores, Esteban Flores. "Post-Bracero Undocumented Mexican Immigration and Political Recomposition." PhD diss., University of Texas, Austin, 1982.

Flores, Lori. *Grounds for Dreaming: Mexican Americans, Mexican Immigrants and the California Farmworker Movement*. New Haven: Yale University Press, 2016.

Foley, Neil. "Becoming Hispanic: Mexican Americans and the Faustian Pact with Whiteness." In *Reflexiones: New Directions in Mexican American Studies*, edited by Neil Foley, 53–70. Austin: University of Texas Press, 1998.

Galarza, Ernesto. "Mexicans in the Southwest: A Culture in Process." In *Plural Society in the Southwest*, edited by Edward H. Spicer and Raymond H. Thompson, 261–97. New York: Weatherhead Foundation, 1972.

Gamio, Manuel. *The Life Story of the Mexican Immigrant: Autobiographical Documents*. Chicago: University of Chicago Press, 1931.

———. *Mexican Immigration to the United States*. Chicago: University of Chicago Press, 1930.

García, Alma. *Chicana Feminist Thought: The Basic Historical Writings*. New York: Routledge, 1997.

García, Ignacio. *United We Win: The Rise and Fall of the La Raza Unida Party*. Tucson: University of Arizona Press, 1989.

García, Juan Ramón. *Operation Wetback: The Mass Deportation of Mexican Undocumented Workers in 1954*. Westport, CT: Greenwood Press, 1980.

García, Laura E., Sandra M. Gutiérrez, and Felicita Nuñez, editors. *Teatro Chicana: A Collective Memoir and Selected Plays*. Austin: University of Texas Press, 2008.

García, Mario T. *The Chicano Generation: Testimonies of the Movement*. Berkeley: University of California Press, 2015.

———. *Memories of Chicano History: The Life and Narrative of Bert Corona*. Berkeley: University of California Press, 1994.

———. *Mexican Americans: Leadership, Ideology and Identity, 1930–1960*. New Haven, CT: Yale University Press, 1989.

——, ed. *The Chicano Movement: Perspectives from the Twenty-First Century.* New York: Routledge Press, 2014.

García, Mario, and Sal Castro. *Blowout! Sal Castro and the Chicano Struggle for Educational Justice.* Chapel Hill: University of North Carolina Press, 2011.

García, Matthew. *From the Jaws of Victory: The Triumph and Tragedy of Cesar Chavez and the Farmworker Movement.* Berkeley: University of California Press, 2014.

Gómez, Alan Eladio. *The Revolutionary Imaginations of Greater Mexico: Chicana/o Radicalism, Solidarity Politics, and Latin American Social Movements.* Austin: University of Texas Press, 2016.

Gómez-Quiñones, Juan. *Chicano Politics: Reality and Promise, 1940–1990.* Albuquerque: University of New Mexico Press, 2000.

——. "Notes on the Interpretation of the Relations between the Mexican Community in the United States and Mexico: Historical and Political Contexts of a Dialogue Renewed." In *Mexico-United States Relations: Conflict and Convergence,* edited by Carlos Vásquez and Manuel García y Griego, 417–39. Los Angeles: Chicano Studies Center and Latin American Research Center Publications, 1983.

——. "Piedras contra la luna, México en Aztlán y Aztlán en México: Chicano-Mexican Relations in the Mexican Consulates, 1900–1920." In *Contemporary Mexico: Papers of the IV International Congress of Mexican History,* edited by James W. Wilkie, Michael C. Meyer and Edna Monzón de Wilkie, 494–527. Mexico City: El Colegio de México and UCLA Latin American Studies Center, 1975.

Gonzales, Alfonso. *Reform without Justice: Latino Migrant Politics and the Homeland Security State.* New York: Oxford University Press, 2014.

Gonzalez, Deena. *Refusing the Favor: The Spanish-Mexican Women of Santa Fe.* Oxford: Oxford University Press, 2001.

Gonzales-Berry, Erlinda, and David R. Maciel, eds. *Contested Homeland: A Chicano History of New Mexico.* Albuquerque: University of New Mexico Press, 2000.

Gramsci, Antonio. *Selections from the Prison Notebooks.* Edited and translated by Quentin Hoare and Geffrey Nowell Smith. 1935. Reprint, London: Lawrence and Wishart, 1971.

Grayson, George W. "The Mexican Oil Boom." In "Mexico-United States Relations," *Proceedings of the Academy of Political Science* 34, no. 1 (1981): 146–57.

Griswold del Castillo, Richard. "From Revolution to Economic Depression." In *Chicano San Diego: Cultural Space and the Struggle for Justice,* edited by Richard Griswold del Castillo, 68–96. Tucson: University of Arizona Press, 2007.

——. "Natives and Settlers: The Mestizo Heritage." In *Chicano San Diego: Cultural Space and the Struggle for Justice,* edited by Richard Griswold del Castillo, 12–39. Tucson: University of Arizona Press, 2008.

Gutiérrez, David G. "CASA in the Chicano Movement: Ideology and Organizational Politics in the Chicano Community 1968–1978." Working Paper Series, no. 5. Stanford, CA: Stanford Center for Chicano Research, Stanford University, 1984.

———. "Citizens, Noncitizens and the Shell-Game of Immigration Policy Reform: A Response to Dan Tichenor." *Labor: Studies of Working-Class Histories of the Americas* 5, no. 2 (2008): 71–76.

———. "Globalization, Labor Migration, and the Demographic Revolution: Ethnic Mexicans in the Late Twentieth Century." In *A Columbia History of Latinos in the U.S. since 1960*, edited by David G. Gutiérrez, 43–86. New York: Columbia University Press, 2004.

———. "Sin Fronteras? Chicanos, Mexican Americans, and the Emergence of the Contemporary Immigration Debate." *Journal of American Ethnic History* 10, no. 4 (Summer 1991): 5–37.

———. *Walls and Mirrors: Mexican Americans, Mexican Immigrants and the Politics of Ethnicity.* Berkley: University of California Press, 1995.

Gutiérrez, David G., and Pierette Hondagneu-Sotelo. "Introduction: Nation and Migration." *American Quarterly* 60, no. 3 (2008): 503–21.

Gutiérrez, Ramón. "Community, Patriarchy and Individualism: The Politics of Chicano History." *American Quarterly* 45, no. 1 (March 1993): 44–72.

Hall, Stuart. "Gramsci's Relevance for the Study of Race and Ethnicity." *Journal of Communication Inquiry* 10, no. 5 (1986): 5–27.

———. "Old and New Identities, Old and New Ethnicities." In *Culture, Globalization, and the World System*, edited by Anthony D. King, 41–68. Binghamton: SUNY Department of Art and Art History, 1991.

———. "Race, Articulation and Societies Structured in Dominance." In *Sociological Theories: Race and Colonialism*, edited by UNESCO, 305–45. Paris, 1980.

Haney López, Ian. *Racism on Trial: The Chicano Fight for Justice.* Cambridge, MA: Belknap Press at Harvard University, 2003.

Herzog, Lawrence. *Where North Meets South: Cities, Space and Politics on the U.S.-Mexico Border.* Austin: Center for Mexican American Studies/University of Texas Press, 1990.

Holloway, John. *Change the World without Taking Power: The Meaning of Revolution Today.* Chicago: Pluto Press, 2002.

Hondagneu-Sotelo, Pierrette. *Gendered Transitions: Mexican Experiences of Immigration.* Berkeley: University of California Press, 1994.

hooks, bell. *Ain't I a Women: Black Women and Feminism.* Boston: South End Press, 1981.

Horne, Gerald. *Fire This Time: The Watts Uprising and the 1960s.* Charlottesville: University Press of Virginia, 1994.

Ignatiev, Noel. *How the Irish Became White.* New York: Routledge, 1995.

Isin, Ian. *Being Political: Geneologies of Citizenship.* Minneapolis: University of Minnesota Press, 2001.

Jacobo, José Rodolfo, and Richard Griswold del Castillo. "World War II and the Emerging Civil Rights Struggle." In *Chicano San Diego: Cultural Space and the Struggle for Justice*, edited by Richard Griswold del Castillo, 97–114. Tucson: University of Arizona Press, 2007.

Jacobson, Matthew Frye. *Whiteness of a Difference Color: European Immigrants and the Alchemy of Race*. Cambridge, MA: Harvard University Press, 1999.

Johnson, Gaye Theresa Johnson. *Spaces of Conflict, Sounds of Solidarity: Music, Race and Spatial Entitlement in Los Angeles*. Berkeley: University of California Press, 2013.

Jung, Moon-Ho. *Coolies and Cane: Race, Labor and Sugar in the Age of Emancipation*. Baltimore: John Hopkins University Press, 2008.

Kelley, Robin D. G. *Hammer and Hoe: Alabama Communists during the Great Depression*. Chapel Hill: University of North Carolina Press, 1990.

Krochmal, Max. *Blue Texas: The Making of a Multiracial Democratic Coalition in the Civil Rights Era*. Chapel Hill: University of North Carolina Press, 2016.

Larralde, Carlos M. "El Congreso in San Diego: An Endeavor for Civil Rights." *Journal of San Diego History* 50, nos. 1–2 (Winter/Spring 2004): 17–29.

———. "Roberto Galvan: A Latino Leader of the 1940s." *Journal of San Diego History* 52, nos. 3–4 (Summer/Fall 2006): 155–56.

Larralde, Carlos M., and Richard Griswold del Castillo. "Luisa Moreno and the Beginnings of the Mexican American Civil Rights Movement in San Diego." *Journal of San Diego History* 43, no. 3 (Summer 1997): 159–75.

———. "San Diego's Ku Klux Klan 1920–1980. *Journal of San Diego History* 46, no. 2 and 3 (Spring/Summer 2000): 69–88.

Lee, Erika. *At America's Gates: Chinese Immigration during the Exclusion Era, 1882–1943*. Chapel Hill: University of North Carolina Press, 2003.

Levins Morales, Aurora. *Medicine Stories: History, Culture and the Politics of Integrity*. Cambridge, MA: South End Press, 1998.

Lipsitz, George. "Abolition Democracy and Global Justice." *Comparative American Studies: An International Journal* 2, no. 3 (2005): 271–86.

———. "Not Just Another Social Movement: Poster Art and the Movimiento Chicano." In *American Studies in a Moment of Danger* by George Lipsitz, 169–84. Minneapolis: University of Minnesota Press, 2001.

Lloyd, David, and Laura Pulido. "In the Long Shadow of the Settler: On Israel and U.S. Colonialisms." *American Quarterly* 62, no. 4 (December 2010): 795–809.

Lorde, Audre. *Sister Outsider: Essays and Speeches*. Trumansburg, NY: Crossing Press, 1984.

Lowe, Lisa. *Immigrants Acts: On Asian American Cultural Politics*. Durham, NC: Duke University Press, 1996.

———. *The Intimacies of Four Continents*. Durham, NC: Duke University Press, 2016.

Lubhéid, Eithne. *Entry Denied: Controlling Sexuality at the Border*. Minneapolis: University of Minnesota Press, 2002.

Lytle Hernández, Kelley. "Amnesty or Abolition: Felons, Illegals and the Case for a New Abolition Movement." *Boom: A Journal of California* 1, no. 4 (2011): 54–68.

———. *Migra! A History of the U.S. Border Patrol*. Berkeley: University of California Press, 2010.

———. "The Crimes and Consequences of Illegal Immigration: A Cross-Border Examination of Operation Wetback, 1943 to 1954. *Western Historical Quarterly* 37, no, 4 (Winter 2006): 421–44.

MacKinnon, Catharine. *Sexual Harassment of Working Women: A Case of Sex Discrimination*. New Haven, CT: Yale University Press, 1979.

Mantler, Gordon K. *Power to the Poor: Black-Brown Coalition and the Fight for Economic Justice, 1960–1974*. Chapel Hill: University of North Carolina Press, 2014.

Mariscal, George. *Brown-Eyed Children of the Sun: Lessons from the Chicano Movement, 1965–1975*. Albuquerque: University of New Mexico Press, 2006.

Márquez, Benjamin. *LULAC: The Evolution of a Mexican American Political Organization*. Austin: University of Texas Press, 1993.

Martínez, Roberto L. "The Border and Human Rights: A Testimony." In *Chicano San Diego: Cultural Space and the Struggle for Justice*, edited by Richard Griswold del Castillo, 222–45. Tucson: University of Arizona Press, 2002.

McC. Heyman, Josiah, and Howard Campbell. "Recent Research on the U.S.-Mexico Border." (Review Essay). *Latin American Research Review* 39, no. 3 (2004): 205–20.

McWilliams, Carey. *North from Mexico: The Spanish-Speaking People of the United States*. New York: Lippencott, 1948.

Miles, Tiya. *The Ties That Bind: The Story of an Afro-Cherokee Family in Slavery and Freedom*. Berkeley: University of California Press, 2005.

Montejano, David. *Anglos and Mexicans in the Making of Texas*. Austin: University of Texas Press, 1987.

———. *Quixote's Soldiers: A Local History of the Chicano Movement, 1966–1981*. Austin: University of Texas Press, 2010.

Moreno, Luisa. "Caravans of Sorrow: Noncitizen Americans of the Southwest." In *Between Two Worlds: Mexican Immigrants in the United States*, edited by David G. Gutiérrez, 119–23. 1940. Reprint, Wilmington, DE: SR Books, 1996.

Muñoz, Carlos. *Youth, Identity, Power: The Chicano Movement*. New York: Verso Books, 1989; rev. ed., 2007.

Muñoz, Carlos, and Mario Barrera. "La Raza Unida Party and the Chicano Student Movement in California." *Social Science Journal* 19, no. 2 (April 1982): 109–19.

Navarro, Armando. *La Raza Unida Party: A Chicano Challenge to the U.S. Two-Party Dictatorship*. Philadelphia: Temple University Press, 2000.

———. *Mexicano Political Experience in Occupied Aztlán: Struggles and Change*. New York: Alta Mira Press, 2005.

Nevins, Joseph. *Operation Gatekeeper: The Rise of the "Illegal Alien" and the Making of the U.S.-Mexico Boundary*. New York: Routledge, 2002.

———. *Operation Gatekeeper and Beyond: The War on "Illegals" and the Remaking of the U.S.-Mexico Boundary*. New York: Routledge, 2010.

Ngai, Mae. "The Architecture of Race in American Immigration Law: A Reexamination of the Immigration Act of 1924." *Journal of American History* 86, no. 1 (June 1991): 67–92.

———. *Impossible Subjects: Illegal Aliens and the Making of Modern America.* Princeton: Princeton University Press, 2004.

Odom, Mychal Matsemela-Ali. "From Southern California to Southern Africa: African Americans and African Liberation, 1960–1994." PhD diss., University of California, San Diego, La Jolla, forthcoming 2017.

Olguín, Ben. "Caballeros and Indians: Mexican American Whiteness, Hegemonic Mestizaje, and Ambivalent Indigeneity in Proto-Chicana/o Autobiographical Discourse, 1858–2008." *MELUS* 38, no. 1 (Spring 2013): 30–49.

Omi, Michael, and Howard Winant. *Racial Formation in the United States: From the 1960s to the 1990s.* New York: Routeledge, 1994.

Oropeza, Lorena. ¡*Raza Si! ¡Guerra No!: Chicano Protest and Patriotism in the Viet Nam War Era.* Berkeley: University of California Press, 2005.

Ortiz, Isidro. "'¡Sí, Se Puede!' Chicana/o Activism in San Diego at Century's End." In *Chicano San Diego: Cultural Space and the Struggle for Justice,* edited by Richard Griswold del Castillo, 129–57. Tucson: University of Arizona Press, 2007.

Pagan, Eduardo. *Murder at Sleepy Lagoon: Zoot Suits, Race, and Riot in Wartime L.A.* Chapel Hill: University of North Carolina Press, 2003.

Paredes, Américo. *With a Pistol in His Hands: A Border Ballad and Its Hero.* Austin: University of Texas Press, 1958.

Patiño, Jimmy. "'All I Want Is That He Be Punished': Border Patrol Violence, Women's Voices, and Chicano Activism in Early 1970s San Diego." In *The Chicano Movement: Perspectives from the Twenty-First Century,* edited by Mario T. García, 21–46. New York: Routeledge, 2014.

Pawell, Miriam. *The Crusades of Cesar Chavez: A Biography.* New York: Bloomsberry Press, 2014.

———. *A Union of Their Dreams: Power, Hope and Struggle in Cesar Chavez's Farmworker's Movement.* New York: Bloomsberry Press, 2010.

Pérez, Emma. *The Decolonial Imaginary: Writing Chicanas into History.* Bloomington: Indiana University Press, 1999.

Pessar, Patricia R. "Engendering Migration Studies: The Case of New Immigrants in the United States." *American Behavioral Scientist* 42 (1999): 577–600.

Pitti, Stephen. *The Devil in Silicon Valley: Northern California, Race and Mexican Americans.* Princeton: Princeton University Press, 2001.

Prieto, Norma Iglesias. *Beautiful Flowers of the Maquiladora: Life Histories of Women Workers in Tijuana.* Austin: University of Texas Press, 1997.

Pulido, Laura. *Black, Brown, Yellow and Left: Radical Activism in Los Angeles.* Berkeley: University of California Press, 2006.

Ramirez, Catherine. *The Woman in the Zoot Suit: Gender, Nationalism and the Cultural Politics of Memory.* Durham, NC: Duke University Press, 2009.

Reina, Leticia, Elisa Servín, and John Tutino. "Introduction: Crises, Reforms, and Revolutions in Mexico, Past and Present." In *Cycles of Conflict, Centuries of Change: Crisis, Reform, and Revolution in Mexico,* edited by Leticia Reina, Elisa Servín, and John Tutino, 1–22. Durham, NC: Duke University Press, 2007.

Robinson, Cedric. *Black Marxism: The Making of the Black Radical Tradition.* 1983. Reprint, Chapel Hill: University of North Carolina Press, 2000.

Rodríguez, Néstor. "The Battle for the Border: Notes on Autonomous Migration, Transnational Communities, and the State." *Social Justice* 23, no. 3 (Fall 1996): 21–37.

Rodríguez, Richard T. *Next of Kin: The Family in Chicano/a Cultural Politics.* Durham, NC: Duke University Press, 2009.

Roediger, David. *Wages of Whiteness: Race and the Making of the American Working Class.* New York: Verso, 1999.

Rosales, F. Arturo Rosales. *Chicano! The History of the Mexican American Civil Rights Movement.* Rev. ed. Houston: Arte Público Press, 1997.

Ruiz, Vicki. *Cannery Women, Cannery Lives: Mexican Women, Unionization, and the California Food Processing Industry, 1930–1950.* Albuquerque: University of New Mexico Press, 1987.

———. "La Nueva Chicana." In *From Out of the Shadows: Mexican American Women in the Twentieth Century,* 99–127. 1998. Reprint, New York: Oxford University Press, 2008.

Sánchez, George J. *Becoming Mexican American: Ethnicity, Culture and Identity in Chicano Los Angeles, 1900–1933.* New York: Oxford University Press, 1993.

San Miguel, Guadalupe. *"Brown, Not White": School Integration and the Chicano Movement in Houston.* College Station: Texas A&M University Press, 2001.

Santillan, Richard. *La Raza Unida.* Los Angeles: Tlaquilo, 1973.

Sassen, Saskia. "America's Immigration 'Problem.'" *World Policy Journal* 6, no. 4 (Fall 1989): 811–32.

———. "U.S. Immigration Policy Toward Mexico in a Global Economy." In *Between Two Worlds,* edited by David G. Gutiérrez, 213–27. Wilmington, DE: Scholarly Resources, 1998.

Saunt, Claudio. *A New Order of Things: Property, Power and the Transformation of the Creek Indians, 1733–1816.* New York: Cambridge University Press, 1999.

Saxton, Alexander. *The Rise of the White Republic: Class Politics and Mass Culture in Nineteenth-Century America.* New York: Verso, 1990.

Schmidt Camacho, Alicia. *Migrant Imaginaries: Latino Cultural Politics in the U.S.-Mexico Borderlands.* New York: New York University Press, 2008.

Shah, Nayan. *Contagious Divides: Epidemics and Race in San Francisco's Chinatown.* Berkeley: University of California Press, 2001.

Sierra, Christine Marie. "In Search of National Power: Chicanos Working the System on Immigration Reform, 1976–1986." In *Chicano Politics and Society in the Late Twentieth Century,* edited by David Montejano, 131–53. Austin: University of Texas Press, 1999.

Slayden, James L. "Some Observations on the Mexican Immigrant." *Annals of the American Academy of Political and Social Science* 93 (January 1921): 121–26.

Streeby, Shelley. *American Sensations: Class, Empire and the Production of Popular Culture.* Berkeley: University of California Press, 2002.

Taylor, Paul S. *An American-Mexican Frontier: Nueces County, Texas*. Chapel Hill: University of North Carolina Press, 1934.

———. *Mexican Labor in the United States*. 7 vols. Berkeley: University of California Publications in Economics, 1928–1932.

Tenayuca, Emma, and Homer Brooks. "The Mexican Question in the Southwest." *The Communist*, March 1939.

Torres, Edén. *Chicana Without Apology: The New Chicana Cultural Studies*. New York: Routledge Press, 2003.

Uggen, Christopher, and Amy Blackstone. "Sexual Harassment as a Gendered Expression of Power." *American Sociological Review* 69, no. 1 (February 2004): 64–92.

Usener, Daniel. *Indians, Settlers and Slaves in a Frontier Exchange Economy: The Lower Mississippi Valley before 1783*. Chapel Hill: University of North Carolina Press, 1992.

Vargas, Zaragoza. *Labor Rights Are Civil Rights: Mexican American Workers in Twentieth Century America*. Princeton: Princeton University Press, 2005.

———. "Tejana Radical: Emma Tenayuca and the San Antonio Labor Movement during the Great Depression." *Pacific Historical Review* 66, no. 4 (November 1997): 553–80.

Williams, Eric. *Slavery and Capitalism*. 1944. Reprint, Chapel Hill: University of North Carolina Press, 1994.

Wolfe, Patrick. "Settler Colonialism and the Elimination of the Native." *Journal of Genocide Research* 8, no. 4 (December 2006): 387–409.

Yung, Judy. *Unbound Feet: A Social History of Chinese Women in San Francisco*. Berkeley: University of California Press, 1995.

Index

Abolition democracy, 223–24, 305n7
Abolitionist perspective, 3, 223
Accountability, 167, 260
Activism: against brutality, 60; Center for Autonomous Social Action studying immigration, 67; Chicano community engagement in, 83; Chicano movement development of, 65, 101–2; Chicano movement early stage of, 152–53; Committee on Chicano Rights community based, 183–84; confrontation promoted by, 101; of Congress of Spanish-Speaking People, in San Diego, 27–29; Federal Bureau of Investigation informant surveying, 153, 162; formal compared to informal, 70; ideological tools for, 104; influence of, 256; language of, 94; local context of, 133–34; MAPA National City as vehicle for, 43; memory as motivation for, 80; Moreno practice of, 43; organizations on, 232; for racial justice, 37; as radical, 25, 84; San Diego as pole for, 188; as survival method, 38; for women's rights, 11, 40; as working-class, 78–79; of youth, 283n49
Ad Hoc Committee on Chicano Rights. *See* Committee on Chicano Rights
African Americans, 95–96; community histories of, 208; Mexican Americans historic relationship with, 234
Akili, Greg, 179, *193*, 209, 235
Alatorre, Soledad "Chole," 1, 5, 54, 242, 256; CASA Justicia described by, 70;

Center for Autonomous Social Action resignation of, 83
American Federation of Labor and Congress of Industrial Organizations (AFL-CIO), 12
Amnesty: alongside repressive legislation, 233; approach to, 262; in Carter immigration proposal, 206; Corona interest in, 308n74; defining of, 207; extension of, 265; as false, 259; humane position on, 204; as limited, 255
Árbenz, Jacobo, 40–41
Asociación Nacional México-Americana (ANMA), 22, 38, 40, 41
Assembly Bill 528, 12–13, 111–22, 135, 142–43, 290n110
Authenticity, 23, 147
Authority: of Committee on Chicano Rights, 229; of law enforcement, 155
Avalos, David, 185–86, 225, 228, 247
Aztec Print Shop, 74, 106, 166–67, 180
Aztlán, 103, 123, 186, 214

Baca, Herman, 1–2, 12, 53, *191*, *193*, *196*; accusations towards, 128; background of, 98; CASA Justicia described by, 72; as Chacón campaign manager, 106–7, 109, 288n67; Chávez, C., embraced by, *189*; Chávez, C., met by, 90; Chicano community presence of, 169; class struggle relationship of, 284n58; Coalition of Human Rights leadership of, 209; Committee on Chicano Rights organized by, 151;

Baca, Herman (cont.)
 Committee on Chicano Rights spoken
 for by, 177; concerns articulated by,
 16; with Corona, *189*; Corona
 criticized by, 265; defending of,
 160–61; emotional reaction from,
 227; family history of, 81; García,
 Alberto, asking assistance of, 57;
 Gutiérrez communication with,
 123–24, 149; Immigration Reform and
 Control Act rejected by, 258–59;
 investigations urged by, 59; Ku Klux
 Klan speech made by, 212–13;
 leadership of, 4, 160, 263; letter of
 concern to, 134–35; letter to presidents from, 249; meetings facilitated
 by, 153–54; Mexican American
 Political Association experience of,
 127; Mexico criticized by, 214; organization need per, 253; as pessimistic,
 262; policy concerns outlined by, 204;
 as potentially dangerous, 153; protests
 led by, 60, 117; resignation of, 109–10;
 Rivera shooting commented on by,
 168–69; solutions asked for by, 230;
 solutions explained by, 233–34;
 Trump phenomenon according to,
 252; as undemocratic, 84–85;
 undocumented immigration argument of, 91; urgency demanded by,
 229–30; Vásquez relationship with,
 98–99; walkout by, 145; Wilson
 attacking character of, 161; Wilson
 frustrated by, 158–59
Badillo, Herman, 174–75
Bagley, David, 33
Battle for the Border, 202
Belonging, 221, 244, 254, 274n23
Bilingual Education School, 157
Black Freedom movement, 94, 224
Black Power, 99, 101–2, 178, 208
Bloody Border, the *(La Frontera en
 Sangre)*, 225–29, 247

Border Industrialization Program, 50–51
Borderlands, 279n47; child fatalities in,
 226–29; enforcement of, 34; enforcement of, as threat, 208; life experience in, 206; Mexican immigrants
 crossing of, 41; militarization of, 44,
 61, 201; racism in, 56, 147; realities
 of, 250; as transnational space, 213,
 270n11; voices of, 66
Border Patrol *(migra)*, 2; abolishment
 of, 133, 223, 239, 257; as anti-
 Mexican, 259; apprehensions by, 49;
 brutality from, 15, 26, 47–50, 55–61,
 119–20, 141, 150, 201, 228, 244;
 creation of, 10–11; family disrupted
 by, 59, 63; fatal emergencies ignored
 by, 226–27; forum for brutality
 victims of, 246–47; Hoobler revealing
 interworkings of, 157–58; invasions
 by, 150, 201; Ku Klux Klan assisting,
 201, 207; legal violence by, 127; media
 covering brutality from, 56; police
 cooperation with, 184; police entanglement with, 13; power increase
 for, 205; racist practices of, 211; raids
 by, 41; repression from, 140; sexual
 harassment by, 47–50, 53, 55, 57–58,
 60, 140, 174; threats from, 48–49;
 violence, Chicano movement and,
 53–55; youth relationship with, 184
Bracero Program, 30, 38–41; Chávez, C.,
 and, 111; end of, 49, 51; as exploitative,
 51, 111; undocumented immigration
 exacerbated by, 39
Brophy, Bill, 115–16
Brown, Pat, 92, 95, 96, 108
Brutality: activism against, 60;
 alleviation of, 219, 229; from Border
 Patrol, 15, 26, 47–50, 55–61, 119–20,
 141, 150, 201, 228, 244; deportation
 and, 53; examples of, 247; forum for
 victims of Border Patrol, 246–47;
 from Immigration and Naturalization

Service, 151; from Ku Klux Klan, 21, 27–28, 29; MAPA National City addressing, 112; media covering Border Patrol, 56; of Mexican Americans, 6, 55; of Mexican immigrants, 6; protests against, 60; publicizing of, 56; recorded testimonies of, 222; unity from, 179. *See also* Sexual harassment

Canneries, 30
Capitalism: critique of, 25; deportation connection to, 38; growth of, 6–7, 271n18; immigration influencing development of, 7; mutilation of human lives by, 228; practices of, 120–21; as racial, 6–10
Cardenas, Lazaro, 27
Carter, Jimmy, 14, 15, 187–88, 245; Chicano Federation meeting invitation with, 219; Chicano/Mexicanos showdown with, 202
Carter Curtain, 202; Corona on implications of, 216; implications of, 216; Ku Klux Klan and, 204–13; mobilization against, 203; National Protest against, *196*; protests against, *196*, 213; as racism symbol, 206
Carter immigration proposal, 203, 205, 233; amnesty in, 206; campaign against, 210–11; failure of, 213, 245; ideological shift from, 302n18; protest against, *195*
CASA Justicia, 136; Alatorre describing, 70; Baca describing, 72; board members of, 78, 85; CASA San Diego compared to, 88; Chicano community used by, 73, 74; Chicano movement influenced by, 79; Corona support for, 85–86; emergence of, 136; family separation fought against by, 76; formation of, 68, 70–73; funding for, 85; identification methods of, 72–73;

leadership of, 83; legal services provided by, 71; location of, 69, 166; members of, 130; phasing out of, 89; radicalization of, 88; as resource, 72, 73; social services role of, 75; transitions within, 83–85
CASA San Diego, 84; CASA Justicia compared to, 88; emergence of, 79; failures of, 87; social service transition by, 86
Castillo, Leonel J., 204–5
Cazares, Norma Mena, 80–81, 85, 137, *190*
Cazares, Roger, 81, 101–2, *190*
Center for Autonomous Social Action (Centro de Acción Social Autónomo; CASA), 2, 11–12, 104, 284n56; Alatorre resignation from, 83; chapter development of, 85–87; conflicts within, 83–84; Corona resignation from, 83; dissolving of, 87; founding of, 54; immigration activism studied through, 67; leadership shift in, 68; Marxist shift of, 68–69; recomposition of, 82; youth strategy for, 83. *See also* CASA Justicia; CASA San Diego; Young Turks
Central Intelligence Agency (CIA), 40
Central Labor Council, 43
Chacón, Peter, 12, 91; Baca as campaign manager for, 106–7, 109, 288n67; background of, 105–6; dislocation argument by, 119; fundraising for, 107; MAPA National City and campaign for, 92, 104–11; Mexican American Political Association assistance for, 92; obligation of, 116; retirement of, 110
Chapman, Leonard F., 204
Chávez, César, 12, 96; Baca embracing, *189*; Baca meeting, 90; Bracero Program and, 111; support for, 156
Chávez, Leo, 58

Cocke, Kenneth, 47–49, 61, 63
Cold War, 22, 34–38, 93
Colonization, of Southwest, 273n6
Committee for the Protection of the
Foreign-Born, 38
Committee on Chicano Rights (CCR), 2;
authority of, 229; Baca organizing,
151; Baca speaking for, 177; community based activism of, 183–84;
compromise refusal of, 267; creation
of, 13–14, 150, 165; decision-making
process desired by, 231; decline of,
257, 262; emergence of, 185–88;
employer sanctions stance of, 206;
immigration position of, 219;
Immigration Reform and Control Act
criticized by, 259–60; international
prominence of, 14; law enforcement
struggled with by, 164; legacy of,
261–67; legal violence struggled with
by, 150–51; members of, 181; Nia
dialogue with, 235; protection from,
186; recall effort of, 173, 177–83;
self-determination processes
developed by, 201; support for,
171–72; threats towards, 172; violence
protested by, 224–25; Walk for Rights
sponsored by, 255
Communist Party of the United States
of America (CPUSA), 23, 25, 275n40
Community Service Organization
(CSO), 38, 93
Confederación de Trabajadores
Mexicanos (CTM), 27
Congress of Industrial Organizations
(CIO), 11, 21, 38
Congress of Spanish-Speaking People
(*Congreso del Pueblo que Habla
Español*), 11, 21, 305n7; cease of, 34;
demise of, 35; resurrection of politics
of, 42; San Diego activism of, 27–29;
as transnational entity, 26; women in,
25, 29, 31; World War II and, 30–34

Constitution, U.S., 36
Coombs, Richard E., 36
Corona, Bert, 1–2, 12, 43, 54, *196*, 256;
amnesty interest of, 308n74; as
Asociación Nacional Mexicana
organizer, 40; Baca criticizing, 265;
Baca with, *189*; canvassing of, 294n75;
on Carter Curtain implications, 216;
CASA Justicia support from, 85–86;
Center for Autonomous Social Action
resignation of, 83; Chicano movement
activist organizations called on by,
127; essays by, 125–27, 134–35;
Immigration Reform and Control Act
supported by, 261; influence of, 81; on
Ku Klux Klan violence, 28; Mexican
American Political Association
position of, 92, 125, 291n10; as
teacher, 82, 262; unity vision of, 143
Coyote (smuggler), 205, 274n27
Criminalization, 187, 212, 252, 266
Cross-citizenship: solidarity and, 40;
survival of, 38; transnational
resistance and, 22–27
Cuban Revolution, 94
Cuevas, Antonio, 56–57
Cuisine, 81
Cultural identity: of Mexicans, 214;
at National Chicano Immigration
Conference, 237–38
Culture: authenticity of, 23; barriers to,
67; as celebrated, 6; debates sur-
rounding authenticity of, 147

Dail, Charles C., 33
Davila, Armando, 31
Decolonization, 94
Deferred Action for Childhood Arrivals
(DACA), 251
Democratic Party, 90, 204; alternatives
to, 92; frustrations with, 96; leadership
taken by, 108; loyalty to, 93; Mexican
Americans tensions with, 96–97;

Democratic Party (cont.)
protests against, 125; La Raza Unida Party challenging, 124; separation from, 130; as unsupportive, 107–8
Democratic practice, 229–31
Deportation regime, 2, 269n4; abolishment of, 267; as attack on Mexicans, 66; brutality and, 53; capitalist interest with, 38; of children, 239; disruption from, 247; end to, 132; family unification destroyed by, 228–29; fight against, 115; of Galvan, 37; of illegal aliens, 203; illegal participation in, 156; immigration based on, 9, 79, 223; increase in, 254; as intimidation tactic, 140; local police interconnected with, 150; mechanisms of, 35–36, 38, 239; Mexican immigrants influenced by, 206; of Moreno, 36–37; policies on, 164; racial capitalism and, 6–10; resistance interconnected with, 10; struggle against, 133, 267; support for, 40; threat of, 24, 143; threat of, as federal offense, 143; as voluntary, 272n28; as weapon, 93
Diaz, Porfirio, 9
Displacement, 202, 212
Division of Adult Education of San Diego, 156
Dixon Arnett Bill, 12–13, 111–22, 135, 142–43, 290n110
Dream movement, 251
Drugs, 279n42; Mexico association with, 52; youth use of, 176
Duffy, John C., 151, 152, 154
Duffy memorandum, 151–65
Duke, David, 207, 212

Economy: Gonzales opinion on structure of, 149; Mexico development of, 9
Education: as bilingual, 110; in Chicano/a studies, 26; as

consciousness-raising, 131; police negatively influencing, 157; scholarships given to Mexican Americans for, 304n53; through writing, 132
Employer sanctions, 206
Encounter sites (encuentros), 10, 22, 67, 147–48, 272n30
Ethno-racial terminology, 269n2
Executive Order 9066, 31
Exploitation, 284n58; from Bracero Program, 51, 111; human rights needed to eliminate, 216; of immigrant workers, 39, 121, 205, 234; of Mexican Americans, 26; of Mexican immigrants, 26; Mexico role in, 214; resistance to, 65

Family (La Familia): Baca history of, 81; Border Patrol disrupting, 59, 63; CASA Justicia fighting against separation of, 76; deportation destroying unification of, 228–29; fragmentation of, 76; gender roles within, 138–40; immigration histories surrounding, 79; as immigration motivator, 75; notion of nuclear, 63; priority of unification of, 266; unity and, 136
Federal Bureau of Investigation (FBI), 36, 153, 162
Feminism, 100, 271n14
First Symposium on Immigration, 243–44
Freedom: demand for, 224; of human movement, 269n4; movements towards, 234
Frontera en Sangre, la (the Bloody Border), 225–29, 247

Galvan, Roberto, 31, 35, 37
García, Alberto, 54, 57, 59, 239
García, Alex, 105, 114–15, 119
Gender, 5; Chicanos/as roles of, 100, 138–40; Chicano movement dimen-

sions of, 59, 80, 101; Chicano movement struggling for justice of, 62;
family roles regarding, 138–40; labor
inequity, racism and, 61–62; leadership and hierarchy of, 139, 148, 263;
legal status and, 61; Parra López
revealing discrimination of, 61;
sexuality, family and, 242; traditional
roles of, 63–64. *See also* Women
Genocide, 202
Gomez, Anna Nieto, 99–100
Gonzales, Rodolfo "Corky," 123–24,
148, *196*, 241; economic structure
opinion of, 149; Gutiérrez rivalry
with, 129–31, 146; human rights
advocated by, 215
Gordillo, José, 40
Great Depression, 22–23, 44
Gutiérrez, José Ángel, 148; Baca
communication with, 123–24, 149;
Gonzales rivalry with, 129–31, 146

Hermandad Mexicana, La (the Mexican
Brotherhood), 11, 38, 41–44, 70, 261–62
Heteronormativity, 76–77, 99, 139, 242
Hitler, Adolf, 30
Homosexuality, 76–77, 99
Hoobler, Ray, 155; Border Patrol
interworking revealed by, 157–58;
forced resignation of, 164; police
defended by, 158; resignation
requested of, 157–58, *191*
Hoobler memorandum, 151–65
Huerta, Dolores, 71, 96, 111
Human rights, 6; denial of, 213;
exploitation eliminated by, 216;
Gonzales commenting on, 215;
violation of, 201, 230, 236, 244, 246
Hurtado, Juan, 156–57

Identity: of Chicanos/as, 102–3, 231,
285n2; of Chicanos/Mexicanos, 4, 60,
81, 82; determining of, 223; develop-

ment of, 81; as feminized, 264;
Mexican Americans having white, 95;
of Mexicans, 43–44; of Mexicans
connected to Chicanos/as, 217;
organizing based on ethno-racial, 94;
repression and, 5; self-determining
of, 225; solidarity and, 242; strategy,
power and, 2–3; as transnational, 4,
82; utilization of ethnic, 25; during
wartime, 31–32
Illegal aliens, 9, 32; apprehending of,
201; Chicanos/as displaced by, 113–14;
Chicano community participation of,
126; construction of, 254, 304n49;
crisis created by, 52–53; deportation
of, 203; fear of, 38; invention of, 11;
Mexican Americans distinguished
from, 119; policies targeting, 81; as
problematic, 144; removal of, 278n12;
right to detain, 154, 155; roundups
of, 21; stereotype of, 151; as strike
breakers, 142–47; structure of, 234;
targeting of, 150, 201, 222, 228; taxi
drivers identifying, 151; term
replacement of, 143; unemployment
influenced by, 120–21; youth accused
as, 184–85
Immigrant workers, 1; Bill of Rights for,
249; citizenship exclusion of, 42;
exploitation of, 39, 121, 205, 234;
need for, 51; shortage of, 39; suffering
of, 21
Immigration, 1; capitalism development influenced by, 7; Center for
Autonomous Social Action studying
activism of, 67; Chicanos/Mexicanos
perspective on, 255; Chicano movement struggle with, 16–17, 135; Chicano
perspective on, 252; Committee on
Chicano Rights position on, 219;
communication of policies for, 74–75;
confrontation with policies of, as necessary, 126; controversy surrounding,

Party taking, 108; empowering of new, 264; gender hierarchy in, 139, 148, 263; government failure to provide, 177; of Ku Klux Klan, 207; as male, 62; of Mexican American Political Association, 104; of Mexican Americans, 162; Mexicans access to, 97; at National Chicano Immigration Tribunal, 248; new generation of, 82; of women, 80, 242; for women's rights, 22, 264

League of United Latin American Citizens (LULAC), 23, 40, 95, 274n18

Legal violence, 141, 265, 278n24; awareness of, 208; by Border Patrol, 127; challenging of, 89; Committee on Chicano Rights struggle with, 150–51; forms of, 61; increase in, 69; towards Mexicans, 50; struggle with, 151

López, Yolanda, *195*, 202, 219–20, 263

López Portillo, Jose, 213, 239, 248

Malcolm X, 94, 102

Maoist August Twenty-ninth Movement (ATM). *See* La Raza Unida Party

MAPA National City, 59; as activism vehicle, 43; Baca experience with, 97, 103; board of, 137; brutality addressed by, 112; Chacón campaign and, 92, 104–11; elitist politics of, 71; focus of, 105; women involvement in, 137

Marriage, 75–77, 139

Martinez, Ester, *196*

Marxism, 68–69, 284n58

Marxist-Leninism, 68–69, 79, 82

Masculinity: of Chicanos/Mexicanos, 63; National Chicano Immigration Conference demonstrating, 242; violence associated with, 63

Media: Border Patrol brutality covered by, 56; immigration debate in, 253

Mega Marches, 251, 267

Memorial March, 231–44

Memory, 80

Mexican American Advisory Council (MAAC), 72

Mexican American Political Association (MAPA), 1, 38; Baca experience with, 127; Chacón assistance from, 92; chapters of, 92; Corona position in, 92, 125, 291n10; Dixon Arnett Bill stance by, 114; electoral politics focus of, 93–94; frustrations of, 95–96; imploding of, 125–28; leadership of, 104; as mechanism for self-determination, 96–97; progressives of, 94; underrepresentation claims from, 130. *See also* MAPA National City

Mexican Americans, 2, 3, 4; African Americans historic relationship with, 234; brutality of, 6, 55; criticism of, 252; Democratic Party tensions with, 96–97; Dixon Arnett Bill influence on, 116–17; exploitation of, 26; as farm workers, 96; fear of, 32; fragmentation of, 91, 132; as gang members, 32; illegal aliens distinguished from, 119; leadership of, 162; loyalty suspicions of, during World War II, 34; Mexican immigrants against, 79, 134–35; military conflict with, 32–33; new generation of, 44; political tradition of, 224; scholarships given for education for, 304n53; solidarity between Mexican immigrants and, 16; title importance of, 95; white identity of, 95. *See also* Pachucos

Mexican-American War, 8, 10, 22, 52, 241

Mexican Brotherhood, the *(La Hermandad Mexicana)*, 11, 38, 41–44, 70, 261–62

Mexican immigrants, 2, 3; borderlands crossed by, 41; brutality of, 6; Chicanos/as engagement with, 89; deportation influencing, 206;

Mexican immigrants (cont.)
engagement with, 69; exploitation of,
26; identifying as, 80; increase in,
during World War II, 30; legal
benefits for, 258; Mexican Americans
against, 79, 134–35; population of,
50; protection for, 41; solidarity
between Mexican Americans and, 16
Mexican Revolution, 238
Mexicans: cultural identity of, 214;
historical citizenship rights of, 241;
identity of, 43–44; Identity of
Chicanos/as connected to, 217;
Immigration and Naturalization
Service removing citizenship of,
38–39; leadership access for, 97; legal
violence towards, 50; taxi drivers
ignoring, 152
Mexico: assistance from, 218; Baca
criticizing, 214; defense lacking in,
239; drugs associated with, 52;
economic development of, 9;
exploitation role of, 214; Latin
America connected to, 203–4; United
States engagement with, 14–15
migra. See Border Patrol
Militarization: of borderlands, 44, 61,
201; end to border, 239; furthering of,
257; of immigration policies, results
of, 218; protests on, 215; results of,
225–26; as violent, 206
Miller, Edwin, 63–64, 173–75
Mobilization: against Carter Curtain,
203; of Chicanos/Mexicanos, 201; of
Chicano movement, 2, 5–6, 60–61,
68, 141, 285n2; difficulty with, 87;
experimentation with, 188; lack of,
263; local officials pressured by, 174;
for petition signatures, 178–80; La
Raza Unida Party needing, 126–27; of
resources, 74; of solidarity, 174; at
state level, 146; of United Farm
Workers, 102

Moreno, Luisa, 28–29, 30, 33, 305n7;
activism practice of, 43; deportation
of, 36–37; harassment of, 35–36
Morgan, Kile, 170, 174–75, 178
Movimiento Estudiantil Chicano de
Aztlán (MEChA), 79, 98–101, 103,
287n42
Msemaji, Ken, 179, *193*, 209, 235
Multiculturalism, 202

National Chicano Immigration
Conference, 15, *196*, 222, 224, 231,
244, 250; cultural identity at,
237–38; influence of, 243; masculin-
ity demonstrated at, 242; organ-
izations participating in, 232–33;
speakers at, 232–33; women and
immigration neglected at, 242;
workshops at, 239–42
National Chicano Immigration Tribu-
nal, *197*, 222, 225, 245–50
National Chicano Political Caucus, 128
National Coalition for Fair Immigration
Law and Practices, 256
National March Against the Militariza-
tion of the Border and the Carter
Curtain, 218–19
Natividad, Luis, 159–60
Naturalization Act of 1790, 8, 272n23
Navarro, Armando, 142–43, 145, *196*,
294n62
Nia Cultural Organization, 178, 208,
234, 235–36, 307n44
Nixon, Richard, 102

Operation Wetback, 38–41

Pachucos, 32
Parra López, Martha Elena: advocating
for, 63; gender discrimination
revealed by, 61; influence of, 54;
sexual harassment of, 47–50, 53, 60,
140, 174

Partido Revolucionario Institucional (Institutional Revolutionry Party; PRI), 214, 304n64

Petroleum industry, 218, 304n64

Plan Espiritual de Aztlán, El (Spiritual Plan of Aztlán), 97, 103

Police: Border Patrol cooperation with, 184; Border Patrol entanglement with, 13; deportation interconnected to local, 150; education negatively influenced by, 157; Hoobler defending, 158; negligence of, 173; public criticism of, 162; raids by, 157; Rivera killing by, 150, 165–86; as trigger-happy, 176; violence from, 14, 141, 165–66, 175–76, 179; Wilson defending, 158. *See also* San Diego Police Department; San Diego Sheriff's Department

Politicization, 73, 130, 141

Power, 2–3, 241

Proletarianization, 9

Protests, 27; Asociación Nacional México-Americana staging, 41; Baca leading, 60, 117; against brutality, 60; against Carter Curtain, *196*, 213; against Carter immigration proposal, *195*; Chicano community demanding, 169; Committee on Chicano Rights, on violence, 224–25; against Democratic Party, 125; of Hoobler memorandum, 163; against Immigration and Naturalization Service, 41; against Ku Klux Klan, *194*; of Latinos/as, 251; on militarization, 215; for Rivera killing, 173, *192*; at San Diego Sheriff's Department, 153. *See also* National March Against the Militarization of the Border and the Carter Curtain; Unity March

Race: citizenship, class struggle and, 118, 120, 242; material experience of, 170; radicalization of issue of, 165

Racialization: of Chicano community, 208; history of, 260; of violence, 166, 179

Racism: in borderlands, 56, 147; of Border Patrol, 211; Carter Curtain as symbol of, 206; Ku Klux Klan representing, 220; labor inequity, gender and, 61–62; legalization of, 211; as oppressive system, 97; as root of problems, 105; San Diego Sheriff Department as obsessed with, 152; sexism intersection with, 63; sexual harassment related to, 61–62; struggle against, 38, 101; understanding of, 22

Ramos, Enrique, 74

Rape. *See* Sexual harassment

Raza Unida Party, La (LRUP), 2, 13, 53–54, 122; chapter participation of, 144–45; competing visions of, 124, 146; Democratic Party challenged by, 124; encounter sites of, 147–48; fractures in, 142–47; as gathering space, 131; infiltration of, 163; launching of, 126; members of, 130; mobilization needed by, 126–27; newsletter of, 131–33, 136–37, 140–41; reflections from, 136–37; roots of, 129; strategy limitations of, 148; transition to Maoist August Twenty-ninth Movement, 294n63; walkout initiated by, 128

Reagan, Ronald, 16, 96, 113, 246, 248, 254

Recall, 173, 177–83

Red Scare, 34–35, 37, 38, 276n63

Repatriation, 24

Repression, 265; from Border Patrol, 140; Cold War rise of, 34–38; efforts towards, 181; Identity and, 5; through immigration, 130; transnational communities experience of, 239

Resistance: Cross-Citizenship and transnational, 22–27; deportation interconnected with, 10; to exploitation, 65; history of, 131; time for, 202

CPSIA information can be obtained
at www.ICGtesting.com
Printed in the USA
LVHW101621230422
717055LV00008B/315